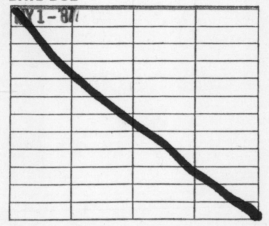

COLD WAR POLITICAL JUSTICE

Recent Titles in
Contributions in American History
Series Editor: Jon L. Wakelyn

COLD WAR
POLITICAL
JUSTICE

The Smith Act, the Communist
Party, and American
Civil Liberties _____

Michal R. Belknap

Contributions in American History, Number 66

 GREENWOOD PRESS
WESTPORT, CONNECTICUT   LONDON, ENGLAND

Library of Congress Cataloging in Publication Data

Belknap, Michal R.
    Cold war political justice.

    (Contributions in American history; no. 66)
    Bibliography: p.
    Includes index.
    1. Communism—United States—1917-
2. Communist trials—United States. 3. Trials
(Political crimes and offenses)—United States
I. Title. II. Series.
KF4856.C6B44   342'.73'087   77-4566
ISBN 0-8371-9692-2

Library of Congress Catalog Card Number: 77-4566
ISBN: 0-8371-9692-2
ISSN: 0084-9219

First published in 1977

Greenwood Press, Inc.
51 Riverside Avenue, Westport, Connecticut 06880

Printed in the United States of America

For TRICIA

Contents

Preface

The genesis of this book was a luncheon conversation with Stanley Kutler in the fall of 1969, when one of the biggest stories in the nation's newspapers was the chaotic trial of the Chicago Conspiracy, antiwar activists indicted for allegedly inciting riots during the 1968 Democratic National Convention. The case was a fascinating one, not only because it featured dramatic battles pitting Judge Julius Hoffman against the defendants and their lawyers, but also because it was in many respects— from the composition of the group that the government had singled out for prosecution to the demonstrations organized by friends of the accused —so obviously a political event. Because of our mutual interest in legal history, Kutler and I soon wandered from discussing the Chicago Conspiracy trial itself to considering similar judicial proceedings in the past. Although it was obvious to both of us that America had produced other criminal cases with decidedly political overtones, we were struck by the dearth of literature on this facet of the country's legal history. Out of this conversation developed the idea of a work on American political trials.

The kind of comprehensive study that we had in mind proved impractical, in part because too little research had yet been done in many areas of this large subject, but even more because of the impossibility of precisely defining the topic. Many people deny that there are political trials, at least in the United States, and even among sophisticated scholars who realize that such things occur, there is no agreement concerning the location of the boundary line that divides this special category of cases from other judicial proceedings. Even though it seemed impossible to write the history of something for which no generally accepted definition was available, a case study—one that might contribute to scholarly understanding of the subject as a whole while identifying the issues with which a comprehensive work on American political justice must one day deal— did appear feasible.

I selected the Smith Act prosecutions of the Communist Party for in-depth examination. In addition to a number of highly publicized trials, these had given rise to several Supreme Court decisions, at least one or two of which were familiar to most beginning students of constitutional law and history. Besides being well known, these cases had left in their wake an almost endless amount of evidence, both legal and nonlegal. Also, the organization to which the defendants belonged was, at least during the period of the prosecutions, probably the most reviled dissenting minority in American history. If this country had ever produced political trials, then surely these Smith Act cases were among them.

After seven years of research and writing, I am convinced that American political justice does exist and that the Smith Act prosecutions are a prime example of that phenomenon. There are those who would prefer to accept neither of these contentions, but the evidence refutes them. American justice may at other times and for other litigants have performed with the neutrality promised by the blindfold that its symbol wears, but, at the height of the Cold War and for the leaders of the Communist Party, it did not. These radicals suffered unjustly, and the Bill of Rights suffered along with them.

Because readers are likely to view a work that reaches such conclusions and that was admittedly inspired by the Chicago Conspiracy trial as a last gasp from the New Left of the 1960s, perhaps it is desirable for me to say something about my own background. While the protests against the Vietnam War were at their height, I was investigating them as a special agent for army intelligence. If this book betrays a certain cynicism with respect to investigative agencies and a certain skepticism concerning alleged threats to internal security, it is because of my experiences as a government detective, not because of any association with the causes or ideology of the New Left.

My service with army intelligence, an organization that did most of its "domestic spying" by clipping items from the newspapers, has also made me somewhat dubious about the supposedly unique value to scholars of investigative agency files. Largely for financial reasons, this book makes very little use of confidential FBI documents. During more than fifty years of intense investigation, the Bureau has compiled immense files on the Communist Party, which are indexed in such a way as to make it impossible to identify readily those items relevant to a study of the Smith Act cases. Locating such documents would require screening what the Bureau has "conservatively" estimated as 1,275,000 pages. For undertaking this task, it requested $300,000, with no advance commitment to release any of the documents in question. While FBI files would

almost certainly enrich an account of the Smith Act cases, the drama with
which this book deals is essentially a public one, and my examination of
those Bureau-originated items available at the Truman Library and in the
report that the Senate's Church Committee prepared after its investigation of U.S. intelligence agencies leads me to believe that greater utiliza-
tion of such documents would not change my conclusions. With two exceptions, this FBI material reveals nothing of significance that one could
not learn by carefully reading the Communist press.[1]

The most pleasant aspect of finishing a project such as this is the opportunity it gives an author to acknowledge and thank all of those who
have helped him along the way. I owe a particular debt of gratitude to
Stanley Kutler, both for suggesting that I undertake this study and for
carefully directing the dissertation which grew out of it. I would also
like to thank the other members of my University of Wisconsin doctoral
committee, Professors Ted Finman and Paul Glad, for their advice and
criticism. Stanley N. Katz of the University of Chicago and my University of Texas colleagues Clarence Lasby and Thomas K. McCraw (aided
by his wife Susan) carefully read an overly long manuscript and furnished
invaluable advice for condensing and improving it, while Professors
Thomas Philpott, Richard Ryerson, Edward Steinhart, and Edward
Rhoads of the University of Texas and William Harbaugh of the University of Virginia also offered helpful suggestions. Particularly valuable
was the brutal but effective editing done by my father, Robert Belknap,
whose savage pencil made this book far more readable than would otherwise be the case.

I am also indebted to David Wigdor of the Library of Congress, Ann
Fagan Ginger of the Meiklejohn Civil Liberties Institute, Nancy Bressler
of the Seeley G. Mudd Manuscript Library at Princeton University, Terry
L. Birdwhistell of the University of Kentucky Library, Erika Chadbourn
of the Harvard Law School Library, and the staffs of the Harry S. Truman
and Dwight D. Eisenhower Presidential libraries for the help they have
given me in my research. Albert Kahn was kind enough to loan me a copy
of the galley proofs of his as yet unpublished book *A National Scandal*,
and Eugene Freedheim opened his home to me so that I might examine
material collected by the Cleveland Bar Association while he was its president. Gerald Gunther of Stanford University, who is working on a biography of Learned Hand, graciously provided me with copies of all of the
relevant documents in that judge's papers, and Woodford Howard, who is
writing about the life of Harold Medina, made available to me some items
from the Princeton University collection of that jurist's papers, which are
presently in his possession. I would also like to thank the editors of *Ohio*

History and *The National Journal of Criminal Defense* for granting permission to use material which appeared first in the pages of those publications. In addition, I owe a very large debt of gratitude to Earline Lago, Rebecca Horn, and Betty Nims, good friends and fine typists, who transformed often illegible drafts into finished manuscript. The contributions of these individuals and organizations made this book possible, and, for whatever virtues it has, they deserve much of the credit. For its shortcomings, I alone am responsible.

In conclusion, I wish to say a special word of thanks to my wife, Patricia, partly for the help she, like many others, has given me, but even more for enduring seven difficult years during which I devoted far too much time to the Smith Act and the Communist Party and far too little to her.

NOTE

1. Clarence Kelley to the Author, 16 January 1974.

Abbreviations Used in Notes

ACLU	American Civil Liberties Union
Cong. Record	*Congressional Record*
CF	White House Central Files
CPUSA	Communist Party, United States of America
DEL	Dwight D. Eisenhower Library
DW	*Daily Worker*
GPO	Government Printing Office
HApp	U.S. Congress, House, Committee on Appropriations
HJC	U.S. Congress, House, Committee on the Judiciary
HLS	Manuscript Division, Harvard Law School Library
HTL	Harry S. Truman Library
HUAC	U.S. Congress, House, Committee on Un-American Activities
ISC	U.S. Senate, Subcommittee to Investigate the Administration of the Internal Security Act and Other Internal Security Laws of the Committee on the Judiciary
Justice	U.S. Department of Justice
LC	Manuscript Division, Library of Congress
NA	National Archives
NYT	*New York Times*
OF	Official File

PA	*Political Affairs*
PW	*Daily People's World*
RTC	"The Right to Counsel" (a collection of correspondence, reports, and clippings assembled by the Cleveland Bar Association)
SApp	U.S. Congress, Senate, Committee on Appropriations
SJC	U.S. Congress, Senate, Committee on the Judiciary
Whitman File	Dwight D. Eisenhower: Papers as President of the United States (Ann Whitman File)

COLD WAR
POLITICAL
JUSTICE

Introduction

On Christmas Eve 1962, unnoticed by most Americans, an obscure radical named Junius Scales walked out of federal prison, bringing down the curtain on a quarter-century drama, the confrontation between the Communist Party of the United States (CPUSA) and a criminal law known as the Smith Act.[1] By then, American communism, once a feared revolutionary movement, was virtually moribund, and few Americans remembered the statute which had cut it down. But the story that ended so obscurely on that December day was far more significant than its quiet conclusion would suggest, for the guard who slammed the prison gate behind Scales was closing the book on one of the classic chronicles of American political justice.

In a sense, of course, all justice is political. Courts are, after all, agencies of the state, and, even when trying civil suits between private individuals, they enforce the values and implement the policies of those who rule society. In all criminal cases the government is actually a party, prosecuting, in the name of "the people," and attempting to remove from circulation defendants accused of antisocial conduct. But, as perceptive scholars such as Otto Kirchheimer and Theodore Becker have observed, some justice, besides involving the state and its policies, also serves partisan ends. In most nations, throughout history, those in control of the government have occasionally employed legal machinery for the purpose of directly affecting power relationships within society. They have used the courts to eliminate from political competition both potent rivals who threatened to upset the prevailing pattern of value distribution and symbolic threats to the status quo. In addition, power elites have exploited judicial procedure to enhance their own reputations. While it is theoretically possible for courts confronted with such cases to act as neutral arbiters, just as they do when handling routine civil and criminal matters, all too often in these political situations they align themselves with the forces of the prosecution, masking partiality behind the accepted formalities of legal procedure. When judges favor "the establishment" over

its victims, while continuing to pay lip service to the ideal of equality
before the law, the judicial system performs dishonestly. Because such
hypocrisy is not the kind of thing that loyal citizens like to associate
with their government, political justice has long enjoyed a bad reputation.[2]

Americans, assured by high school civics teachers that theirs is a government of laws and not of men, are loath to acknowledge that this
country's legal system is, or ever has been, used for partisan purposes.
But political justice—as H. Rap Brown once said of violence—is as American as apple pie. From the Federalists in the 1790s to the Nixon administration in the 1970s, those in control of governments in this country
have used judicial machinery to harass partisan opponents and critics
of their policies. The military trial of Copperhead Congressman Clement
Vallandigham during the Civil War, the prosecution of anarchists for the
1886 Haymarket bombing, the jailing of radicals, pacifists, and German
Americans in World War I, and the more recent legal proceedings against
Black Panthers and anti-Vietnam activists—although occurring in widely
differing circumstances and presenting as many contrasts as similarities,
all involved (as the writers who have chronicled them make clear) the
use of criminal law for political purposes. Clearly, they are examples of
the phenomenon which Kirchheimer and Becker characterize as political justice.[3]

A catalog of repression, of course, captures only one facet of American legal history. Political justice is commonly associated with social
and economic conflict, and in the United States this phenomenon has
most commonly manifested itself when the nation was under considerable stress, as during wars and periods of extreme racial tension or bitter confrontations between labor and capital. In calmer times Americans
have often repudiated political justice and practiced as well as professed
the principles embodied in their Bill of Rights. The popularly demanded and judicially sanctioned incarceration of the West Coast Japanese
during World War II and the almost universal condemnation of that action and the court decisions which allowed it after the fighting ended are
perhaps the best illustration of the contrast. Few judges, legal scholars
or historians would today defend the Alien and Sedition Acts or the sweeping attack on peaceful dissent which accompanied World War I and the
Red Scare that followed it. But, despite repeated condemnation of past
excesses, the use of legal machinery for partisan purposes by those who
control the government continues.[4]

The concept of political justice, however, embraces more than just
official abuse of dissenting minorities, for litigation can serve the inter-

ests of the attackers as well as the defenders ıf the status quo. American radicals have employed it to facilitate and escalate their ongoing ideological war with the established order, taking advantage of the attention which the media generally focus upon spectacular trials to convey their movements' messages to the public and to build support for their organizations. Although some dissidents, such as Clement Vallandigham and Eugene V. Debs, have invited prosecution, most have entered into judicial proceedings (at least those of a criminal nature) only under compulsion. Once forced into battle, though, they have frequently counterattacked with demonstrations, rallies, leafleting, and other forms of mass political activity, intended both to inform a watching world and to bring the weight of popular opinion to bear on judicial institutions regarded as so biased that, unless pressured, they would never give members of dissident minorities a fair trial. Carrying their propaganda activities into the courtroom, such litigants, frequently aided by their lawyers, have attempted to make legal proceedings themselves vehicles for the conversion of the masses.[5]

The resistance of establishment prosecutors and judges to such tactics has often produced disruptive confrontations, such as those which marred the 1969 Chicago 7 trial. Attorney William Kunstler, who represented several of the defendants in that proceeding, attributes these outbursts to the impossibility of trying a political case "within the strictures that apply to ordinary criminal trials." More accurately, the cause of such disruptions is the attempted exploitation of the judicial process for political purposes it was not designed to serve, and responsibility for the turmoil generally rests as much with the defendants and their lawyers as with the prosecution.[6]

Certainly this was true of the first Smith Act case involving leaders of the Communist Party. In that respect, as in many others, it was a typical political trial. Although the Smith Act attack on the CPUSA is a chapter in the chronicle of the Cold War, the story of that legal assault on a small radical organization, and of the way in which the judiciary, the general public, and the victims themselves responded to it, embodies themes which recur throughout the history of American political justice. It is a narrative which reveals both the kinds of pressures and considerations that inspire partisan use of the judicial process and the consequences of such exploitation, for both the targets of prosecution and the civil liberties of the nation as a whole.

The Smith Act came into being because some anti-Communists were determined to mobilize the legal order against the CPUSA. Their initial efforts to secure enactment of legislation proscribing that organization met with little success, but on the eve of World War II, with strong anti-foreign sentiment gripping the country, Congress responded to their entreaties by passing the Smith Act.

For several years the wartime alliance between the United States and the USSR protected the Party from the new law, but by 1948 Russian-American relations had deteriorated badly. Bent on rallying the public behind an anti-Soviet foreign policy, the Democratic Truman administration employed arguments which projected international communism as the threat to national security. Its rhetoric, as historians Athan Theoharis and Richard Freeland have pointed out, aroused public concern about the domestic wing of the movement which was supposedly menacing America from abroad.[7] Exploiting an issue on which their rivals had focused attention, Republicans condemned the Democrats for not doing enough to combat communism at home, and the Truman administration, acting a bit more defensively than its critics would acknowledge, set out to repress the CPUSA. In July 1948, Truman's Attorney General secured an indictment charging the members of the Party's National Board with violation of the Smith Act.

The CPUSA responded to this political prosecution with a political defense. Bent on rescuing its leaders from the clutches of a hostile legal system, it mounted around the case a massive propaganda campaign, intended to mobilize the public behind a demand that the government drop the charges against the indicted men. When this effort failed to achieve the desired results, Communists carried their political struggle into the courtroom, endeavoring to make it a forum for criticism of American society and government. The prosecution presented an equally political case, largely ignoring the defendants, and instead attacking the CPUSA, which it sought to characterize as a disloyal, dangerous, and dishonest organization, whose disclaimers of intent to overthrow the government by violence could never be taken at face value. With both sides determined to wage ideological warfare in the courtroom and willing to employ disruptive tactics in order to achieve the ends they sought, the proceedings quickly degenerated into a disorderly spectacle.

Courtroom chaos was not the only consequence of this political trial, for after the jury returned guilty verdicts against the defendants, they appealed. Influenced by the Cold War atmosphere around them, appellate courts, in order to uphold the convictions of Communists, affirmed the constitutionality of the Smith Act. This they could do only by modifying the accepted interpretation of the First Amendment in such a way as to significantly constrict the freedom of expression which that constitutional provision supposedly guaranteed to all Americans.

Having secured judicial approval of the Smith Act, the Department of

Justice mounted a nationwide campaign designed to destroy the CPUSA, but also calculated to advance its own institutional interests. Although the Republican Eisenhower administration replaced the Democratic Truman one, the prosecutions continued, for bureaucratic as well as partisan reasons. Students of American communism have tended to underestimate the impact of this legal assault, but the fact of the matter is, it was one of the major reasons for the virtual collapse of the CPUSA by 1958.[8]

The nation paid a high price for the debilitation of a small radical organization, for the methods used to incapacitate it seriously endangered rights lying at the heart of the American constitutional system. As the nature of the Cold War changed and international tensions eased somewhat, many people began to express concern about abuses such as the use of perjured testimony by the government, and, when a number of lawyers offered their services to Communists who could not otherwise have obtained adequate representation, the public applauded them for doing so. The Supreme Court, also manifesting a renewed concern for civil liberties, handed down a decision which construed the Smith Act far more narrowly than had government attorneys conducting the attack on the CPUSA. When the Justice Department sought new ways to continue its war on the Party, a now-resistant judiciary barred the prosecutors' path.

By 1963 Junius Scales was out of prison, and the Smith Act story was concluded. Today only aging veterans of the battered American Communist movement think much about that law and the damage that it did. Perhaps their fellow citizens should also, for although the Smith Act prosecutions were a product of circumstances unique to the early years of the Cold War, the kind of political justice which they represent is not. As old as the Alien and Sedition Acts and as contemporary as the Angela Davis case, it is a phenomenon which should be of continuing concern to all Americans who value their civil liberties.

NOTES

1. 54 Stat. 670 (1940). The Smith Act is also known as the Alien Registration Act of 1940.

2. Otto Kirchheimer, *Political Justice: The Use of Legal Procedure for Political Ends* (Princeton, N.J.: Princeton University Press, 1961), pp. 6, 49-53; Theodore L. Becker, ed., *Political Trials* (Indianapolis, Ind., and New York: Bobbs-Merrill, 1971), pp. xi-xv.

3. On the Federalists' use of the Alien and Sedition Acts against their Jeffersonian rivals see James Morton Smith, *Freedom's Fetters: The Alien and Sedition Laws and American Civil Liberties* (Ithaca, N.Y.: Cornell University Press, 1956). The best account of the Vallandigham

case is Frank Klement, *The Limits of Dissent: Clement L. Vallandig-ham & the Civil War* (Lexington: University of Kentucky Press, 1970); Henry David, *The History of the Haymarket Affair: A Study in the American Social Revolutionary and Labor Movements* (New York: Russell & Russell, 1958), is the classic account of that incident. On World War I political justice see the incredibly detailed H. C. Peterson and Gilbert Fite, *Opponents of War 1917-1918* (Seattle: University of Washington Press, 1957). Donald Freed, *Agony in New Haven: The Trial of Bobby Seale, Erika Huggins and the Black Panther Party* (New York: Simon and Schuster, 1973), and Peter L. Zimroth, *Perversions of Justice: The Prosecution and Acquittal of the Panther 21* (New York: Viking Press, 1974), contain informative accounts of Black Panther cases. Jessica Mitford, *The Trial of Dr. Spock* (New York: Alfred A. Knopf, 1969), William O'Rourke, *The Harrisburg 7 and the New Catholic Left* (New York: Thomas Y. Crowell, 1972), and Jason Epstein, *The Great Conspiracy Trial: An Essay on Law, Liberty and the Constitution* (New York: Random House, 1970), deal with three of the most important trials of opponents of the Vietnam War. The Daniel Ellsburg prosecution and the Gainesville trial of members of the Vietnam Veterans Against the War are probably the best known examples of Nixon administration political justice.

    4. Nathan Hakman, "Political Trials in the Legal Order: A Political Scientist's Perspective," *Journal of Public Law* 21 (1972): 95, 99.

    5. Hakman, "Political Trials," pp. 95, 102-15, and "Old and New Left Activity in the Legal Order: An Interpretation," *Journal of Social Issues* 27 (1971): 117; Klement, *The Limits of Dissent*, pp. 150-51; Peterson and Fite, *Opponents of War*, pp. 249-51; David J. Danielski, "The Chicago Conspiracy Trial," in Becker, ed., *Political Trials*, pp. 162-64, 173.

    6. "Playboy Interview: William Kunstler," *Playboy* 17 (October 1970): 78.

    7. Richard Freeland, *The Truman Doctrine and the Origins of McCarthyism: Foreign Policy, Domestic Politics and Internal Security 1946-1948* (New York: Alfred A. Knopf, 1972); Athan Theoharis, *Seeds of Repression: Harry S. Truman and the Origins of McCarthyism* (Chicago: Quadrangle, 1971) and "The Rhetoric of Politics," *Politics and Policies of the Truman Administration*, ed. Barton Bernstein (Chicago: Quadrangle, 1970), pp. 196-241.

    8. The leading studies of the Communist Party in this period are David A. Shannon, *The Decline of American Communism: A History of the Communist Party of the United States Since 1945* (New York: Harcourt, Brace and Company, 1959) (cited hereafter as *Decline*), and Joseph R. Starobin, *American Communism in Crisis, 1943-1957* (Cambridge, Mass.: Harvard University Press, 1972). For a discussion of the explanations for the collapse of the CPUSA offered by these authors, see Chapter 7.

1

A Law for
the Communists

This bill is aimed directly at the Communists. . . . We have
been coddling that outfit too long in my opinion.
                                    —Representative John McCormack
                                    1 March 1935

"[J]ustice is a sharp weapon in the hands of our reactionary enemy,"
complained an imprisoned radical in 1926, and so it seemed to those
who marched in the ranks of American communism during the decade
and a half which followed World War I.[1] Subjected to repeated legal
harassment, members of the CPUSA developed a strategy designed
to protect their organization from attack and to turn persecution to
their political advantage. The Party owed its survival, however, largely
to the fact that its enemies lacked the federal criminal statute with
which they might have dealt it a fatal blow. Not until the eve of World
War II, when a fear of all things foreign gripped the country, could anti-
Communists persuade Congress to adopt the legislation which they wanted—the Smith Act.

I

Their target, a product of the coalescence of several radical factions
that broke away from the Socialist movement during the post-World War I
Red Scare, had endured legal attack since its inception. During the infamous Palmer raids of early 1920, federal authorities rounded up several
thousand Bolsheviks, with the aim of deporting them. The states were
equally vigorous, as nearly thirty of them enacted "red flag" laws, pro-

scribing symbolic expression of radical sentiments, and more than twenty adopted criminal syndicalism statutes, also useful for attacking communism. Using these and already existing anti-radical measures, the states sent approximately 300 dissidents to prison during 1919 and 1920. This prosecution forced communism underground and by 1922 had deprived the movement of nearly nine-tenths of its original 40,000 followers. In August of that year federal agents organized a raid against a secret meeting of the Party's top leaders and secured the indictment of those in attendance under a Michigan criminal syndicalism law. Fortunately for the Communists, bad luck and legal technicalities thwarted the prosecution, and none of those arrested went to prison. As America subsided into the comfortable normalcy of the Coolidge era, popular concern with radicalism declined, and so did governmental harassment of the Party. By the end of the 1920s, not a single Communist remained in jail for his political beliefs.[2]

Freed from the pressure of constant attack by the legal order, the Party should have been able to concentrate on expanding its size and influence. Instead, throughout the middle and late 1920s, its members devoted most of their attention to unproductive factional infighting, which ultimately made Earl Browder—inept, but suitably submissive to the Russians—the head of the organization. Not until the onset of the Great Depression did American communism experience a genuine revival. Between April 1930 and May 1935, the membership of the Party quadrupled, rising from 7,500 to around 30,000. Hard times made a wide variety of people susceptible to Communist appeals, so that the CPUSA, once composed largely of workers from abroad, now acquired both a native-born majority and a substantial middle-class element. Marxist ideology ignited the imaginations of many young people, and, despite the fact that the Party, bent on "proletarianizing" itself, tended to regard students as dubious characters, the Young Communist League established strong units on a number of college campuses. Communism also gained support among the millions of Americans thrown out of work by the Depression. For the first time, blacks, too, began to join the CPUSA in substantial numbers.[3]

During the early Depression years, Communists made only limited gains in the labor field, but their advances laid a solid base for explosive progress in the late 1930s. During the strike wave that began in 1933, competent Party members working in factories and mines found it easy to rise to top positions in newly created unions. Here they gained visibility, and when the Congress of Industrial Organizations (CIO) began its organizing drive in 1935, John L. Lewis tapped many of them for important jobs in his new labor federation. While laying the groundwork for future advances in the union movement, Communists also entered the federal government in significant numbers. The extensive need for public servants which developed in the early days of the New Deal created an immediate demand for 250,000 new bureaucrats. Thus a qualified Communist, or for that matter any competent person, could easily obtain a federal job, and many Party members did so.[4]

Although the Great Depression enabled Communists to advance on many fronts, it also revived the countervailing passions of the postwar Red Scare. By 1935, as Representative Emanuel Celler (D., N.Y.) noted, there seemed "to be a general hysteria of fear gripping the nation against communism. . . ." Public anxiety manifested itself in legal action, particularly at the state level, where Nevada (1929), Indiana (1933), and Tennessee (1934) all enacted new sedition legislation, and Illinois amended its statute on the subject.[5]

These revived fears of radicalism expressed themselves most forcefully in prosecutions under laws already on the books. There existed an almost infinite variety of measures which could be used, in Communist terms, to "crush all labor's class struggle organizations." For example, between January 1929 and November 1930, Boston police arrested 35 Communists for assault and battery, 15 for violation of park rules, 7 for disturbing the peace, 1 for stealing a police captain's club, and 1 for common law nuisance, and apprehended 102 other radicals for violation of miscellaneous city ordinances.[6]

The multitude of state and local laws employed against Communists included the red flag statutes enacted just after World War I. Using such measures, authorities successfully prosecuted radicals in California, Michigan, and New York. Although the Supreme Court overturned the California conviction, its ruling was too narrow to withdraw all red flag laws from the anti-Communists' arsenal.[7]

These measures threatened no very fundamental Party activity, but the same was not true of sedition statutes, which were aimed directly at communism's proselytistic activities. New Jersey authorities used such a law against nine "workers" taken into custody during a raid on a meeting of the unemployed at a Newark Party headquarters. In Pennsylvania, law enforcement officials prosecuted numerous radicals for distributing handbills and making speeches, while in Colorado police arrested two teenagers for passing out Communist literature to troops near Fort Logan and charged them with violation of a 1919 anarchy-sedition act.[8]

State authorities also dusted off criminal syndicalism laws, little used since 1925, for employment against strikers and Communists. In 1929,

Ohio convicted two "workers" of criminal syndicalism, and the following year California jailed eight Communist agricultural organizers on the same charge. Oregon, which had thirty-two prosecutions under way in 1934, proved even more vigorous. A report issued in March of that year noted other criminal syndicalism cases in progress, apparently against Communists, in Utah, Washington, Iowa and Upper Michigan. By October 1934, California, Illinois, and Georgia were also prosecuting radicals for that offense. Many of these prosecutions were products of labor-management confrontations. During the West Coast maritime dispute of 1934, a supporting general strike in San Francisco, involving 127,000 workers, led to the trial of 17 Communists in Sacramento and the conviction of 8. When Party members in Portland, Oregon, staged a public assembly to protest the beating and shooting of longshoremen and raids by police on workers' homes and meeting halls, the authorities seized the chairman, one of the speakers, and four other participants, and at least three of those arrested were ultimately convicted of criminal syndicalism. The high-handed use of these laws ultimately produced a widespread reaction, which expressed itself in demands for their repeal and in appellate court decisions freeing radicals convicted under them.[9]

Criminal syndicalism laws were far less severe than the nineteenth-century insurrection statutes, originally designed to prevent slave revolts, which two Southern states resurrected for use against Communist organizers. Virginia pioneered this approach to the radical problem with a single arrest in 1929, but it was Georgia that made the most extensive use of one of these antiquated laws, charging at least twenty-five persons under it between 1930 and 1936. The most notable victim of the Georgia insurrection statute was a youthful Communist organizer named Angelo Herndon, a man guilty of nothing more than recruiting a few new members for the CPUSA and having some Party pamphlets in his possession. Although the state never managed to prove that Herndon had openly advocated the subversion of governmental authority, or even that he had distributed any literature that did so, a jury nevertheless convicted him, and only the intervention of the U.S. Supreme Court saved the young radical from a lengthy stay in prison.[10]

The national government failed to match the anti-Communist vigor of states such as Georgia, but, during the first six years of the Depression, it did step up its use of the deportation laws. Apparently, in some instances federal authorities acted at the request of state judges, who referred to the Immigration Service the cases of alien radicals convicted in their courtrooms.[11]

II

The Communists countered the assaults upon them with "labor defense," an aggressive strategy based on the proposition that all government is class government. As far as members of the CPUSA were concerned, the state was nothing more than force organized to serve the interests of the ruling class; and in America that meant the capitalists. The governmental institutions of this country were bourgeois instruments for the exploitation of the working class. As for the law, it was simply a codification of rules for the protection of the capitalists, their possessions, and their system. It was, naturally, the very embodiment of injustice against the workers.[12]

Regarding both the law and the institutions that created and applied it as merely instruments of one segment of society for the oppression of the rest of the people, Communists concluded that all justice was class justice. "With unfailing regularity," one of them declared, "constitutional provisions are applied one way for the employing class and another way for the workers." Members of the CPUSA accepted this situation as natural and did not "accuse" such justice; they expected to play by the same rules when the power of the state was at last in their hands. This outlook divided Communists from true civil libertarians, with whom they were willing to make common cause in defense of their own rights, but not those of their political opponents.[13]

The class nature of so-called justice meant that workers and their Communist leaders could hope for neither fair nor impartial treatment from the machinery of criminal justice. The "bosses" controlled the entire judicial apparatus, even the jury system; therefore, as Party leader John Gates put it, "those who labored for the cause of the workers could expect nothing but injustice in a capitalist court."[14]

Consequently, proletarian prisoners had to win their freedom outside the legal process. Because the important thing was the political defense of the accused, in most cases, it was desirable that he represent himself. The Party offered classes in the rudiments of courtroom self-defense, and the Communist-controlled International Labor Defense (ILD) published detailed instructions on the subject. If a proletarian prisoner found it necessary to employ an attorney, the role of the lawyer should be kept strictly secondary. He was just a courtroom technician, responsible only for ensuring that the juridical aspects of the case were handled properly.[15]

According to William Patterson (for many years head of the ILD and the chief Communist spokesman in this field), popular protest, rather

than legal skill, was needed to free a proletarian defendant. Success depended upon the political mobilization of the working class and its sympathizers. In Patterson's words: "The court rooms of the working class
are the streets. It is in the streets they must pass their verdict of innocence on a class war victim. When they, in sufficient number, have done
this, that verdict will be reflected by judge and jury in capitalist courts."[16]

The Party valued trials only for the opportunity which they afforded
to generate effective revolutionary propaganda; thus Communist writers
urged their comrades to employ courtroom tactics not of defense, but of
attack. Through trials, they argued, Party members could expose to their
fellow workers the true nature of the courts. Indicted radicals should take
advantage of their situations to make the institutions of American justice
look as weak and ridiculous as possible and to bring an indictment against
the entire capitalist regime.[17]

To exploit trials for propaganda purposes and mobilize the masses behind proletarian defendants, Communists relied on the International Labor
Defense (ILD). The ILD was the successor to a number of special and local
defense committees, some of them independently established groups with
which Communists had cooperated and others creations of the Party itself.
In existence since 1925, it was the American affiliate of the International
Red Aid. By the end of 1926, the ILD claimed 156 branches, with 25,000
individual members, and enough affiliated groups to add another 75,000
names to its rolls.[18]

The organization published the monthly *Labor Defender* and in many
states also put out pamphlets, adapted to local law, which explained to
workers what to do if they were arrested. The ILD also agitated for repeal of statutes that it considered anti-Communist and anti-working class
and labored to prevent the passage of new ones. By far its most important activity, however, was exploiting the courts to advance the revolutionary objectives of the CPUSA, through the offensive use of criminal defense.
The organization would seize upon a case with major propaganda value
and exploit it continuously during the arrest, trial, appeal, clemency,
imprisonment, and even post-imprisonment stages.[19]

In some instances this exploitation involved cases, such as that of
Angelo Herndon, in which Communists themselves were the defendants.
Around the victim of the Georgia insurrection statute, the ILD built up
a mass campaign, designed both to pressure authorities into freeing him
and to assist Party recruiting among blacks by advertising Communist
efforts to promote unity between Negro and white workers in the South.[20]
Often, though, the ILD exploited prominent cases which did not directly concern the Communist Party, working to free labor activists Tom

Mooney and Warren Billings and anarchists Nicola Sacco and Bartolomeo
Vanzetti and mounting an impressive nationwide campaign to save the
Scottsboro boys, innocent black teenagers unjustly convicted in Alabama
of raping two white women.

While the ILD may have taken up such cases in part because of the
opportunity which they afforded to solicit money from supporters of
the defendants, its major reason for plunging into them was to win con-
verts among the members of some large group—such as blacks, organized
labor, the foreign born, or intellectuals—deeply concerned about the fate
of the accused. Above all, the ILD took up the causes of nonmember
victims of capitalist justice because of their value as vehicles of education. By involving itself in cases of this type and propagandizing them
heavily, the International Labor Defense hoped to heighten the class
consciousness of the masses while teaching them important revolutionary lessons. Scottsboro, for example, demonstrated the futility of seeking freedom for blacks without first overthrowing the social system of
the South. Probably the biggest lesson such cases could teach was the illusionary nature of the "justice" promised by the capitalist legal order.[21]

The Communists were convinced that the best defense was always a
protest movement of the masses. Under the influence of ILD principles,
they came to regard the legal process as fundamentally irrelevant and to
see the preservation of their movement as dependent upon fighting strength
rather than the ability to use the tools provided by the law. Their analysis
was faulty, and one day the Party would pay dearly for its deficiencies.

III

These were not readily apparent as long as no federal criminal law
menaced the movement. During the Red Scare, the national government
had bloodied bolshevism with the deportation statutes, but in the 1920s
and early 1930s—because the courts imposed stiffer standards of evidence
and procedure on immigration officials, because the Bureau of Investigation stopped collecting information on dissident political activity, and because the percentage of native-born Americans in the Party rose—this anti-
radical artillery lost much of its effectiveness. Criminal syndicalsim, criminal anarchy, sedition, and red flag laws enabled local prosecutors to harass
Communists, but as each of these operated only within a single state, they
posed no serious threat to a national organization, such as the CPUSA.
Only a federal criminal statute, effective wherever Communists became
active, could seriously endanger the Party.[22]

During the tenure of Attorney General A. Mitchell Palmer (1919-1921), the Department of Justice attempted to provide the national government with such an anti-radical instrument. The results of its experiments with section 6 of the Penal Code, embodying an 1861 seditious conspiracy law which made it a crime to attempt the overthrow of the government, were disappointing. When the department brought a test case against the anarchist El Artie Society, Federal District Judge John Raymond Hazel ruled that Congress had not intended to proscribe attempts to overthrow the government by means of propaganda. Because American Bolshevists rarely went beyond revolutionary rhetoric, this decision left the Justice Department empty-handed.[23]

A federal sedition statute, similar to the wartime measure adopted in 1918, appeared to be the solution to the problem, for armed with such a law, the national government could move forcefully against those who endeavored to promote its overthrow through speech and writing. During the winter of 1919-1920 members of Congress introduced approximately seventy peacetime sedition bills, and both Attorney General Palmer and President Wilson worked to secure passage of such legislation. Its proponents had the support of many patriotic groups and radical-hunting state officials, but they faced opposition from a Harvard Law School professor, Zechariah Chafee, Jr., a number of clergymen, and the American Federation of Labor. The press, viewing sedition legislation as at least an indirect threat to its own freedom, overwhelmingly condemned it, while congressional skepticism steadily increased, and the House Rules Committee reported unfavorably on the two most prominent bills, thus killing them. By February 1920, all hope for a federal sedition law was gone.[24]

Not until the Depression-stimulated revival of the CPUSA did Congress again focus attention on internal communism. In 1930, at the suggestion of Representative Hamilton Fish, Jr. (R., N.Y.), the House created a special committee to study the subject. That body listened mainly to spokesmen for right-wing and patriotic organizations but also took testimony from labor leaders and from William Z. Foster of the CPUSA. In addition to a report, it produced numerous legislative proposals, among them recommendations for outlawing the Party and for barring Communist propaganda from interstate commerce and the mails. Several bills embodying the suggestions of the Fish Committee were introduced, but none achieved passage.[25]

In 1934 Congressman Samuel Dickstein (D., N.Y.) proposed creation of a second special committee to investigate "un-American activities," and the House adopted his suggestion, placing John McCormack (D., Mass.) in charge of the new investigating body. When the committee began hearings on 5 June, McCormack informed the public that the House "keenly sensed and fully realized the danger of vicious propaganda . . . aimed at the subversion of those fundamental principles upon which our Constitution rests. . . ." The objective of the investigation, he said, would be to find some means of "protecting this country and its people from its dissemination."[26]

IV

The report that the McCormack-Dickstein Committee submitted to the House of Representatives in February 1935 was a call for legislative action to defend the rights and liberties of the American people. Essential to their preservation, the committee argued, was a statute making it a crime to advocate political or social change in a manner which might incite violent overthrow of governmental authority. The report called also for legislation making it a crime to advise, counsel, or urge members of the armed forces to disobey the law or military regulations.[27]

Assisted by allies in the Senate, members of the McCormack-Dickstein Committee set out to secure enactment of these proposals. Representative Charles Kramer (D., Calif.) introduced a sweeping measure designed to punish persons advocating overthrow of any government in the United States by force, violence, or assassination, setting up organizations to do such things, or deliberately defending those who did. He later withdrew this bill in favor of a more limited one outlawing advocacy of violent revolution and the distribution of literature urging it, while Richard B. Russell (D., Ga.) submitted a companion measure to the Senate. Meanwhile, McCormack was introducing in the House legislation to carry out those recommendations of his committee involving the armed forces, and Millard E. Tydings (D., Md.), chairman of the Senate Naval Affairs Committee, was offering an identical bill in the upper chamber.[28]

Their target was the CPUSA, for although the McCormack-Dickstein Committee ostensibly had investigated fascism and nazism, as well as Stalinism, it devoted over two-thirds of its report to left-wing activities. McCormack made his own purposes quite clear when he informed the House Committee on Military Affairs that his bill was "aimed directly at the Communists." Although the Massachusetts congressman denied it, so too was the sedition measure sponsored by his colleague Charles Kramer.[29]

These anti-Communist proposals recruited many supporters. The Army endorsed the disaffection measure, and the Navy became the most enthusiastic backer of that legislation. The American Legion, the Veterans of Foreign Wars, the Disabled American Veterans, the National Republic, the Daughters of the American Revolution, the American Coalition, and the ROTC Association all threw their support behind McCormack's bill, and well over a hundred such organizations endorsed Kramer's too. Both proposals received backing from the business community, with the Chamber of Commerce of the United States officially endorsing military disaffection legislation, while a number of its local affiliates also urged adoption of a law against sedition.[30]

Although generating considerable support, the proposals of the McCormack-Dickstein Committee aroused potent opposition too. The Communists condemned the sedition and military disaffection bills, as did a number of "front" groups,[31] the most vocal being the American League Against War and Fascism. Outside the Communist orbit the most active opponent of this legislation was the American Civil Liberties Union, which sent two representatives before the House Military Affairs Committee to urge rejection of McCormack's measure. In late March the ACLU joined with the American League Against War and Fascism in sponsoring a Madison Square Garden rally against "alien and sedition bills." At a 24 April meeting in New York 150 ACLU members unanimously adopted a resolution condemning the "gag" legislation then before Congress, and during the summer spokesmen for the organization continued to speak out against such measures.[32]

The ACLU did not stand alone. Karl Llewellyn of the Columbia Law School testified against the McCormack bill, and a group of 150 of his students signed a resolution condemning both that measure and Kramer's. The disaffection proposal also drew fire from Harvard's scholarly civil libertarian, Zechariah Chafee, Jr. The press and publishing industry, regarding the proposed legislation as a threat to freedom of expression, proved equally hostile to it, with even the conservative *Wall Street Journal* joining the chorus of protest. Sedition and military disaffection bills elicited support only from the Hearst newspapers, and even they did not push it strongly.[33]

The vigorous opposition of the publishing industry, most of the press, students, professors, and the ACLU proved effective, so that while disaffection and sedition legislation made limited progress in the Seventy-fourth Congress, it failed to win enactment. During the first session, a badly divided House Judiciary Committee endorsed the Kramer bill by a one vote margin, but Speaker Joseph Byrns (D., Tenn.) refused to allow the suspension of the rules sought by its proponents, and the measure never reached the floor. After some acrimonious hearings, McCormack's bill died in committee, but its Senate counterpart made greater progress. Tydings, acting for the Naval Affairs Committee, reported his disaffection measure without holding any hearings on it, maneuvered the bill onto the unanimous-consent calendar—supposedly reserved for minor and non-controversial legislation—and secured its passage while the Senate chamber was nearly empty. Boosters of the bill then rammed it through the House Military Affairs Committee in the absence of a quorum. Their efforts, as well as Tydings's, went for naught, since the Rules Committee, unwilling to see a fight over military disaffection legislation interfere with efforts to pass several important administration measures, kept the bill off the floor for the remainder of the first session. Neither Tydings's proposal nor Kramer's made any progress in the second session, as even their sponsors lost enthusiasm for them.[34]

Such measures met with even less success in the Seventy-fifth Congress. With many of its members swept into office by the Roosevelt landslide of 1936, that body was liberal in character and utterly unreceptive to anti-Communist legislation. When the persistent McCormack introduced a bill "to prohibit statements and publications advocating overthrow of the government by violence," he excited no one but the CPUSA. The Judiciary Committee quietly buried his measure and similar ones introduced by Malcolm C. Tarver (D., Ga.) and J. Will Taylor (R., Tenn.), declining even to schedule hearings on them. The Navy, the driving force behind the Tydings and McCormack bills, apparently considered the climate on Capitol Hill so unfavorable that for two years it did not even bother to request disaffection legislation.[35]

V

Although Congress was for the moment unreceptive to proposals for anti-Communist laws, domestic and foreign events were combining to produce in Americans, and in their senators and representatives, a fear of foreigners and alien ideologies which would eventually make such legislation irresistible. This was ironic, for there was now less danger of a Communist attack on the U.S. government than at any time since the Party's birth. In 1935 the CPUSA abandoned revolutionary isolationism in favor of accommodation with the nation's liberal leadership. The Moscow-controlled Comintern, fearful of the growing strength of the implacably anti-Soviet Fascist powers and anxious to secure allies for Russia among the Western democracies, called upon Communists everywhere to enter into Popular Fronts, broad coalitions that would unite all pro-

gressives in the fight against fascism. The CPUSA, excluded by the realities of American politics from any direct participation in the government, responded by stepping up its work with front groups, through which it hoped to exercise some indirect influence over national policy. It pushed the long-range objectives of Marxism-Leninism into the background and concentrated on issues of immediate concern to liberals, labor, and racial minorities. Stalinists proved to be among the hardest-working members of the new CIO and consequently, although a small minority within the labor federation, soon gained control over many of its affiliates and substantial influence in the national headquarters as well. In the political arena Communists were among the most vocal and least critical supporters of the New Deal, and this stance, coupled with their unrestrained anti-fascism, made them respectable in the eyes of many liberals. The CPUSA could muster considerable support for its causes from left-leaning intellectuals, and even from well-known political figures, such as Frances Perkins, Harold L. Ickes, and Robert Jackson.[36]

Nevertheless, Americans came to favor its proscription. This occurred not because a Stalinist attack upon the government was imminent, but rather because the Party was an organization with foreign ties, which espoused a foreign ideology. Throughout American history nativism had been a persistent problem, and, as the Great Depression settled over the country, many people, angered and frustrated by high unemployment, vented their emotions on the aliens whom they incorrectly blamed for the nation's economic ills. Events abroad, particularly the rise of dictatorships and the aggressive exploits of the Fascist powers, also fanned the fires of xenophobia. By the late 1930s most of Europe was no longer democratic, and Americans came to fear for the safety of their own popular government, a fact that became apparent in 1937 when President Roosevelt proposed legislation authorizing him to pack the Supreme Court and reorganize the executive branch. One of these measures was designed to remove an undemocratic barrier to popular economic and social reforms, and the other simply to promote administrative efficiency, but Roosevelt suffered humiliating defeats on both. The major reason was fear of presidential despotism.

Regarding both dictatorship and war as foreign phenomena, Americans reacted to their threatening advance by pulling into a protective shell. While both contemporaries and scholars have characterized this conduct as isolationism, it involved more than a refusal to interact with the other countries of the world. Also apparent was a deep distrust of anyone or anything which intruded into the United States from abroad.

A Gallup poll conducted in January 1939 revealed that 87 percent of the population favored requiring all noncitizens to register with the government.[37] This inward-looking and defensive form of nationalism manifested itself in hostility toward foreign individuals, institutions, and ideologies.

In Congress it produced not only neutrality legislation but also an environment ripe for exploitation by anti-Communists. On 10 May 1938 the House passed, by a vote of 194 to 41, a resolution introduced by Representative Martin Dies, Jr., of Texas, which called for the creation of another special committee to investigate un-American propaganda. Some of those who supported this measure were primarily interested in spotlighting Nazi activities, but Dies, who combined xenophobia with an intense hostility toward radicalism, was more interested in the Communists. After becoming chairman of the new committee, he made left-wing extremism the subject of its first public hearings. These, held in the summer of 1938, would have been ludicrous, had they not been so serious, for a parade of witnesses, many of them irresponsible, pinned the Communist label on 640 organizations, 483 newspapers, and 280 labor unions.

Despite the character of these hearings, Dies and his colleagues commanded tremendous support, and, during the 1938 elections, a number of liberal candidates whom they opposed went down to defeat. The committee's activities drew sharp criticism from Roosevelt, but, despite his attack, a December Gallup poll revealed that 79 percent of those familiar with the work of the Dies group favored continuation of its investigations. In February 1939 a resolution to extend the life of the committee passed the House 344 to 35. Support for the Dies Committee arose mainly from concern about war propaganda and Nazi activities, but, as Congress and the public grew ever more fearful of alien dangers, the likelihood that attacks on any un-American influence would achieve success mounted steadily. As a California congressman noted in July 1939, "the mood of this House is such that if you brought in the Ten Commandments today and asked for their repeal and attached to that request an alien law, you could get it."[38]

The Communists had hoped to make the Seventy-sixth Congress their forum, but clearly the Party, with its ties to the Soviet Union, was likely to arouse hostility rather than support in a legislature such as this. By mid-July, senators and representatives had introduced more than a hundred anti-alien proposals. Among them was H.R. 5138. A measure ideally suited to capitalize on the country's fear of foreign influences, it would become the Smith Act.[39]

VI

As Representative Howard Smith (D., Va.) readily acknowledged, he could take no pride of authorship in the bill which bore his name, a measure that, the *New York Times* observed, simply drew together "most of the anti-alien and anti-radical legislation offered in Congress in the last twenty years. . . ." H.R. 5138 provided for everything from expanding the jurisdiction of the U.S. Courts of Appeals to the registration and fingerprinting of aliens.[40]

Two of its provisions simply reincarnated anti-Communist proposals that had died in the Seventy-fourth Congress. Title I was a slightly reworded version of the first and harshest of Charles Kramer's two sedition bills. Smith also resurrected McCormack's military disaffection measure. Early in 1939, the Navy, the most enthusiastic champion of such legislation, drew up a bill and sent it to Congress, including with the copy that went to the House a letter from Acting Secretary Charles Edison which argued for its passage in terms almost identical to those that had failed to produce results four years earlier. Smith incorporated the Navy's proposition into his alien and sedition measure, because, he said, of a desire "to make this a comprehensive piece of legislation. . . ."[41]

His omnibus proposal, embracing as it did the provisions of the 1935 sedition and disaffection bills, naturally drew support from similar sources. The Navy, the Army, and veterans' groups all backed the Smith bill. Inspired by a mixture of anti-communism and nativism, a long list of patriotic societies and two immigration restriction leagues also endorsed it.[42]

While support for the Smith bill closely resembled that which its ancestors had received, the character of the opposition had changed considerably. Correspondence received by the House Judiciary Committee, to which H.R. 5138 was referred, ran fifty to one against it, but this protest, unlike that aroused by the 1935 measures, lacked geographic and political breadth. Almost all opponents of the Smith bill lived in the New York City area. In the rest of the country the press and radio ignored H.R. 5138, and only around Pittsburgh, Milwaukee, and Buffalo did there develop anything resembling organized efforts to defeat it. Besides being limited to a single metropolitan area, most of the opposition to the Smith bill was Communist inspired. The Party press urged readers to register vigorous protests with their senators and representatives, and much of the correspondence received by the Judiciary Committee was obviously modeled on a message from Eleanor Doddridge, New York division chairwoman of the American League for Peace and Democracy, a front group. The International Workers Order and the American Committee for the Protection of the Foreign Born, also Party puppets, registered their objections, and a number of Communist-influenced labor unions urged defeat of H.R. 5138. Lee Pressman, the Stalinist who served as general counsel for the CIO, managed to put that organization on record against the Smith bill.[43]

While substantial within the Communist orbit, opposition to H.R. 5138 was slight outside the Party's sphere of influence. The American Federation of Labor and local and national officers of a number of trade unions apparently free of Stalinist influence did come out against the bill, and the Foreign Language Information Service, an organization interested mainly in the education of aliens, denounced those provisions directed at its constituency. The major source of independent opposition, however, was the ACLU.[44]

Those determined to defeat H.R. 5138 found few members of Congress sympathetic to their cause. In the House opponents of the Smith bill, led by radical Vito Marcantonio (American Labor Party, N.Y.) and liberal Emanuel Celler (D., N.Y.), subjected the measure to critical analysis and employed delaying tactics to slow its progress, but they could not stop it. Too many congressmen agreed with Chauncey Reed (R., Ill.) that their constituents would no longer tolerate "criminal alien enemies" who "tear down American ideals and institutions." Smith's proposed disaffection and sedition sections would apply to citizens as well as foreigners, but his colleagues seemed oblivious to this fact, endorsing them by a vote of 179 to 32 and supporting the entire bill by an even more impressive margin of 272 to 40.[45]

The measure that the House passed and sent to the Senate on 29 July 1939 was, in the words of the *Daily Worker*, "one of the most dangerous threats to democratic liberties this county has ever faced"; yet few Americans objected to it. While the New York press added its protests to those of the Communist Party and the International Labor Defense, throughout most of the nation newspapers ignored what the House had done, apparently regarding the Smith bill as a routine expression of prevailing public opinion.[46]

H.R. 5138 received a powerful boost from events in Europe and the Communist Party's reaction to them. On 24 August 1939, Hitler and Stalin concluded an alliance, and nine days later German panzer divisions rolled into Poland. The outbreak of war made the possibility of subversion by foreigners and their ideas seem even more threatening than before. Then too, after learning of the Nazi-Soviet pact, the CPUSA executed a policy somersault, abandoning the programs of the Popular Front to become the champion of peace and isolationism. A substantial proportion of its membership quit in disgust, and many fellow travelers also walked away. Liberals, who had made common cause with Stalinists in the crusade against fascism, turned with a vengeance on their former allies. The American Labor Party, represented in Congress by Marcantonio, condemned the policies of the CPUSA, and the ACLU expelled Communist Elizabeth Gurley Flynn, formerly one of its top leaders.[47]

Not surprisingly, legal harassment of Communists increased. In 1940 thirteen states arrested more than 350 Party members and charged them with offenses ranging from election fraud and disorderly conduct to criminal syndicalism and possession of explosives. Under pressure from the Republican National Committee, the Justice Department indicted Earl Browder for an old passport offense, obtained a conviction, and sent him off to prison. The government also arrested other Communists on passport charges and prosecuted the Stalinist leaders of the furriers unions under the antitrust laws. Federal courts denaturalized California Party leader William Schneiderman and convicted several comrades of contempt of Congress for refusing to answer questions before the Dies Committee. Equally hostile to Communism, a number of state legislatures enacted statutes barring the CPUSA from the ballot. Meanwhile Dies and his colleagues also zeroed in on Stalinism, and Congress passed laws excluding advocates of violent revolution from federal employment and requiring agents of foreign powers to register with the government. The House even went as far as to adopt an undoubtedly unconstitutional bill to deport Harry Bridges—alleged Communist leader of the West Coast dock workers—and came within three votes of deleting from the budget the salary of the American ambassador to Russia.[48]

This legal activity reflected an emotionalism which made the Smith bill irresistible. There had never been much doubt that H.R. 5138 would pass, but prior to the Hitler-Stalin pact and the outbreak of war in Europe, it had encountered a minor roadblock. Tom Connally (D., Tex.) and the Senate Judiciary Committee had attempted to rush the omnibus alien and sedition measure through the upper chamber without hearings, actually drafting a favorable report on the bill before the House passed it, but many liberal senators objected to their "unseemly haste." By threatening a fight that might delay adjournment, they forced backers of H.R. 5138 to let it ride over until Congress reconvened in 1940.[49]

The delay gave opponents of the measure time to mobilize, but those seeking to defeat it could rally few new supporters. Although *Publishers' Weekly* denounced H.R. 5138, and the National Council of Jewish Women and a number of its local affiliates enlisted in the fight, most expressions of opposition continued to come from habitual allies of the Communist

Party. Some organized protest developed in Michigan, Baltimore, and Philadelphia, but hostility to the Smith bill remained primarily a New York phenomenon. Although a number of prominent Americans expressed doubts about this type of legislation, the hostility to communism gripping the country was so intense that neither the Party and its supporters nor the persistent but ineffective ACLU could translate generalized libertarian sentiments into votes against the Smith bill.[50]

Only a handful of witnesses appeared before the Senate Judiciary Committee to oppose H.R. 5138. That body finally decided to have a subcommittee consisting of Connally, John Danaher (R., Conn.), and John Miller (D., Ark.) redraft the bill, but concern about the structure of the measure, rather than any objection to its purposes, inspired this action. Title I of the revised measure, reported on 10 June, included provisions aimed at both sedition and incitement of disaffection in the armed forces. The first of that title's five sections made it unlawful for any person to advocate or cause insubordination, disloyalty, mutiny, or refusal of duty by a member of the Army or Navy with intent to impair the loyalty, morale, or discipline of the country's military or naval forces. It also forbade distribution of literature urging such misconduct. The second section prohibited knowingly or willfully advocating, advising, abetting, or teaching the duty, necessity, desirability, or propriety of overthrowing any level of government within the United States by force or violence and made it illegal to publish or circulate written or printed matter urging such revolutionary action (provided this was done with the intent to bring about the result advocated). In addition, in what Connally characterized as probably the broadest provision in the bill, section 2 made it a crime to organize any society which advocated overthrow of the government by force or violence, or to belong to such a group with knowledge of its purposes. Danaher had contended at one point that, unless such a provision were operable only in time of war or national emergency, it would violate the right of free speech. Connally and Miller won him over only by making it explicit that this part of the bill would punish no other advocacy than that involving force and violence. A third section provided for punishing conspiracy to violate either of the preceding ones, while a fourth authorized seizure of printed matter intended for use in violation of the act. A fifth established penalties for the offenses created by Title I.[51]

In reporting the Smith bill Connally called upon his colleagues to take immediate action to assure the people that Congress was "doing something about the so-called 'fifth column' " and "correcting subversive activities." When H.R. 5138 came up for final action on 15 June, the Senate responded to his appeal, passing it on a voice vote after only a few minutes of deliberation. Because the upper chamber had substantially altered the bill, a conference was necessary to reconcile its version with the House one. Senate conferees Connally, Danaher, and Miller persuaded Congressmen Hatton Sumners (D., Tex.), Sam Hobbs (D., Ala.), and Clarence Hancock (R., N.Y.) to accept almost all of the changes they had made, and the conference committee reported out essentially the same bill passed by the Senate.[52]

On 22 June, without any real debate, the upper chamber accepted the committee's report on a voice vote. In the House there was a fight. Hobbs, who submitted the conference report, lauded Title I, saying that it went as far as Congress constitutionally could toward outlawing Communist, Nazi, and Fascist organizations. On the other side, Marcantonio made an impassioned plea for free speech, but, as he himself realized, his was "just a voice in the wilderness." Fear of alien fifth columns, which could destroy the country through espionage, sabotage, and subversion, was simply too strong for an argument based on civil liberties to prevail, and when the vote came, there were 142 in favor of H.R. 5138 and only 4 opposed. Marcantonio insisted on a roll call, but succeeded only in expanding a rout into a massacre. Still able to muster just 4 nays, he listened while 382 representatives voted aye.[53]

The legislation that anti-Communists had sought for years now needed only the signature of Franklin Roosevelt to become the law of the land. Hopeful that a torrent of letters and telegrams might persuade the President not to sign, the CPUSA mounted a last-ditch correspondence campaign against the bill. The ACLU telegraphed the White House, urging Roosevelt to refer the sedition and disaffection sections to the Attorney General for an opinion on their constitutionality and expressing hope that he would "carefully consider the wisdom of vetoing . . . provisions striking so openly at freedom of speech and the press."[54]

There was some reason to believe that Roosevelt might withhold his signature from H.R. 5138, for he shared with his wife a sincere interest in the problems of aliens and a distaste for the kind of assault upon their rights which this legislation represented. Nevertheless, on 28 June, the President signed the Smith Act. He did so in part because the Justice, State, Navy, and War Departments all endorsed the measure, the Army even terming it "urgent." More important was the hostility Roosevelt felt toward the Communists. After conclusion of the Hitler-Stalin pact, the CPUSA, once among the President's most enthusiastic backers, had loosed upon the interventionist chief executive a flood of abuse. Believing that Browder had flirted with a charge of conspiracy against the government, Roosevelt gave his approval to legislation which could be used to silence the Stalinist leader and his comrades. At the time he signed the Smith Act, the President urged officials to exercise restraint in administering its alien registration provisions, but he made no such attempt to soften the impact of Title I.[55]

The new law faced continued opposition from Congressman Marcantonio, but his proposals for its repeal got nowhere, for what Congress and the President had done reflected the wishes of the American people. The Communist Party, although enduring legal harassment from its earliest days, had long evaded a confrontation with the type of federal criminal statute which could do it really serious harm. In calm times those who called for enactment of such a law found it impossible to arouse substantial support for their proposals, and they faced the opposition of influential citizens who considered such legislation a threat to freedom of expression. By the summer of 1940 few Americans were thinking much about civil liberties. Alien influences appeared to threaten national security, and people were prepared to do whatever seemed necessary to save the country from subversion. Bent on protecting the United States from foreign dangers, Congress passed a law proscribing the speech of domestic radicals. In an attempt to preserve democracy, it enacted a statute which was itself a major threat to democratic values. The Communist Party would be the principal victim of that law but not the only one. A nation had sacrificed a slice of liberty for the illusionary security of the Smith Act.[56]

NOTES

1. A Class War Prisoner, "We Accuse," *Labor Defender* 1 (May 1926): 74.
2. Robert K. Murray, *Red Scare: A Study in National Hysteria 1919-1920* (Minneapolis: University of Minnesota Press, 1955), pp. 53, 234, 251; *Digest of the Public Record of Communism in the United States* (New York: Fund for the Republic, 1955), pp. 307-14 (cited hereinafter as *Public Record*); Eldridge Foster Dowell, *A History of Criminal Syndicalism Legislation in the United States*, Johns Hopkins University Studies in Historical and Political Science, Series 57, No. 1 (Baltimore: Johns Hopkins Press, 1939), p. 21; Theodore Draper, *American Communism and Soviet Russia: The Formative Period* (New York: Viking Press, 1960), pp. 18-19; Irving Howe and Lewis Coser, *The American Communist Party: A Critical History (1919-1957)* (Boston: Beacon Press, 1957), pp. 91-92; Michal R. Belknap, "The Smith Act and the Communist Party: A Study in Political Justice," (Ph.D. diss., University of Wisconsin, 1973), pp. 20-25.

3. Nathan Glazer, *The Social Basis of American Communism* (New York: Harcourt, Brace & World, 1961), pp. 92-93, 99-100, 114-16, 174-75 (cited hereinafter as *Social Basis*); J. Edgar Hoover, *Masters of Deceit: The Story of Communism in America and How to Fight It* (New York: Henry Holt & Co., 1958), pp. 4-5; Howe and Coser, *American Communist Party*, pp. 192-96, 205, 211; Glazer, *Social Basis*, is excellent on changes in the size and ethnic and class composition of the Party. See particularly pp. 92-93, 99-100, 114-16, and 174-75.

4. Glazer, *Social Basis*, p. 107; Howe and Coser, *American Communist Party*, pp. 371-77; Earl Latham, *The Communist Controversy in Washington: From the New Deal to McCarthy* (Cambridge, Mass.: Harvard University Press, 1966), pp. 75-78.

5. *Public Record*, pp. 272-73, 280, 286. For Celler's remarks, see HJC, *Report on H.R. 6427 . . .* , 74th Cong., 1st sess., 1935, H. Rept. 1869, p. 6.

6. Louis Coleman, "Criminal Syndicalism—A Political Crime," *Labor Defender* 10 (October 1934): 5; *Public Record*, p. 315.

7. *Public Record*, pp. 307-14; Stromberg v. California, 283 U.S. 359 (1931); People v. Immonen, 271 Mich. 384, 261 N.W. 59 (1935).

8. J. Louis Engdahl, "113 Workers Face 1105 Years in Prison," *Labor Defender* 5 (March 1930): 47; Sam Strong, "Boys Who Face 20 Years," *Labor Defender* 7 (November 1931): 212.

9. "Federal Sedition Bills: Speech Restriction in Theory and Practice," *Columbia Law Review* 35 (June 1935): 917-27; Lawrence Emery, "Mass Action—To Defeat C. S. Laws," *Labor Defender* 10 (March 1934): 6-7; "Deportations, Prison Terms in Portland; Northwest Bosses Seek to Deport 14 and Jail 12; Throw Young Worker into Insane Asylum," *Labor Defender* 6 (January 1931): 9; William Z. Foster, *History of the Communist Party of the United States* (New York: International Publishers, 1952), p. 301; People v. Chambers, 22 Cal. App. 2d 687, 72 P. 2d 746 (1937); De Jonge v. Oregon, 229 U.S. 353 (1937); Anna Damon, "The Struggle Against Criminal Syndicalist Laws," *The Communist* 16 (March 1937): 279; Zechariah Chafee, Jr., *Free Speech in the United States* (Cambridge, Mass.: Harvard University Press, 1941), pp. 384-86; Dowell, *State Criminal Syndicalism Legislation*, pp. 120-22.

10. "The Atlanta Six," *Labor Defender* 5 (August 1930): 154; J. Louis Engdahl, "No Death, No Prison," *Labor Defender* 5 (July 1930): 134; Untitled, *Labor Defender* 10 (July 1936): 3; Herndon v. Lowry, 301 U.S. 242 (1937); Chafee, *Free Speech*, pp. 388-89; Charles H. Martin, *The Angelo Herndon Case and Southern Justice* (Baton Rouge: Louisiana State University Press, 1976), is an excellent account of the most important of the insurrection cases.

11. William Z. Foster, "Deportation Doak Wants You," *Labor*

Defender 8 (May 1932): 87; Anita Whitney, "Deportation Activities in California," *Labor Defender* 4 (April 1929): 76.

12. Clinton Rossiter, *Marxism: The View from America* (New York: Harcourt, Brace & World, 1960), p. 264; Robert Minor, "An Old Prison Speaks," *The Workers Monthly* 4 (February 1925): 158; Jay Lovestone, "The Supreme Court and the Workers," *The Labor Herald* 2 (June 1923): 17; *DW*, 9 March 1935; "Editorials," *The Communist* 6 (May 1927): 130-37.

13. Clarissa S. Ware, "The Anti-Labor Courts," *The Labor Herald* 2 (July 1923): 25, 32; William L. Patterson, "The I.L.D. Faces the Future," *The Communist* 13 (July 1934): 719.

14. "Notes of the Month," *The Communist* 9 (August 1930): 675-76; John Gates, *The Story of an American Communist* (Edinburgh: Thomas Nelson & Sons, 1958), p. 31 (cited hereinafter as *The Story*).

15. William L. Patterson, "How We Organize the International Labor Defense and Courtroom Techniques," *Labor Defender* 9 (May 1933): 54; "What to Do When Arrested," *Labor Defender* 9 (March 1933): 35; ISC, *The Communist Party of the United States of America: What It Is and How It Works; A Handbook for Americans*, 84th Cong., 1st Sess., 1955, Committee Print, p. 89.

16. "How We Organize," p. 54.

17. ISC, *Communist Party of the United States*, pp. 87-89; Hoover, *Masters of Deceit*, p. 306.

18. Foster, *History of the Communist Party*, pp. 209-10; Draper, *American Communism and Soviet Russia*, pp. 180-81; Thurber Lewis, "A Solid Line of Proletarian Defense," *The Worker's Monthly* 4 (August 1925): 460; Benjamin Gitlow, *I Confess: The Truth About American Communism* (New York: E. P. Dutton Co., 1940), pp. 223-25; James P. Cannon, *The First Ten Years of American Communism: Report of a Participant* (New York: Lyle Stuart, 1962), p. 162.

19. "What to Do When Arrested," p. 17; Damon, "Criminal Syndicalist Laws," pp. 284-85; Hoover, *Masters of Deceit*, pp. 297-99.

20. Angelo Herndon, *Let Me Live* (New York: Arno Press and New York Times, 1969), pp. 215-41, 307-22, 330; Benjamin Davis, *Why I Am a Communist* (New York: New Century Publishers, 1947), pp. 11-12.

21. Dan T. Carter, *Scottsboro: A Tragedy of the American South* (Baton Rouge: Louisiana State University Press, 1969), pp. 51-52, 138, 143, 248; James Oneal and G. A.Werner, *American Communism: A Critical Analysis of Its Origins and Development* (New York: E. P. Dutton & Co., 1947), pp. 230-31; Gitlow, *I Confess*, pp. 471-72; Francis Russell, *Tragedy in Dedham: The Story of the Sacco-Vanzetti Case* (New York: McGraw-Hill, 1962), p. 332; "Mooney Still in Jail," *The Labor Herald* 1 (November 1922): 28; Richard H. Frost, *The Mooney*

Case (Stanford, Calif.: Stanford University Press, 1968), p. 436; Harry Haywood, "The Scottsboro Decision: Victory of Revolutionary Struggle over Reformist Betrayal," *The Communist* 11 (December 1932): 1065-75; James P. Cannon, "A Living Monument to Sacco and Vanzetti," *Labor Defender* 2 (October 1927): 153.

22. Jane Perry Clark, *Deportation of Aliens from the United States to Europe* (New York: Arno Press and New York Times, 1969), pp. 222-27; William Preston, Jr., *Aliens and Dissenters: Federal Suppression of Radicals* (Cambridge, Mass.: Harvard University Press, 1963), pp. 242-43.

23. Stanley Coben, *A. Mitchell Palmer: Politician* (New York and London: Columbia University Press, 1963), p. 217.

24. Murray, *Red Scare*, pp. 198-202, 245-46; Chafee, *Free Speech*, pp. 168-69.

25. Latham, *Communist Controversy in Washington*, pp. 28-34.

26. U.S., Congress, House, Special Committee on Un-American Activities, *Investigation of Nazi Propaganda Activities, . . . Hearings . . .*, 73rd Cong., 2d sess., 1934, pp. 1-2.

27. U.S., Congress, House, Special Committee on Un-American Activities, *Investigation of Nazi and Other Propaganda*, 74th Cong., 1st sess., 1935, H. Rept. 153, pp. 23-24.

28. HJC, *Crime to Promote Overthrow of the Government: Hearings . . . May 22, 1935*, 74th Cong., 1st sess., 1935, pp. 1-2 (cited hereinafter as HJC, *1935 Hearings*); "Legislation," *Columbia Law Review* 35 (June 1935): 917; *Cong. Record*, 74th Cong., 1st sess., 18 February 1935, p. 2154, 14 March 1935, p. 3592, and 9 April 1935, p. 5286.

29. U.S., Congress, House, Committee on Military Affairs, *Hearings . . . on H.R. 5845, to Make Better Provision for the Government of the Military and Naval Forces of the United States by Suppression of Attempts to Incite the Members Thereof to Disobedience*, 74th Cong., 1st sess., 1935, pp. 7, 41-44; HJC, *1935 Hearings*, pp. 3-4, 18, 23, 26-33.

30. House Military Affairs Committee, *Hearings on H.R. 5845*, pp. 2, 6, 14-24, 29, 31-39; U.S., Congress, Senate, Committee on Naval Affairs, *To Make Better Provision for the Government of the Military and Naval Forces of the United States by Suppression of Attempts to Incite Members Thereof to Disobedience*, 74th Cong., 1st sess., 1935, S. Rept. 714, pp. 2-3 (cited hereinafter as Senate Naval Affairs Committee, *To Make Better Provision*); U.S., Congress, House, Committee on Military Affairs, *To Punish Mutinous Influences upon the Army and Navy*, 74th Cong., 1st sess., 1935, H. Rept. 1603, p. 11; Maury Maverick, "The Gag Threatens: Shall Congress Mangle the Bill of Rights?" *Forum* 95 (May 1936): 296; HJC, *1935 Hearings*, p. 39; W. G. Hamilton to Rep. Hatton Sumners, Chairman, HJC, 19 July 1935, File on H.R. 4313, Record Group 233, HJC, NA (cited hereinafter as HJC H.R.

4313). For the views of the Chamber of Commerce see D.A. Skinner to
R. Ewing Thomason, 1 March 1935, printed in full in House Military
Affairs Committee, *To Punish Mutinous Influences*, p. 12, and the
dozen letters from local chambers in HJC H.R. 4313.
    31. By a front group I mean an organization under the influence
of, or entirely controlled by, the Communist Party.
    32. *DW*, 9 July 1935, 13 July 1935, and 19 August 1935; Howe
and Coser, *American Communist Party*, pp. 348-51; *NYT*, 25 March
1935, p. 10, 28 March 1935, p. 1, 5 April 1935, p. 3, 25 April 1935,
p. 29, and 8 July 1935, p. 4; House Military Affairs Committee, *Hearings on H.R. 5845*, pp. 69-76. For the views and activities of the American League Against War and Fascism see Carl Levy, 30 April 1935, and
Carl Porter, 27 April 1935 to Hatton Sumners, HJC H.R. 4313. For
position statements by another front, the Finnish Workers Order, see
the letters from its Chicago, Illinois, Marengo, Wisconsin, and Berkeley,
California, clubs in HJC H.R. 4313.
    33. Roger Baldwin to Sumner, 19 April 1935, and W. W. Norton
to Sumners, 29 March 1935, HJC H.R. 4313; House Military Affairs
Committee, *Hearings on H.R. 5845*, pp. 50-52, 67-69, 73-74; *East Bay
Labor Journal*, 23 August 1935; "Making America Safe for Martial
Law," *The Nation*, 31 July 1935, p. 117; *NYT*, 16 February 1935, p.
12, 2 April 1935, p. 18, 24 July 1935, p. 12, and 11 August 1935, sec.
4, p. 12; Maverick, "The Gag Threatens," p. 300.
    34. *DW*, 3 July 1935, 13 July 1935, 18 July 1935, 26 July 1935,
14 August 1935, 15 August 1935, 17 August 1935, and 22 August
1935; HJC, *Report on H.R. 6427: A Bill to Make It a Crime to Advocate the Overthrow of the Government by Force and Violence*, 74th
Cong., 1st sess., 1935, H. Rept. 1869, pp. 1-8; House Military Affairs
Committee, *Hearings on H.R. 5845*, pp. 5-64; Senate Naval Affairs
Committee, *To Make Better Provision*, pp. 1-3; *Cong. Record*, 74th
Cong., 1st sess., 24 June 1935, p. 9972; House Military Affairs Committee, *To Punish Mutinous Influences*, pp. 12-27; *NYT*, 23 July 1935,
p. 4; Maverick, "The Gag Threatens," p. 295; Morrie Ryskind, "The
Hollywood Tea Party," *The Nation*, 6 May 1936, p. 581.
    35. *Cong. Record*, 75th Cong., 1st sess., 1 February 1937, p. 670,
5 January 1937, p. 24, and 6 January 1937, p. 101; "Let Your Congressman Hear from You," *Labor Defender* 11 (May 1937): 5.
    36. Howe and Coser, *American Communist Party*, pp. 352-60;
Shannon, *Decline*, pp. 83-85; Wilson Record, *Race and Radicalism: The
NAACP and the Communist Party in Conflict* (Ithaca, N.Y.: Cornell University Press, 1969), pp. 85-86.
    37. "Recent Anti-Alien Legislative Proposals," *Columbia Law Review* 39 (November 1939): 1214.
    38. August Raymond Ogden, *The Dies Committee: A Study of the
Special House Committee for the Investigation of Un-American Activi-*

ties (Washington, D.C.: Catholic University Press, 1945), pp. 43-47, 62, 78-85, 101, 113-14; William E. Leuchtenburg, *Franklin D. Roosevelt and the New Deal* (New York: Harper & Row, 1963), pp. 280-81; James T. Patterson, *Congressional Conservatism and the New Deal: The Growth of the Conservative Coalition in Congress, 1933-1939* (Lexington: University of Kentucky Press, 1967), p. 167; *Cong. Record*, 76th Cong., 1st sess., 28 July 1939, p. 10370.

39. Earl Browder, "Mastery of Theory and Methods of Work," *The Communist* 18 (January 1939): p. 20; *Cong. Record*, 76th Cong., 1st sess., Appendix, p. 3686.

40. HJC, *Crime to Promote the Overthrow of the Government: Hearings . . . April 12 and 13, 1939*, 76th Cong., 1st sess., 1939, p. 71 (cited hereinafter as HJC, *1939 Hearings); NYT*, 13 April 1939, p. 9; *Cong. Record*, 76th Cong., 1st sess., 20 March 1939, p. 3013; Chafee, *Free Speech*, Chapter 12, provides a legislative history of the Smith Act, but the author's research is limited to published sources and is incomplete even with respect to those.

41. HJC, *1939 Hearings*, pp. 1-5. For Smith's comment see SJC, *Crime to Promote Overthrow of Government: Hearings . . . May 17, 1940*, 76th Cong., 3rd sess., 1940, p. 6 (cited hereinafter as HJC, *1940 Hearings*).

42. HJC, *1939 Hearings*, pp. 41-57, 81-87, 93-95; Mrs. John S. Heaume, Recording Secretary General of the National Society of the Daughters of the American Revolution, 27 April 1939, Grace Hurd, National Treasurer of the Daughters of Union Veterans of the Civil War, 21 April 1939, General Secretary, General Society of Mayflower Descendants, 24 April 1939, and Susan Hardy, Chairman, Legislative Committee, Rhode Island Association of Patriots, 2 May 1939, to Sumners, File on H.R. 5138, HJC, Record Group 233, NA (cited hereinafter as HJC H.R. 5138).

43. *DW*, 29 June 1939; *PW*, 30 June 1939, 5 July 1939, and 20 April 1939; Doddridge, telegram to Sumners, 26 May 1939, and Pressman to Sumners, 11 May 1939, HJC H.R. 5138; HJC, *1939 Hearings*, pp. 76-78. The correspondence on which conclusions concerning the geographic sources of opposition to the bill are based is found in HJC H.R. 5138. On the silence of the media see Chafee, *Free Speech*, p. 443. For examples of the opposition of the American League for Peace and Democracy and letters setting forth the position of more than twenty lodges of the International Workers Order and those of the Furriers Joint Council of New York City, the Allis-Chalmers local of the United Auto Workers, and assorted affiliates of the CIO Farm Equipment Workers, United Furniture Workers, United Electrical, Radio, and Machine Workers, United Office and Professional Workers, United Wholesale and Warehouse Employees, and the Federation of State, County, and Municipal Workers see HJC H.R. 5138. For a list of those

CIO unions influenced or controlled by the CPUSA see Max M. Kampelman, *The Communist Party vs. the CIO: A Study in Power Politics* (New York: Frederick A. Praeger, 1957), pp. 45-46. This list represents the situation as of 1946, but previous Communist involvement in many of the unions on it is discussed earlier in the book.

44. HJC, *1939 Hearings*, pp. 7-14, 18-21, 69-70; Harry F. Ward, John Haynes Holmes, and Arthur Garfield Hays to Sumners, 3 June 1939, HJC H.R. 5138. For numerous expressions of apparently non-Communist labor sentiment see HJC H.R. 5138.

45. *Cong. Record*, 76th Cong., 1st sess., 19 July 1939, p. 9532, 28 July 1939, pp. 10355-73, 29 July 1939, pp. 10452-56, and Appendix, p. 3293, and 2d sess., 22 June 1940, p. 9035 (Reed's remark appears at 1st sess., p. 10361); ACLU Weekly Bulletin no. 870, 27 May 1939, p. 2; *NYT*, 28 June 1939, p. 4; HJC, *Suppression of Certain Subversive Activities*, 76th Cong., 1st sess., 1939, H. Rept. 994, pp. 1-9.

46. *Cong. Record*, 76th Cong., 1st sess., 29 July 1939, pp. 19455-56; *DW*, 31 July 1939; "What the Washington Bureau Says," *Equal Justice* 13 (August 1939): 6-7.

47. Stanley High, "Termites in America," *Vital Speeches* 6 (1 December 1939): 120-22; *PW*, 16 February 1940; *DW*, 6 October 1939 and 28 February 1940; SJC, *1940 Hearings*, p. 52; Howe and Coser, *American Communist Party*, pp. 387-405; Jerold S. Auerbach, "The Depression Decade," in *The Pulse of Freedom: American Liberties 1920-1970s* (New York: W. W. Norton, 1975), ed. Alan Reitman, pp. 92-102; Ogden, *Dies Committee*, p. 179.

48. "Interference with Freedom of Political Thought," *Equal Justice* 15 (Winter 1941): 43-46; Foster, *History of the Communist Party*, pp. 391-92; Ogden, *Dies Committee*, pp. 123-29, 153, 192-201; Howe and Coser, *American Communist Party*, pp. 400-01; Robert D. Gibbons, "Recent Legislative Attempts to Curb Subversive Activities in the United States," *George Washington Law Review* 10 (November 1941): 116-17, 123-24; Chafee, *Free Speech*, pp. 490, 577; *DW*, 13 March 1940; *PW*, 15 June 1940; *NYT*, 8 February 1940, p. 1.

49. *Cong. Record*, 76th Cong., 1st sess., 31 July 1939, p. 10487, and 5 August 1939, p. 11124; SJC, *Suppression of Certain Subversive Activities*, 76th Cong., 1st sess., 1939, S. Rept. 1154, pp. 1-4, and *1940 Hearings*, p. 5; "What the Washington Bureau Says," p. 6.

50. Frederic C. Melcher, "Editorial: Civil Rights Again an Issue," *The Publishers' Weekly*, 9 March 1940, p. 1069; "The Washington Bureau Says," *Equal Justice* 13 (September 1939): 26; Elsa C. Beck et al., "National Lawyers Guild Brief Against H.R. 5138," (unpublished), pp. 1-7 and George Beerman, Secretary, American Youth Committee, 20 May 1940, and Martin Worbow, Fur Market Employees Union Local 64, 16 February 1940, to Senator Henry Ashhurst, Chairman, Senate Judiciary Committee, File on H.R. 5138, SJC, Record Group 46, NA

(cited hereinafter as SJC H.R. 5138); *NYT*, 7 December 1939, p. 25;
PW, 18 April 1940; ACLU, *Defeat the Omnibus Gag Bill* (New York:
ACLU, 1939); ACLU Weekly Bulletin no. 908, 17 February 1940,
p. 1-2; "What Shall We Do About Un-American Activities?" *Current
History* 51 (December 1939): 45-48. Comments on the geographical
distribution and political coloration of opposition to the bill are based
on correspondence contained in SJC H.R. 5138.

    51. SJC, *1940 Hearings*, pp. 6-8, 17-21, 44-49, 51-61, 67, and
*Providing Punishment for Promoting Overthrow of Government, to
Require Deportation of Certain/Aliens, to Provide Registration and
Fingerprinting of Aliens*, 76th Cong., 3rd sess., 1940, S. Rept. 1721,
pp. 1-3; *Cong. Record*, 76th Cong., 3rd sess., 10 June 1940, p. 7818,
and 15 June 1940, pp. 8340, 8344-45; SJC, *Prevention of Subversive
Activities and Registration of Aliens*, 76th Cong., 3rd sess., 1940, S.
Rept. 1796, pp. 1-2.

    52. *Cong. Record*, 76th Cong., 3rd sess., 10 June 1940, p. 7818,
15 June 1940, pp. 8340-47, 17 June 1940, p. 8426, and 22 June 1940,
pp. 8950-52, 9032-33; U.S., Congress, House, Committee on Conference, *Alien Registration Act of 1940*, 76th Cong., 3rd sess., 1940, H.
Rept. 2683, pp. 8-10; *NYT*, 16 June 1940, p. 23.

    53. *Cong. Record*, 22 June 1940, pp. 8950-52 and 9032-36.

    54. *DW*, 28 June 1940; *PW*, 27 June 1940; ACLU Weekly Bulletin
no. 927, 29 June 1940, p. 2.

    55. *NYT*, 23 November 1939, p. 30, and 3 March 1940, sec. 1,
p. 22; Attorney General, 25 June 1940, Cordell Hull, Secretary of
State, 25 June 1940, Lewis Compton, Acting Secretary of the Navy,
24 June 1940, and Louis Johnson, Secretary of War, 26 June 1940 to
Harold D. Smith, Director, Bureau of the Budget, Series 39.1, Box 125,
File 017, Bureau of the Budget Files, Record Group 51, NA; Franklin
D. Roosevelt, "Statement by the President on Signing the Alien Registration Act, June 20, 1940," *The Public Papers and Addresses of Franklin D. Roosevelt*, 13 vols. (New York: Macmillan & Co., 1938-1950),
comp. Samuel I. Rosenman, vol. 9, pp. 274-75.

    56. For commentary on the lack of public protest against passage
of the Smith Act see Chafee, *Free Speech*, pp. 440-41. On Marcan-
tonio's efforts to repeal it see Vito Marcantonio, "Repeal the Alien
Registration Act," *Equal Justice* 14 (Autumn 1940): 3, and *Cong.
Record*, 76th Cong., 3rd sess., 29 August 1939, p. 11267, and 77th
Cong., 1st sess., 3 January 1941, p. 21.

2
The Politics
of Prosecution

As though being a victim of the cold war was not enough, the Communist Party also had the misfortune to be caught in the crossfire of big-time partisan politics.
—John Gates
The Story of an American Communist

Although an anti-Communist sedition law became part of the *United States Code* in 1940, eight years were to pass before the CPUSA would feel its sting. In June 1941 Germany turned on Russia, and when the United States joined the war against the Axis the following December, it found itself fighting side by side with the Soviet Union. As long as this alliance lasted, American Communists, although under constant scrutiny by the Federal Bureau of Investigation (FBI), were safe from prosecution. The government used the Smith Act against the Party's Trotskyist and fascist enemies, while Stalinists cheered wildly from the sidelines. After the war, though, Russian-American relations deteriorated badly, and a new President committed the United States to an anti-Soviet foreign policy. Because Harry Truman sought to mobilize support for this program by characterizing it as a crusade against communism, his administration soon found itself under irresistible political pressure to take action against the domestic disciples of that creed. Harassed by Republicans, Truman's Attorney General lashed out at the CPUSA, and by July 1948 the leaders of that once safe organization were under indictment, charged with violation of the Smith Act.

I

By then nearly twelve years had passed since August 1936, when the FBI began the investigation which led to their arrest. At that time Franklin Roosevelt had asked the Bureau to provide him with a comprehensive picture of what certain allegedly subversive groups were doing, only to learn that it lacked the authority to probe dissident activity which violated no federal law. Director J. Edgar Hoover offered the helpful suggestion that an appropriations act, authorizing the Bureau to undertake general investigations in support of the State Department, could provide a legal basis for the type of inquiry Roosevelt had in mind. The President enlisted the cooperation of Secretary of State Cordell Hull, and, after the three men agreed that the FBI would restrict itself to collecting information for intelligence purposes, rather than gathering evidence suitable for presentation in court, Hoover sent out word to his field offices to begin quiet inquiries on the CPUSA. In September 1939, Roosevelt assigned the Bureau additional responsibilities in the national security field. At about the same time, in an effort to ensure the loyalty of federal employees, Congress passed the Hatch Act, which also increased the authority of the FBI to probe domestic communism.[1]

As the Bureau's responsibilities grew, so did its size, the number of special agents increasing from 851 in 1939 to 4,600 by 1943. But the war, which was primarily responsible for this expansion, brought the FBI even more work than people to do it, so that the agency managed to continue its investigation of Communist activities only by relying heavily on informants. These were sometimes disillusioned members of the CPUSA, who had volunteered to spy on their comrades, but often they were persons whom the Bureau inserted into the Party specifically to collect information for the government. From the FBI point of view the use of informants had a great deal to recommend it, for such persons, because circumstances had already placed them on the fringes of the Communist movement, could gain entrance into the Party far more easily than could FBI agents, who needed elaborate cover stories to hide their past activities from their Stalinist associates. These semiprofessional spies were paid only for their expenses, and, while they almost certainly padded these, they still cost the government far less than an equal number of salaried detectives. Finally, if an informant was caught in the act, only the operation for which the Bureau had recruited him would suffer, whereas the unmasking of an agent could ruin a permanent employee in whom the government had invested considerable time and training. Because of the mental strain undercover work involved and the unpleasantness of constantly informing on intimate associates, the dropout rate among FBI plants was extremely high. Nevertheless, for a variety of reasons—ranging from patriotism through inertia to greed and a romantic fascination with playing secret agent—some stuck with the job year after year, filling the Bureau's files with thousands of reports on the Communist Party.[2]

The FBI continued to collect such information even while the United States and the Soviet Union were allies. In February 1944, for example, two agents convinced a New York photographer, Angela Calomiris, to join the Communist movement, spy on its activities, and submit written reports to the government. Calomiris, who later testified against the Party at a Smith Act trial, was only one of several future government witnesses recruited during the honeymoon of Soviet-American cooperation.[3]

II

She found perplexing the fact that the FBI's sustained investigation produced no prosecutions. In part this was because Hoover took the position that the FBI should only collect facts, not evaluate them or make recommendations for or against legal action in particular cases. This meant that the attorneys assigned to the Criminal Division of the Justice Department who reviewed the Bureau's investigative reports had to decide for themselves whether or not to seek indictments against the CPUSA. Because the vastly expanded FBI developed such tremendous amounts of information during the war, these lawyers fell far behind in their analysis of it.[4]

Even more important in protecting the Party from prosecution were considerations of national policy. Attorney General Francis Biddle had no use for Communists, but President Roosevelt was determined that nothing should be done to the CPUSA which might adversely affect the war against the Axis. Party members burned with desire to save the Soviet Union and were willing to do anything to strengthen Russia's ally, the United States. Putting war production ahead of their Marxist principles, they opposed strikes and slowdowns and even endorsed piecework, incentive pay, and a labor draft. The CPUSA elevated national unity to the level of religious dogma, preaching cooperation with capitalists and declining to support, because it considered them disruptive, the demands for equality made by the racial minorities whose cause it had long championed. In promoting concord, the Party even went to the extreme of abolishing itself in 1944 and reconstituting as the Communist Political Association (CPA), an identity it maintained until the following year. At one point Browder even attempted to have the word "Communist" deleted from the name of the organization.

As the head of the American Stalinist movement, he endeavored to promote not only national unity but also Soviet-American cooperation, and during the war sympathy for the USSR did increase markedly in this country. Both the Russians and American Communists actively fostered hopes that what had begun as an alliance of necessity might ripen into permanent friendship. As part of this effort, in 1943 the Soviets abolished the Communist International, the organization through which they had long sought to promote world revolution.

In common with many other Americans, Franklin Roosevelt was more than willing to do his part to strengthen the Russian-American alliance. He also recognized that Stalinist strength in the CIO made Communist support, whatever the motivation behind it, vital to the national war effort. The President was not about to allow criminal law to impair either U.S.-Russian relations or the production and distribution of defense material; thus in May 1942, over Biddle's objections, he commuted the sentence of the imprisoned Browder.[5] Criminal Division lawyers were not likely to challenge the President by prosecuting other American Stalinists.

III

The Communists, safe from the Smith Act themselves, watched with delight while the government used that law to harass their enemies. The prosecutions that they cheered were not Biddle's idea, for the Attorney General considered the extravagant use of sedition statutes one of the worst features of the home front hysteria that had accompanied World War I, and he was determined to avoid any repetition of what had happened in 1917-18. The FBI, although conducting thousands of investigations, demonstrated the kind of moderation and restraint that he wanted, and the Justice Department's prosecutors moved even more cautiously than the Bureau. Biddle directed U.S. attorneys to initiate sedition prosecutions only with his personal written approval and made it clear that permission would be granted "only when public safety was directly imperiled." So reluctant was the Attorney General to see freedom of speech endangered, that during fiscal 1944 he granted the necessary approval in only 1 of the 660 cases referred to Washington. The following year the Justice Department initiated no sedition prosecutions at all.[6]

When Biddle authorized legal action against the Trotskyist Socialist Workers Party, he did so because of pressure from the White House. Roosevelt owed a political debt to Dan Tobin, head of the Teamsters Union, and when Minneapolis Local 544, controlled by the Dunne brothers and other Trotskyists, threatened a revolt against Tobin's authority, he appealed to the President for help, claiming subversives were out to damage the union because of the support he had given FDR during the 1940 campaign. Two weeks later, federal marshals raided the New York headquarters of the Socialist Workers Party.

They brought to the bar of justice an organization which had once adopted a declaration of principles explicitly advocating the forceful overthrow of capitalist society and government. The Socialist Workers Party had published and disseminated literature intended to convert others to this position and had circulated reading matter calculated to incite insubordination in the armed forces. After Congress passed the Smith Act, the party suspended and withdrew its declaration of principles, but the continued existence of the Workers Defense Guards, the street-fighting arm of the organization, indicated that the Trotskyists had not abandoned their revolutionary purposes.

The government indicted twenty-nine of them under the 1861 seditious conspiracy statute and Title I of the Smith Act. After a lengthy trial the judge directed verdicts of acquittal for four of the accused, and the jury found the others innocent of seditious conspiracy. It convicted eighteen on the Smith Act charge, however. Twelve of these received sixteen-month sentences, and the remainder received a year and a day.

When the Trotskyists appealed, Judge Patrick Stone of the Eighth Circuit Court of Appeals rejected their contentions that the indictment and the evidence against them were insufficient, and also upheld the constitutionality of the Smith Act. Stone denied that section 10 of that law, the one directed at attempts to incite violent overthrow of the government, was excessively broad or vague, and that it made guilt a matter of association rather than personal conduct. He also rejected the contention that the application of the Smith Act to these defendants violated their First Amendment rights. Stone refused to concede that Justice Oliver Wendell Holmes Jr.'s famous "clear and present danger" test—under which punishment of expression was permissible only if the words used created a "clear and present" threat of some substantive evil which a legislative body possessed the authority to prevent—had any relevance in this case. Citing the Supreme Court's 1925 decision in *Gitlow* v. *New York*, he reasoned that, because Congress had already decided the type of speech employed by the defendants was dangerous, Holmes's test could not apply. As far as Stone was concerned, the power of a nation to restrict the kind of expression proscribed by the Smith Act was beyond question. The Trotskyists asked the Supreme Court to review his decision, but it refused to do so.[7]

By the time the Socialist Workers had exhausted their appeals, a German alien and an advocate of a black-Japanese alliance to subjugate the white race had also been convicted under the Smith Act.[8] Thereafter,

Biddle's restraint held the 1940 sedition law in check—with one notable exception. In July 1942, again under pressure from the President, who was angry about scurrilous attacks from right-wing critics, the Attorney General persuaded a District of Columbia grand jury to indict a large group of Nazi sympathizers. Legal minds found the indictment wanting, and government attorneys had to redraw it twice, alter the list of defendants, and even reopen the grand jury proceedings before obtaining a satisfactory version in January 1944. As finally written, it accused an odd collection of thirty-one neo-Fascists of conspiring with one another and with officials of the Nazi Party and German government to cause insubordination in the armed forces and to prepare and disseminate literature intended to promote military disaffection. Among those hauled into court by the Justice Department were Elizabeth Dilling, author of *Red Network*, a book that branded as Communists many leading liberals, Joseph E. McWilliams, head of the Christian Mobilizers, and Lawrence Dennis, a former diplomat and the resident intellectual on the American far right.

The trial of this group, which began in April 1944, quickly degenerated into one of the most bizarre spectacles in the history of American law. An oversized defense staff, which included a number of court-appointed attorneys unfamiliar with criminal procedure, talked and argued constantly, attacked every document submitted by the prosecution, and objected to every piece of evidence. Some of the defendants became as disorderly as their attorneys, and no one at the defense table showed the slightest respect for Judge Edward C. Eicher. Although that jurist went out of his way to be fair, the only thanks he received were two motions to disqualify himself for bias and an attempt by one defense attorney to secure his impeachment. The tumult in the courtroom grew steadily worse, and the proceedings dragged on and on. By late November, although the record already stretched to 18,000 pages, the prosecution still had not managed to finish presenting its case. By then the trial had become a brutal campaign on the part of the defendants and their counsel to wear out Eicher. On 30 November, exhausted, the judge died.

His death produced a mistrial, and although prosecutor O. John Rogge wished to continue the case, hardly anyone else could develop much enthusiasm for doing so. The war was drawing to a close, and the pro-Axis propaganda which had roused Roosevelt's ire had long since ceased. The Justice Department procrastinated, and in January 1946 the defendants, claiming denial of their constitutional right to a speedy trial, moved for dismissal of the indictment. Judge Boetha Laws, convinced that the handling of their case had violated the Sixth Amendment, dismissed all charges against them, and the Court of Appeals sustained his action.[9]

Its ruling evoked sharp criticism from the Communists, for they had been enthusiastic supporters of the government's effort to jail right-wing propagandists, an effort they regarded as an important campaign in the world war against fascism. Stalinists had also endorsed the prosecution of the Socialist Workers, whom they considered anti-Soviet and hence worthy of extermination. The Party's callous disregard for the rights of the Trotskyists would return to haunt it, for when the CPUSA became the target of the Smith Act, many people who thought that law was unconstitutional but who remembered how Stalinists had applauded the attack on the Socialist Workers would spurn their pleas for help.[10]

The American Civil Liberties Union understood the folly of the Party's position. The ACLU worked hard to win the release of the convicted Socialist Workers, and in June 1944 its director, Roger Baldwin, announced that if the case of the native fascists, who were then on trial, went to a higher court, his group would take the unpopular position of defending them also. As he saw it, the two cases were inseparable, because they were the only ones then being conducted under the Smith Act. In both the ACLU's objective was the same: the invalidation of that law. Its attitude contrasted sharply with that of the Communists, who supported both prosecutions because, they argued, each was directed at enemies guilty of aiding Hitler. Stalinists seemed unable to grasp Baldwin's message, that constant resistance to the Smith Act was necessary, regardless of whom the defendants in any given case might be, for as long as that statute remained on the books, it threatened all dissenting minorities.[11]

IV

Soon enough, events made the Smith Act a menace to the Party itself. As allied troops advanced toward the final destruction of Axis power, the Soviet-American alliance began to deteriorate. The Russians, determined to ensure the future security of their country by providing it with a buffer against attack from the West, sought to create a sphere of influence in those areas liberated by the Red Army; and the United States, motivated in part by a sincere commitment to traditional American principles such as democracy and self-determination, but influenced also by a longstanding fear of bolshevism and a desire to keep the door to Eastern Europe open for its own commerce, objected vigorously. Until his death in April 1945, Roosevelt attempted, through personal diplomacy, conducted in a spirit of accommodation, to ease the developing tensions between the two allies. But his successor, Harry Truman, quickly concluded that the Soviets were untrustworthy and that the only language they understood was force. In early 1946, having decided that accommodation was impossible, he dug in his heels and began "talking tough" to the Russians.

His administration developed a foreign policy whose essence, soon christened "containment," was the economic, political, and military encirclement of the Soviet Union. Its principal features were the Truman Doctrine, a commitment to support "free peoples" resisting subjugation by armed minorities and outside pressures, and the Marshall Plan, a program of massive economic assistance to war-torn Western Europe. The aim of these policies was to stabilize the political situation in nations such as Greece, Italy, and France, thus thwarting the drive for power of Communist groups in those countries. In this way the United States would contain the Soviet Union.

Fundamental to this American grand strategy was the assumption that communism and Russian imperialism were in fact synonymous. At best a gross oversimplification, that proposition was nevertheless useful, because Americans, particularly in the twentieth century, had tended to define foreign policy issues in moral terms, and because fear of radicalism, particularly any strain with foreign roots, had long been endemic to the United States. Had Truman confronted the country with nothing more than a Russian threat to American influence ánd markets in distant lands, it is doubtful whether he could have aroused much enthusiasm for the sort of massive involvement in world affairs and the kind of sharp break with the country's isolationist heritage which containment necessarily involved. Realizing this, the President talked not of imperialism, but of communism, representing the efforts of the USSR to dominate Eastern Europe as part of a Red plot to crush freedom and impose bolshevism on the entire globe.[12]

Eventually, a Republican Congress, and indeed the entire country, rallied behind his foreign policy. But events abroad, particularly the Soviet-backed coup that toppled the democratic government of Czechoslovakia in early 1948, probably did more than presidential rhetoric to generate support for containment, and Truman's persistent characterization of the developing Cold War as an ideological conflict between communism and democracy had its greatest impact on domestic politics. During the late 1940s, partisan debate would have become overheated in any case, as conservatives, frustrated by their unnaturally long exclusion from presidential power during the two decades after 1933 when liberal Democrats controlled the White House, grew increasingly vitriolic and irresponsible in their criticism of the executive branch, more and more lacing their attacks with the epithet "Communist." Republican charges of subversion and disloyalty did not reach their maximum volume and viciousness until after Senator Joseph R. McCarthy (R., Wis.) leaped to prominence in February 1950, but, as early as 1944, GOP orators, led by their party's vice-presidential candidate, John Bricker, were attempting to link the New Deal with Stalinism, to picture the Democratic Party as a front group, and to portray Roosevelt as a tool of the CPUSA.[13]

During that year's campaign, such talk aroused so little enthusiasm that a disappointed Senator Arthur Vandenberg (R., Mich.) lamented, "a majority of our electorate does not seem to be very worried about [communism]." Within a few years it was. By April 1947, according to the Gallup poll, 61 percent of the American people wanted to outlaw the CPUSA, a figure that rose to 68 percent in November 1949. Thus by the time Truman ran for a term of his own in 1948 a subject that had aroused only apathy in 1944 had become a major political issue. Communism did not dominate that campaign, as it would those of the next few years, but the issue had grown sufficiently important to the electorate that the Democrats could not ignore it. They felt compelled to respond to Republican charges and to profess loudly their own hostility to Stalinism. For example, early drafts of a campaign speech that Truman delivered in Boston on 27 October 1948 did not discuss communism. Then Jim Goggin, an aide to the Democratic candidate for governor of Massachusetts, warned the President's organization that their man was in trouble in the Bay State, because Irish voters there considered his Republican challenger, Governor Thomas Dewey of New York, more likely to clean the Reds out of Washington. "When Truman comes here . . . if he will really nail that Communism issue, he will pick up a hell of a lot of votes that don't seem to be going to him now," Goggin advised. The President's staff heeded this counsel, and in the Boston address Truman professed hatred for communism and promised to "continue to fight it with all my strength."[14]

The President had little choice but to take a hard line on this issue, for, while not himself worried about the tiny Stalinist organization in this country, he confronted an electorate that was both hostile to and fearful of the CPUSA. Its animosity was understandable, given the development of the Cold War and the Party's recent policies. After Soviet-American relations began to deteriorate at the end of World War II, Jacques Duclos, a prominent French Communist, acting under orders from Moscow, published a letter sharply critical of Earl Browder, the accommodationist leader of the American movement. On 2 June 1945 the National Board of the Communist Political Association adopted a draft resolution repudiating both Browder and his policies, after which a special national convention, meeting from 26 to 28 July, dissolved

the CPA and reconstituted the Communist Party. Under the leadership
of William Z. Foster the resurre ted CPUSA embarked upon a course of
unwavering support for Soviet foreign policy and truculent opposition
to the American position on almost all international issues.[15]

While the Party's close association with Russia readily explains the
hostility Americans directed at the organization, it does not provide sufficient explanation for the exaggerated concern about domestic communism which engulfed the country during the late 1940s. By February
1948, according to a *Fortune* poll, 10 percent of the American people
believed the CPUSA was rapidly reaching the point where it could dominate the country, and another 35 percent thought it controlled important segments of the economy and was getting stronger all the time. To be
sure, the public's overblown fears had some basis in fact, for in 1948 two
witnesses before the House Committee on Un-American Activities (HUAC),
Elizabeth Bentley and Whitaker Chambers, did reveal that American Communists had spied for the Soviet Union. But these revelations, which concerned crimes committed several years in the past, would hardly have produced the excitement they did had it not been for the persistent agitation
of the Communist issue by Republican politicians, particularly those associated with HUAC. In 1947 the committee staged a headline-grabbing
foray into Hollywood in search of Reds in the motion picture industry,
and the following year it paraded Chambers and Bentley before the country, while ᵗts rising young star, Congressman Richard Nixon (R., Calif.),
linked Alger Hiss, once a prominent New Dealer, with both the Party and
Soviet e: pionage.[16]

Although Republicans portrayed the threat of domestic communism
as something far larger and more frightening than the facts warranted,
they could never have made it the politically explosive issue it became
without the assistance provided by the rhetoric the Truman administration useᴄ to win support for its foreign policy. By calling on the country
to enlist in a crusade against communism abroad, the President buttressed the arguments of those who claimed that America was menaced from
within. Unlike Clark Clifford, a principal architect of the administration's
anti-Soviet policy who seems to have entertained some serious concerns
about the CPUSA, Truman believed that the threat which the United
States confronted was almost entirely a foreign one. The President dismissed the Communist Party as "a contemptible minority in a land of
freedom. . . ." "The greatest danger to us does not come from Communism in the United States," he told an Oklahoma City audience on 28
September 1948. "The greatest danger has been that Communism might
blot out the light of freedom in so much of the rest of the world that the

strength of its onslaught against our liberties would be greatly multiplied."
Although Truman wanted only to arouse public concern about what he
regarded as a Soviet challenge to American interests abroad, by identifying an ideology which had disciples in the United States as the enemy
the nation must combat, he encouraged acceptance of the notion that
American Communists must be extremely dangerous. Presidential
rhetoric made even the wildest Republican charges seem worthy of serious attention.[17] Realizing that the GOP was exploiting a phony issue,
Truman, Attorney General Tom Clark, and other members of the administration attempted to downplay the Communist problem, but their efforts,
repeatedly undercut by their own speeches on foreign policy, proved unsuccessful. The public gave increasing credence to charges emanating from
the Republican right, and the administration, despite initiating a loyalty-
security program for federal employees, found itself under constant pressure
to demonstrate its patriotism and competence by doing something about domestic communism. Not surprisingly, its members surrendered to the
temptation to protect their political position by attacking a non-threat.
"[W]e have all been influenced in our thinking, although perhaps uncon-
sciously, by loud shouts from some quarters, notably the House Un-
American Activities Committee . . . ," an administration authority on
internal security, Stephen Spingarn, admitted in October 1948. By then
Secretary of Labor Lewis Schwellenbach, testifying before a GOP-con-
trolled congressional committee, had called for the outlawing of the
CPUSA, and Attorney General Clark, who considered the Party a mini-
mal threat to national security, had secured the indictment of its leaders for violation of the Smith Act.[18]

V

Even before politics drove Clark to initiate his legal assault on the Communist Party, the Department of Justice had begun quietly building a
Smith Act case against the CPUSA. Attorneys for the Criminal Division
seem to have begun work on the matter sometime prior to Biddle's resig-
nation as attorney general in June 1945. While discontinuing most of its
sedition investigations after the war ended, the FBI continued to check
on the Communists, apparently believing their prosecution on Smith Act
charges was imminent.[19]

This assumption proved erroneous, but, nevertheless, under Biddle's
successor, Clark, who had formerly headed the Criminal Division, investigation of the Party continued. In February 1947, the new Attorney

General told a House committee that the FBI was devoting considerable
time to monitoring Communist activity and that each of its offices had
an "excellent set-up" for handling this problem. Director Hoover considered the Bureau's program an intelligence-gathering one, and for him prosecution, at least in mid-1947, was only a side issue. As a later attorney
general would note, however, the kind of operation that the FBI had
mounted was ideally suited to gathering evidence of statements made in
private which might constitute violations of the Smith Act.[20]

After the war ended, the number of new cases arising under statutes
administered by the Internal Security Section of the Criminal Division
decreased sharply, and in some instances nearly ceased. As its war-related
business declined, Internal Security, casting about for other activity to
justify its continued existence, gave increasing attention to information
about the CPUSA which the Bureau had collected. In fiscal 1947, the
section handled only five cases involving Party members, most of them
growing out of Communist refusal to cooperate with HUAC, but Clark's
replacement as head of the Criminal Division, Theron Caudle, saw this
as a "compensating type of business" which could assume substantial
proportions in the future.[21]

During 1946 and 1947, the FBI cooperated with the Internal Security Section in assembling a Smith Act case against the Communist Party.
Although Hoover insisted that the Bureau was strictly a fact-finding organization which limited itself to collecting information, it would, at
the request of a U.S. attorney or the Criminal Division, do some analytical work in particularly involved cases, preparing a prosecutive summary, which included only evidentiary information. In this instance the
Bureau assembled a brief that ran 1350 pages, contained 546 exhibits,
and reported all the evidence which it had gathered against the Communist Party and its leaders. After putting together the basic document,
Hoover's men added two supplements, probably intended to fill in evidentiary gaps noted by Internal Security lawyers. The final product,
1850 pages long and including 846 exhibits, represented the most complete summary of the activities and aims of American communism ever
assembled.[22]

While this brief was still being put together, Clark decided to move
against the Party. In late 1947, he discussed his plans with former Justice Department attorney O. John Rogge, mentioning the possible use of
a New York federal grand jury then conducting inquiries into Soviet espionage. Rogge, a liberal, who did not like what he had heard, went to
the press, and the resulting stories, which wildly exaggerated Clark's intentions, sent the Communists into what an FBI informant described as
a "swift dive for cover."[23]

The early months of 1948 witnessed a Justice Department campaign against the CPUSA, but Clark's initial tactic had nothing to do with the New York grand jury. The Attorney General turned instead to the deportation laws. As early as the spring of 1947, the Justice Department had intensified its efforts to expel alien Communists from the country, but with the exception of Californian Frank Carlson, all those arrested were insignificant individuals, better known for their work in front groups or labor unions than for their rank in the CPUSA. During early 1948, Clark's forces zeroed in on the leadership of the American Communist movement, first arresting Alexander Bittleman and Claudia Jones, both members of the Party's National Committee, and then moving against the National Board, the directorate of the CPUSA, by seizing John Williamson on 10 February and Irving Potash on 1 March. At Ellis Island, where immigration officials took them to await expulsion from the country, Williamson and Potash joined Gerhard Eisler, a mysterious figure reputed to be the American representative of the world Communist movement. Jack Stachel, the fourth-ranking man in the CPUSA, also spent a short time on Ellis Island before posting a $3,500 bond and going home to await return to his native Poland.[24]

Clark seems to have considered the expulsion of alien Communist leaders sufficient action against the CPUSA. In conjunction with the administration's loyalty-security program for federal employees and the tightening of a few existing laws, he contended, deportation would provide the nation with all the protection it needed. Many Republicans did not agree. They favored new legislation explicitly outlawing the Communist Party and criticized the Attorney General for failing to enforce statutes already on the books. On 5 February 1948, when the Republican-controlled Un-American Activities Committee demanded to know why the Justice Department had failed to use the Smith Act against the CPUSA, Clark answered evasively, saying that frequent changes in the Party "line" made employment of that law impractical. After surviving this roasting, Clark moved to protect himself against future criticism. That very day, at his request, the FBI transmitted a copy of its massive brief on the Communist Party to the Attorney General's office, where that document received the attention of Clark's top deputy, Peyton Ford.[25]

T. Vincent Quinn and Thomas J. Donegan, two special assistants to the Attorney General, who had been presenting evidence to the federal grand jury in New York that was investigating Soviet espionage, also took an interest in the brief. Sitting intermittently since June 1947, that body had listened to more than a hundred witnesses but had returned no indictments. When it recessed for a month in December 1947 and

January 1948, the press began reporting, on the basis of leaks from
inside sources in Washington and New York, that the case was washed up
and the grand jury would soon be dismissed.[26]

Quinn and Donegan were reluctant to see it go home, and so was Tom
Clark. The Attorney General, sensitive about his agency's reputation as
guardian of the nation's internal security, was shrewd enough to realize
that the Republican-dominated Eightieth Congress would make partisan
capital out of the impending failure in New York. Because of the grand
jury hearings, the Un-American Activities Committee had postponed a
planned inquiry into Communist espionage in the federal government,
but it stood ready to leap into action should the Justice Department fail
to produce results. Quinn apparently suggested seeking Smith Act indictments from the New York grand jury, and Clark approved the proposal.[27]

Fearful of criticism, the Attorney General and the two lawyers decided to let a leading liberal attorney, possibly Morris Ernst, study the
FBI brief and determine whether or not it would support an indictment.
The Bureau objected to this idea, arguing that, if its summary of evidence
were turned over to a law firm, the government's plans would surely leak
out. Consequently, the department turned instead to John F. X. McGohey,
the U.S. Attorney for the Southern District of New York, who accepted
the assignment on 8 April. McGohey proved something of a disappointment
to his superiors, for he opposed submitting the new case to the espionage
grand jury and, because the brief was so long, could not read and analyze
it as rapidly as they desired.

When McGohey traveled to Washington for a conference on 29 April,
Clark opened the meeting by asking, "What are you going to do about
Commies?" He insisted, as did Quinn and Donegan, that the U.S. attorney present and try the case at the earliest possible date. Opposed to
such haste, McGohey argued that thorough preparation was essential,
but Peyton Ford alone supported him, and he managed to prevail only
by threatening to withdraw from the case. A few days later, Quinn informed McGohey that the grand jury, anxious to conclude its business
and go home, had reluctantly agreed to adjourn subject to call.

On 6 May, McGohey met with a Justice Department lawyer named
Kneip, who had taken on the assignment of drafting the proposed indictment. They decided to consider as targets for prosecution only the leaders of the CPUSA and those members responsible for the Party's publications. The two lawyers agreed that a conspiracy charge would be desirable, because it would make admissible as evidence acts committed in
various parts of the country, but neither favored trying a large number
of defendants at one time. They had no desire to repeat the mistake which
the government had made in the Washington Sedition Trial. McGohey re-

quested that the FBI supply them with all the evidence it had of teaching and advocacy, as well as the distribution of literature by top Party leaders. Over the next month agents and lawyers, spurred on by Quinn's repeated calls for greater speed, worked furiously to prepare the case. McGohey demanded weekend labor from the six attorneys assigned to the project, and the FBI struggled to cull useful evidence from its massive files on the Party. Then suddenly the mounting pressure abated.[28]

The reasons were political. In early April, after an attack on the home of a Stalinist labor leader in Ohio, the president of the United Auto Workers, Walter Reuther, spoke out about what he saw as the need to protect the civil liberties of everyone, including Communists. Asked about the Reuther statement during an 8 April press conference, Truman stressed constitutional limitations on the President's powers to deal with local violence and displayed a rather flippant attitude toward the problem which had agitated the auto union official. His response contrasted sharply with the views of former Vice-President Henry Wallace, as expressed in a speech he delivered just two days later. Wallace, who favored a revival of Russian-American cooperation, had broken with the administration over its anti-Soviet foreign policy and was mounting a third-party campaign for the presidency, which he hoped would attract liberal elements of the old New Deal coalition away from Truman and the Democrats. He vigorously condemned "highly emotional attacks on communists which provoke violence and lead to the suppression of civil liberties." Besides a defense of free speech, Wallace offered anti-Stalinist liberals like Reuther a positive solution to the problem posed by the CPUSA: preservation and extension of the American democratic system. "The only way to compete with the Communists is to solve the problems for which they offer radical solutions," he said.[29]

Threatened from the left by a rival with a policy likely to inspire New Deal liberals, Truman and his advisers watched while the leading contender for the Republican nomination, Thomas Dewey, and his GOP rival, Harold Stassen, clashed over the desirability of outlawing the CPUSA. In this sparring match, which culminated in a nationwide radio debate on 17 May, Dewey came out strongly against proscription. Because Senator Robert Taft supported his position, the challenge from the right, to which Clark had reacted in February, now seemed less menacing than the one from the left.[30]

In a memorandum written the previous November, Truman's trusted political adviser, Clark Clifford, had proposed neutralizing the Wallace threat by systematically exposing the extent to which members of the CPUSA, attracted to the former Vice-President by his foreign policy, had involved themselves in his campaign. But, with respect to civil liberties,

this approach played directly into Wallace's hands, so administration
leaders now decided to adopt their rival's position on domestic communism. During a press conference on 13 May, Truman told reporters
that outlawing a political organization was contrary to American principles and expressed the opinion that splinter parties were harmless. Five
days later, with the President looking on, Attorney General Clark informed a White House audience, consisting of five hundred delegates to the
National Conference on Citizenship, that the way to combat the threatening ideology of communism was to make the ideals of democracy a
living fact, by reducing squalor, disease, and distressed housing. During
a 4 June speech in Chicago, Truman stressed the same theme, assuring
his audience that "the menace of Communism" lay not in "the activities
of a few foreign agents or the political activities of a few isolated individuals," but rather "in those areas of American life where the promise of
democracy remains unfulfilled."[31]

The Democratic Party soon adopted the same line as the President
and his Attorney General, for the "extend democracy" theme was perfectly suited to its needs. The policy had an obvious appeal for liberals
and also challenged those Republicans inclined to make an issue of the
administration's alleged softness on communism to prove their own determination to combat the "red menace" by enacting some of the President's social legislation. But the rapidly developing Smith Act prosecution
was inconsistent with this positive approach to communism. It could
easily reawaken liberal fears for freedom of speech, thus allowing Wallace
to mount a challenge to Truman on that issue.[32]

On 18 June, Peyton Ford, who apparently had lost track of what was
going on in New York, learned that McGohey planned to present his case
to the grand jury four days later. He immediately ordered the U.S. attorney to Washington for a conference with Clark. At a luncheon meeting
the Attorney General expressed surprise that McGohey would go to the
grand jury without consulting him and indicated doubts about the strength
of the prosecutor's case. He also asked whether it would not be possible
to delay prosecution until after the Democratic National Convention,
scheduled for 12-15 July. When informed that the statute of limitations
made this impossible, Clark requested that any indictments which the
grand jury might return be sealed until after the convention to prevent
charges they had been brought out "mainly for political purposes." The
Attorney General was in a difficult position. Both he and Truman had publicly expressed doubts about whether the Communists should be prosecuted. If the government moved against the Party now, Wallace was bound
to charge the administration with fanning anti-Communist hysteria and
endangering civil liberties in order to advance Truman's bid for reelection,

and the President would surely lose liberal support. Yet Clark dared not order McGohey to drop the Smith Act prosecution, because his case was the only thing keeping the "espionage" grand jury alive. Should that body dissolve without producing indictments, the Republican right would again assault the administration for its inability or unwillingness to produce evidence of subversive activities in the federal government, and McGohey could add to the embarrassment of his superiors by revealing the events of the past few weeks, all of which he had carefully recorded. Therefore, Clark had little choice but to submit to the terms dictated by a subordinate. McGohey insisted upon arrest of the proposed defendants by no later than 7 July, and his only concession to the political problems of his superior was an agreement to review the Attorney General's HUAC testimony to ensure that the proposed prosecution was not inconsistent with what Clark had told the committee.[33]

Despite subsequent reassurance from McGohey that the prosecution did not conflict with the administration's position, the Attorney General kept up the pressure for delay. In a telephone conversation on 28 June, Clark again urged sealing the indictments until after the convention, saying he had promised "someone else" this would be done. Quinn then asked McGohey to send the indictments to Washington for examination by the solicitor general's office. Although the U.S. attorney did not consider such a review necessary, he was unwilling to take responsibility for preventing it, so, when the grand jury met on 29 June and voted to indict on the charges presented, he prevailed upon its members to delay filing until 20 July.[34]

In the meantime the solicitor general's staff and the Appeals Section of the Criminal Division carefully examined the indictments, one of which charged that from on or about 1 April 1945 the twelve members of the CPUSA's National Board had conspired with one another and with unknown persons to

> ... organize as the Communist Party of the United States, a
> society, group, and assembly of persons who teach and advo-
> cate the overthrow and destruction of the Government of
> the United States by force and violence, and knowingly and
> willfully to advocate and teach the duty and necessity of over-
> throwing and destroying the Government of the United States
> by force, which said acts are prohibited by ... the Smith Act.

The grand jury alleged that the CPUSA had been an organization of the prohibited type since 26 July 1945. The other indictments charged individual defendants with violation of the Smith Act's membership clause.[35]

Having secured Washington's approval, the grand jury reassembled on 20 July and quickly handed up true bills. At 5:55 p.m. that day, a dozen FBI men charged into the national headquarters of the CPUSA on New York's East 12th Street, where they arrested William Z. Foster, Eugene Dennis, John Williamson, Henry Winston, and Jack Stachel, all of whom, alerted that their arrest was imminent, were quietly awaiting the arrival of the agents. Subordinates of the Communist leaders immediately began distributing a two-page press release denouncing the indictments.[36]

Publicity was not what Washington wanted, for at the moment this case was a political liability, and the less attention it received the better. At their convention the previous week the Democrats had adopted a platform that condemned the Republicans for attempting "to impose thought control upon the American people and to encroach on the freedom of speech and press" and that promised to combat communism by extending economic and social democracy. This document, embodying White House views carried to the Resolutions Committee by Clark Clifford, also contained a strange paragraph that combined a promise vigorously to enforce "the laws against subversive activities" with a pledge of constant adherence to the constitutional guarantees protecting speech, press, and "honest political activity." Although presented to the public almost a week before the FBI struck against the Communists, it read very much like an attempt to justify the Smith Act prosecution and to assure liberals that this case was not a threat to civil liberties.[37]

The administration remained concerned about their views, for on 23 July Henry Wallace's Progressive Party would assemble in Philadelphia for its first national convention, and some Democrats believed it still might be possible to persuade the former Vice-President not to run and to tempt his followers back into the Truman camp. They were trying to arrange a meeting between the Progressive leader and the President. Because even the non-Communists in the Wallace organization despised Red-baiting, a political and highly visible attack on the CPUSA might well ruin these delicate negotiations. The Justice Department sought to downplay the arrests by having deputy marshals quietly serve the warrants, but McGohey insisted on using the FBI, thereby assuring plenty of headlines and the further alienation of the Progressives. Wallace loudly condemned the indictments, and his campaign manager, Beanie Baldwin, one of the men with whom the Democratic high command had been in contact, wondered sarcastically whether the timing of the arrests "could perhaps be anything more than a coincidence."[38]

Despite its political impact, the FBI raid netted less than half of the Communists whom the grand jury had indicted. The Bureau seized Benjamin Davis elsewhere in New York and that night took Carl Winter into custody in Detroit. On 21 July John Gates turned himself in, and Irving Potash, who was vacationing in New England, notified McGohey that he would appear for arraignment the following day. A week later Robert Thompson surrendered in New York, and Gil Green gave himself up in Chicago. The last of the twelve taken into custody was Gus Hall, who turned himself over to the authorities in Cleveland on 4 August.[39]

All of the Communist leaders were soon out on bail, some posting $10,000, and the rest only $5,000, but their speedy release did not lessen the fury of the Party's reaction to the indictments. At a press conference the day after his arrest William Z. Foster branded the case a frame-up. Spokesmen for the CPUSA accused the administration of illicit motives and charged the government with trying to outlaw their organization. Most of their explanations for the indictments were wrong, but the Communists understood one thing perfectly: They were the victims of a political prosecution inspired by the Cold War. For a time an alliance between the United States and Russia had encouraged the government to aim the Smith Act at other targets, but the developing Soviet-American conflict and the rhetoric used to elicit public support for a crusade against communism abroad had generated pressure which the Truman administration could not ignore. Political motives initially inspired Clark to seek indictments against the leaders of the Communist Party; political considerations caused top Democrats to delay the indictments; and ultimately political reality dictated that this case must go forward, for to call it off would have been suicidal. Because the Truman administration could not wage Cold War abroad and shrink from fighting it at home, the Communist Party would have to battle for its life in the New York courtroom of Judge Harold Medina.[40]

NOTES

1. Don Whitehead, *The F.B.I. Story: A Report to the People* (New York: Random House, 1956), pp. 157-60, 171; Earl Latham, *The Communist Controversy in Washington: From the New Deal to McCarthy* (Cambridge, Mass.: Harvard University Press, 1966), p. 363.

2. Frederick L. Collins, *The F.B.I. in Peace and War* (New York: G. P. Putnam's Sons, 1943), p. 37; Angela Calomiris, *Red Masquerade: Undercover for the FBI* (Philadelphia and New York: J. B. Lippincott Co., 1950), p. 44. For general information on the informant system and the life of a plant, see Calomiris's *Red Masquerade*, Herbert A. Philbrick's *I Led 3 Lives: Citizen, "Communist," Counterspy* (New York: McGraw-Hill, 1952), and the less reliable *The Big Decision* (Hollywood: Matt Cvetic, 1959), by Matt Cvetic.

3. Calomiris, *Red Masquerade*, pp. 11, 15, 28-29; Philbrick, *I Led 3 Lives*, pp. 1-65; United States v. Schneiderman, No. 22131—Crim.

(S.D. Cal. 1952), Transcript of Proceedings, page 1645, opinion report in 106 F. Supp. 941 (S.D. Cal. 1952) (hereinafter cited as *Yates Transcript*, because of the name that the case assumed on appeal).

4. Calomiris, *Red Masquerade*, p. 217; Francis Biddle, *In Brief Authority* (Garden City, N.Y.: Doubleday & Co., 1962), p. 257; J. Edgar Hoover, *Masters of Deceit: The Story of Communism in America and How to Fight It* (New York: Henry Holt & Co., 1958), p. 313; SApp, *Second Supplemental National Defense Appropriations Bill: Hearings . . .*, 77th Cong., 1st sess., 1941, pt. 2: 72.

5. Biddle, *In Brief Authority*, pp. 299-303.

6. Ibid., pp. 234-35; Whitehead, *F.B.I. Story*, pp. 208-09; Fred J. Cook, *The FBI Nobody Knows* (New York: Macmillan Co., 1964), p. 267; Justice, "Annual Report of the Attorney General of the United States for the Fiscal Year Ended June 30, 1943" (Washington, D.C.: Department of Justice, 1943), pp. 255-56 (hereinafter cited as Justice, *Annual Report for 1943*, or other year as appropriate). (Although these reports are normally published, during the war and immediate postwar years they were sometimes not published or were published only in part. A complete discussion of this matter appears in the bibliographical essay at the end of the book. For the sake of consistency, titles will be italicized in all future citations to these reports, whether the report in question was actually published or not.) Justice, *Annual Report for 1944*, pp. 6-7, 107-08, 315; Justice, *Annual Report for 1942*, p. 3; and Justice, *Annual Report for 1945*, p. 111.

7. Thomas L. Pahl, "G-String Conspiracy, Political Reprisal or Armed Revolt?: The Minneapolis Trotskyite Trial," *Labor History* 8 (Winter 1967): 30-47; Justice, *Annual Report for 1942*, pp. 160-61; Dunne v. United States, 138 F. 2d 152 (8th Cir. 1943), *cert. denied*, 320 U.S. 790 (1943).

8. Justice, *Annual Report for 1943*, p. 161.

9. Ibid., pp. 166-67; Biddle, *In Brief Authority*, pp. 237-43; United States v. McWilliams, 54 F. Supp. 791 (D.C. 1944); Maximilian St. George and Lawrence Dennis, *A Trial on Trial: The Great Sedition Trial of 1944* (Washington [?]: National Civil Rights Committee, 1944), pp. 16, 311, 337; United States v. McWilliams, 69 F. Supp. 812 (D.C. 1946), *aff'd.*, 163 F. 2d 695 (D.C. 1947); *DW*, 14 July 1944.

10. *PW*, 26 July 1944, 31 August 1944 and 3 July 1947; Max M. Kampelman, *The Communist Party vs. the CIO: A Study in Power Politics* (New York: Frederick A. Praeger, 1957), p. 114; Gates, *The Story*, p. 127; Joseph R. Starobin, *American Communism in Crisis 1943-1957* (Cambridge, Mass.: Harvard University Press, 1972), p. 47; "An Open Letter to Attorney General Biddle," *Equal Justice* 16 (Spring 1942): 3-7; *DW*, 4 January 1944, 20 April 1944, 23 July 1944, and 2 August 1944.

11. *PW*, 17 May 1944 and 7 July 1946; *DW*, 6 June 1944, 10 June 1944, and 12 June 1944.

12. John Lewis Gaddis, *The United States and the Origins of the Cold War 1941-1947* (New York and London: Columbia University Press, 1972), pp. 34-51.

13. Ibid., pp. 57-61; Latham, *Communist Controversy in Washington*, pp. 3-7.

14. George H. Gallup, *The Gallup Poll: Public Opinion 1935-1971*, 3 vols. (New York: Random House, 1972), 1: 640 and 2: 873; Goggin to Bill [Boyle], 11 October 1948, Boyle to Goggin, 13 October 1948, and speech drafts, all in Box 4, Charles Murphy File, Truman Papers, HTL; U.S., Presidents, *Public Papers of the Presidents of the United States: Harry S. Truman*, 8 vols. (Washington, D.C.: GPO, 1961-66), 4: 884. Vandenberg is quoted in Gaddis, *Origins*, p. 61.

15. Presidents, *Public Papers: Truman*, 4: 254-55; Justice Tom C. Clark, personal interview with the Author at Supreme Court Building, Washington, D.C., 17 August 1976; Shannon, *Decline*, pp. 3-33; Starobin, *American Communism in Crisis*, pp. 71-120.

16. "The Quarter's Polls," *Public Opinion Quarterly* 12 (Summer 1948): 350-51; Walter Goodman, *The Committee: The Extraordinary Career of the House Committee on Un-American Activities* (Baltimore: Penguin Books, 1969), pp. 190-271.

17. "Address of the President in Oklahoma City, Oklahoma, September 28, 1948," Box 23, Stephen J. Spingarn Papers, HTL; Clark Clifford, "American Relations with the Soviet Union: A Report to the President by the Special Counsel to the President," TOP SECRET (24 September 1946), pp. 67-68, Box 15, Files of the Administrative Assistant to the President, Truman Papers, HTL.

18. Clark interview; Memorandum for the President, 15 October 1948, Box 31, Spingarn Papers; *NYT*, 12 March 1947, p. 19, 2 April 1947, p. 32, and 11 May 1947, p. 35. Both Athan Theoharis and Richard Freeland emphasize the relationship between Truman's foreign policy and the rhetoric used to enlist support for it, on the one hand, and the development of public anxiety about domestic communism, on the other. But both of these scholars characterize the administration's actions in the loyalty-security field as deliberate efforts to quicken this hysteria rather than as attempts to protect itself from Republican criticism. See Freeland's *The Truman Doctrine and the Origins of McCarthyism: Foreign Policy, Domestic Politics and Internal Security 1946-1948* (New York: Alfred A. Knopf, 1972) and Theoharis's book *Seeds of Repression: Harry S. Truman and the Origins of McCarthyism* (Chicago: Quadrangle Books, 1971), and his articles "The Rhetoric of Politics: Foreign Policy, Internal Security and Domestic Politics in the Truman Era, 1945-1950," and "The Escalation of the Loyalty Program," both in Barton J. Bernstein, ed., *Politics and Policies of the Truman Administration* (Chicago: Quadrangle Books, 1970), pp. 196-241 and 242-68 respectively. Alan D. Harper, *The Politics of Loyalty: The White House and the Communist Issue 1946-1952* (Westport,

Conn.: Greenwood Publishing Co., 1969), pp. ix-x and 1-83, is a pro-Truman account that is fundamentally sound, but presents the adminis-tration in an excessively favorable light, because the author fails to dis-cuss some of its actions, such as the Smith Act prosecutions of the CPUSA.

19. Justice, *Annual Report for 1946*, pp. 13, 359; letter from the Author to Justice Tom C. Clark, dated 19 January 1971, annotated with answers to questions asked and returned in franked envelope carrying no postmark.

20. HApp, *Hearings . . . on the Department of Justice Appropria-tion Bill for 1948*, 80th Cong., 1st sess., 1947, p. 17; Justice, *Annual Report for 1947*, p. 396, and *Annual Report for 1949*, p. 7; HUAC, *Menace of Communism: Statement of J. Edgar Hoover Before Commit-tee on Un-American Activities, House of Representatives, March 26, 1947*, 80th Cong., 1st sess., 1947, S. Doc. 20, pp. 1, 12.

21. Justice, *Annual Report for 1946*, p. 128, and *Annual Report for 1947*, pp. 353-61.

22. HApp, *Hearings . . . on the Department of Justice Appropria-tion Bill for 1946*, 79th Cong., 1st sess., 1945, p. 272; Justice, *Annual Report for 1949*, p. 581; Kevin T. Maroney, personal interview with the Author in his office at the Internal Security Division, U.S. Department of Justice, Washington, D.C., 22 January 1971; Whitehead, *F.B.I. Story*, pp. 294-95.

23. Philbrick, *I Led 3 Lives*, pp. 252-53.

24. Freeland, *Truman Doctrine*, p. 217; *NYT*, 17 January 1948, p. 1, 21 January 1948, p. 1, 22 January 1948, p. 28, 11 February 1948, pp. 1, 21, 2 March 1948, pp. 1, 3, 2 June 1948, pp. 1, 5, and 21 July 1948, p. 3.

25. HUAC, *Hearings on Proposed Legislation to Curb and Control the Communist Party*, 80th Cong., 2d sess., 1948, p. 21; "File of the Facts" (unpublished), file no. 1, pp. 4-5, Box 62, J. Howard McGrath Papers, HTL; handwritten notes on Communist case prepared by John F.X. McGohey between 18 April and 2 July 1948 (hereinafter cited as McGohey Notes) and unsigned memorandum dated 25 June 1948, Box 1, John F. X. McGohey Papers, HTL. Clark later denied that Republi-can political pressures had caused him to initiate the prosecution (Clark interview).

26. Cabell Phillips, *The Truman Presidency: The History of a Triumphant Succession* (New York and London: Macmillan Co. and Collier-Macmillan, 1966), pp. 365-66; "The Case of Mary and the Spy Ring Shrinks to the Case Against the Reds," *Newsweek*, 2 August 1948, pp. 23-24; *NYT*, 21 July 1948, p. 3, and 3 August 1948, p. 13. Phillips and the *Times* say the grand jury began work in June; *Newsweek* claims 22 March. I have accepted the majority's version. Clark (interview) now maintains that the subject of the grand jury's investigation was always communism rather than espionage.

27. Justice, *Annual Report for 1948*, pp. 8-24; HUAC, "Interim Report on Hearings Regarding Communist Espionage," *Hearings Regarding Communist Espionage in the United States Government*, 80th Cong., 2d sess., 1948, p. 1353; McGohey Notes. Clark (interview) denies the prosecution was politically motivated, insisting that he initiated it only because "the evidence indicated they were violating the Smith Act."

28. McGohey Notes.

29. For Truman's remarks see Presidents, *Public Papers: Harry S. Truman*, 4: 209. For Wallace's, see *NYT*, 11 April 1948, p. 40.

30. *NYT*, 9 May 1948, p. 46, 13 May 1948, p. 19, and 18 May 1948, pp. 1, 16.

31. Clark Clifford, Memorandum for the President, 19 November 1948, Box 21, Clark Clifford Papers, HTL; *NYT*, 19 May 1948, p. 7. For the Truman speech see "File on the Facts," file no. 2, p. 2. With respect to the interrelated issues of domestic communism and civil liberties Allen Yarnell's contention (*Democrats and Progressives: The 1948 Presidential Election as a Test of Postwar Liberalism* [Berkeley: University of California Press, 1975] p. 79) that at the national level Democrats paid only slight attention to Wallace is clearly incorrect.

32. "File on the Facts." file no. 2. p. 2.

33. McGohey Notes.

34. Ibid.; McGohey to Clark, 28 June 1948 and 27 September 1948, Box 1, McGohey Papers.

35. McGohey Notes; copy of indictment in Box 1, McGohey Papers.

36. John Williamson, *Dangerous Scot: The Life and Work of an American Undesirable* (New York: International Publishers, 1969), pp. 179-80; *NYT*, 21 July 1948, pp. 1, 3; *DW*, 21 July 1948; *PW*, 21 July 1948. Williamson says Benjamin Davis and Robert Thompson were also present at national headquarters, but his memory seems to have failed him on this point.

37. *NYT*. 12 July 1948. p. 4, and 14 July 1948, p. 9.

38. Curtis D. MacDougall, *Gideon's Army*, 3 vols. (New York: Marzani & Munsell, 1965), 2: 544-45; McGohey to Clark, 15 July 1948, Box 1, McGohey Papers; NYT, 22 July 1948, p. 2. Generally overlooked is the fact that in his famous 19 November 1947 memorandum Clifford stated that "some lines should be kept out so that if the unpredictable Henry sees the light and can be talked into supporting the administration, he will have a handy rope to climb back on the bandwagon. . . . "

39. *NYT*, 21 July 1948, p. 1, 22 July 1948, p. 1, 23 July 1948, p. 1, 30 July 1948, p. 5, 4 August 1948, p. 3, 5 August 1948, p. 2, and 6 August 1948, p. 3.

40. *PW*, 21 July 1948, 22 July 1948, and 24 July 1948; *DW*, 22 July 1948; Henry Winston, "For a Fighting Party Rooted Among the Industrial Workers," *PA* 27 (September 1948): 837.

3
Delaying the
Day of Reckoning

*It is . . . not the outcome of the coming trial on which demo-
cratic-minded Americans must fasten their attention, but on
demanding that the Administration end its plan to hold the infamous trial at all.*

—Daily Worker
14 December 1948

The Communist response to the indictments fell short of what labor defense demanded. Americans wanted a trial of the CPUSA, and, had that
organization remained true to its creed, it would have welcomed the day
in court which the public wished to provide. But, rather than seizing this
opportunity for a highly publicized confrontation with the capitalist
state, the Party opted for a bastard compromise with its traditions, seeking, besides some incidental propaganda gains, only to pressure the Truman administration into calling off the trial.

I

Such caution was understandable, for reaction to the July 1948 indictments was overwhelmingly favorable, with almost the only criticism coming from sources close to the CPUSA. The organization that protested
loudest and did the most to mobilize opposition to the prosecutions was
the Civil Rights Congress (CRC), a successor to the International Labor
Defense. Protests came also from the National Lawyers Guild, the American Veterans Committee, the American Labor Party, and a number of
Communist-dominated components of the CIO. No group expressed greater outrage than did the Henry Wallace Progressive Party.[1]

Though much of the opposition to the indictments was Stalinist inspired, a number of individuals and groups having no obvious Communist connections did speak out against them. Sociologist Max Weber, ACLU counsel Arthur Garfield Hays, attorney Charles Garry, Socialist Party leader Norman Thomas, and *The Nation* editor Freda Kirchwey all joined the ACLU in condemning the government's action. The Communist press filled column after column with the names of seemingly independent individuals who had denounced the arrest of the Party's leadership, and, although many of these persons were probably fellow travelers, it is doubtful that all were. The Los Angeles County Democratic Central Committee condemned the prosecutions, and the Communists also received undeserved support from the Socialist Workers Party.[2]

The supportive position of these civil libertarians was decidedly a minority one. Newspapers ranging from the reactionary *Chicago Tribune*, through the moderate *San Francisco Chronicle*, to the liberal *New York Times* all gave the idea of a Communist trial their editorial endorsement. Although many papers expressed a willingness to withhold judgment on the guilt or innocence of the accused until the evidence was in, the press definitely wanted them tried—and the sooner the better. Most editorial writers recognized what the *New York Times* expressed openly: that the real defendant in this case was the CPUSA. The press welcomed these proceedings as an opportunity to settle conclusively the legal position of American communism.[3]

Stalinists angrily accused the newspapers of helping the government, the Republicans, and the Democrats inflame public opinion against their Party. They had considerable justification for charging the press with creating a false impression that their leaders had been accused of violent acts aimed at the overthrow of the government rather than merely of conspiring to teach and advocate revolutionary doctrine. Spokesmen for the CPUSA also found objectionable the fact that many newspapers had run FBI photographs which pictured the defendants with police numbers beneath their faces, thus subtly implying that they were hardened criminals. While the press doubtless did allow some distortions to creep into its coverage, on the whole the nation's newspapers probably reflected public opinion much more than they inflamed it. Most Americans who gave the matter any thought wanted a Smith Act trial of the CPUSA.[4]

II

So did William Z. Foster. Deeply committed to the Party's traditional labor defense strategy, he welcomed the opportunity that this prosecu-

tion offered. Elizabeth Gurley Flynn, a veteran labor defender, who was
elected the month after the FBI raid to serve with the defendants on a
now thirteen-member body, renamed the National Committee, shared
Foster's fighting spirit. "Our comrades will make the trial court a mighty
tribunal of the people so that the accused become the accusers and the
enemies of the people find themselves on trial before the huge court of
public opinion in America—and the world," she assured readers of the
Daily Worker. Not all Communist leaders were as combative as Flynn
and Foster, for the lack of popular opposition to the indictments hinted that the consequences of a trial might be disastrous. The defendants
were almost certain to suffer conviction, and the chances for a compensating propaganda victory did not look promising. Many top Communists
concluded that a suicidal courtroom showdown must be avoided, and, as
early as 22 July, the *Daily Worker* ran a front-page editorial urging its
readers to bombard President Truman with letters and telegrams demanding dismissal of the charges against the Twelve. At the CPUSA's national
convention the following month General Secretary Eugene Dennis urged
a mass campaign to "secure the dismissal of the Grand Jury indictments
against our Party. . . ."[5]

Proponents of this cautious approach eventually prevailed, and, while
the CPUSA did not entirely abandon labor defense, it did modify that
strategy. The Party mounted a mass campaign around the case, but made
the objective of its efforts prevention of the trial rather than freedom
for the accused after a courtroom propaganda triumph. At a 21 September rally near the courthouse in New York's Foley Square, sponsored
by the Civil Rights Congress and addressed by defendants Winston and
Green, supporters of the Twelve urged the government to drop its case
against them. The next day the CRC held a press conference in the Washington office of Congressman Vito Marcantonio. Demanding that President Truman use his executive power to have the charges dismissed, representatives of that group announced plans for a campaign aimed at obtaining 250,000 signatures from rank-and-file trade unionists on a petition urging him to do so.[6]

Meanwhile, the Party, besides ordering its own members to bombard
Truman and Clark with telegrams, had asked sympathetic organizations
to do this too, and also to prepare statements for distribution to the press.
At the same time, the CRC set out to broaden support for the campaign
against the prosecutions, by bombarding the public with leaflets, fliers, and
speeches, which sought to link the prosecution of the Communist leaders
to abuses of blacks and labor, and thus to convince many non-Communist
Americans that they had a stake in the fate of the CPUSA. The CRC also

contacted many prominent persons, trying to persuade them to sign petitions urging Truman and Clark to dismiss the indictments. Its national office directed local affiliates that "On October 14, the day before the trial starts, hundreds of thousands of telegrams *must* be sent to Attorney General Tom Clark, from all over the country, demanding that the indictments against the 12 Communist Party leaders be dropped."[7]

The position of the CPUSA was that this prosecution endangered the exclusive right of the electorate to pass on political parties and their programs and that, consequently, democracy would suffer a serious blow if a trial was held, regardless of its outcome. Even Flynn, initially eager for a traditional labor defense fight, eventually adopted this cautious line. Although able to agree among themselves on how the Party should approach the case, the leadership found it difficult to explain its position to rank-and-file members. Despite many authoritative statements on the subject, ordinary Communists seemed unable to comprehend what the CPUSA was trying to accomplish. For years labor defense had been the Party's strategy in criminal prosecutions, and they continued to think in terms of achieving its objectives. Returning from a speaking tour on which he had talked with numerous ordinary members, Carl Winter reported that the rank and file was cheering on its leaders as if the Twelve were gridiron heroes headed out to win a football game against the capitalists, a situation he found alarming.[8]

On 14 December the *Daily Worker* informed its readers in no uncertain terms: "It is . . . not the outcome of the coming trial on which democratic-minded Americans must fasten their attention, but on demanding that the Administration end its plan to hold the infamous trial at all." West Coast Communists received similar counsel from Dennis in the form of an open letter to the Los Angeles CRC, which appeared in the *People's World.* Winter added his voice to that of his codefendants. "The time to 'show them' is now, in a tremendous coast-to-coast demand to dismiss this indictment," he declared.[9]

III

The popular protest on which these Party spokesmen pinned their hopes never materialized, and although the defendants managed to avoid trial until January 1949, it was routine legal maneuvering which delayed matters that long. Elizabeth Gurley Flynn worked tirelessly to obtain the substantial sums needed to finance legal and extralegal defense of the Twelve, but returns from her fund-raising campaigns were disappointingly

small. There were a few substantial contributions and one reception yielded $20,000, but the CRC generally had a difficult time finding people
willing to contribute to the defense of Communists. In late October supporters of the Twelve picketed federal buildings in seventeen major cities
and also places where the President and Attorney General made public
appearances. There were other demonstrations on their behalf, but none
represented more than strenuous exertion by the faithful. Expressions of
support still came mainly from long-time allies of the CPUSA, and, despite Communist insistence that numerous "prominent individuals" were
protesting the indictments, most of those denouncing them continued to
be fellow travelers of no great stature.[10]

Ironically, in view of the fact that it was emphasizing extralegal defense, the Party achieved greater success in the courtroom than outside
it. Attorneys for the Twelve enabled them to take their case to the people by overcoming prosecution attempts to confine the defendants, despite their release on bail, within the jurisdiction of the U.S. District Court
for the Southern District of New York, and also waged a modestly productive fight to prevent a trial. On 16 August, lawyer Abraham Unger
went before Judge Harold Medina to ask for an additional ninety days
in which to file motions. Medina, dealing for the first time with a case
he would eventually try, seemed considerably less than objective, for
when McGohey argued that delay would allow the defendants to continue the activities which had resulted in this indictment, he observed,
"If we let them do that sort of thing they'll destroy the government. . . ."
It would be better for all concerned, the judge said, if the case was disposed of quickly. Medina did agree, however, to extend the deadline for
filing motions to 22 September.[11]

On 23 August Unger was back, arguing that the court should postpone
the trial until after the November elections, because the case had become
a political football. Medina, who considered this "just another criminal
case," saw no reason why it should be handled in any special way and
granted the government's motion for a 15 October trial date.[12]

Efforts to obtain a postponement proved unsuccessful, and on 6 October argument opened before Judge Murray Hulbert on defense motions
attacking the indictments. Lawyers for the Communist leaders, contending that the prosecution had presented no legally competent evidence to
the grand jury, attributed that body's action against their clients to pressure from the press and government officials. Counsel for the Communists
went on to contend that the grand jury had been improperly constituted
and, along with the ACLU and the National Lawyers' Guild, which filed
briefs as amici curiae, to attack the constitutionality of the Smith Act.
The constitutional issue received further attention in a lengthy defense

brief, which argued that this prosecution was an attempt to outlaw a political party.[13]

Argument before Judge Hulbert dragged on for three days and left the jurist with so many problems to resolve that he could not possibly finish his labors before the trial was due to begin, thus forcing him to reschedule opening day for 1 November. The lawyers had gained a brief respite, but nothing more, for on 22 October Hulbert denied all their motions. Relying primarily on Judge Stone's opinion in the Trotskyist case, he ruled in favor of the constitutionality of the Smith Act, upheld the indictment, rejected as unproved the Communist contention that the grand jury had been improperly constituted, and turned down both a defense motion for a bill of particulars and a prosecution one for consolidation of the indictments.[14]

It seemed, as Elizabeth Gurley Flynn observed, that the decks were now "cleared for action for the biggest and most important political trial this country has ever seen."[15] The Communist press whipped up the faithful and on 1 November three hundred pickets, mobilized by the CRC, appeared in front of the Foley Square courthouse, ready for a showdown. Again, defense counsel managed to postpone the day of reckoning, this time by persuading Judge Medina to push jury selection back to 15 November, so that he might hear oral arguments on a defense claim that the anti-Communist hysteria gripping the country necessitated indefinite postponement of the trial. Along with their two-week delay the Communists received some bad news: Medina, who had displayed less sympathy for the Twelve than any other judge they had yet confronted, would try the case.[16]

Their attorneys immediately demanded his removal, but Medina, insisting that he was not biased against the defendants, refused to disqualify himself. "I have not now nor have I ever had any thoughts or opinions relative to the facts of the case," he asserted. The defense asked the Second Circuit Court of Appeals to order the judge to remove himself, but it refused, concluding that nothing in his past remarks supported the charge of bias.[17]

While attempting to force Medina off the case, the lawyers also continued their efforts to delay the trial. On 8 november Harry Sacher, armed with piles of anti-Communist literature, spent four hours arguing that such material had created a hysterical atmosphere which made a fair proceeding impossible, and another defense attorney, Abraham Isserman, added that his side needed more time to prepare its case. While neither argument impressed Medina, the judge did grant a delay, based on the ill health of William Z. Foster. The aging Party leader had a long history of heart trouble, and, after two court-appointed physicians determined that the rigors of a trial might kill him, Medina agreed to a postponement, announcing on 17 November that the trial would begin exactly two months later.[18] While giving the defense until 17 January, he rejected most of its arguments. "I have concluded there is no such state of inflamed public opinion that would preclude a fair trial," Medina announced.[19] In a written opinion filed a few days later, he observed that the affidavit and exhibits indicated "hostility toward Communism" but made "little mention of the defendants personally." The judge also rejected the contention that the defense needed more time in which to prepare.[20]

Still committed to preventing a trial, lawyers for the Twelve decided to argue that, if Foster remained too ill to participate, because his testimony was vital to the other defendants, Medina must postpone the whole case. While awaiting the results of a court-ordered medical examination of their client, they also went to the Supreme Court, asking it to disqualify the judge and also to void the indictments, because of the alleged exclusion of workers, low-rent families, and blacks from juries in the Southern District. On 10 January, the high tribunal rejected both petitions, and four days later Medina, unimpressed with the Foster argument and unwilling to countenance further delay, announced that the trial would go on as scheduled on 17 January.[21]

Party efforts to block the wheels of justice continued down to the last minute, as a long-planned January 1949 march on Washington in support of black rights became a protest against the trial of the Twelve. On 17 January an estimated seven hundred "civil rights fighters" showed up in the capital, demanding that Truman dismiss the indictments. The next day the crowd of protestors, now swelled to several thousand, concentrated its attention on senators and representatives. The group that received the most encouraging reception was the one that visited the junior senator from Wisconsin. Joseph R. McCarthy, who had not yet realized how much political profit there could be in attacking Communists, told them that he opposed trying people for their political beliefs and expressed interest in learning what evidence the government had of force and violence.[22]

His sympathetic response was about the only positive result of the march on Washington. Like earlier efforts to smash the indictments with mass pressure, this one was a failure. Legal maneuvering had accomplished more than labor defense, but the lawyers could delay the inevitable no longer. The Party would have the day in court it did not want.

IV

On 17 January 1949 the curtain rose on the legal drama which would decide the fate of the National Committee, and perhaps the entire Communist Party. The stage was the largest available: room 110 of the Foley Square courthouse, with seating for 140 spectators. Its high ceiling, paneled walls, and majestic judge's bench and jury box gave the place an impressive—but somehow morbid—look, like a funeral parlor, defendant John Gates thought. [23]

Perhaps his impression arose from a premonition that within its walls doom awaited such leaders of the CPUSA as William Z. Foster. The Party's National Secretary and its ranking official, Foster was one of the patriarchs of American radicalism. Born of working-class parents in 1881 and reared in the slums of Philadelphia, he had joined the Socialist Party while in his early twenties, and later, after flirting with the Industrial Workers of the World, had founded his own short-lived Syndicalist League of North America. After organizing meat packers for the AFL and leading the gigantic 1919 steel strike, Foster visited Russia in 1921. Upon returning to the United States, he cast his lot with the infant American Communist movement and fought his way through the fierce intra-Party leadership struggles of the 1920s to the top spot in the CPUSA, only to have the Soviets ease him aside in favor of the inept, but subservient, Earl Browder. After World War II, when the international situation changed and Foster's form of militant opposition to capitalism and the U.S. government became more suitable to Russian purposes than Browder's accommodationism, control of the Party again passed into his hands.

Because of Foster's poor health, General Secretary Eugene Dennis now directed the day-to-day operations of the CPUSA. Originally known as Francis X. Waldron, he was a graduate of the Lenin Institute in Moscow and a veteran of Comintern work in South Africa, the Philippines, and China. Although at one time a protégé of Browder, who brought him into the national office from the Wisconsin state organization, Dennis wisely backed Foster during the Party's postwar power struggle, and in 1946 his new patron rewarded him with the post of general secretary.

Facing trial along with Foster and Dennis were all of their top subordinates but Flynn. Three of the accused—National Organizational Secretary Henry Winston, Trade Union Secretary John Williamson, and New York Party Chairman Robert Thompson—comprised, with Foster and Dennis, the secretariat which supervised all activities of the CPUSA. Below them in official status, but nevertheless a figure of such power that his name inspired awe among the rank and file, was National Educational Director Jacob (Jack) Stachel, a man whose mastery of bureaucracy and skills as a boss and fixer had enabled him to survive innumerable leadership struggles during a lengthy career at the top of the Communist hierarchy. Stachel's codefendant, Irving Potash, lacked his influence within the organization but was far better known outside it. Head of the Furriers Joint Council of New York, he had, during a colorful career as a union leader, survived a brutal knifing, assisted Thomas Dewey in his crackdown on New York labor racketeering, and served time in prison for criminal anarchy and tampering with a witness in an antitrust case. Even more familiar to the public was Benjamin Davis, the only Communist on the New York City Council, where he had served since 1943. The list of indicted National Committee members also included the chairmen of the Party's Illinois, Michigan, and Ohio organizations: Gil Green, Carl Winter, and Gus Hall. Finally, there was Gates, the editor of the semiofficial Communist newspaper, the *Daily Worker.*

While presenting a diverse appearance, these men had more in common than membership on the National Committee. All were male, and most were between thirty-five and fifty years of age. Foster, at sixty-seven, was almost twenty years older than any of the others, and Thompson, the youngest member of the group, was thirty-three. At least three-quarters of these Communists were American-born citizens (the exceptions being Stachel, a native of Poland, Potash, from Russia, and Williamson, who had emigrated to the United States from Scotland). Only two of the defendants, Winston and Davis, were nonwhite. The group included more Jews than members of any other ethnic group, although Green (born Gilbert Greenberg), Winter (formerly Phillip Carl Weisburg), and Gates (originally Israel Regenstreif) had disquised their heritage by Americanizing their names. As befit self-styled leaders of the working class, most of these Communists came from poor families. Davis, the exception, was the son of a well-to-do Atlanta publisher and Republican Party leader and had attended Amherst and the Harvard Law School. His radicalism was a product of white racism, rather than of poverty.

Although most of the defendants were products of the lower classes, few could justifiably claim to speak for American labor. Only Foster and Stachel had ever had any real status in the trade union movement. Four members of the group—Winston, Thompson, Gates, and Hall—had served in the armed forces during World War II, and Thompson had won the Army's second highest decoration, the Distinguished Service Cross, for heroism in the South Pacific. Both he and Gates had done their first military service with the International Brigade during the Spanish Civil War, and all four had joined the American armed forces less out of traditional patriotism than because of their commitment to the worldwide struggle against fascism. At least half of the defendants had entered the Party from radical youth organizations, and two, Green and Winston. had once been top officials of the Young Communist League. The Twelve were a group of professional revolutionaries with long and deep commitments to communism.[24]

Assisting them in their confrontation with the government was a team
of attorneys led by Harry Sacher and Abraham Isserman, both of whom
had been identified as Communists by witnesses before the Un-American
Activities Committee. The most combative of their associates was Richard
Gladstein, a tough labor lawyer from California, who had represented
Harry Bridges, the alleged-Communist chieftain of West Coast dockwork-
ers, in two deportation cases. Probably, he too was a Party member. Also
associated with the defense team was a black attorney from Detroit,
George Crockett, the first Negro ever employed in a legal capacity by the
U.S. Department of Labor and also a former employee of the Fair Employment Practices Commission. Although less politically radical, and
generally more restrained in his courtroom conduct, than Isserman, Sacher,
and Gladstein, Crockett hated white racism with a passion that often boiled
to the surface. The most calm and dignified of the defense attorneys
was Louis F. McCabe, a gray-haired, distinguished-looking barrister from
Philadelphia. Assisting these five as staff counsel, although not participating in the trial proper, was the only woman on the team, Mary Kaufman.[25]

Most of the attorneys accepted the subordinate role which labor defense
assigned to lawyers in a criminal trial. As counsel for Communist leaders,
they practiced in support of a mass movement and used their legal skills
largely to advance the propaganda efforts of the Party. Although it was
the attorneys who possessed expertise in courtroom tactics, the men directing this defense were the leaders of the CPUSA, and even though the attorneys might advise against things which the defendants proposed, in
the end they always deferred to the wishes of their clients.[26]

The Twelve and their counsel confronted a five-man team of government lawyers headed by U.S. Attorney John McGohey, who had decided
to prosecute this case himself. Serving McGohey as special assistants were
Frank Gordon of New York and Irving Shapiro of Washington. The Attorney General's office had contributed Edward C. Wallace to the prosecution staff, and the Criminal Division had sent Lawrence K. Bailey up
from the capital to oppose the Communists.[27]

Although the adversary system of justice supposedly pitted the Twelve
and their lawyers against this team of prosecutors, the man with whom
they ultimately fought their most bitter battles was the judge. Harold
Medina, who bore a striking resemblance to actor Adolph Menjou, was a
brilliant lawyer who had ranked near the top of his class at Columbia Law
School, from which he graduated in 1912 and where he later taught for
twenty-five years. No mere legal academic, Medina also achieved great
success as a practicing attorney. Specializing in appellate work, he argued
about 1,400 appeals in his four decades at the bar, more than any other
lawyer in New York. Although not undertaking trial work until 1931, he

proved equally adept at it, not losing a single case over a period of fourteen years. In addition to engaging in private practice and teaching at Columbia, Medina also, for over a quarter of a century, operated a bar review course, through which countless New York attorneys passed. He came to the bench endorsed by numerous prominent members of the legal profession and by the American Bar Association.

Although a great lawyer, Medina was the wrong man to try the Communist case, for he had been on the bench for only about eighteen months, and this was his first criminal trial. Apparently because of his inexperience, he found it necessary to lean on the U.S. attorney for advice, with the result that at times the court did not appear entirely neutral. Then too, his background was an unfortunate one for a jurist asked to deal objectively with a case involving the American Communist movement. Medina's father, although a Mexican immigrant, was quite well-to-do, and Harold had attended Holbrook Military Academy and Princeton University prior to enrolling at Columbia Law School. In adult life, the son became a wealthy man in his own right. Having a judge from such a background on the bench gave the defendants sufficient cause to complain about class justice, adding to the problem created by the fact that, whether he was objective or not, Medina had already managed to create a distinct impression of bias.

Perhaps the judge's biggest liability was his personality. As a boy during the Spanish-American War, he had received a great deal of abuse from other children because of his Latin surname and appearance and, forced to fight his way to and from school, had grown up combative. As a Princeton freshman, young Harold established a reputation for being argumentative, which made him the target of unmerciful hazing by older students. Later, as an attorney, he achieved respect, but not popularity, among his colleagues, for in the courtroom he was aggressive, sarcastic, and an "insufferable egoist." On the bench Medina remained abrasive, demonstrating a flippant attitude, a fondness for wisecracking with and at attorneys, and a readiness to use language that was often caustic and sometimes downright rude. Although often lashing others with a biting tongue, he was extremely sensitive and reacted strongly against what he interpreted as insults from the bar.[28]

Chief Judge John Knox had what he considered good reasons for overlooking these negative traits and assigning Medina to the Communist trial. One was the fact that Medina already knew something about the case. Hulbert did too, but he was in poor health, and Knox, remembering Eicher's death during the Washington Sedition Trial, felt it necessary to have a man of undoubted physical strength handling this proceeding. The chief judge wished to avoid naming a Catholic, because of the strong anti-Com-

munist stand that church had taken, and Medina, despite his Mexican ancestry, was a Presbyterian. Finally, while aware that his choice had been
on the bench for only a short time, Knox felt sure that the wide experience Medina had acquired during a distinguished career at the bar would
compensate for this deficiency.[29]

Although Medina appeared to be a sensible selection, events soon demonstrated that the chief judge had erred in choosing him. After getting
the case, the already hypersensitive jurist made a careful study of the
Washington Sedition Trial, which agitated him considerably. Medina grew
fearful that, like Eicher, he might collapse from exhaustion, and, in order
to conserve his strength, he eliminated all social life and rigidly scheduled
his entire day. Haunted by thoughts of Eicher, the judge soon concluded
that the defendants and their lawyers were plotting to wreck his health
and sanity through their persistent efforts to delay resolution of the case.
The longer the proceedings dragged on, the more "wearing" the experience became, and the more it seemed to him that only a desire to break
his mind and body could explain the tactics of the Communists and their
attorneys. Medina's resentment of the defense grew and grew, until he became more adversary than arbiter, with the result that many of the most
spectacular scenes in the drama which unfolded at Foley Square involved
battles between the Communist side and an antagonist on the bench.[30]

V

The courtroom theatrics began on 17 January 1949 when the Party
launched a challenge to the court's jury selection system, intended to
put off the trial while simultaneously discrediting American government.
The Communists scored a small propaganda triumph that day, for the
New York City Police Department stationed four hundred men in and
around the courthouse, giving Foley Square the appearance of a military
camp. The only "hostile" activity on 17 January was a peaceful noon-
hour demonstration by about five hundred pickets; hence this occupy-
ing army had nothing to do, and liberal newspapers joined the Communist press in expressing outrage at its presence. Unfortunately for the
Party, defense delaying tactics soon alienated the allies which this incident had recruited.[31]

Convinced that Communists could win only outside the legal system,
the CPUSA continued to stall in order to give itself time to mobilize the
masses. Flynn, Party lobbyist Simon Gerson, and New York District official William Norman set up an eighteen-member provisional leadership

group. It in turn brought about creation of a permanent "spark plug" organization, the Communist Committee for the Defense of the Twelve, which included several veteran labor defenders and much of the second-echelon leadership of the CPUSA. The defendants kept up a heavy speaking schedule around the country. Benjamin Davis sought support from his New York City Council colleagues, and the Party continued trying to convince trade unionists and liberals that they too had a stake in what was going on at Foley Square. As in the past, favorable response came mainly from long-time allies of the CPUSA.[32]

Lack of popular backing failed to destroy the Party's faith in the efficacy of mass pressure. From all over the country delegations purporting to speak for organized labor, veterans, blacks, trade unionists, and other interest groups flocked to Foley Square in an effort to force Medina to rule as the CPUSA desired. At first the judge was receptive to these groups, twice even giving up his midday meal to confer with them. When, eventually, he grew tired and refused to see any more, the delegations stopped coming, but a deluge of correspondence, some of it quite obscene, then rained down upon him. Although Medina did not read all of this mail, he did make an effort to keep up on its contents and was not impressed by what he recognized as a manufactured substitute for public opinion. About all the correspondence blitz accomplished was to irritate the judge.[33]

Nevertheless, the Communists convinced themselves that these were winning tactics. Believing that public protest would free the Twelve, they felt that all they had to do was prevent adjudication of the case until the mass campaign could arouse the people—so defense counsel stalled furiously. First the attorneys renewed their request for a postponement until public opinion moderated. Medina was not impressed by the arguments in favor of this, which, he felt, amounted to a claim that anyone accused of advocating the overthrow of the government by force and violence, because that subject would always arouse interest and discussion, could not be tried at all. A plea for postponement of the entire case until Foster was healthy enough to stand trial aroused no greater sympathy, the court rejecting it in favor of a prosecution motion for severance. The judge also turned down defense requests for ninety- and fifteen-day continuances.[34]

Thwarted in their attempts to obtain a postponement, lawyers for the Communist leaders turned to a jury challenge which they had initiated earlier. Endeavoring to convince the court that the now-eleven defendants had been indicted by a body selected in a way which violated the accused's rights under the Fifth and Sixth Amendments, they argued

that the Southern District grand jury was an organ of the well-to-do.
Those responsible for its selection had systematically excluded, in whole
or in part, the poor, slum dwellers, manual laborers, wage workers, blacks,
members of other racial and national minorities, and persons affiliated
with the Communist and American Labor Parties, the defense contended.
As the grand jury did not represent a cross section of the population, its
composition was illegal. Because the defendants belonged to various of
the excluded groups, had devoted themselves to the interests of the dis-
advantaged, and were known antagonists of the wealthy, the attorneys
argued, the way in which the jury had been selected violated their rights.[35]

This challenge was designed to postpone trial of the case itself and
thus give mass protest time to get the prosecution "thrown out of court."
At the same time it provided the Communists with an opportunity to
characterize the federal district court and its grand jury as "instruments
of a capitalist class intent on clamping a police state on the people."
Party leaders, such as Eugene Dennis, seem to have felt that with this tactic the CPUSA could rally the population behind its cause.[36]

Because the objectives of the challenge dictated the manner of its conduct, the course that the defense pursued was showy but circuitous. As
a lawyer Medina had argued a well-known case attacking New York's
jury selection system. But while favoring panels that represented a cross section of the population, he realized that the law, as laid down by the Supreme Court, did not require this. It demanded only that there be no willful, deliberate, or systematic exclusion of any identifiable group. Medina
felt that in order for the challenge to succeed, the defense would have to
prove that those who selected panel members in the Southern District
had been guilty of the practices the law forbade. He indicated to defense
counsel that this could best be established by questioning the jury commission clerk and his deputy, but the lawyers would have nothing to do
with such a direct approach.

Instead, they called as witnesses a succession of grand and petit jurors
to demonstrate that Southern District panels were nonrepresentative ag-
gregations of middle- and upper-class, white, male professionals. While
succeeding in establishing this, they failed to demonstrate the *deliberate*
exclusion of blacks, women, or the poor and thus could not sustain their
legal challenge. Finally, on 27 January, Medina, convinced that he was
confronted with a deliberate attempt to frustrate the judicial process,
put an end to this stall, ordering the lawyers to call no more jurors until
they had offered some other proof in support of their allegations.[37]

Although compelled by the judge to change direction, counsel still refused to take the course which he had recommended. Instead of exam-

ining court officials, they called to the stand Doxey Wilkerson, director of faculty and curriculum at the Jefferson School of Social Science, a New York educational institution controlled by the CPUSA. Wilkerson, who held a master's degree, had previously taught at Howard University, worked for two government agencies, and participated in a widely acclaimed study of American racial problems. Claiming skill and experience in the use of statistical methods, he arrived in the courtroom weighted down with an impressive collection of social science visual aids and attempted, as an expert witness, to establish the same things which the defense had tried to prove with the testimony of the jurors. Because Medina not only considered the points Wilkerson was trying to make irrelevant but also had little understanding of statistical methodology, the professor's chances of swaying him were never good. Wilkerson made his job even more difficult by acknowledging under cross-examination that he had not personally prepared or verified the accuracy of his exhibits and did not even know all of the people who had worked on them. Equally damaging in Medina's eyes was his admission of deep involvement in the Communist movement.

When it became apparent that Wilkerson was making a bad impression on the judge, the defense attempted to shore up his sagging presentation by interjecting supporting testimony from other witnesses. It called three more jurors—all well-to-do white property owners—and then, in an effort to convince Medina that Wilkerson's methodology and data were more reliable than he suspected, put on the stand researchers for the *New York Times* and the Commonwealth Edison Company. Apparently for publicity purposes, Vito Marcantonio appeared, billed as an authority on the social composition of his congressional district. The defense also called two men who had once compiled a report on the Southern District jury system for the Administrative Office of the United States Courts.[38]

Even buttressed by the contributions of these other witnesses, Wilkerson's testimony did not impress Medina, and as it dragged on and on, the judge began casting about for some way to keep the challenge from becoming an interminable proceeding. On Friday, 11 February, he instructed counsel for the Eleven to prepare a detailed statement of what they intended to prove and how they proposed to go about doing it. The following Monday, finding their memorandum wholly insufficient, Medina "in the exercise of [his] discretion as to the order of proof, and without prejudicing counsel for the defendants as to what they [might] later do," directed "that . . . the government proceed with its proof."[39]

This judicial bombshell did not substantially accelerate the proceedings, for defense counsel now dragged out cross-examination of government witnesses. After listening for three tedious days while they interrogated

Jury Clerk Joseph McKenzie, Medina remarked acidly that their questioning was getting rather prolonged. When the lawyers ignored such hints, he imposed a time limit, giving them one more day in which to finish with the witness. The defense took the position that "the essential consideration of the Court is with justice, and if justice and examination of the facts require an extensive proceeding, the proceeding must be extensive." Medina, who disagreed, was by now "looking for some reasonable way to take what is essential here and stop." When the defense attempted to drag out cross-examination of McKenzie's assistant, William J. Borman, the judge again imposed a time limit.[40]

By now the proof had persuaded Medina that the facts were the exact opposite of what the defense claimed, and he announced that he was putting "a termination to this preliminary proceeding. . . ." He ordered the Eleven to present the rest of their case by the following Tuesday or Wednesday and informed counsel that the trial would begin the Monday after that. Under this severe judicial pressure, the grumbling lawyers at last got down to business, and in the time that remained they called and examined with dispatch a number of significant witnesses, whose testimony bore directly on the issues.[41]

It was already too late, though. On 4 March, after reading briefs submitted by the parties, Medina overruled the challenge and denied all defense motions. "[N]ot only have the defendants failed to prove this charge," he said, "but the evidence largely adduced by them conclusively refutes it." The challenge, he felt, came down to an assertion that those responsible for administering the jury selection system had to ensure proportional representation of blacks, the poor, manual workers, and members of all racial and religious groups. This contention was contrary to precedent, and if such a procedure were adopted, it would, he felt, breed the very intolerance that everyone wished to avoid.[42]

The jury challenge had failed, and the mass campaign had yet to force dismissal of the indictments. Eleven of the Twelve were going to stand trial, and they would do so before a judge made hostile by the tactics which they and their lawyers had employed. Although legal maneuvering and courtroom stalling had bought them time, the Communists had managed to do no more than delay their day of reckoning.

NOTES

1. Elizabeth Gurley Flynn, "The Militant Traditions of Labor Defense Inspire Our Fight Today," *PA* 30 (February 1951): 127; *NYT*, 22 July 1948, p. 2; *PW*, 22 July 1948, 23 July 1948, and 26 July 1948; *DW*, 22 July 1948, 23 July 1948, 26 July 1948, 28 July 1948, 29 July 1948, and 2 August 1948.

2. *DW*, 22 July 1948, 23 July 1948, 27 July 1948, 29 July 1948, 3 August 1948, 11 August 1948, and 23 August 1948; *NYT*, 22 July 1948, p. 2; *PW*, 30 July 1948; *Militant*, 26 July 1948 and 17 January 1949; ACLU Weekly Bulletin no. 1344, 26 July 1948, p. 1.

3. *Chicago Tribune*, 23 July 1948; *San Francisco Chronicle*, 22 July 1948; *NYT*, 22 July 1948, p. 22; *Appleton* (Wis.) *Post-Crescent*, 22 July 1948; *New Orleans Times-Picayune*, 22 July 1948; *St. Louis Post-Dispatch*, 21 July 1948; *Los Angeles Times*, 22 July 1948; *Cleveland Plain Dealer*, 22 July 1948; Roscoe Drummond, "Are Communists Traitors to America?" *American Mercury* 67 (October 1948): 389-96.

4. *DW*, 21 July 1948, 23 July 1948, 26 July 1948, and 27 July 1948.

5. *DW*, 22 July 1948 and 1 September 1948; William Z. Foster, "Concluding Remarks at the Convention," *PA* 27 (September 1948): 832; Eugene Dennis, "The Fascist Danger and How to Combat It," *PA* 27 (September 1948): 795-96.

6. *NYT*, 23 September 1948, p. 9; *DW*, 21 September 1948 and 22 September 1948.

7. Federal Bureau of Investigation, "Communist Party, USA (Action of CP re Arrest of National Board Members), Internal Security—C," 23 July 1948, typescript, and "Communist Party, USA (Action of CP re Arrest of National Board Members), Internal Security—C.," 26 July 1948, typescript, both in Box 167, President's Secretary's Files, Papers of H. S. Truman, HTL; Herbert A. Philbrick, *I Led 3 Lives: Citizen, "Communist," Counterspy* (New York: McGraw-Hill, 1952), pp. 268-70; HUAC, *Hearings . . . Exposé of the Communist Party of Western Pennsylvania Based upon Testimony of Mathew Cvetic*, 81st Cong., 2d sess., 1950, pp. 1290-97, 1306 (quote on p. 1295).

8. *DW*, 8 December 1948, 10 December 1948, and 20 December 1948; *PW*, 24 December 1948.

9. *DW*, 14 December 1948 and 20 December 1948; *PW*, 17 December 1948.

10. *DW*, 26 July 1948, 3 August 1948, 25 August 1948, 21 September 1948, 23 September 1948, 27 September 1948, 6 October 1948, 11 October 1948, 16 October 1948, 20 October 1948, 21 October 1948, 25 October 1948, 12 November 1948, 29 November 1948, 3 December 1948, 22 December 1948, 28 December 1948, and 7 January 1949; *PW*, 26 July 1948, 30 July 1948, 22 September 1948, 25 September 1948, 8 October 1948, 15 October 1948, and 18 October 1948; *NYT*, 26 September 1948, p. 8, and 12 November 1948, p. 25.

11. *NYT*, 12 August 1948, p. 7, 17 August 1948, p. 3, and 2 September 1948, p. 4; *DW*, 2 September 1948; United States v. Foster, 79 F. Supp. 422 (S.D.N.Y. 1948). The quote is from the 17 August *NYT* story.

12. *NYT*, 24 August 1948, p. 3; *DW*, 21 September 1948.

13. *NYT*, 7 October 1948, p. 5, 8 October 1948, p. 5; *DW*, 21 September 1948, 8 October 1948, and 11 October 1948; ACLU Weekly Bulletin no. 1355, 11 October 1948, p. 1; "From the Briefs on the Unconsti-

tutionality of the Smith Act: Submitted by Defense Attorneys for the Indicted Twelve Communist Party National Committee Members," *PA* 27 (November 1948): 1013-14, 1030.

14. *DW,* 18 October 1948; United States v. Foster, 80 F. Supp. 479 (S.D.N.Y. 1948).

15. *DW,* 1 November 1948.

16. Ibid., and 2 November 1948; *NYT,* 2 November 1948, p. 18; Hawthorne Daniel, *Judge Medina: A Biography* (New York: Wilfred Funk, 1952), pp. 217-19.

17. United States v. Foster, 81 F. Supp. 280 (S.D.N.Y. 1948), at 280-81; Foster v. Medina, 170 F. 2d 632 (2d Cir. 1948), *cert. denied,* 335 U.S. 909 (1948).

18. *DW,* 9 November 1948, 15 November 1948, 18 November 1948, p. 2; *NYT,* 13 November 1948, p. 32.

19. *NYT,* 18 November 1948, p. 2.

20. United States v. Foster, 81 F. Supp. 280 (S.D.N.Y. 1948) (quote at 283).

21. *NYT,* 3 January 1949, p. 12, 4 January 1949, p. 10, 8 January 1949, p. 13, 11 January 1949, p. 3, 12 January 1949, p. 4, 14 January 1949, p. 4, and 15 January 1949, p. 2.

22. *DW,* 18 January 1949 and 19 January 1949; Angela Calomiris, *Red Masquerade: Undercover for the FBI* (Philadelphia and New York: J. B. Lippincott Co., 1950), pp. 240-41.

23. *NYT,* 7 January 1949, p. 5; Gates, *The Story,* p. 119.

24. These sketches of and comments about the defendants are based on Shannon, *Decline,* pp. 9-19; Irving Howe and Lewis Coser, *The American Communist Party: A Critical History (1919-1957)* (Boston: Beacon Press, 1957), pp. 79-81; Theodore Draper, *American Communism and Soviet Russia: The Formative Period* (New York: Viking Press, 1960), pp. 62-94, 234-35; Benjamin Gitlow, *I Confess: The Truth About American Communism* (New York: E. P. Dutton & Co., 1940), pp. 326-31; Philbrick, *I Led 3 Lives,* p. 183; Benjamin Davis, *The Path of Negro Liberation* (New York: New Century Publishers, 1947), p. 6, *Communist Councilman from Harlem: Autobiographical Notes Written in a Federal Penitentiary* (New York: International Publishers, 1969), pp. 21-39, 53-144, and *Why I Am a Communist* (New York: New Century Publishers, 1947), pp. 8-10; Julia Brown, *I Testify: My Years as an Undercover Agent for the FBI* (Boston and Los Angeles: Western Islands Publishers, 1966), pp. 169-70; Gates, *The Story,* pp. 3-118; Max M. Kampelman, *The Communist Party vs. the CIO: A Study in Power Politics* (New York: Frederick A. Praeger, 1957), p. 215; *NYT,* 21 July 1948, p. 3, and 30 July 1948, p. 5; *PW,* 22 October 1948, 29 October 1948, 12 November 1948, 19 November 1948, 26 November 1948, 3 December 1948, 10 December 1948, and 17 December 1948; Joint Appendix to Brief for Appellants and Brief for the Appellee, United States v. Dennis, 183 F. 2d 201 (2d Cir. 1950), pp. 6352-410, 7183-220, and 12073 (cited hereinafter as *Joint Appendix).*

    25. *Joint Appendix*, pp. 54-55; Daniel, *Judge Medina*, pp. 23-31;
PW, 12 October 1948; George Marion, *The Communist Trial: An Ameri-
can Crossroads* (New York: Fairplay Publishers, 1950), pp. 180-81; HUAC,
Communist Legal Subversion: The Role of the Communist Lawyer, 86th
Cong., 1st sess., 1959, H. Rept. 41, pp. 41-61; Abraham Isserman to the
Author, 9 December 1976.
    26. Gates, *The Story*, p. 126; Isserman to the Author, 9 December
1976.
    27. United States v. Foster, 9 F.R.D. #367 (S.D.N.Y. #1949).
    28. Daniel, *Judge Medina*, pp. 4-12, 53-71, 89-177, and 207-13; Jack
Alexander, "The Ordeal of Judge Medina," *Saturday Evening Post*, 12 Au-
gust 1950, p. 84; Irwin Ross, "Harold Medina—Judge Extraordinary,"
Reader's Digest 66 (February 1950): 87-88; "Trial: His Honor, Judge
Patience," *Newsweek*, 23 May 1949, pp. 21-22; Felix Frankfurter to
Learned Hand, 24 April 1951, Box 64, Felix Frankfurter Papers, LC;
Joint Appendix (18 February 1949), p. 2083, and (25 February 1949),
p. 2276; *NYT*, 24 August 1948, p. 3.
    29. Daniel, *Judge Medina*, pp. 217-19.
    30. Ibid., pp. 231-33.
    31. *NYT*, 18 January 1949, pp. 1, 22; *PW*, 18 January 1949; *Wash-
ington Post*, 18 January 1949.
    32. *PW*, 21 January 1949 and 7 February 1949; *DW*, 1 February
1949, 11 February 1949, 22 February 1949, 28 February 1949; *NYT*,
14 February 1949, p. 3, and 16 February 1949, p. 20; *Joint Appendix*
(2 February 1949), pp. 877-80.
    33. Harold Medina, "A Look at America," in *The Anatomy of Free-
dom* (New York: Henry Holt & Co., 1949), ed. C. Waller Barrett, pp. 2,
4-5; Daniel, *Judge Medina*, pp. 231-34.
    34. *Joint Appendix* (18 January 1949), pp. 55-141, 158-200.
    35. Ibid. (18 January 1949), pp. 221-25.
    36. Arnold Johnson, "The Politics of the Truman Administration,"
PA 27 (March 1949): 12; Eugene Dennis, "For Communist Clarity and
Resoluteness to Forge Working-Class and People's Unity," *PA* 29 (May
1950): 54.
    37. *Joint Appendix* (19-21 and 26-28 January 1949), pp. 286-624
and 772; United States v. Foster, 83 F. Supp. 197 (S.D.N.Y. 1949).
    38. *Joint Appendix* (28 January-11 February 1949), pp. 748-1645;
NYT, 1 February 1949, p. 4.
    39. *Joint Appendix* (11 February 1949), p. 1610, and (13 February
1949), p. 1657; *NYT*, 15 February 1949, p. 8.
    40. *Joint Appendix* (15-25 February 1949), pp. 1703-2275 (quotes
on pp. 2121 and 2150).
    41. Ibid. (28 February—1 March 1949), pp. 2293-547 (quote on
p. 2293).
    42. *NYT*, 3 March 1949, p. 7; United States v. Foster, 83 F. Supp.
197 (S.D.N.Y. 1949) (quote on p. 201).

4

The Battle
of Foley Square

> *A trial is not an industrial dispute, nor is it a political cam-*
> *paign. It is an attempt to reach a reasoned judgment in the*
> *light of evidence that can be fully and impartially explored.*
> —*New York Times*
> 28 August 1949

"Hey judge, we won't budge until the twelve are free." Chanting their
determination, hundreds of demonstrators marched around a little island
in the middle of Foley Square in a noon-hour rally called by the Civil
Rights Congress. They wore armbands damning Jim Crow juries and cry-
ing out for the preservation of the Bill of Rights. Between chants they
sang, mingling the strains of "America" and "The Battle Hymn of the
Republic" with the sounds of New York traffic. It was 7 March 1949,
and the pickets had come to protest the beginning of the Communist
trial. After six months of preliminary skirmishing, the symbolic Cold
War battle that would decide the fate of the CPUSA was at last under
way.[1]

I

Commencement of the trial proper changed little. Foreign leftists
went on demanding that the government dismiss the indictments, while
a dozen placard-carrying CRC demonstrators launched a daily vigil outside the courthouse. Inside, defense lawyers filed more motions, many
of them duplicating others rejected earlier, some as long ago as the hearing before Judge Hulbert. An exasperated Medina, complaining that "This
must be almost a world's record of motions," rejected every one. If what

the lawyers were doing was not stalling, he fumed, "I never observed it in my life."[2]

Despite the judge's growing annoyance, the defense lawyers continued to raise objections and drag their feet, so that selecting a jury took more than a week. With the trial expected to be a long one, many potential jurors did not wish to serve, and the court had to devote considerable time to hearing their excuses, but much of the delay was attributable to the defense. "If justice in this case has not been speedy, it is not the fault of the prosecution or of the court," the *New York Times* observed on 10 March. By then Medina, pleading exhaustion, had shortened the trial day, and the press, alienated by the conduct of the defense lawyers, had begun to make a martyr of the judge.[3]

While the man on the bench was hardly the blameless victim the public came to know, he did, during the early stages of the trial, exhibit considerable restraint in the face of great provocation. The Communists' counsel complained incessantly about the way the jury was being selected and on at least two occasions provoked Medina into sharp criticism of their conduct. Believing that the intent of his tormentors was to goad him into interrupting the trial to initiate contempt proceedings against them, he restricted himself to issuing verbal reprimands and warnings of future punishment, and both his temper and the situation remained reasonably well under control.[4]

The jury selection process, which dragged on until 17 March, resulted in the seating of a group of individuals that differed markedly from the aggregation of rich, white, male capitalists the Communists had pictured as typical of juries in the Southern District. Seven of its members were women, three were black, and none was truly wealthy. The foreman, Thelma Dial, was a black housewife and part-time dressmaker, whose husband worked as a musician. Her fellow jurors included two other housewives, two secretaries, a department store clerk, a beauty operator, an industrial engineer, and a retired beer salesman. One, James F. Smyth, belonged to the strongly anti-Communist American Legion, but as a member of the Communications Workers of America, he was also the only trade unionist on the jury. The last man chosen was perhaps the most interesting of the lot; Russell Janney, who entered the box after the defense had exhausted its preemptory challenges (most of which it expended on persons having some present or past connection with the armed forces), was a writer and theatrical producer, well known for his authorship of *The Miracle of the Bells*. Not even the Communist press could find much reason to criticize this jury.[5]

On 21 March McGohey rose to address its members. The government

intended to prove, the prosecutor said, that, after dissolving the Party
in 1944 and abandoning the struggle to establish socialism through violence in favor of an effort to accomplish that objective by peaceful democratic means, the defendants had reconstituted the CPUSA, in order to
alter American economic, political, and social institutions "according
to the Marxist-Leninist teaching." That meant, according to McGohey,
the establishment of socialism "by the violent overthrow and destruction of our constitutional form of government through the smashing of
the State government and the setting up of the dictatorship of the proletariat by violent and forceful seizure of power under the leadership of
the Communist Party." The prosecution would show, he continued, that
the defendants had held numerous high-level positions in the CPUSA and
that since 1947 they had comprised the entire membership of its National Board. Party clubs, he claimed, were "in reality and in fact classes for
the indoctrination of their members with the theory and practice of
Marxist-Leninist principles of the overthrow and destruction of the government of the United States by force and violence." According to the
U.S. attorney, the Party taught that during times of unrest or disorder,
brought about by severe depression or war, Communists who had managed
to obtain positions of influence in the key trades and basic industries would
receive orders from the National Board and, in compliance with these,
would lead the proletariat in revolt. "They teach that this revolution cannot be without violence," McGohey said, "for to be successful the entire
apparatus of the Government must be smashed." Communists instructed
their followers that, "Every vestige of the bourgeois state and class must
be wiped out. Only when this has been accomplished can the program of
Marxian Socialism be carried out."[6]

The first reply came from Eugene Dennis. As a defendant, he would
have had no right to make an opening statement, had not Louis McCabe,
Abraham Unger, and David Friedman withdrawn from his case four days
earlier, in order that he might act as his own attorney and personally "defend the principles and practices of the Communist Party. . . ."[7] Dennis
readily acknowledged that he and his comrades were leaders of the CPUSA
but denied that there was any resemblance between that organization and
the "fantastic conspiracy" described by the indictment. He pointed out
that the prosecution had accused the defendants of neither overt acts nor
direct advocacy of violent revolution and that the Smith Act had been on
the books for eight years before the government charged a Communist
with violating it. This was, Dennis claimed, a prosecution for political
beliefs, intended to destroy his Party.

He attempted to defend the CPUSA by enumerating its virtues and accomplishments, but Medina would have none of this. The charge was advocating the overthrow of the government by force and violence, the judge said, and it was irrelevant what "very good boys" the defendants "were in some respects." Tongue-lashing Dennis for what seemed to him an attempt to take over his courtroom and use it for propaganda purposes, Medina compelled the Communist leader to abandon this line of argument.

The General Secretary then turned to the subject of Marxism-Leninism. He denied that the Party's principles implied the duty or necessity of forcefully overthrowing the U.S. government and promised the defense would prove that it was reactionary minority groups bent on halting the march of social progress who resorted to violence. The constitution of the CPUSA called for the institution of socialism by free choice of the American people, and the defendants, Dennis insisted, had simply urged labor and the masses to work toward the peaceful establishment of a new economic and political order.[8]

After the General Secretary came the defense lawyers. Crockett claimed that this was a trial of political beliefs, McCabe argued that the CPUSA could not be held responsible for outdated Communist literature nor for every word uttered by all its members, and Sacher stressed the defendants' longstanding opposition to force and violence. When, after some routine remarks by Isserman, Gladstein launched into a fiery labor defense appeal, Medina exploded, "Now you are not going to try in this court anybody accused by the defendants." When Gladstein concluded with another assertion that the Eleven were on trial for their thoughts, Medina again intervened, admonishing the jury that, no matter what kind of ideas were involved, a conspiracy such as the indictment charged was criminal. An angry defense promptly moved for a mistrial, but the judge denied its motion, leaving the prosecution free to present its case against American communism.[9]

II

That case was not a strong one, for as the *Washington Post* had suspected from the beginning, the real purpose of this prosecution was "not so much the protection and security of the state as the exploitation of justice for the purpose of propaganda." Because the government had no proof of serious wrongdoing by the CPUSA, in order to dramatize its own anti-communism, it had to resort to the Smith Act, a statute that, despite many ominous-sounding references to "overthrow of the government by force and violence" proscribed only the teaching and advocacy of revolutionary doctrine. If the

Justice Department had possessed evidence that the CPUSA was plotting a revolt, it could have prosecuted the organization's leaders for seditious conspiracy. "However, it is highly doubtful—at least on the basis of presently available evidence—" a government lawyer had advised McGohey in the spring of 1948, "that a case could be made out against such individuals." The authorities could not prosecute the Communists for violation of the Voorhis Act, which required subversive groups to register with the attorney general, for in order to make a case against them under the two most important provisions of that law, federal prosecutors had to be able to prove that the CPUSA was controlled by the Soviet government or that it had engaged in military activity, and they could do neither. Nor did the Justice Department have any evidence which would justify a prosecution of the Party's officers for violation of the Foreign Agents Registration Act.[10]

Indeed, even under the Smith Act, federal prosecutors did not have as strong a case as they might have wished. After reading the FBI's massive brief on the Party, McGohey's adviser informed him that the government would "be faced with a difficult task in seeking to prove beyond a reasonable doubt in a criminal prosecution, that the Communist Party advocates revolution by violence." Fortunately for McGohey, the Smith Act did not require a prosecutor to establish actual advocacy of armed revolt but only that the defendants were guilty of creating a group to engage in such activity or of conspiring to advocate or organize.[11]

Unable to prove actual incitement, let alone revolutionary deeds or plots, the authorities attacked the Party with the conspiracy provisions of the Smith Act. For prosecutors short of evidence, the choice was a shrewd one. In the words of Supreme Court Justice Robert Jackson, "The modern crime of conspiracy is so vague that it almost defies definition." Two or more persons commit that offense when they enter into a combination to accomplish an unlawful purpose or to achieve a lawful objective by illegal means. But in order to obtain a conspiracy conviction, a prosecutor does not have to establish that the alleged participants executed any kind of formal agreement, or even that each knew all of the others or their roles in the enterprise. In 1949, the law insisted only that he prove a given defendant had engaged in affirmative conduct that either aided the proposed unlawful act or in some way indicated his agreement with the other conspirators. Furthermore, if a prosecutor could establish the existence of a conspiracy, he freed himself from having to prove individual defendants guilty of substantive offenses, because each member of a conspiracy was criminally liable for all declarations made and acts done by his confederates in furtherance of their common purpose.[12]

The indictment returned by the federal grand jury in New York accused the Eleven of conspiring to teach and advocate the violent overthrow of the government and of conspiring to organize the Communist Party to engage in such activity. It thus made the CPUSA the real defendant in this case, even though, technically, the Party and the conspiracy were distinct. The indictment actually alleged that the Stalinist organization was an instrument fashioned by a small group of plotters for use in accomplishing their unlawful purposes, but as the Eleven constituted almost the entire top leadership of the Party, the public, and even the prosecutors, easily forgot this technical point. Then too, although the CPUSA was not the conspiracy, its character was crucial, for if that organization was not what the government claimed, planning to establish it could not possibly constitute a violation of the Smith Act. Once the nature of the Party became an issue, there was no effective way of preventing it from overshadowing all others. Because the prosecution's real target was the CPUSA, rather than the Eleven, and because it could muster far more evidence against the organization than against its current leaders, the government encouraged this development.

McGohey's men devoted about 90 percent of their attention to building a case against the CPUSA and only about 10 percent to establishing the defendants' complicity in the alleged conspiracy. The theory behind their case was that sometime prior to 1935 there had existed in America a Communist Party, which belonged to the Third International and followed the revolutionary doctrines of Marxism-Leninism. According to the prosecution, that philosophy included among its tenets the use of force and violence to overthrow the capitalist system and the governments it spawned, including that of the United States. About 1935 the world Communist movement had adopted the Popular Front policy of cooperation with many capitalist regimes, and, nine years later, the chief American exponent of the new line, Earl Browder, had brought about the dissolution of the CPUSA, replacing it with the Communist Political Association. Sometime prior to 1 April 1945, under orders from Moscow, the Popular Front idea was dropped, and the international Communist apparatus reverted to its pre-1935 policy. The defendants, as leaders of the Stalinist movement in this country, repudiated Browder's collaborationist program and replaced his CPA with a reconstituted CPUSA, which then created a network of schools to teach Marxism-Leninism.

The nature of that doctrine was crucial, because the Smith Act made illegal only instruction involving the forcible overthrow of governments in the United States. The prosecution hoped to prove, through the introduction of numerous books, pamphlets, and articles—most notably Marx and Engels's *The Communist Manifesto* (1848), Lenin's *State and Revolution* (1917), Stalin's *Fundamentals of Leninism* (1929), *The History of the Communist Party of the Soviet Union (Bolsheviks)* (1925), and *The Program of the Communist International* (1928)—that the education provided by the CPUSA was of the forbidden type. This dated literary evidence was the guts of McGohey's case, and the primary mission of his witnesses was to introduce the literature, interpret it, and explain how these aged books and pamphlets manifested themselves in the activities of the Party. The prosecution regarded oral testimony as merely corroborative of its printed evidence. As for proof that Communist theory was about to translate itself into revolutionary action, the U.S. attorney would not offer any— because he had none.[13]

In examining their first witness, McGohey and Frank Gordon concentrated on securing exposition and interpretation of Marxism-Leninism, and by the time they finished, the prosecution had for all practical purposes made its case. The individual whose testimony served the government so well was Louis Francis Budenz, an assistant professor of economics at Fordham University, and a former Party member, who had already established a national reputation and profitable career as an anti-Communist lecturer, writer, and government witness.

Although never one of the really top individuals in the American Stalinist movement, Budenz had been close enough to those who were to lend weight to his claims of expertise concerning its operations and secrets. A Catholic trained in the law, he had drifted into the labor movement as a young man and for a number of years during the 1920s and early 1930s had edited a radical socialist magazine. When his American Workers Party took up with the Trotskyists, Budenz broke with it and joined the CPUSA, where his first assignment was on the staff of the *Daily Worker*. Later he moved to Chicago, took over the *Midwest Daily Record*, and became a member of the Illinois State Committee. After his newspaper folded in 1940, Budenz returned to New York to become president of the dummy corporation ostensibly responsible for publication of the *Daily Worker*, and later managing editor of that paper. In 1945, he left the CPUSA, returned to the Catholic Church, and assumed a teaching post at Notre Dame. He had been a member of the National Committee from 1936 until 1945 and, although not on the National Board, had attended many of its meetings in his capacity as a journalist.[14]

During his first three days on the stand, this seemingly knowledgeable witness identified numerous books, pamphlets, and articles, from which McGohey and Gordon then read at length. Although some of these contained expressions of violent revolutionary sentiments, others, such as "To Comrade Stalin," which consisted mainly of lavish praise for the Soviet leader, while prejudicial to the defendants, had little or nothing to do with the charges. Despite his supposedly intimate involvement with the alleged conspiracy, Budenz often seemed to be just an appendage to the prosecution's case, whose only real function was to satisfy the legal requirements which had to be met in order to get its literary evidence before the jury.

Many of the documents introduced through him, over strenuous defense objections, had been published prior to the 1945-1948 period covered by the indictment, and a number even predated the passage of the Smith Act, but Medina turned a deaf ear to protests against their admission. He agreed to allow this aged material to become evidence because of what it purportedly demonstrated about the intent with which the person who had supplied it to Budenz, generally Jack Stachel, had acted during the period covered by the indictment. Although the judge admitted these documents for that purpose only and against a single defendant, as the defense pointed out, whatever the legal merits of his rulings they were psychologically dubious, because for jurors to compartmentalize evidence in this manner demanded a nearly impossible mental operation. As a practical matter, Medina allowed the prosecution to build a case against the existing Communist Party with evidence of considerable age and rather questionable relevance.[15]

Although the first few days of Budenz's testimony taught some excellent lessons about how a political trial can abuse the legal process, they were not particularly important in determining the fate of the Eleven. But 29 March was different. That afternoon, McGohey quoted the first sentence from the constitution of the CPUSA—"The Communist Party of the United States is the political party of the American working class, basing itself upon the principles of scientific socialism, Marxism-Leninism"—and then asked Budenz to explain it.[16] Before the witness could answer, the defense lawyers were on their feet objecting.

They had good reason to be agitated, for the Eleven's leadership of the CPUSA and the Party's commitment to the principles of Marxism-Leninism were acknowledged facts. The major issue in the case was whether the Communist creed included among its tenets the overthrow of the government by force and violence. Only if it did, could the defendants be guilty. The prosecution had asked Budenz to settle this crucial matter for the jury, and Medina, unable to see why the witness should not testify as to the common understanding of Communists concerning the meaning of the sentence, permitted him to answer.

This sentence as is historically meant throughout the Communist movement, is that the Communist Party bases itself upon so-called scientific socialism, the theory and practice of so-called scientific socialism as appears in the writings of Marx, Engels, Lenin and Stalin, therefore as interpreted by Lenin and Stalin, who have specifically interpreted scientific socialism to mean that socialism can only be attained by the violent shattering of the capitalist state, and the setting up of a dictatorship of the proletariat by force and violence in the place of that state. In the United States this would mean that the Communist Party of the United States is basically committed to the overthrow of the Government of the United States as set up by the Constitution of the United States.

Isserman moved to strike this answer, but Medina denied his motion.[17] In a few short minutes Budenz had devastated the defense. In a savagely critical book, published soon after the trial, George Marion charged that by "smuggling that [last] sentence into the record" Medina had helped to perpetrate an "ugly legal swindle." The judge's ruling, though not as clearly wrong as Marion maintained, was at least highly questionable, because it allowed Budenz to report on the mental attitudes of other people, something about which he could have had no direct knowledge. Assuming the role of expert witness, he also commented judgelike on the evidence and summed up the essence of the prosecution's case. His testimony was devastating, and Marion went very little beyond the truth when he concluded that by letting "this sentence into evidence, Judge Medina ended the trial for all serious purposes."[18]

Budenz followed a hard blow with a knockout punch. While explaining another passage from the Party constitution, he stated that the words "The Communist Party of the United States is the political party of the American working class, basing itself upon . . ." implied that those provisions which conflicted with Marxism-Leninism were null in their effect. "They are merely window dressing asserted for protective purposes, the Aesopian language of V. I. Lenin," Budenz told the jury. The term, he explained, came from Aesop's fables and referred to roundabout protective wording. The following day Medina read to the witness a section of the Party constitution which stated that any Communist who adhered to a group or faction guilty of conspiring or acting to subvert or overthrow the institutions of American democracy was liable to immediate expulsion. When the judge asked the witness what the passage meant to him, Budenz replied that, in view of the document's first sentence, this was merely Aesopian language, intended to protect the Party from American courts. By equating the creed of the CPUSA with the violent overthrow of the government, while defining anything that tended to contradict this conclusion as a lie, Budenz had, if the jury believed him, sealed the fate of the Eleven.[19]

Hit hard by his testimony, the Communist side attempted to draw attention away from it, and perhaps goad the court into prejudicial error, by accelerating its warfare against the judge. By continuing their provocative behavior, the defense attorneys succeeded in arousing the hypersensitive Medina, who complained bitterly about their smiling, sneering, and smirking.[20] "This is the doggondest trial I ever saw . . . ," the judge exclaimed.[21]

Antagonizing Medina cost the Communists dearly, for his hostility ruined what at times seemed likely to prove a highly successful crossexamination. When Gladstein asked Budenz if he himself had ever advocated violent revolution, the witness replied that it was not the line of the CPUSA to do this openly, but that he had done it through the use of Aesopian language. "[I]n one article in April [1945] I recommended the Political Affairs for that month, which contains an article by John Williamson. . . ." The piece to which he referred his readers, Budenz explained, "begins to stress again the reading of the History of the Communist Party of the Soviet Union." As proof that the CPUSA advocated the forcible overthrow of American political institutions, this revelation was absurd, but when Gladstein closed in on the vulnerable witness, McGohey interposed an objection, and Medina saved Budenz by sustaining the prosecutor. Later, when the Communist side, through questioning Budenz about a series of articles he had written for the *Daily Worker*, tried to establish that in the past he had not equated scientific socialism and Marxism-Leninism with the violent overthrow of the U.S. government, the judge, thinking he detected another attempt to score propaganda points, again thwarted the defense.[22]

After Budenz, a series of witnesses, neither so well known as the former *Daily Worker* official nor so important to the prosecution's case, paraded to the stand. The first of these was Herbert A. Philbrick, an advertising executive from Melrose, Massachusetts, destined to become famous as the hero of the television series, "I Led 3 Lives," but, at the time he testified, an obscure middle-level official of the Communist Party, familiar only to the men at the defense table. His appearance on the stand horrified them. When the initial shock wore off, Isserman leaped

to his feet pleading unfair surprise. As Philbrick revealed that he had
been in regular contact with the FBI since 1940, Winter's jaw tightened,
Davis glared angrily, and Potash, Green, and Hall grew tense with rage.[23]

The witness had been preparing for this dramatic moment since short-
ly after the indictment of the Communist leaders when Don Richards,
his FBI contact, had revealed to him that the prosecution might need
his testimony. Philbrick had reservations about taking the stand, for although the idea of escaping from his nerve-wracking triple life as busi-
nessman, Communist, and spy appealed to him, he felt that, having bored
deep into the Party, he could serve his country better as an informant
than as a witness. Traveling under the alias Hubert Brooks, he made three
secret trips to New York, conferring there, in the back seat of a moving
car, with Justice Department attorney Irving Shapiro. Then for a time
Philbrick heard nothing. Finally, Richards informed him that he would
probably be subpoenaed. There followed further conferences with government lawyers in both New York and Washington, through all of which
the FBI kept his identity a secret, so that, if for any reason the lawyers
did not use him, the informant could slip quietly back into his former
role. Finally, legal minds decided that Philbrick should take the stand,
and on 5 April, after arranging to send his wife out of town, he headed
for New York. There he called a blind telephone number and was directed to a rendezvous with an FBI man. After an all-day conference with
McGohey and a night in a small hotel under Bureau protection, Philbrick
slipped into the Foley Square federal building via a cellar ramp and remained in an out-of-the-way room until the moment arrived for his dramatic entrance into court. The shock of his sudden appearance on the
stand temporarily paralyzed the Party. But soon the CPUSA launched a
determined campaign of vilification designed to discredit Philbrick.[24]

Despite the shock and outrage which his testimony produced, it was
not particularly devastating. The prosecution sought through Philbrick
to establish the conspiratorial nature of American communism, by showing that the Party operated in secret and spread its doctrines by subter-
fuge, but his only real contributions in this area were a description of
some security measures which the District I Professional Group had initiated when Congress seemed about to outlaw the CPUSA and a report
that a few officers had once talked about going underground. The informant was considerably more successful in satisfying the government's
desire for damning evidence about Communist teaching and advocacy,
for he had served on the Massachusetts state educational commission
and also attended a number of Party classes and training sessions. He
was able to identify literature and study outlines employed by Commu-

nist instructors during the period covered by the indictment and to testify that teachers had told him the government could not be taken over peacefully, and consequently that American workers would have to arm themselves for the struggle against the capitalists.

Most of what Philbrick had to say about the Party's educational program supported the prosecution's case, but one facet of his testimony undercut Budenz's Aesopian-language theory. After eliciting from the witness testimony that *The Communist Manifesto* was current Party doctrine, Gordon read from it a passage intended to establish that Communists supported every revolution against the existing political and social order. But the quoted segment also stated in very explicit terms that Marxists *decline to conceal their views*, thus directly contradicting Budenz. Rather than exploiting such inconsistencies in the prosecution's case, the defense lawyers continued to press their running fight with Medina, relying heavily on what the *New York Times* recognized as "delaying tactics" and efforts to distract attention from the charges. Again, they managed only to overshadow and obscure their own cross-examination.[25]

The government's next three witnesses were far less impressive than Philbrick. Frank S. Meyer, a British-born writer and lecturer, was a former Communist. He had a great deal to say about the organization, operation, and supervision of the Party's educational system, but this information was considerably less than current, his affiliation with the CPUSA having ended in December 1945. Eugene H. Stewart and Fred G. Cook were FBI agents who in 1941 had attended a public meeting at which Carl Winter was one of the speakers. The defendant had said nothing that even approached the bounds of illegality, but Tim Buck, head of the Canadian Stalinist movement, had declared that the time was coming when Communists would smash their way to victory. At best the prosecution did not have much here, and on cross-examination Crockett drew from Cook the damaging admission that FBI reporting of such functions was unbalanced and biased.[26]

While the testimony of Meyer, Stewart, and Cook was unimpressive, they were at least more respectable and responsible witnesses than William Odell Nowell and Charles Nicodemus. Nowell, an employee of the Immigration and Naturalization Service, who had once worked as a labor spy for the Ford Motor Company, filled the record with inflammatory testimony about the Communist program for the creation of a black republic in the South and also discussed training in revolutionary theory and the conduct of civil warfare which he had received at Moscow's Lenin Institute—in 1929. Nicodemus, a textile union official from Dawson, Maryland, had as recently as January 1948, been arrested in a Pittsburgh motel room, where police found him and a married lover armed with guns probably intended for protection against her husband. Nicodemus apparently avoided punishment for carrying a concealed weapon only because the FBI, with which he had been cooperating in an investigation of Communist activities at the Cumberland, Maryland, plant where he worked, intervened on his behalf with a police magistrate. This witness offered the most inflammatory and implausible testimony of the entire trial when he stated that, during a 1945 meeting, National Committee member Al Lannon had said that, in order for the revolution to succeed in the United States, the Red Army might have to march from Siberia through Alaska and Canada to Detroit. The defendants roared with laughter when they heard this tale of a logistically unfeasible military operation, but Medina took it quite seriously.[27]

As he demonstrated during the testimony of government witness Garfield Heron, the judge had by now, for all practical purposes, aligned himself with the prosecution. Heron, an active FBI informant, who had been operating inside the Communist movement since 1944, spent most of his time on the stand identifying and explaining various pieces of Marxist-Leninist literature, which he represented as guides to revolutionary action. The selections from these read by the prosecution supported that characterization, but the defense contended that, rather than passages ripped out of context, the complete books should go into the record, along with other works by the quoted authors. To comply with this request would have greatly prolonged the trial, but to refuse it meant denying principles of fairness and balance. Experience dictated Medina's reaction. "I am not going to have this trial carried on for the purpose of pushing out propaganda," he informed Sacher. Although the judge's analysis of the Communists' motives was almost certainly correct, his insistence that the defense might offer only those parts of books and articles which directly refuted the government's accusations enabled the prosecution to overemphasize greatly the importance of violence in Marxist-Leninist theory.[28]

This overemphasis and the spy thriller drama provided by Angela Calomiris were both part of the Justice Department's propaganda attack on communism. Calomiris, a professional photographer and long-time FBI informant, had remained active in the CPUSA down to the moment she took the stand, even participating in a Washington rally protesting the trial and contributing $50 of the government's money to save the Eleven. Her appearance on the witness stand evoked expressions of surprise and distaste from the defendants, who shot derogatory gestures at her, as she calmly identified the nine she knew, smiling and shaking her head, as if pitying them. Despite the drama that surrounded her testimony, Calomiris did not add a great deal to the prosecution's case. The photographer-spy reported that during one Communist class the instructor had told her socialism could be achieved only by violent overthrow of the existing government, and she also managed to identify a piece of literature which seemed to deny that America could ever arrive at socialism through peaceful evolution. On the whole, though, her performance was notable less for what she said than for the drama which surrounded it and for an accompanying increase in the level of discord between the defense staff and its enemies.[29]

In characterizing the witnesses who followed Calomiris to the stand as a "dreary procession of petty . . . police informants," the *Daily Worker* was not far off the mark. Thomas Aaron Younglove, an FBI plant from St. Louis, who had spied on the Party from 1945 to 1947, added little to the picture already sketched by Philbrick, Heron, and Calomiris. Nor did William Cummings, an inveterate collector of reports and intra-Party correspondence, who, in part through establishing his feigned dedication to the Stalinist cause by recruiting three relatives into the CPUSA, had managed to work his way up the Party ladder to membership on the Ohio State Committee. Cummings yielded the stand to John Victor Blanc of Cleveland, a rather inactive Communist during the 1930s, who had become a Bureau informant when he reentered the movement in 1944, and who had little to say that was not either repetitious or irrelevant.[30]

Because on the whole the prosecution's case had been running downhill ever since Budenz left the stand in early April, both reporters and outside lawyers present at the trial felt certain that the government would finish with a real "atomic bomb," a superwitness steeped in Marxist theory, who could provide the jury with an incisive analysis of the defendants' line and activities. Cast in this role, Balmes Hidalgo, Jr., another low-level FBI informant who had held a number of minor Party offices, was a considerable disappointment. Although not a weak witness, he made a much less than atomic impact. Small wonder that when the prosecution rested on 19 May, courtroom observers experienced a letdown.[31]

In calling a halt to its case at 3:30 p.m. that day, the government took counsel for the Communist leaders completely by surprise, as they had not expected the prosecution to rest for at least ten days. The defense attorneys tried to secure an adjournment, but Medina, recognizing another effort to delay the proceedings, forced them to make and argue motions that very afternoon. While rejecting all requests for declaration of a mistrial, he did agree to consider both directing verdicts of acquittal—because of the alleged failure of the prosecution to establish the existence of a clear and present danger—and striking the testimony of FBI informants.[32]

The next day, arguing the first of these issues, Isserman contended that the Supreme Court had staked out an area within which, no matter how great and present the danger, the government had no choice but to tolerate speech. Besides, he said, prosecution for conspiracy to use words in the future was utterly absurd, since any danger such a combination might create was extremely remote. Sacher contended that evidence gathered by FBI informants was inadmissible, because this method of collecting information violated the First, Fourth, and Fifth Amendments and, further, because the use of private citizens as police spies was contrary to public policy. On Monday, 23 May, Medina rejected the arguments of both attorneys, denying all defense motions.[33]

Most Communists had entertained no hopes that he would do anything else, for they remained convinced that only mass pressure could save their leaders. The little band of CRC pickets kept up its vigil in Foley Square, and Stalinists continued to hope that thousands of Americans would soon join these few men and women in their protest. Branding the FBI informants who had testified at the trial as "labor spies," the CPUSA worked diligently to convince trade unionists that this prosecution of Communist leaders was only the prelude to a full-fledged attack on their own movement. Simon Gerson, director of public relations for the defense campaign, argued in a letter to *The Nation* that liberals dared not "sit by idly while books are placed on trial and a political party outlawed," and the *Daily Worker* and the CRC hammered away at the theme that this prosecution threatened the liberties of all Americans. The Party and its front groups invested a substantial amount of money in these efforts to mobilize the public, actually spending two to three times as much on propaganda as on legal services.[34]

But despite their large expenditures of cash and hard work, supporters of the Eleven could not build much of a mass movement, for the public, gripped by the emotions which the world situation and domestic politics had aroused, refused to identify with the defendants at Foley Square. In Pittsburgh an angry crowd of 5,000 persons set upon 250 men and women leaving a meeting called by the Western Pennsylvania Party to protest the trial. Only the intervention of about 200 policemen saved the Communists from serious bodily injury.[35]

Even though they had been unable to enlist the support of the masses, the Eleven were not in a hopeless situation. Numerous thoughtful observers considered the prosecution's evidence unimpressive. In early April, Robert Bendiner of *The Nation* had written: "Whatever the legal technicalities of the case, the public in general, I think, will expect the prosecution to show a more concrete conspiracy to advocate overthrow of the government than the agreement to circulate and expound, through the party apparatus, certain books which may be found in almost any library." McGohey and his assistants never managed to do this, and certainly they failed to bring forth any solid evidence of Communist revolutionary action done or even contemplated. Indeed to some people the most disturbing thing about the whole case was the fact that, under the terms of the Smith Act, the government had not had to prove the commission of overt acts of any kind. Many persons found distasteful the prosecution's heavy reliance on informers and were also distressed by the fact that very little of the evidence seemed to have anything directly to do with the defendants. "Clearly," wrote the liberal *New Republic*, "the government has failed to make out the overwhelming case that many people anticipated before the trial began."[36]

III

Although the evidence against the Eleven was unimpressive, the defendants and their lawyers refused to concentrate on rebutting it. Instead, true to the traditions of labor defense, they launched a prosecution of their own. On 23 May their first witness, John Gates, stepped to the stand, determined to seize the offensive. Gates described his life and how he had become a Communist, identifying in the process a summary of *Das Kapital* which he had prepared long ago and still used. As Sacher argued for the admission of this document, it became apparent that the witness intended to present a comprehensive exposition of the philosophy and program of the CPUSA. The lawyer sought to justify this enterprise by contending that Marxism-Leninism was an integrated body of thought and that *Das Kapital* was its economic and political foundation. When he urged the court to admit Gates's summary because it would help the jury see the Communist creed in its entirety, Medina replied that he would permit the defense to show to a limited extent what the Eleven had done and what they said they had taught, but he insisted that the approach which counsel advocated would only confuse the issues. In the end, the summary was not admitted.[37]

Responding to the outcome of this exchange, the *People's World* attempted to demonstrate the weakness of Medina's evidentiary theories by pointing out the absurd consequences that would result if they were applied in an ordinary criminal case:

A man is accused of a crime. But as a matter of fact he was nowhere near the scene of the crime at the time it was committed. He was fishing. However, he is not allowed to introduce any evidence to prove that he was fishing as that is irrelevant because obviously fishing has no connection with the nature of the alleged crime. . . .

Judge Medina has ruled the defendants must be confined to introducing evidence that they did not conspire to advocate or teach forcible overthrow of the government, without at the same time being permitted to demonstrate what they actually did teach and advocate.

That's not a trial. That's a legal straight jacket.[38]

Despite this initial setback, Gates did not abandon his efforts to use the witness stand as a political platform. Now, however, he camouflaged them by blending the propaganda into accounts of his own activities and by working it into his direct rebuttals of prosecution allegations. Also, borrowing an effective trick from the prosecution, Gates and the defense attorneys quoted extensively from Party publications. On 1 June, the *Daily Worker* editor turned to the prosecution's charge that the CPUSA taught and advocated the overthrow of the U.S. government by force and violence, maintaining that during the period covered by the indictment he had not considered the establishment of socialism an immediate question for the American people. Since 1935, Gates said, Communists had seen the rise of fascism as the main issue confronting the world, and in according top priority to preventing the growth of that menace, they had put forward the idea of popular front governments, which would unite all opponents of fascism. These did not include as part of their program the replacement of capitalism with socialism. In 1949, according to Gates, fascism and the related danger of war were still the major issues confronting the American people, so that the immediate objective of the CPUSA remained the creation of a united front and the peaceful election of a government representing it. Only at some time in the future, when threatened with overthrow by reactionary interests, would such an anti-fascist peace administration attempt to abolish capitalism and move toward socialism. Having studied the lessons of history, Gates testified, members of the CPUSA naturally assumed that Wall Street and big business would violently resist this step. But while fighting was likely to accompany the institution of socialism, Communists did not advocate force and never had. Gates vigorously denied that he and the

other defendants were participants in any kind of conspiracy to overthrow the U.S. government by force.[39]

During this testimony, the defense and the judge battled constantly
over the nature and permissible breadth of the Communist case, with
Benjamin Davis protesting so vociferously on 26 May against the court's
refusal to admit a document that Medina threatened to jail him for contempt.[40] Five days later Crockett, angered by the judge's unwillingness
to allow the admission of a declaration adopted at a Communist veterans'
encampment, complained that Medina was destroying the Eleven's defense, which was "to show the whole body of Marxist-Leninist doctrine
and from that let the jury conclude whether . . . there is any teaching or
advocacy of the overthrow of the Government by force and violence."
Such an approach, the judge replied, would prolong the trial for years.
All he wanted to hear was the defendants' version of what was taught
and advocated at those schools. "I submit what you are in effect telling
me is that it is all right for the Government to prepare the framework
within which the defense must be brought and that the defense must accept that framework or it can't put in any case," Crockett retorted, sum-
marizing in one sentence the inherent bias of Medina's evidentiary theories.[41]

The wrangling that accompanied Gates's direct testimony was only the
prelude to a really serious conflict sparked by the cross-examination tactics McGohey used when he began to question the witness on 2 June.
The prosecutor, seemingly far less interested in discrediting Gates's
statements than in asking him about other Communists, wanted to know
what post Dennis had held in January 1946. When Gates responded that
he would testify about himself but would not become a "stool pigeon"
by discussing other members of the Party, Medina insisted that the witness answer the question, despite the fact that Dennis expressed his willingness to stipulate those positions he had held at the time in question—
and the fact that this information was a matter of public record anyway.[42]

Crockett protested, pointing out that, "[T]he difficulty with which
the court is now confronted stems from the sheer impossibility of trying to fit a political trial into the framework of common law procedure."
Medina maintained, the defense attorney noted, that in an ordinary case,
it was perfectly normal for a witness to be asked who a certain individual
was. But this was no ordinary case. To reveal what position Dennis held
would also be to identify him as a Communist, and, although being publicly linked to the CPUSA could do no harm to the general secretary of
the organization, it might have disastrous consequences for other persons
whom the government could later connect with the Party through the
use of similar questions.[43]

Crockett's argument did not impress Medina, for in the judge's eyes
the only issue here was judicial power and prerogative. If he sustained
the objection raised by counsel, he said, the defendants and their witnesses would be free to testify about what they wished and to refuse to
discuss anything else. That the court could not allow.

After caucusing with their attorneys, the defendants announced they
were prepared to stipulate, for purposes of the present proceeding, all
offices which any of them had held during the period covered by the indictment. McGohey refused to accept this compromise, and Medina supported him. The jurist agreed to accept a memorandum from Sacher on the
the issue, but insisted that in the meantime Gates must answer what was,
in his opinion, clearly a relevant and material question. Left with little
choice but to talk, the witness enumerated all the Party offices which
Dennis had held in January 1946 and even identified the other members
of the secretariat.

McGohey wanted more. When the prosecutor asked Gates to identify
those who had served with him on the Party's National Veterans Committee, Sacher and Gladstein immediately objected. After some discussion,
the two sides and the judge all agreed it might be best to recess until the
defense had a chance to file its memorandum, and Medina could make a
definitive ruling on the propriety of this line of questioning.[44]

The following morning, a crowd, composed mainly of persons supporting the defendants, began to gather in Foley Square some two and one-
half hours before the day's proceedings were scheduled to commence.
While a hostile throng milled about outside, Medina, who had spent the
previous evening studying the problem, secreted himself in his chambers,
where he waded through the lengthy memorandum which the defense
had prepared and heard arguments from counsel. By 10:30 he had reached
a decision. Waiting to hear it was an unfriendly audience, comprised
mainly of people from the crowd outside. When McGohey again inquired
about the members of the National Veterans Committee, Medina ordered
Gates to answer.

The witness supplied his own name and those of Thompson and Winston. After some sparring over constitutional rights, the prosecutor demanded to know the identities of the men responsible for helping Gates
prepare a pamphlet entitled "Who Ruptured Our Duck?" The witness
refused to supply them, claiming that these individuals worked in private industry and would lose their jobs if he named them. Medina directed him to respond, but Gates, invoking the First and Fifth Amendments,
again refused. The judge excused the jury and advised the defendant that
he did not have the rights he was asserting. Dennis then delivered a flam-

ing oration, but the court, unmoved, held Gates in contempt and remanded him to jail for thirty days or until he chose to answer.[45]

The room immediately exploded.[46] An angry roar went up from the
crowd, and almost everyone present leaped to his feet. Henry Winston,
perhaps advancing a few steps toward the bench, shouted something about
lynching and loudly condemned the government for initiating such a mon-
strous case. The judge promptly remanded him for the remainder of the
trial. By this time deputy marshals and bailiffs were beginning to converge
on Medina's courtroom from all over the building. Gus Hall screamed at
the bench that he had seen more law and constitutional rights in a kan-
garoo court. "Mr. Hall," the judge replied, "you are hereby remanded
for the balance of the trial."[47]

The shouting onlookers fell silent and resumed their seats, as Gladstein took issue with the bench, then gave way to Dennis, who attacked
the judge for outrageous, contemptible, and unconstitutional conduct.
Medina warned the General Secretary that although his status as one of
the attorneys would protect him from a contempt sentence while the
trial lasted, he might anticipate eventual punishment for such behavior.
Apparently realizing the futility of argument, and also aware that his
comrades faced jail if they joined him in his protest, Dennis finally turned to the other defendants, urging them to be silent, and the judge recalled the jury.

Medina subsequently experienced some doubts about the wisdom of
his actions, but other jurists endorsed them. Later in the day Samuel H.
Kaufman refused to restore the three jailed defendants to bail, and on
Monday, after giving Medina a bad scare by asking him to state the grounds
for his action, Judge Vincent Lubell also upheld his handling of the incident. Augustus Hand of the Circuit Court of Appeals rejected an application on behalf of Gates, and after Medina turned down defense motions
to set aside the orders remanding Hall and Winston, the Court of Appeals
also endorsed his handling of their cases. In addition, it rejected an appeal of Gates's sentence, denying that the privilege against self-incrimination justified his refusal to answer.[48]

The jailing of the three defendants produced an immediate outcry
from the Communists and their allies. The next day five hundred pickets
marched in protest before the House of Detention. Henry Wallace, Vito
Marcantonio, and O. John Rogge all condemned Medina's action, as did
a number of other persons from around the country, most of them affiliated with the CRC, the Progressive Party, or leftist labor unions.[49]

Medina had presented the CPUSA with something it had sought for
months: a dramatic issue that could be used to rally the public behind

the Foley Square defendants and indirectly to build support for the crusade to halt the trial. The Party immediately launched a well-organized campaign to exploit the incident. The National Committee issued a statement urging trade unions, churches, the legal profession, blacks, and all democratic individuals to join in demanding the immediate release of Gates, Winston, and Hall. On 6 June, 500 pickets staged a noisy four-hour demonstration in Foley Square, and the next few days saw additional protests in both New York and Philadelphia. A brief lull followed this initial burst of activity, but when Medina sent Gil Green to jail in mid-June, the rallies and demonstrations resumed. Highlighting this phase of the mass campaign was a 28 June assembly in Madison Square Garden, sponsored by the Civil Rights Congress, which dispatched a wire to Medina calling for release of the four jailed defendants and also adopted and sent to Truman a resolution demanding that he bring about the immediate dismissal of the indictments against the Twelve.[50]

In early August efforts to exploit the jailings reached their climax in "Free Henry Winston Week," a widespread and coordinated protest, carefully orchestrated by the National Organization Department of the CPUSA, which published detailed instructions for local Party units. As editorials in the Communist press made clear, and as information which the FBI received about Simon Gerson's efforts to enlist the support of Congressman Adam Clayton Powell confirmed, the free Henry Winston movement was a device to win black backing for the defendants. Its ultimate objective, like that of the campaign as a whole, was "to move 'Main Street' to register the demand for the immediate release of Winston, Hall, and Green, and for the dismissal of the indictments against all the defendants."[51]

Despite the expenditure of much time and effort, the men Medina sent to jail stayed there, and, worse yet, the crusade for their freedom failed to mobilize the public against the trial. The Committee to Defend the Twelve, unable to secure needed contributions, slid steadily deeper into debt, and the Party press, always prone to exaggerate the extent of support for Communist causes, rarely found any for this one outside the ranks of habitual fellow travelers.[52]

While his comrades labored unsuccessfully to mobilize the masses, Gates remained on the witness stand, where McGohey attempted a few more times to question him about the involvement of other persons with the CPUSA. Every time he did so, amnesia seemed to strike the witness. "I don't remember" and "I don't recall" became Gates's stock replies to such inquiries. The U.S. attorney had more success when he stuck to attacking the integrity of the Communist leader. He managed to develop the fact that on several occasions, in filling out government forms, Gates had provided false information and then sworn to the truth of it. McGohey even got the witness to admit that he considered it proper to lie under certain circumstances, thereby calling into question the truthfulness of all his testimony. Clearly, it was possible for the prose- . cution to cross-examine most effectively without fishing for names of Communists who had little or nothing to do with the case.[53]

The government demonstrated this again with Gilbert Green. The second defendant to take the stand devoted most of his lengthy direct testimony to rebutting the prosecution's charges, but the Communist side continued to do enough stalling and introduce enough propaganda to irritate Medina, who, exasperated with the tactics of labor defense and convinced that he was in danger of entirely losing control of the trial, cracked down hard on the comparatively innocent Illinois Communist.[54] On 20 June, when the court refused to admit an article from *The Communist*, Green burst out: "I thought we were going to be given a chance to prove our case. The article is germane to the very heart of the issue." Medina, who had given the Party leader several prior warnings, did not hesitate for a moment. "Mr. Green," he told the witness, "you are hereby remanded for the balance of the trial." Protests from Isserman and Dennis elicited the comment that perhaps some had misunderstood the court's past leniency; there would be no more of it. Refusing to reverse himself, the judge declared emphatically, "Now, I am running this court, not the defendants, or their lawyers." The Court of Appeals upheld Medina's action, expressing complete agreement with his assessment of what was going on at Foley Square. "This record," it observed, "fairly presents a series of events which if allowed to continue in the courtroom unchecked might well so disrupt the trial and so flout the authority of the court that its effectiveness as an instrument of the judicial process would be much impaired if not destroyed."[55]

Medina had vindicated his authority, but regaining control of the trial proved more difficult, since the Communists continued to insist that he must allow them to demonstrate what the CPUSA really taught and advocated. According to Isserman, Budenz had presented a false characterization of Marxism-Leninism, and now it was necessary for the defense to demonstrate the true nature of the Communist creed. Medina was willing to permit brief explanations of the Party's position on veterans' affairs, unemployment, and the like, but he regarded such matters as peripheral and wanted no unnecessary repetition of evidence concerning them. While making it clear that the court would not tolerate week after week of testimony about how the Party had met various grievances, Medina said he would admit resolutions relating to the setting up of Communist schools and teaching directives and curricula from such institutions, an opening that Green and his lawyer promptly exploited to get more propaganda into evidence. On 30 June, noting that direct examination of this witness was now in its eleventh day, the judge warned that he might soon feel compelled to curtail it, as he had the jury challenge, and threatened to put counsel under "a lot more pressure than I am doing now before I get through . . . . "[56]

Following Green's direct testimony came about a week of relatively quiet cross-examination and redirect. McGohey managed to show that this witness, like Gates, had supplied false information in filling out several official and unofficial forms, and to establish that during a 1936 debate Green had said if the Soviet Union were attacked, he and his comrades would defend it. But the prosecutor refrained almost entirely from fishing for names.[57]

Consequently, relative calm prevailed. It continued after Green yielded the stand to Benjamin Davis, who, like his predecessors, began by telling the jury why he had become a Communist. His account was a moving tale of a talented black youth impelled into radicalism by a racist white society which too often frustrated and abused him, and it evoked a sympathetic response, even from *Time* magazine. After finishing his story, though, Davis reverted to the role of Party propagandist, emphasizing, as befit his color, the Communist position on racial matters. Because he was a politician, Davis had a natural cover for such material: He attempted to introduce it as what he had said during campaigns for office or by referring to bills and resolutions which he had sponsored.[58]

His efforts were not entirely successful, because Medina, continuing to oppose repetition, sustained a number of objections to this type of evidence. On one occasion Dennis interrupted the judge to point out that the prosecution could put an end to testimony on this subject if it would stipulate "that our activities in defense of the rights of the Negro people . . . are typical of our activities and constitute the . . . application of the principles of Marxism-Leninism. . . ." Medina simply ignored the General Secretary, apparently considering his argument only rationalization.[59]

Soon after the defense handed Davis over to the prosecution, the witness found himself in trouble, as McGohey proved that he had supplied false information on applications for everything from a driver's license to admission to the bar. The prosecutor also established that in a speech this Harvard-trained lawyer had misrepresented statements about the Party which the Supreme Court had made in a 1943 citizenship case in-

volving Communist leader William Schneiderman. On 13 July, bloodied
by his encounter with McGohey, Davis retreated to the defense table.[60]

The next six weeks produced bitter controversy but only a little significant testimony. During that period, the only defendant to take the
stand was Robert Thompson, who testified for about a week in early August, primarily for the purpose of laying out for the Communist faithful
and the rest of the country the Party line on a number of questions raised
by the trial. The *Daily Worker* published a four-page supplement, consisting of excerpts from his testimony, and advertised it as a fighting statement, having special educational value. Although Thompson used the
witness stand as a political platform, he comported himself so well, consistently complying with Medina's admonitions to be brief, that his propagandizing produced little real trouble.[61]

In that respect his days on the stand were exceptional, for from mid-
July until late August defense efforts to accuse the accusers, coupled
with prosecution demands for names, kept the court in almost constant
turmoil. The Communists sometimes carried their propaganda campaign
far indeed, as when witness Anthony Krechmarek attempted to get into
evidence the contents of fifty-three radio broadcasts dealing with conditions in the coal fields of Ohio and West Virginia and with the Party's
work among miners. Medina eventually cracked down hard on this kind
of thing. After witness Yolanda Hall spent most of two days attempting
to make political speeches, the judge announced that he was going to
begin curtailing somewhat the expansiveness of defense testimony, and
when she persisted in propagandizing, he brusquely cut her off. Medina
responded to the proselytistic efforts of Edward Joseph Chaka and Ger-
aldine Lightfoot by taking over examination of these witnesses from the
defense attorneys. Despite counsel's bitter objections to his interference,
the judge gave no quarter. once even instructing a marshal to escort the
protesting Isserman to his seat.[62]

During a meeting of lawyers and defendants in the judge's chambers
on 4 August, the defense attorneys attempted to justify their conduct
by explaining that they had started from the major premise that Marxism-Leninism was an integral science and with the assumption that advancing proof about its character would be permissible. Once it became
apparent that Medina did not share their views, the lawyers said, they
had tried to determine what he would admit, but had found this most
difficult, because his position on the amount and type of proof that
was allowable kept changing. Medina, who acknowledged that there
had been some "evolution" in his rulings, insisted that consistency was
not the greatest of virtues and indicated that he had made adjustments,

both in order to prevent cumulative evidence and to terminate the case within bounds consistent with his health and that of the jurors.[63]

The trial had by now become a considerable strain on the judge, whose chronic bad back kept him in constant pain and whose strength had been sapped by the intense heat and humidity of the New York summer. Medina was pale and tired, and because he blamed the defense lawyers for the state of his health, he was utterly intolerant of their tactics. He was, Medina told them, physically and mentally incapable of going through any more wrangling. "It is more than any human being can stand," the judge complained. When, on 1 August, Gladstein, defying instructions from the bench, insisted upon arguing an objection, Medina summoned a marshal to put him in his place and announced to the protesting defense staff that its "field day" was over. His meaning was clear: Continued defiance would result in immediate imprisonment.[64]

Because of his hostility toward the defense, Medina refused to allow Communist historian Herbert Aptheker to give expert testimony on the meaning of Marxism-Leninism and would not let Abner Berry, editor of the Harlem edition of the weekly *Worker*, respond to questions identical to ones that Budenz had answered earlier. He also blocked an attempt by the defense to demonstrate that one of its witnesses, Dr. Herbert Phillips, had taught exactly the same material at a Communist school which he had previously presented to a philosophy class at the University of Washington. "I think there must be some connection now between the defendants and this course he gave before anything should go in as to the details . . . ," the judge declared. Had Medina applied this standard earlier, most of the government's evidence would never have gotten into the record.[65]

Far less strict with the prosecution than with the defense, the judge tolerated the government's repeated demands for the identification of Communists unconnected with the case, even though these were quite as disruptive as the tactics of the Communists and their lawyers. During Davis's testimony, McGohey and his staff had temporarily abandoned their quest for names, but they returned to it with the parade of middle-level Party functionaries who followed the councilman to the stand. Apparently lacking for these obscure figures anything like the mass of FBI-assembled documentary evidence with which they had attacked the credibility of defendant witnesses, government lawyers asked them questions they knew no Communist would answer, hoping that their failure to reply would cause the jury to discount their testimony. McGohey also sought to make the CPUSA look bad by trapping Krechmarek into admitting that his refusal to identify other Communists was ordered by the

Party, and also by establishing, through asking for the name of a full-time functionary, who obviously was in no danger of losing his job with the CPUSA, that something more than their professed concern about economic reprisal against the persons whom they might identify motivated Communists who declined to "stool." In an attempt to block the defense from presenting evidence, prosecutors urged the court not to let one witness testify about statements made at a Party school until he had identified those who ran it, and also asked it to bar another from talking about a meeting of the *Daily Worker* staff until he had named all those in attendance, despite the fact that Budenz had discussed the same gathering earlier. Medina, taking the position that the jury might hear what such witnesses had to say and then consider their refusal to answer in deciding how much weight to give their testimony, declined to give the government everything it wanted. But, generally, he condoned the prosecution's name hunting. Because government lawyers had no real need for the information they were requesting and did not press hard for answers, no contempt citations resulted from their employment of this tactic, but innumerable courtroom conflagrations did, and these, like labor defense, prolonged the trial and obscured the real issues in the case.[66]

On 23 August, an already troubled trial staggered into major crisis when the defense brought to Medina's attention that morning's edition of the *Daily Compass*. It reported that juror Russell Janney had discussed the trial at length with an entertainer named Carol Nathenson. The next day, just after court convened, Crockett filed a motion for mistrial, based not only on these conversations, but also on an anti-Communist speech which Janney allegedly had delivered several months earlier in Macon, Georgia. In support of this document, the defense submitted a sworn affidavit from Nathenson and copies of a newspaper published in the Southern city. According to the 25 February issue of the *Macon Telegraph*, Janney had declared, during his address, that communism was antithetical to the spirit of brotherhood and that those who stirred up religious and racial hatred were a fifth column for Stalin. While in Macon, the juror also had told reporter George Landry that "we're already fighting a war with Communism and it should be a fight to the death." The affidavit, which reported in great detail numerous conversations between Janney and Nathenson about the general subject of Stalinism and about the trial itself, contained many direct quotations, suggesting that the girl had deliberately encouraged the juror to talk about forbidden subjects and then written down everything he said. Nathenson had a record of past association with left-wing causes and might have undertaken such a job for the defense, but much of the mountain of information she reported was legally useless, and her story did appear first in the *Daily Compass* rather than the Party press. More probably, that paper, inspired by the fact that Janney had been rather loose-tongued about the trial in an interview with the *New Yorker*, had decided to see whether a good-looking woman who had frequent professional contact with the writer-producer could get him to say enough about a forbidden subject to provide it with a sensational story. Whatever her motive, Nathenson trapped the juror into talking at length about matters which he clearly had no business discussing.[67]

The CPUSA welcomed news of Janney's indiscretions, for it needed something to fuel the mass campaign. Despite the efforts of Communists and their allies to dramatize the plight of jailed defendants and arouse the public against the biased and sometimes dictatorial conduct of Judge Medina, it had been going badly. By mid-July the defense was $20,000 in debt. Even more disturbing was the fact that the primary target of its pressure tactics had thus far ignored them. Neither the great piles of mail that he received nor the delegations that descended on Foley Square impressed Medina. Only one tactic had any real effect on him. After Secretary of Defense James Forrestal committed suicide by leaping from a hospital window, courthouse pickets began carrying signs which read "Medina Will Fall Like Forrestal." These, and cards, letters, and anonymous phone calls urging the judge to jump, rattled him, for he suffered from a pronounced fear of heights. But Medina endured and the trial continued.[68]

Inspired by the Janney incident, the CPUSA unleashed a blitz intended to smash the prosecution once and for all. Arguing that "The defense demand for a mistrial . . . should be supported by the entire country," the *Daily Worker* urged its readers: "Wire your demand to Judge Medina." The *People's World* added a call for letters to Truman and J. Howard McGrath, Tom Clark's successor as attorney general. Even before the defense lawyers filed a motion, hundreds of wires urging a favorable ruling were on their way to Foley Square. Leaders of leftist trade unions and the American Labor Party joined Communists in demanding a mistrial, and pickets marched before the courthouse. [69]

In spite of all this pressure, the judge denied the defense motions, Janney remained on the jury, and the trial continued. Rather than persuading Medina, the Party had simply made him angry. Referring to the barrage of correspondence, the judge declared: "I am not affected by any influence or pressure from any source whatsoever." Picketing, like correspondence, he considered an improper method of influencing judicial decisions. "I will not be intimidated . . . ," Medina announced defiantly.[70]

His ruling angered supporters of the Eleven, but it was the Communists' efforts to coerce the court which aroused the ire of other Americans. Indicative of popular reaction to the Janney incident was a *New York Times* editorial demanding immediate passage of legislation to outlaw the picketing of federal courts and condemning organized correspondence campaigns intended to influence or intimidate judges. Communist efforts to strong-arm the legal system succeeded only in alienating those who might otherwise have found some merit in a quite legitimate grievance.[71]

Having failed to halt the proceedings, the defense returned to the business of the trial worse off than ever and with no choice but to resume the tedious parade of minor Party figures which the excitement of the Janney incident had temporarily interrupted. Predictably none of these had anything very important to say. Only on 26 August, when Max Weiss took the stand, did the proceedings again assume some significance. Active in the Stalinist movement for nearly twenty years, Weiss had served on the National Committee since 1940. Having been a member of the Party's educational committee and also its educational director, he was knowledgeable about matters which were central to the case, and for the most part Medina let him talk. At one point the judge gave Weiss an hour in which to deliver what amounted to a lecture on the Communist theories of the state and the dictatorship of the proletariat, and later he let him talk at length about Aesopian language, something the witness claimed never to have heard of until he read about Budenz's testimony in the newspapers. According to Weiss, the CPUSA intended none of its documents to express anything other than what the plain meaning of their words conveyed.[72]

After Weiss, the defense summoned Arthur Schusterman and William Boyde Coleman, a couple of small-time Communists from Cumberland, Maryland, who had belonged to the same union local and Party club as the prosecution's Charles Nicodemus. Between them they denied the truth of practically everything he had said. Next to take the stand was defendant Carl Winter, who, after two days of uneventful testimony, was interrupted by the long Labor Day weekend.[73]

By the time court reconvened, the trial was again threatened with disruption. On Sunday, 4 September, about 15,000 persons gathered on a golf course at Peekskill, New York, for an open-air concert by Paul Robeson, widely regarded as a rally in support of the Foley Square defendants. Aware that a week earlier a disturbance had prevented the radical singer from performing at the nearby Lakeland Acres picnic grove, authorities braced for trouble, and, under direct orders from Governor Thomas Dewey, eight hundred law enforcement officers saturated the area. Unfortunately, this massive show of force proved insufficient to prevent serious trouble, for five hundred veterans, determined to express their hostility toward communism, showed up at the concert, bringing with them enough brass bands to drown out the singing. Because a security force from the Furriers and National Maritime unions, armed with baseball bats and bottles, barred the way, they were unable to get at the audience, but after the festivities ended and the crowd started home, violence erupted. The veterans stoned buses and overturned private cars. One person suffered a brain concussion, another lost a finger, and a third was stabbed. At least 8 persons required hospitalization, and the total number injured approached 150. Among the casualties was Irving Potash, hit in the eyes with flying glass when the rampaging veterans stoned out the windshield of his car.[74]

When court reconvened on Tuesday, the injured defendant was still in the hospital undergoing examination. Crockett suggested a two-day adjournment, and after several hours of hesitation Medina agreed, despite some reluctance, inspired by suspicion of defense motives. The rioting veterans, the judge was sure, had played into the hands of the Communists, who wanted to create a situation which would force him to halt the trial. His analysis gave the CPUSA credit for more foresight than it possessed, but certainly once the disturbance had taken place, the Party seized upon it eagerly as an excuse for demanding that authorities free the Eleven. "[T]he first job of all those in our country shocked by the violence at Peekskill," the *People's World* insisted, "is to hit back by demanding an end to the trial of the Communist leaders in Foley Square."[75]

When court reconvened on 8 September, the defense filed a mistrial motion and demanded that the U.S. attorney immediately investigate and prosecute this violation of federally protected rights. It also urged the judge to inquire into all the circumstances surrounding the riot. After considering the matter, Medina announced that he found no merit in the application for a mistrial, but he declined to rule on the other defense requests, thus leaving open the possibility of their renewal before an outside judge. While characterizing what had happened at Peekskill as an outrage, he expressed determination to let nothing disrupt the trial. When the Communist side pressed its demands for an investigation, Medina exploded at what seemed to him "part and parcel of the endeavor to make this counterattack on society, instead of trying the issue against these defendants. . . ."[76]

The judge having washed his hands of Peekskill, Carl Winter returned to the witness stand. Following two days of uneventful direct testimony, McGohey initiated cross-examination and another round in the battle over names began. Attempting to represent Winter's motives for refusing to identify a particular individual as sinister, the U.S. Attorney introduced a 1940 *Daily Worker* article which urged Communists to protect their comrades from conviction and to give no testimony that might aid the state. McGohey also tried to force the witness into linking his father-in-law, Alfred Wagenknecht, to the CPUSA, but Winter refused, citing the First Amendment as justification. Medina, taking care to consult legal authorities, informed him that he did not have the right he claimed. If "this so-called stool pigeon rule" existed, the judge said, "our system of courts and justice" could not "function in the traditional manner. . . ." He disciplined Winter with a thirty-day contempt sentence.[77]

The turmoil generated by the prosecutor's quest for names and the Communists' efforts to employ the trial as a propaganda vehicle continued to overshadow the real issues in the case until 16-20 September, when Gates and others read to the jury a deposition from William Z. Foster, who offered what the Communists had thus far failed to present: a coherent and reasonably concise defense of the Party. Its impact was enhanced by the fact that the reading of the deposition precluded the noisy interaction between defense lawyers and trial judge which in the past had distracted attention from more important matters. According to Foster, the CPUSA sought to achieve Communist objectives by educating the masses in the need to build a political organization and by persuading them, when a majority of the country was ready, to adopt socialism. The quotations presented by the government, he contended, failed to reflect properly the teaching and advocacy of the CPUSA, for they had been torn out of context and related to remote times and to circumstances quite different from those existing in the America of 1949. Worst of all, these quotations failed to take into account the fundamental changes in strategy and tactics which the CPUSA had developed after the Seventh World Congress of the Comintern in 1935. Since then, the Party had proceeded on the theory that the rise of fascism made possible the election of peoples' governments in the capitalist democracies, which would have the capacity to move in the direction of socialism and which would eventually use their legal powers to establish it. Books written prior to 1935 (and this included many of the Marxist-Leninist "classics" stressed by the prosecution) were now tactically obsolete. Even though Communists had once expected the ruling classes to protect their position violently, they themselves had never advocated force. Although the government's cross-interrogatories cast some doubt on Foster's credibility, nothing brought out by the prosecution directly contradicted his testimony.[78]

After presenting this effective deposition, the defense returned to the kind of grandstanding which had characterized most of its efforts since late May, calling as a witness Paul Robeson. It quickly became apparent that the singer had no knowledge of any facts relevant to the case and that his appearance was just a publicity stunt. Medina sustained objections to practically every question Crockett asked him and eventually forced the lawyer to withdraw his famous witness. The Communist side next offered the director of the New York Public Library, who testified briefly that anyone could obtain from the shelves of his institution the books which the government had characterized as tools of subversion.[79]

The defense, which for months had geared its courtroom tactics to the needs of a mass campaign, decided to make black Organizational Secretary Henry Winston, martyred hero of the summer's biggest propaganda spectacular, its last witness. He no doubt hoped to finish his Party's case on a high note, but his four days on the stand produced little more than a tiresome rerun of the worst features of almost four months of defense testimony. Winston devoted some attention to rebutting prosecution evidence and some to denying the allegations set forth in the indictment, but clearly his overriding purpose was to fight for the Communist Party in the labor defense tradition. After lulling Medina into dropping his guard, he began responding to questions with long polemic speeches. Cross-examination also provided a last display of abuses already seen in gross excess. Although Frank Gordon had considerable information with which to demonstrate that in the past Winston had shown a rather casual regard for the truth, he displayed the same fascination with names which had afflicted government lawyers since early June.[80]

All in all, Winston's testimony, which he concluded on 23 September, was a bad end to a bad four months. Although California Communist William Schneiderman praised the "magnificent defense conducted by our Party leadership at the trial," the CPUSA had little cause for celebration. Accusing the accusers had not helped the Eleven's chances of acquittal, and it had further alienated a public already hostile to communism when the trial began. Even defendant John Gates would later admit that the Party's strategy had been a mistake. By continuously demanding that witnesses identify other Communists, the prosecution had managed to serve its immediate interests, but only at the cost of disrupting the proceedings and lending the prestige of the Justice Department to a tactic with which anti-Communist extremists would terrorize America for a decade. The government's performance, too, had been far from magnificent.[81]

IV

In October 1949, with the courtroom confrontation finally drawing to a conclusion, the leaders of the CPUSA called upon their supporters for one last effort, and the faithful responded by circulating more petitions and staging additional demonstrations. On 10 October, a delegation, headed by Paul Robeson and O. John Rogge, attempted to see the Attorney General, but, despite the fact that Congressman Marcantonio had requested an appointment for the group, McGrath refused to meet with it, and the protesters had to content themselves with handing a petition to Assistant Attorney General Alexander Campbell. The failure of the Robeson-Rogge delegation was a fitting conclusion to this last-ditch drive to halt the trial, for an air of futility had hung over the enterprise from its inception, and by 3 October the CRC had already launched a campaign to raise a million-dollar bail fund.[82]

The pessimism that inspired this action was fully warranted, for the judicial machinery ground on without interruption, and the Eleven suffered one courtroom setback after another. On 4 October, Medina turned down defense motions for dismissal of the indictment, for withdrawal of a juror and declaration of a mistrial, and for directed verdicts of acquittal. Counsel for the Communist leaders had contended that the evidence presented was insufficient to establish the guilt of their clients and that in any case it consisted of activities protected by the First Amendment, but Medina did not share their belief that submitting this case to the jury would violate the rights of the accused. He also rejected a defense request that Benjamin Davis be permitted to dismiss Sacher and act as his own attorney for the balance of the trial. Medina suspected the councilman of planning to deliver as his summation a political speech, covering subjects he had been forbidden to discuss as a witness, and the judge was not about to let Davis get away with that.[83]

When their lawyers began final arguments on 7 October, it was obvious that things were not going well for the Eleven. Isserman tried to reverse the tide by pointing out to the jurors that the CPUSA was the real defendant in this trial and that their verdict would decide its fate. He reminded them that the indictment charged not a single overt act and ridiculed the alleged conspiracy. McCabe supported his colleague with a brief summation, in which he attacked the prosecution's use of testimony supplied by paid informers, and also attempted to persuade the jury that a verdict of not guilty would constitute neither aid and comfort to Stalinism nor an expression of approval for Communists' proselytizing. After a weekend recess Gladstein entered the lists, emphasizing the Smith Act's failure to make communism expressly illegal or to forbid holding or imparting its creed. He reminded jurors that the New York Public Library displayed books which advocated Marxism-Leninism, and, noting that in 1943 the Supreme Court had said it was a tenable conclusion that Communist literature did not urge force and violence, argued that Party members had

relied on this decision. On the other hand, Budenz's interpretation of Marxism-Leninism was his own, Gladstein argued, and it was not reasonable to
attribute his views to other Communists, nor to hold each member of the
CPUSA responsible for every word of all the others. Sacher added little
of significance to what his colleagues had said, but Crockett offered a defense of the Party's secretiveness and also criticized the prosecution for
inconsistency, reminding jurors that the government was arguing simultaneously that the CPUSA followed the teachings of Marx, Engels, and
Stalin with literal exactness and that its leaders wrote just the opposite
of what they meant. Finally, Crockett tried to persuade the jury not to
hold the Party or the defendants responsible for the tensions between
the United States and Russia.[84]

After the lawyers came Eugene Dennis, who began his summation by
reiterating the charge, made repeatedly by the defense, that this was a
political and thought control trial. Given the nature of the evidence, he
argued, only a desire to repress a peaceful party and its ideas could explain this prosecution. He attacked the government for pressing guilt by
association, demanding names, and trying to substitute extraneous issues
like passport fraud for real evidence. The General Secretary also insisted
that, although he and his comrades considered Socialist revolution inevitable, the Party's principles did not include the duty or necessity of overthrowing the U.S. government by force and violence. In the postwar period,
he said, Communists had sought to achieve their objectives by advocating
the establishment of democratic antiwar and antitrust peoples' governments. The prosecution had dug into the archives of their movement to
dredge up outdated ideas. Dennis argued that he and his comrades should
be judged by the deeds which flowed from their Marxist-Leninist principles and attacked the prosecution for trying to exclude evidence of these.
He concluded with a plea for tolerance and a confident assertion that,
whatever the outcome of this trial, Communists would march on to inevitable victory.[85]

On 12 October Dennis finished, and the prosecution had its turn
before the jury. For the most part McGohey simply reviewed evidence
presented earlier. Although quoting extensively from Marxist-Leninist
literature, he denied that the government was prosecuting books, insisting that, because study outlines prepared by the defendants assigned the
works of Marx, Engels, Lenin, and Stalin, these authors' ideas were not
on trial. In dealing with the issue of free speech, McGohey sought to distinguish this form of liberty from unbridled license and argued that the
Constitution was no bar to punishment of those who abused it. He emphasized Party secrecy, obviously hoping that his listeners would accept

it as proof of conspiracy, and concluded by criticizing those witnesses who had refused to identify other Communists.[86]

The summations ended, Medina then proceeded to charge the jury, reading to its members a set of instructions 15,000 words in length.[87] Although the indictment seemed to allege two conspiracies, the judge said, it actually accused the defendants of participation in one conspiracy having two objects: (1) the organization of the Communist Party as a group or assembly of persons to teach or advocate the overthrow and destruction of the U.S. government by force and violence and (2) the actual teaching and advocacy. He endeavored to explain to the jurors the complexities of conspiracy law and also offered them guidance in a number of areas where controversy had arisen during the trial. The defendants, he said, were responsible for the declarations of all other Communists who had acted on behalf of the conspiracy to further the common purpose of those participating in it. He instructed the jurors to consider evidence from the period prior to that covered by the indictment only for the purpose of determining the intent with which those of the Eleven to whom it specifically applied had acted later. According to the judge, it was not the jury's place to decide the philosophical validity of any theories or the "miscellaneous matters" injected into the case by the defense. In evaluating the credibility of witnesses, he said, jurors might consider their refusal to answer certain questions. Medina also emphasized the importance of not allowing passion, prejudice, or public opinion to influence the forthcoming deliberations.

Turning to the crucial freedom of speech issue, he charged that the defendants had the right to advocate peaceful change of the laws and the Constitution, to criticize the U.S. government and its officers and policies, and to say that Russian democracy was superior to the American variety. If, said Medina, "the defendants did no more than pursue peaceful studies and discussions or teaching and advocacy in the realm of ideas, you must acquit them."[88] But, the judge added, no person had an absolute and unbridled right to say, write, or publish whatever he chose under all circumstances. To convict, Medina told the jurors, they must feel satisfied beyond a reasonable doubt that the defendants had entered into their conspiracy with the ultimate aim of bringing about the violent overthrow of the government. In determining Communist purposes, he said, they might consider the secrecy of Party operations. Next the judge told them:

In further construction and interpretation of the statute
I charge you that it is not the abstract doctrine of overthrow-

ing or destroying organized government by unlawful means
which is denounced by this law, but the teaching and advocacy of action for the accomplishment of that purpose, by language reasonably and ordinarily calculated to incite persons to
such action. Accordingly, you cannot find the defendants or
any of them guilty of the crime charged unless you are satisfied beyond a reasonable doubt that they conspired to organize a society, group and assembly of persons who teach and advocate the overthrow or destruction of the government of
the United States by force and violence and to advocate and
teach the duty and necessity of overthrowing or destroying
the Government of the United States by force and violence,
with the intent that such teaching and advocacy be of a rule
or principle of action and by language reasonably and ordinarily calculated to incite persons to such action, all with the
intent to cause the overthrow or destruction of the Government of the United States by force and violence as speedily
as circumstances would permit.[89]

The defense had asked Medina to require a finding that Communist
teaching and advocacy had created a clear and present danger of forcible
overthrow, but the judge refused to submit this matter to the jury. If the
defendants had violated the statute, he held, "as a matter of law" there
was "sufficient danger of a substantive evil that Congress [had] a right
to prevent to justify the application of the statute under the First Amendment of the Constitution."[90]

At 3:53 p.m., Medina finished and submitted the case to the jurors.
Under pressure from the defense, he recalled them a short time later to
instruct that, in determining individual intent and state of mind, they
might consider a defendant's loyal military service. After hearing this,
the jury began to deliberate in earnest. About 4:45 p.m. it requested and
received a number of exhibits. At 10:20, still unable to reach a decision,
the jurors asked permission to retire. After spending the night in the
Knickerbocker Hotel, they returned to work at 9:30 a.m. and by 11:00
had arrived at a verdict.[91]

Word that the jury had reached its decision ran like an electric shock
through the courtroom, where a handful of lawyers and reporters lounged,
drinking coffee, reading newspapers, and talking. A large band of deputy
marshals entered the room and ranged themselves along the walls. The
defendants, who had been pacing the corridor, trooped in behind their
attorneys, followed by McGohey and the prosecution staff. Then Judge

Medina swept into the room, his black robe flying. Last of all came the jury.[92]

"Madam Foreman, have you agreed upon a verdict?" the clerk asked the slight, smartly dressed Thelma Dial. "We have," she replied. "The jury finds each of the defendants guilty." Isserman had believed "there was no possibility . . . to obtain an acquittal," and the Eleven themselves had dared to hope for nothing better than a hung jury, but, as John Gates wrote years later, "Although I had expected this outcome, the words were a shock."[93]

Medina now dismissed the jury, and its members, refusing to discuss the verdict with anyone, sought to leave Foley Square as quickly as possible. Several were detained briefly by individuals who sidled up to mutter, "How could you do this to us?" Four of the women, concerned about their safety, asked for and received police escorts out of the area.[94]

After the jurors left, Medina's face hardened. "Now I turn to some unfinished business," he announced, glaring at the defense attorneys. The judge ordered Dennis and the lawyers to rise and, after reviewing the relevant contempt provisions of the *Federal Rules of Criminal Procedure*, read a prepared opinion in which he accused them of entering into an agreement to engage in contemptuous conduct for the purpose of halting the trial by creating delay and confusion, provoking an incident which would require declaration of a mistrial, or impairing his health. Although counsel's conduct constituted deliberate sabotage of the judicial system, Medina said, during the trial he could do nothing more than warn them, because going further would have produced the very results which they sought. Now, however, he was adjudging them guilty of contempt. Attributing twenty-three separate offenses to Sacher, eighteen to Gladstein, nine to Crockett, seven to Isserman, and six each to Dennis and McCabe, Medina imposed sentences ranging from thirty days for the Philadelphia lawyer to six months for Sacher, Gladstein, and Dennis. Only McCabe seemed at all contrite. The others rose defiantly, one after another, to condemn Medina.[95]

The judge had not mellowed either. "You continue in the same brazen manner," he snapped at Sacher. "[Y]ou continue with the same old mealy-mouth way of putting it." Equally harsh with the defendants, Medina refused to release them on bail and instead looked on as marshals handcuffed the leaders of American communism and led them off to jail to await sentencing.[96]

V

From their cells the convicted men watched while Governor Dewey hailed the verdict against them as a vindication of the American system

of justice, and members of Congress as diverse in their political orienta-
tions as South Dakota conservative Karl Mundt and New York liberal
Jacob Javits expressed gratification at the outcome of the trial. John
McCormack, the father of the Smith Act, congratulated the jury for
doing its job courageously, and there was also congressional praise for
Judge Medina. While the statement released by J. Howard McGrath was
cautious, his pleasure with the verdict was obvious. On 15 October came
another expression of administration delight: the appointment of Mc-
Gohey to a federal judgeship.[97]

Medina, now a national hero, received 50,000 congratulatory letters
within a week after the proceedings ended, and mail continued to pour
in from all over the world. Among those writing to praise his performance
were both McGrath and J. Edgar Hoover. Some letters came from groups
of up to 1,000 persons, and the writers represented a complete range of
occupations, educational levels, and religious and political affiliations. Despite the Communists' professed concern for racial minorities, black, Chinese,
and Mexican Americans joined in praising the judge who had presided
over their conviction. Through all the letters ran a common theme:
American justice had prevailed under difficult conditions, providing
even despised radicals with a fair trial in an atmosphere of calm but firm
impartiality. Although this was not an accurate assessment of what had
happened at Foley Square, thousands of people saw the trial that way
and wished to express their gratitude to the judge who had presided over
it.[98]

Medina could not travel to any part of the country where strangers
did not smile, wave, or bustle up to greet him. Callers suggested that he
run for governor, senator, and even president. This judge, wrote Irwin
Ross, was "the stuff of which folk heroes are made." Medina himself
probably explained his popularity about as well as anyone. "There seem
to be millions of people," he told a magazine writer, "filled with a love
of country they don't know quite how to express. They just happened
to pick me, who they saw as a nice fellow with a fair sense of humor, as
a handy and current symbol." This judge, an anti-Communist public
seemed to feel, "had done something that was peculiarly American!"[99]

The nation's press was largely responsible for the popular lionization
of Medina, for all over the country newspapers of every political persuasion
applauded the outcome of the trial, praising both the verdict and the punishment of the defense lawyers. Although pleased with the results of the
case, the press gave little evidence of understanding them. The *Los Angeles Times*, for example, erroneously reported that the verdict had stated
"officially . . . that the Communist Party is a criminal conspiracy against
the United States, run from Moscow." Concerning the nature of the defendants' cabal and whether the jury's action had outlawed the CPUSA,

complete confusion reigned among the nation's newspapers. The readiness of the press to praise the outcome of a trial it did not understand was in part the result of a reaction against the disruptive tactics of the defense. Perhaps even more important was the Russian-American Cold War, which had convinced most editors that the Truman administration was right in refusing, as the *Washington Post* put it, "to permit a tightly organized and conspiratorial agency, drawing its inspiration and a large measure of its strength from the Soviet Union, to operate freely within our 'marketplace of ideas.' "[100]

There were dissenting voices, of course, but these were few and muted. *New Republic* termed the trial a "disaster" and the Smith Act a bad law, but took care to praise the FBI and to give the government credit for proving the CPUSA was not a legitimate political party. Robert Bendiner of *The Nation* avoided specific criticism of the verdict, focusing instead on Medina's failure to leave the clear-and-present-danger issue to the jury. Among the nation's major newspapers, the *St. Louis Post-Dispatch* raised a lonely cry of protest. While admitting that there was no defense for much of what had occurred in Medina's courtroom, it nevertheless warned that the verdict reached there had altered the First Amendment, establishing a new and repressive limitation on freedom of speech. The Socialist Workers spoke out even more strongly than did these liberals, but such independent protest was exceptional. Most criticism of the convictions came from Stalinists and habitual fellow travelers. Even the American Civil Liberties Union refused to go beyond a perfunctory reiteration of its longstanding opposition to the Smith Act.[101]

Although only their close allies and the despised Trotskyists seemed concerned about their fate, the Communists talked bravely of fighting back. William Z. Foster and Elizabeth Gurley Flynn issued a statement declaring that the CPUSA would continue to function and expressing confidence that every member would stand by his post. They called upon their comrades to rally millions of Americans to protest against the verdict and Medina's punishment of defense counsel and to demand that Truman and McGrath release the Eleven immediately. Leafleting began at once, and on 17 October, while the *Daily Worker* announced to the world that a "great campaign" was already under way, Paul Robeson and Howard Fast revealed plans to take the case to the U.N. Commission on Human Rights.[102]

On 20 October, the day set for sentencing, a force of about eight hundred pickets mobilized in Foley Square to continue pressing the Party's labor defense. Seventy-five policemen were on hand, and security personnel locked every courthouse door but one. These precautions proved unnecessary, for the crowd was apathetic, and an air of gloom, as thick as the clouds which darkened the autumn sky above, hung over this last mass protest of the trial.[103]

Inside, Eugene Dennis, beaten but unbowed, vowed that the CPUSA would defend its legality and continue to function and grow, while a defiant Benjamin Davis told Medina, "You cannot kill our Party. . . ." Although the judge probably hated the CPUSA enough to wish it dead, he did not deal as harshly with the Eleven as he might have. The conspiracy section of the Smith Act authorized prison sentences of up to ten years, and McGohey wanted the maximum, because "today, in the atmosphere of the cold war, the potential danger of these men as the leaders of a subversive group is probably incalculable." Since 20 July 1948, however, Congress had revised the *United States Code*, providing a uniform five-year penalty for conspiracy to violate all federal laws. Technically, this change had no bearing on cases initiated earlier, but Medina was reluctant to hand out sentences longer than the legislature considered proper. He ordered all of the defendants, except Robert Thompson, to prison for five years and fined each of them $10,000. In deference to Thompson's military record, the judge imposed only a three-year sentence and the fine on him. The unappreciative war hero promptly announced he took "no pleasure that this Wall Street judicial flunky has seen fit to equate my possession of the D.S.C. with two years in prison."[104]

After Medina imposed sentence, O. John Rogge, now acting for the defense, asked him to release the Eleven on appeal bond. The judge refused, touching off a brief demonstration outside. But soon, in the streets as in the courtroom, the great Communist trial was over. It had been, as *Newsweek* reported, "the longest, dreariest and most controversial" proceeding in the history of American criminal law. The record which recorded its tortuous progress stretched to over 20,000 pages. In addition to a small mountain of testimony and exhibits, the trial had produced some astronomical bills, costing the Communists and their supporters an estimated $250,000 to $500,000 and the people of the United States about $1 million.[105]

Why had the country paid such a price? As *New Republic* noted at the time, the Cold War with Soviet Russia lay in the background, and this trial was "a focal point, for the moment, in a great worldwide struggle . . . ." The Communists were deemed important, not as members of a comparatively small group of American revolutionaries, but as agents of a potential enemy.[106] The political situation which the foreign policy of the Truman administration had helped to create left the government with little choice but to vilify communism, while the ideology of the Party and its members required them to attack American political and social institutions. In form a criminal trial, their confrontation in Medina's courtroom was in fact a Cold War battle, with the opposing forces fighting for propaganda victory. The tactics of both combatants contributed to the chaos which engulfed the proceedings, and though the government decisively defeated the Party, neither side earned much glory on the battlefield at Foley Square.

NOTES

1. *DW*, 8 March 1949; *NYT*, 8 March 1949, p. 1. The *Daily Worker* claimed the crowd numbered 2,500, but the "several hundred" estimate of the *Times* is probably more accurate. The most complete account of the trial is George Marion's extremely biased and polemical *The Communist Trial: An American Crossroads* (New York: Fairplay Publishers, 1950). Hawthorne Daniel devotes a chapter of his undocumented *Judge Medina: A Biography* (New York: Wilfred Funk, 1952) to the Foley Square trial. The first account based on Medina's personal papers will be that in a forthcoming biography of the judge by J. Woodford Howard.
2. *NYT*, 4 March 1949, p. 30, and 8 March 1949, p. 3; *PW*, 4 March 1949; *DW*, 8 March 1949; *Joint Appendix*, pp. 2561-636. For Medina's remarks see *Joint Appendix* (7 March 1949), pp. 2630, 2636.
3. *Joint Appendix* (8 March 1949), pp. 2662-713; *NYT*, 10 March 1949, p. 26.
4. *Joint Appendix* (7-17 March 1949), pp. 2637-3108.
5. Daniel, *Judge Medina*, p. 240; *Joint Appendix* (11-14, 16 March 1949), pp. 2772-938, 3100-02, 3073-74; *DW*, 21 March 1949; *PW*, 18 March 1949.
6. *Joint Appendix* (21 March 1949), pp. 3200-23 (quotes on pp. 3218, 3220, 3223).
7. Ibid. (17 March 1949), pp. 3113-27.
8. Ibid. (21 March 1949), pp. 3225-50; *NYT*, 22 March 1949, p. 13.
9. *Joint Appendix* (21-22 March 1949), pp. 3250-317 (quote on p. 3304).
10. *Washington Post*, 24 July 1948; "The Communist Party of the United States" (unpublished memorandum by Kneip), Box 1, John F. X. McGohey Papers, HTL.
11. "The Communist Party of the United States."
12. 15A C.J.S. *Conspiracy*, sec. 1(1) (1967); "The Conspiracy Dilemma: Prosecution of Group Crime or Protection of Individual Defendants," *Harvard Law Review* 62 (December 1948): 276. For Jackson's remark see Krulewitch v. United States, 336 U.S. 440 (1949), at 446.
13. Herbert L. Packer, *Ex-Communist Witness: Four Studies in Fact*

Finding (Stanford, Calif.: Stanford University Press, 1962), pp. 11-12; Louis Boudin, " 'Seditious Doctrines' and the 'Clear and Present Danger' Rule," *Virginia Law Review* 38 (February 1952): 178-79; McGohey to Clark, 27 September 1948, Box 1, McGohey Papers.

14. Packer, *Ex-Communist Witness*, pp. 121-24; *Joint Appendix* (25 March 1949), pp. 3340-80.

15. *Joint Appendix* (23-25 March 1949), pp. 3340-593.

16. Ibid. (29 March 1949), p. 3632.

17. Ibid., pp. 3632-38. Budenz's answer appears on pp. 3636-37.

18. Marion, *The Communist Trial*, pp. 87, 88.

19. *Joint Appendix* (29, 30 March 1949), pp. 3638-39, 3707.

20. Ibid. (29-31 March 1949), pp. 3714-862; "Communists: 'Doggondest Trial,' " *Time*, 11 April 1949, pp. 23-24.

21. *Joint Appendix* (31 March 1949), p. 3863.

22. Ibid. (1, 4 April 1949), pp. 3897-98, 3971-76, 3987-88 (quotes on p. 3897).

23. Ibid. (6 April 1949), pp. 4144-45; Herbert A. Philbrick, *I Led 3 Lives: Citizen, "Communist," Counterspy* (New York: McGraw-Hill Book Co., 1952), pp. 2-5; "Communists: Unfair Surprise," *Time*, 18 April 1949, p. 24.

24. Philbrick, *I Led 3 Lives*, pp. 262-83, 290; *DW*, 13 April 1949; *PW*, 11 April 1949.

25. Philbrick, *I Led 3 Lives*, pp. 286-87; *Joint Appendix* (6-9, 12 April 1949), pp. 4144-465; *NYT*, 7 April 1949, p. 22.

26. *Joint Appendix* (13, 18 April 1949), pp. 4505-615.

27. Ibid. (18-19, 22 April 1949), pp. 4615-806; Marion, *The Communist Trial*, pp. 9-19.

28. *Joint Appendix* (22, 25, 26 April 1949), pp. 4862-5019 (quote on p. 4968).

29. Ibid. (26-29 April and 2-3 May 1949), pp. 5022-440; *NYT*, 27 April 1949, pp. 1, 11; Angela Calomiris, *Red Masquerade: Undercover for the FBI* (Philadelphia and New York: J. B. Lippincott Co., 1950), pp. 104-5, 244-45. Calomiris says that once she began meeting with a government attorney to prepare her testimony, he advised her to ease out of assignments connected with the defense campaign and to refuse to have anything to do with lawyers representing Party leaders.

30. *DW*, 4 May 1949; *Joint Appendix* (3-6, 9-13, 16-17 May 1949), pp. 5441-6019.

31. Marion, *The Communist Trial*, p. 125; *Joint Appendix* (18-19 May 1949), pp. 6177-250.

32. *Joint Appendix* (19 May 1949), pp. 6257-78.

33. Ibid. (20, 23 May 1949), pp. 6281-351.

34. *DW*, 8 April 1949, 25 April 1949, and 10 May 1949; *PW*, 18 April 1949; "No Immunity for Liberals," *The Nation*, 23 April 1949, pp. 483-84; *NYT*, 24 May 1949, p. 15.

35. *NYT*, 3 April 1949, p. 79.

36. "From Lenin to Dennis," *The Nation*, 9 April 1949, p. 406; "The Court, the Communists and the Liberals," *New Republic*, 20 June 1949, p. 6; Elizabeth G. Flynn, "Freedom for the Communist Leaders!" *PA* 31 (July 1952): 3; Harry Overstreet and Bonaro Overstreet, *The FBI in Our Open Society* (New York: W. W. Norton, 1969), pp. 148-49; Marion, *The Communist Trial*, pp. 137-41.

37. *Joint Appendix* (23 May 1949), pp. 6352-85.

38. 25 May 1949.

39. *Joint Appendix* (23-27, 30-31 May and 1-2 June 1949), pp. 6390-801.

40. Ibid. (26 May 1949), pp. 6595-96.

41. Ibid. (31 May 1949), pp. 6655, 6658.

42. Ibid. (2 June 1949), pp. 6803-13.

43. Ibid., pp. 6814-15.

44. Ibid., pp. 6815-31.

45. Ibid. (3 June 1949), pp. 6833-44; Daniel, *Judge Medina*, pp. 253-54; *NYT*, 4 June 1949, p. 1.

46. The account in this paragraph is based on the following sources: *Joint Appendix* (3 June 1949), pp. 6845-53; Daniel, *Judge Medina*, pp. 256-57; *NYT*, 4 June 1949, p. 1. The only real controversy connected with this outburst involves the question of whether or not Hall and Winston advanced toward the bench. Medina later claimed they did (United States v. Sacher, 9 F.R.D. 394 [S.D.N.Y. 1949]), and Daniel, who probably obtained his information from the judge, supports him. The Communists alleged, however, that Medina did not mention this until five days after the incident and that the press did not report any such action by the defendants until *NYT* described it eight days after that (*DW*, 18 July 1949). Neither the *Times* report of 4 June nor the *Joint Appendix* contains any mention of either Winston or Hall advancing toward the bench.

47. *Joint Appendix* (3 June 1949), p. 6845.

48. Daniel, *Judge Medina*, pp. 258-60; Harold Medina, "A Look at America," in *The Anatomy of Freedom*, ed. C. Waller Barrett (New York: Henry Holt & Co., 1959), pp. 7-11; *NYT*, 4 June 1949, p. 1; United States v. Hall, United States v. Winston, United States ex rel. Hall v. Mulcahy, and United States ex rel. Winston v. Mulcahy, 176 F. 2d 163 (2d Cir. 1949); United States v. Gates, 176 F. 2d 78 (2d Cir. 1949).

49. *NYT*, 5 June 1949, p. 2; *DW*, 6 June 1949.

50. *DW*, 6 June 1949, 9 June 1949, 10 June 1949, 22 June 1949, 27 June 1949, and 29 June 1949; *NYT*, 7 June 1949, p. 12, 8 June 1949, p. 13, 23 June 1949, p. 11, and 29 June 1949, p. 4.

51. *DW*, 2 August 1949, 8 August 1949 (quote on p. 3), and 10 August 1949; *PW*, 11 August 1949; J. Edgar Hoover to Major General Harry Hawkins Vaughn, 11 August 1949, Box 167, President's Secretary's Files, Papers of H. S. Truman, HTL.

52. *PW*, 22 July 1949.

53. *Joint Appendix* (3, 6-9, 13-14 June 1949), pp. 6856-7168.

54. Green's direct testimony is reported in *Joint Appendix* (14-16, 20-24, 27-30 June 1949), pp. 7183-8306.

55. Ibid. (20 June 1949), pp. 7454-59 (quotes on pp. 7456, 7458, and 7459); United States v. Green, 176 F. 2d 169 (2d Cir. 1949), at 172.

56. *Joint Appendix* (21, 22, 30 June 1949), pp. 7545-48, 7563-67, 8008-09 (quoted on p. 8008).

57. Ibid. (30 June, 5-7 July 1949), pp. 8042-332.

58. Ibid. (7-8, 11-12 July 1949), pp. 8333-490; "Communists: Man & Automaton," *Time*, 18 July 1949, p. 17.

59. *Joint Appendix* (11 July 1949), p. 17.

60. Ibid. (12-13 July 1949), pp. 8491-525.

61. Ibid. (9-12 August 1949), pp. 9841-10067; *DW*, 16 August 1949.

62. *Joint Appendix* (26, 28-29 July and 1-3 August 1949), pp. 9112, 9259-343, 9432-86, 9521-35; *NYT*, 4 August 1949, p. 5.

63. *Joint Appendix* (4 August 1949), pp. 9679-91.

64. Daniel, *Judge Medina*, pp. 266-67; *Joint Appendix* (28 July and 1 August 1949), pp. 9220, 9402-06 (quote on p. 9220); *NYT*, 2 August 1949, p. 1.

65. *Joint Appendix* (21 July and 22-23 Aug. 1949), pp. 8978-9002, 10522-625 (quote on p. 8987).

66. Ibid. (14, 19-21, 28 July 1949 and 4, 18 August 1949), pp. 8690-91, 8699-700, 8809-14, 8826-30, 8879-84, 8888-96, 8967-72, 9226-30, 9600-20, 10384-99.

67. Ibid. (23-24 August 1949), pp. 10578-81, 10654-55 and (Exhibits), 13376-421; "Communists: Fizzled Firecracker," *Newsweek*, 5 September 1949, p. 22; *DW*, 26 August 1949. Medina had instructed jurors on 9 and 18 March not to discuss the case (*Joint Appendix*, pp. 2745, 3198).

68. Daniel, *Judge Medina*, pp. 262-64; *DW*, 19 July 1949, 5 August 1949, 9 August 1949, and 15 August 1949; *PW*, 22 July 1949.

69. *DW*, 25 August 1949; *PW*, 25 August 1949; Daniel, *Judge Medina*, pp. 271-72; *Joint Appendix* (25 August 1949), pp. 10656-57; *NYT*, 27 August 1949, pp. 1, 6.

70. *Joint Appendix* (25 August 1949), pp. 10656-57.

71. 28 August 1949, sec. 14, p. 8.

72. *Joint Appendix* (25-26, 29-30 August 1949), pp. 10666-898.

73. Ibid. (30-31 August 1949), pp. 10911-84.

74. Ibid. (6 September 1949), pp. 11087-88; *NYT*, 5 September 1949, pp. 1, 3; Daniel, *Judge Medina*, pp. 275-76; Wilson Record, *Race and Radicalism: The NAACP and the Communist Party in Conflict* (Ithaca, N.Y.: Cornell University Press, 1964), p. 175. For a lively but not entirely accurate account of the Peekskill riot see Roger M. Williams, "A Rough Sunday at Peekskill," *American Heritage* 27 (April 1976): 74-80.

75. Daniel, *Judge Medina*, pp. 274-76; *Joint Appendix* (6 Septem-

ber 1949), pp. 11087-90; *PW*, 6 September 1949.

76. *Joint Appendix* (8 September 1949), pp. 11091-105 (quote on pp. 11104-05).

77. Ibid. (8-9, 12 September 1949), pp. 11108-519 (quotes on p. 11307).

78. Ibid. (16, 19-20 September 1949), pp. 11528-679.

79. Ibid. (20 September 1949), pp. 11686-97.

80. Ibid. (20-23 September 1949), pp. 11701-921.

81. William Schneiderman, "The Defense of the Party," *PA* 28 (October 1949): 24; Gates, *The Story*, p. 127.

82. *DW*, 21 September 1949, 27 September 1949, 29 September 1949, 3 October 1949, 4 October 1949, and 12 October 1949; *PW*, 28 September 1949, 30 September 1949, 4 October 1949, and 6 October 1949; *NYT*, 16 September 1949, p. 12, and 11 October 1949, p. 16.

83. *Joint Appendix* (28-29 September, 4 October 1949), pp. 11925-2062; United States v. Foster, 9 F.R.D. 367 (S.D.N.Y. 1949).

84. *Joint Appendix* (6-7, 10-11 October 1949), pp. 12070-325.

85. Ibid. (11-12 October 1949), pp. 12326-74.

86. Ibid. (12-13 October 1949), pp. 12375-446.

87. The charge is printed verbatim in both *Joint Appendix* (13 October 1949), pp. 12543-94, and United States v. Foster, 9 F.R.D. 367 (S.D.N.Y. 1949). Medina later sent a copy of it to Senator Joe McCarthy (McCarthy to Medina, 31 October 1949, Harold Medina Papers, Princeton University).

88. United States v. Foster, at 390.

89. Ibid., at 391.

90. Ibid., at 392.

91. *NYT*, 15 October 1949, p. 3; *Joint Appendix* (13-14 October 1949), pp. 12496-514, 12556-655; "Communists: Guilty as Charged," *Newsweek*, 24 October 1949, p. 25.

92. "Guilty as Charged," p. 25; "The Presence of Evil," *Time*, 24 October 1949, p. 21; *Joint Appendix* (14 October 1949), p. 12518.

93. *Joint Appendix* (14 October 1949), p. 12519; *NYT*, 15 October 1949, p. 3; Gates, *The Story*, p. 131; Abraham Isserman to the Author, 9 December 1976.

94. *NYT*, 15 October 1949, p. 5; *Joint Appendix* (14 October 1949), p. 12522.

95. *Joint Appendix* (14 October 1949), pp. 12322-27 (quote on p. 12522); *NYT*, 15 October 1949, p. 3; "Guilty as Charged," p. 25.

96. *Joint Appendix* (14 October 1949), pp. 12527-41 (quote on p. 12533); *NYT*, 15 October 1949, p. 3; "Presence of Evil," p. 23.

97. *NYT*, 15 October 1949, pp. 3, 13, and 16 October 1949, p. 1.

98. Jack B. Alexander, "The Ordeal of Judge Medina," *Saturday Evening Post*, 12 August 1949, p. 18; Medina, *Judge Medina Speaks*, pp. 299-302; Jerold S. Auerbach, *Unequal Justice: Lawyers and Social Change in Modern America* (New York: Oxford University Press, 1976), p. 241, and p. 253, n. 33.

99. Alexander, "Ordeal of Judge Medina," p. 18; Irwin Ross, "Harold Medina—Judge Extraordinary," *Reader's Digest* 56 (February 1950): 85.

100. *Chicago Tribune*, 16 October 1949; *Los Angeles Times*, 15 October 1949; *NYT*, 15 October 1949, p. 14, and 16 October 1949, sec. 4, p. 7; *New Orleans Times-Picayune*, 15 October 1949; *Washington Post*, 16 October 1949; *San Francisco Chronicle*, 15 October 1949.

101. "After the Communist Trial," *New Republic* (24 October 1949): 5-6; Robert Bendiner, "Marx in Foley Square," *The Nation* (22 October 1949): 388-89; *St. Louis Post-Dispatch*, 16 October 1949; *NYT*, 16 October 1949, p. 20; "Presence of Evil," p. 24; *DW*, 17 October 1949; *PW*, 17 October 1949; *Militant*, 24 October 1949.

102. *DW*, 17 October 1949; *PW*, 17 October 1949; *NYT*, 18 October 1949, p. 21.

103. *NYT*, 22 October 1949, pp. 1-3.

104. *Joint Appendix* (21 October 1949), pp. 12684-737 (quotes on pp. 12687, 19715). Thompson is quoted in "Communists: The Penalty," *Time*, 31 October 1949, p. 15.

105. "Guilty as Charged," p. 26.

106. "After the Communist Trial," p. 6; Bruce Bliven, "Two Worlds at Foley Square," *New Republic*, 9 May 1949, p. 14.

5
The Communist Case
and the Constitution

> *The cold war was a fact, and it was the cold war rather than the fear of any domestic disorder which became the paramount fact in the Court's consideration of the Dennis case.*
> —Dalton Trumbo
> *The Devil in the Book*

The Cold War ritual that began in Harold Medina's courtroom did not end there. Although the leaders of the CPUSA retained greater faith in labor defense than in litigation, the Party carried its case on to the U.S. Court of Appeals for the Second Circuit and ultimately to the U.S. Supreme Court. Both tribunals rebuffed the Communists. In order to uphold the Foley Square convictions, they massively modified the classic clear-and-present-danger test for determining the limits of constitutionally protected speech, making First Amendment rights dangerously dependent on the identity of the person attempting to exercise them. In this appellate litigation not only the CPUSA but also free speech went down to defeat.

I

The Party's setback at Foley Square did not immediately inflict much injury on it, or even on the Eleven themselves. Because of a state law barring convicted felons from office, Benjamin Davis lost his city council seat, and, as a result of a successful suit by an aroused citizen, the authorities struck John Gates's name from the voting rolls. But Medina could not keep the Communist leaders in jail. On 3 November the government conceded that the defendants had raised a substantial question regarding the constitutionality of their convictions, and the court of appeals promptly set bail for them. Within an hour and a half representatives of the Civil Rights Congress had posted the required $260,000, and the Eleven were again at liberty.[1]

Despite this legal victory and the fact that labor defense had failed the Party at Foley Square, Communist leaders continued to dream of mobilizing the masses. Elizabeth Gurley Flynn announced that the Eleven would take their appeal to the highest court in the land, the American people, and Alexander Bittleman argued that the key to success was to make the public aware that preservation of everyone's rights depended upon a general willingness to fight for those of Communists. But ordinary members did not spring to the colors as they once had. By the time the National Committee met in plenary session on 23-25 March 1950, there were complaints about the "complacency" of the rank and file. Flynn, worried that her fellow Communists were awaiting the outcome of appellate litigation, admonished them that "to sit back and expect the legal appeal by itself to win a verdict" was "contrary to our many years experience in labor defense campaigns." Many members, though, preferred to watch passively from the sidelines while the case moved through the appellate courts. By mid-1950 anti-Communist passions had reached such a level that Harry Truman himself feared a wave of hysteria might sweep the country, and under such conditions a mass campaign seemed to them a hopeless enterprise.[2]

The leadership refused to tolerate the wait-and-see attitude of the rank and file. When Eugene Dennis entered prison on 2 May 1950 to begin serving a one-year sentence for contempt of Congress, he utilized the occasion to warn his fellow Communists against yielding to fatalism or to "legalistic illusions of reliance on the higher courts." He had a point. While some liberals, worried about the repressive nature of the Smith Act, wanted a judicial decision destroying it, even if that meant freeing the leaders of the CPUSA, most Americans, including judges, regarded communism as far more threatening than any sedition statute. If the Eleven were to benefit from appellate litigation, the courts would have to go at least as far as the liberals desired, and given the profoundly illiberal character of public opinion, that did not seem likely.[3]

II

Despite doubts about the utility of the undertaking, the Eleven commenced an appeal. Sacher, Isserman, Gladstein, Crockett, and McCabe, along with Dennis and Davis, both acting as their own attorneys, filed two briefs with the U.S. Second Circuit Court of Appeals. One of these dealt with the jury challenge. Besides reiterating most of the arguments made at Foley Square, it disputed Medina's finding that the challenge had been a deliberate effort to delay the trial.[4]

The other brief, a massive 403-page document, branded prosecution of the Eleven a political act. By punishing speech and belief rather than conduct, the Communists charged, the government had endangered the legal process and even American liberty itself. The Smith Act, they contended, was unconstitutional, both on its face and as construed and applied in this case, for it frustrated the central purpose of the First Amendment: the protection of political expression. Appellants emphatically denied that the Supreme Court's 1925 decision in *Gitlow* v. *New York*, which had held that the legislative branch might declare some kinds of speech inherently dangerous, justified this law. Among the statute's many defects, they contended, was the invalidity of its conspiracy provisions. The Communists accused Medina of revising both the Smith Act and the indictment in such a way as to invade the First Amendment rights of the defendants and of jettisoning the established clear-and-present-danger test in favor of a novel and an unwarranted theory of constitutional interpretation. The indictment, which relied on portions of the statute dealing with protected activities, actually charged no real offense at all, they claimed, so that it was fatally defective. The Communist leaders also contended that the trial court, by admitting into evidence the testimony of informers and by failing to caution jurors that they must scrutinize carefully the stories of such witnesses, had violated their rights under the First, Fourth, and Fifth Amendments. Their brief also argued that Medina's bias and misconduct had deprived them of a fair trial, as had the want of an impartial jury, that the judge had committed numerous reversible errors, particularly in his rulings on the admission of evidence and in his instructions to the jury, and that the trial court had improperly denied a motion for acquittal.[5]

Unlike the wide-ranging briefs of the Communists, the one submitted by the American Civil Liberties Union confined itself to a single issue: freedom of speech. ACLU attorneys argued that the Smith Act violated the First Amendment and that, even if constitutional on its face, the law was invalid as applied to these defendants, because there had been no jury finding of a clear and present danger. The National Lawyers Guild also asked leave to file a brief, but the court of appeals rejected this request.[6]

Beginning on 21 June a three-judge panel, sitting in New York, heard oral arguments in the case. All of its members were Republicans appointed by Calvin Coolidge. Preeminent among them was Chief Judge Learned Hand.

son of one distinguished jurist and grandson of another, Phi Beta Kappa, and honor graduate of the Harvard Law School. In 1909 William Howard Taft had appointed him to a federal district judgeship, and fifteen years later Coolidge had rewarded his distinguished service with elevation to the court of appeals. During his lengthy career Hand had acquired an awesome professional reputation, and although politics, geography, and finally advanced age had denied him the appointment to the Supreme Court which his abilities seemed to merit, Justice Felix Frankfurter, himself a member of the high tribunal, spoke reverently of this judge as "one at whose feet I sat almost from the time I came to the bar and at whose feet I still sit." Hand's colleague Thomas Swan had joined the court of appeals in 1927 after eleven years as dean of the Yale Law School. An expert on commercial litigation, he was notably conservative, as was the third member of the panel, Harrie Brigham Chase, a former state judge from Vermont.[7]

Both Chase and Swan were ill disposed toward the Eleven when the hearing began, because of the defendants' request two weeks earlier for permission to travel throughout the country making speeches. The Communist leaders claimed they needed to explain their views to the nation and raise money to finance the appeal, but Chase was sure their real purpose was to "indulge in widespread propaganda" and "to try their cause in public." That idea, "shocking" to him, left Swan "cold." On 21 June, apparently in anticipation of more labor defense tactics, armed guards took up positions in the courtroom and outside the building. The expected demonstrations failed to materialize, but an obviously alienated Swan entered the hearing prepared to "have all the oral argument we can stomach."[8]

Thus the defense attorneys who spoke for three hours against the constitutionality of the Smith Act faced a tough audience. When Sacher asserted that the government had failed to establish the existence of any clear and present danger, Hand interrupted to ask whether the defense maintained that Congress could not pass laws which forbade revolutionary leaders from making agreements to incite their followers to violence at some propitious time in the future. Sacher conceded that what the jurist had described was a criminal conspiracy, but pointed out that in this case the agreement had involved no substantive crime. It was purely in the realm of speech.

At the end of the day Louis McCabe took up a different subject, arguing that because of certain errors which Medina had committed, the Eleven had been tried by a jury that was biased against them. On 22 June Isserman, Gladstein, and Crockett joined their colleague in criticizing the trial judge, charging him with, among other things, judicial misconduct, favoritism for the prosecution, hostility toward themselves and their clients, and badgering defendants and attorneys. Crockett also attacked the jury selection system, only to have Hand interrupt with a comment which indicated a complete lack of sympathy for his position on the subject.[9]

On 23 June the government responded, requesting that the judges uphold the convictions, because the Eleven were not bonafide political leaders, but rather fifth-column agents guilty of espionage and of conspiring to seize power forcefully and establish a Soviet America. The thrust of the argument put forward by Frank Gordon, Irving Shapiro, and Robert W. Ginnane, all special assistants to the Attorney General, was that whatever abridgement of free speech the Smith Act might involve did not violate the First Amendment, in part because of recent Supreme Court decisions, but also because of the Cold War. Hand expressed concern that this statute might have made criminals of such revered eighteenth-century advocates of the right to revolution as Thomas Jefferson, but Ginnane managed to allay his fears on that score. The government lawyer also issued an ominous warning that unless the court found the imminence of an intended revolt irrelevant, "the entire preparatory stage of recruitment by a modern totalitarian political organization . . . [would] be brought under the protection of the First Amendment."[10]

As a political matter, such a possibility was something no jurist could ignore, certainly not after 23 June 1950. The same papers that reported the final day of oral argument before the court of appeals also carried the first news of the North Korean invasion of South Korea. On 27 June President Truman ordered American air and naval forces to assist the South Koreans, thus plunging the United States into armed combat against a Communist foe.

While the Cold War grew hot on the battlefields of Asia, judges deliberated the fate of Dennis and his comrades. By 4 July the fate of the Eleven was all but sealed, for Chase had declared that he would vote to affirm their convictions and Swan had indicated that he would probably do likewise. Neither of these judges entertained any doubts about the constitutionality of the Smith Act. Swan found none of the Communists' complaints about Medina's conduct of the trial sustainable, and although instructing his clerk to prepare a detailed report on the jury challenge, he did not wait until it was finished to conclude that on this point too "appellants' contentions should not be sustained." Swan considered the CPUSA an obvious "danger to our form of government" and apparently wished to resolve all issues in a manner that would justify the imprisonment of its leaders. So did Chase, who experienced no doubts at all about the propriety of the necessary rulings.[11]

Hand not only voted with Chase and Swan, thus making the decision unanimous, but also wrote the opinion of the court. His role in this case, now known as *United States* v. *Dennis*, surprised many observers, for the Second Circuit's most distinguished jurist enjoyed a reputation as a staunch defender of civil liberties, which he had earned during World War I, by attempting to prevent the Post Office Department from suppressing a radical periodical called *The Masses*. Conventional wisdom attributes Hand's antilibertarian position in the Communist case to his devotion to the principle of judicial restraint, and certainly there is a measure of truth in this analysis. As the judge told Francis Biddle, although ruling in favor of the Smith Act, he disapproved of that law as a means of dealing with the threat of communism. Unlike many jurists, who gladly deferred to the legislature in economic cases, but intervened actively to strike down legislation threatening the First Amendment freedoms to which they assigned a preferred position, Hand insisted that, regardless of the subject matter, courts had no business upsetting the compromises among competing interests which legislators had worked out. But he acknowledged in a letter to Justice Frankfurter, the Supreme Court's leading champion of judicial restraint, that, in his mind, there were some kinds of speech, namely, those that counseled violation of the law, which could never enjoy the protection of the Constitution. He had argued in *Masses Publishing Company* v. *Patton* (1917) that in speech cases the test should be the content of the utterance and that only language which constituted a direct incitement to illegal action should be liable to suppression. Although now willing to acknowledge that Congress could "require the utterer to separate the wheat from the chaff," he still believed the rule he had formulated then was essentially correct. But the *Masses* test had failed to win the approval of the legal profession or the courts, so in *Dennis* Hand bowed to authority, and, although disagreeing with Frankfurter's view that it was "a balance of interest in each case which judges [had] no business to mess in with . . . did follow just that [line] in what [he] wrote. . . ."[12]

Two other considerations, both more important than judicial restraint, dictated his position in *Dennis*. One of these, identified by Marvin Shick, was obedience to the Supreme Court. When Hand wrote his *Masses* opinion, there was little case law on freedom of speech, but by 1950 the high tribunal had spoken a number of times on the subject, and the nature of its rulings was such that only by completely ignoring the obligation to follow precedent could he have based a decision on the principle enunciated in his 1917 opinion. The ruling that bulked largest in Hand's thinking was *American Communications Association* v. *Douds*, in which the Court, only six months before *Dennis*, had upheld the anti-Communist oath provision of the Taft-Hartley Act against a claim that it violated the First

Amendment. While *Douds* differed sufficiently from *Dennis* that, as Hand realized, it was not technically a controlling precedent, this earlier ruling left little doubt about how the Supreme Court would react when confronted with an appeal by Communist defendants.[13] Hand found it easy to decide *Dennis* in a way that his superiors would find acceptable, for, as his opinion demonstrated, he shared the concern about the menace of international communism which animated Chase and Swan.

That opinion, announced on 1 August, conceded nothing to the CPUSA, rejecting every contention the Eleven had advanced.[14] In upholding Medina's disposition of the jury challenge Hand admitted that the Southern District lists did not represent a cross section of the community, but he emphasized the failure of the Eleven to establish that the heavy representation of wealthy persons on them resulted from deliberate discrimination. In an effort to justify the composition of the lists, he pointed to certain provisions in relevant statutes which permitted officials selecting names of prospective jurors to exercise a great deal of discretion and then formulated a number of innocuous hypotheses to explain why they might have chosen more people of some types than others. Such reasons could not justify the total exclusion of any group from the rolls, said Hand, but the poor, blacks, and so on, did participate in the system and in more than merely token numbers. That was sufficient.

Hand also endorsed the district court's conduct of the trial. Besides finding appellants' complaints about informers totally without merit and ruling that Medina's refusal to let Benjamin Davis address the jury had not violated his rights, he also upheld the district court's many rulings on the admission and exclusion of evidence. Medina had not erred in refusing to receive some material concerning the actual content of the defendants' teaching and advocacy, Hand felt, because the charge did not depend upon the extent of force and violence in their propaganda, only on its presence. He also found the trial judge innocent of bias and misconduct. Although conceding that at times Medina had used language which fell short of requisite judicial gravity and had let his emotions get the better of him, Hand denied this was his fault. "The record discloses a judge sorely tried for many months of turmoil . . . who . . . showed considerably greater self-control and forbearance than it is given to most judges to possess. . . ."[15] All Medina had tried to do, he believed, was keep the trial within measurable bounds. That did not constitute favoring the prosecution.

Although acknowledging the existence of heated public feeling against Communists, Hand insisted the jury had been sufficiently impartial. He considered it unlikely that public opinion would change within the foreseeable future, so that the choice was between going ahead with the least prejudiced jury possible or letting the prosecution lapse, an alternative Hand considered unthinkable. Appellants claimed Medina's *voir dire* had been too general to determine whether or not potential jurors entertained any disqualifying biases, but Hand also cavalierly waved aside that objection.

The most important part of his opinion, that dealing with the constitutionality of the Smith Act, began with a lengthy review of Supreme Court decisions on freedom of speech. In the course of this, Hand pushed aside the Court's 1943 ruling in *Schneiderman* v. *United States*, reasoning that since the official opinion in the case actually expressed the views of only three justices, nothing compelled him to accept its declaration that membership in the Communist Party was not necessarily incompatible with attachment to the principles of the Constitution. Hand concluded that under the precedents an utterance could not lose the protection of the First Amendment simply because the purposes of the speaker included inciting his hearers to illegal conduct. The Constitution safeguarded even a "bare appeal to action" as long as it was incorporated into or accompanied by utterances addressed to the understanding and intended to persuade. The phrase "clear and present danger" had developed as a kind of shorthand way of characterizing those among such mixed or compound utterances which that amendment did not protect. "It is," said Hand, "a way to describe a penumbra of occasions, even the outskirts of which are indefinable, but within which, as is so often the case, the courts must find their way as they can." But how? In answering that question, Hand formulated his own new version of Holmes's rule. "In each case they must ask whether the gravity of the 'evil,' discounted by its improbability, justifies such invasion of free speech as is necessary to avoid the danger," he said. "We have," Hand added, "purposely substituted 'improbability' for 'remoteness' because that must be the right interpretation."[16]

This conclusion was far less obvious than he implied, for in *Schenck* v. *United States*, where the phrase "clear and present danger" had made its first appearance, Holmes asserted that in speech cases the question was one of "proximity and degree." There were, he said, things that one might say under ordinary circumstances that became intolerable in times of extreme danger—as when the nation was at war. Hand's formulation, with its emphasis on the gravity of the evil, represented a reasonably accurate rendering of what Holmes seems to have had in mind, but this new rule was not at all consistent with the concurring opinion of Justice Brandeis in *Whitney* v. *California*, often regarded as the classic statement of the clear-and-present-danger principle. In it Brandeis had stipulated that "There must be reasonable ground to believe that the danger apprehended is imminent." As long as there was an opportunity for counterspeech to head off a threatened evil, he argued, suppression was constitutionally impermissible. Hand, however, rather largely wrote the time element out of the formula, substituting "improbability" for "remoteness," because it seemed to him irrational to condone future evils which society would prevent if they were imminent. In his hands the clear-and-present-danger test became a kind of "rule of reason" for balancing the competing values of social security and free speech.[17]

As far as Hand was concerned, what mattered was the gravity of the danger and the likelihood of its eventual occurrence, and he found a sufficiently serious threat in this case. The CPUSA, the judge observed, was a highly articulated, well-contrived, far-spread organization, with thousands of rigidly disciplined adherents, many of them infused with a passionate utopian faith. One article of the Communist creed was the capture of all existing governments. The question, then, was simply how long after discovering the existence of such a conspiracy the government had to wait before moving against it.

Hand was convinced that by 1948 the requisite clear and present danger existed. "We must not close our eyes to our position in the world at that time," he said. Russia's leaders preached a faith as militantly evangelical as Islam and there were important Stalinist factions agitating for control in most Western European countries. Defendants had acted in close concert with this worldwide movement. Hand discussed the growth of international tensions after 1945, citing the Berlin airlift as an example. Given the present world situation, he believed, any border flare-up, diplomatic incident, or difference in interpretation of a modus vivendi might spark war. "We do not understand how one could ask for a more probable danger, unless we must wait till the actual eve of hostilities," he concluded.[18]

In this context, Hand felt, the punishment of the Eleven for conspiring to teach and advocate violent overthrow of the government and to set up the Communist Party to engage in such instruction was constitutionally permissible if the defendants had acted with the intent to bring about forceful revolution. As he would later tell Boston attorney Elliot Richardson, the "purpose of the utter" was the key. If a person sought through speech to bring about a violation of the law, Hand could "see no reason why the Constitution should protect him, however remote the chance . . . of his success."[19] On its face the Smith Act did not mention intent, but in his charge Medina had made a guilty verdict dependent upon a finding that the defendants planned to overthrow the government eventually. Appellants accused him of amending the law, but Hand did not agree.

As far as he was concerned, intent plus conspiracy to advocate, in the context of the Cold War, constituted a clear and present danger—if the accused were Communists. The threat to American society that worried

Hand was a war between the United States and Russia in which the CPUSA would act as a fifth column for the enemy. In his eyes it was their relationship to the Soviet Union, not their Marxist-Leninist philosophy, that made the Communists dangerous. Political scientist Francis Wormuth later accused him of imputing to the Eleven guilt of a pro-Russian seditious conspiracy for which they had been neither indicted nor convicted, and then using the danger created by that plot to justify their punishment for an entirely different conspiracy: one to teach and advocate.[20] Wormuth's criticism was somewhat misdirected, for Hand had discussed international tensions and the Party's relation to them, not to prove the defendants had committed an offense, but only to show the context in which they had agreed to employ a particular kind of speech. The fact remains that it was because the Eleven were pro-Russian Communists that he found a clear and present danger. Its existence, and hence the right of Congress to restrict the exercise of the defendants' First Amendment rights, depended, not on what they said or the context in which they said it, but on who they were. Hand also ruled that Medina's withdrawal of the clear-and-present-danger question from the jury had been proper, because unless decided as a matter of law, the determination of that issue would have been immune from judicial review, a situation that he considered unthinkable.

Disdaining Hand's sophistic reasoning, Chase filed a concurring opinion in which he advocated resting this ruling squarely on the majority opinions in *Gitlow* and *Whitney*. The Supreme Court had never overruled those decisions, but in view of later judicial acceptance of the opposing views of Holmes and Brandeis, most authorities regarded them as obsolete. Chase wished to resurrect these relics of the Red Scare because he was convinced that communism had "by forcible overthrow engulfed or attempted to engulf nation after nation, after preparing for the use of force by just such advocacy as this act forbids." "As this is being written," he noted, "fifth column activities are aiding the North Koreans in their war against the United Nations."[21]

Because the kind of anxieties that animated Chase were commonplace in the summer of 1950, applause greeted the decision of the court of appeals. Although *New Republic* spoke of the ruling as "a cold war [one] and . . . regrettable on that ground," other commentators joined the White House in commending it. The *Columbia Law Review* endorsed Hand's revision of the clear-and-present-danger test, agreeing that the American sympathizers of a hostile power "should not be protected because of the possibility that their scheme will be foiled." Mary Hornaday of the *Christian Science Monitor* made even more explicit the connection between this country's international problems and the favorable reception accorded Hand's opinion. Pointing to the Korean conflict, she observed, "Most civil rights guardians who questioned whether the Smith Act was too stringent a measure for peacetime were sure it wasn't now that war had come."[22]

III

Convinced that the Korean conflict did not justify the ruling against them, the Eleven quickly informed authorities that they would appeal to the Supreme Court. Apparently within the Party leadership there were some who considered mass pressure more likely than further litigation to produce positive results, and the confusing signals sent out by the legal system only complicated this internal debate. First the court of appeals voted two to one to grant a government request for revocation of the convicted Communists' bail. Then Robert Jackson, the Supreme Court justice with responsibility for the Second Circuit, reversed that ruling, allowing the Eleven to remain free while they pressed their appeal. Jackson's colleagues quickly crushed whatever hopes his ruling might have inspired among Stalinists by granting a writ of certiorari to the Eleven but refusing to examine any of the many issues which they had raised except the constitutionality of the Smith Act. Now certain that the high tribunal was just "an instrument in the not-so-cold war," the Party sought to delay final determination of its leaders' fate, focus international attention on the case, and perhaps discredit the Court by asking permission for a British barrister, who already had a conflicting trial date in India, to participate in the oral arguments. The Supreme Court refused to grant the necessary postponement. Unable to turn the case into a labor defense spectacular and apparently convinced that, although capitalist judges were unreliable, the Eleven's only hope now lay in a favorable judicial ruling, the Party finally decided to depend on conventional constitutional adjudication but to bombard the Court with reminders of how "the people" felt the judges ought to rule.[23]

Although its threats that mass protest would greet the wrong decision alienated at least one justice, the Communists had good reason to try something more than a traditional nonpolitical litigation strategy. Within the past year the Court had handed down the *Douds* decision and also refused to reverse Dennis's contempt-of-Congress conviction. Like its recent rulings, the composition of the high tribunal boded ill for the Communists' cause. Fourteen times during the period 1937-48 the Supreme Court had decided cases on the basis of the clear-and-present-danger test, always ruling against the challenged governmental action, but in the summer of 1949 death had claimed Frank Murphy and Wiley Rutledge, half of the four-man liberal phalanx around which the majorities in those cases had formed. As replacements Truman had named Sherman Minton, a former New Deal Democratic senator from Indiana, grown conservative during eight years on the U.S. Seventh Circuit Court of Appeals, and Tom Clark, the attorney general who had initiated the prosecution of the CPUSA. Both new justices were far less committed to the protection of civil liberties than the men they replaced, and although Clark would have to disqualify himself in the *Dennis* case, the Communists' chances would have been far better had Murphy and Rutledge still held the seats that he and Minton now occupied.[24]

Sitting with the newcomers were two other Truman appointees unlikely to respond favorably to the appeal. Harold Burton, a former mayor of Cleveland and a buddy of the President during his Senate days, was a moderately conservative Republican who supported libertarian claims more often than Clark and Minton but less frequently than a majority of the Court. Fred Vinson, secretary of the treasury when named chief justice in 1946, was a former Kentucky congressman who had held several lesser economic posts in the executive branch as well as a seat on the Court of Appeals for the District of Columbia. Highly indulgent toward loyalty programs, he was, with respect to civil liberties claims, among the most negative members of the Court, rejecting challenges to federal action in this area more than 90 percent of the time.[25]

Vinson's views contrasted sharply with those of the two remaining members of the once-dominant liberal bloc. Hugo Black, a former senator from Alabama, had joined the Court in 1937 having no judicial experience other than that gained during a brief term on a police court, and under a cloud of suspicion because of his one-time membership in the Ku Klux Klan. But he proved to be both an able judge and a vigorous defender of the Bill of Rights. His liberal associate, William O. Douglas, who had taught law at Yale and served on the Securities and Exchange Commission before ascending to the bench in 1939, had enough status as a Democratic politician to receive serious consideration for the vice-presidential nomination in 1940, 1944, and 1948. Although hostile to communism, he believed passionately in free speech and was likely to give even members of the CPUSA a sympathetic hearing if they raised claims of its denial.[26]

On the ideological ground between Black and Douglas and the four conservatives stood three other survivors of the "Roosevelt Court" of 1937-48: Justices Stanley Reed, Felix Frankfurter, and Robert Jack-

son. Reed, a Kentuckian, had come to Washington as an attorney for the
Hoover administration and had stayed to serve the New Deal, first as
counsel for the Reconstruction Finance Corporation and later as solicitor general. Appointed to the Court in 1938, he became a swing man between the liberal and conservative blocs. But in cases involving efforts
to combat subversive activities, Reed consistently supported the government.[27]

His ideological position was far easier to define than that of Frankfurter,
a former Harvard Law School professor who had helped to found the
ACLU and whose personal views on individual rights were so liberal that
during his academic days some had considered him a radical. He had joined
with other prominent lawyers in publishing a scathing indictment of the
Justice Department's conduct during the Palmer raids and later nearly
lost his professorial position for championing the cause of Sacco and Vanzetti. Despite his background, on the bench, where he had served since
1939, Frankfurter compiled a distinctly antilibertarian record. The reason was his devotion to the principle of judicial restraint. Believing it was
not a judge's place to impose his will on the popularly elected branches
of government, he often suppressed his personal feelings and voted to sustain laws he would have opposed had he been a legislator.[28]

Jackson, too, defied easy classification. A justice since 1941, he had
joined the Court after service as solicitor general and attorney general. His
voting pattern resembled Frankfurter's, but his written opinions were
erratic. Likely to influence Jackson's thinking on the Communist case
was a deep concern about the capacity of totalitarian groups to seize
power in democratic countries, which he had developed while prosecuting
Nazi war criminals at Nuremberg.[29]

If the Eleven were to achieve reversal, they needed Jackson's vote, as
well as the votes of Black, Douglas, Frankfurter, and Reed. Because Reed
seems to have been committed to affirmance from the beginning, the Communist leaders never really had a chance, but their lawyers made a determined effort. Around 20 November they filed a lengthy brief which argued that no one could make it a crime to advocate ideas and exercise the
rights of speech, press, and assembly and that, even if advocacy was part
of an effort to bring about a substantive evil, the First Amendment protected it, unless there was a clear and present danger. Petitioners went on
to argue that the conspiracy section of the Smith Act was independently
unconstitutional because, by making it a crime to agree to exercise civil
rights at some unspecified time in the future, that provision imposed prior
restraint on speech, press, and assembly. Their lawyers also challenged
Medina's refusal to let the jury consider the clear-and-present-danger ques-

tion and attacked Hand for changing the meaning of Holmes's classic constitutional test. In addition, petitioners accused the prosecution of attempting to convert the statute, the indictment, and indeed the entire case, from one involving speech, press, and assembly into one involving conduct. Their contention was that the Justice Department had suddenly "discovered," *after* Vinson declared in *Douds* that, although the government might not censor political views, it could impose some incidental burdens on free expression in order to regulate dangerous conduct, that the Eleven's conviction was really not for radical advocacy at all, but for forming fifth columns and recruiting revolutionaries to overthrow the government. Petitioners also insisted that their sympathy for the Soviet Union should not deprive them of the constitutional protection to which they would otherwise be entitled, and asserted that "Affirmance here would merely be a confession of our unwillingness to take the risk of permitting political dissent to be heard. This is a suppression of the democratic process itself." Both the ACLU and the National Lawyers Guild echoed this theme in motions requesting permission to file friend-of-the-court briefs.[30]

The Justice Department, on the other hand, denied that freedom of expression was at issue, maintaining that the Smith Act punished not speech but the formation of fifth columns serving the aggressive purposes of foreign nations. Requiring the government to establish the existence of an imminent and immediate danger, even after Congress had explicitly prohibited utterances of this kind, might be appropriate in dealing with unorganized and irresponsible agitators, the government acknowledged. But, "Applied to these petitioners and their Communist Party, it would mean that the First Amendment protects their preparations until they are ready to attempt a seizure of power, or to act as a fifth column in time of crisis." The Justice Department argued that Soviet-sponsored Communist "aggression and disruption" made the highly disciplined CPUSA a clear and present danger, and denied both that the Smith Act was unconstitutionally vague and that it punished conduct excessively distant from actual armed revolt.[31]

The petitioners countered with a devastating reply brief, which charged the Justice Department with falsely representing this as a case involving a conspiracy to overthrow the government rather than one to teach and advocate doctrine. In talking as if recruitment was the target and subject matter of the Smith Act, the Eleven charged, their opponents had misrepresented the nature of that statute and had ignored its legislative history. They bluntly accused the government of dishonesty.[32]

Three days after receiving their reply brief, the Court heard oral arguments in the case. Solicitor General Philip B. Perlman told the justices that Congress had modeled the Smith Act on the New York statute upheld in *Gitlow* and contended that, because the Court had never overruled that decision, the federal law was obviously constitutional. Resorting to a complete non sequitur, he argued that because Communists would eliminate free speech if they gained power, it was not an issue in this case. Perlman sarcastically brushed aside the clear-and-present-danger test, contending that it applied only when the threat from suppression of speech exceeded that of the evil legislated against. His side did not have to establish the existence of a clear and present danger, the Solicitor General argued, as long as it showed that the Communists intended to overthrow the government when the time was ripe. Perlman's colleague, Irving Shapiro, reiterated the contention that the Eleven had been convicted, not for teaching philosophy and organizing a political party, but for training revolutionaries.

After Irving Saypol, John McGohey's replacement as U.S. attorney in the Southern District, and two Justice Department lawyers also argued for the government, George Crockett, Harry Sacher, and Abraham Isserman replied. Isserman contended that the Smith Act deprived petitioners of their right to due process of law and warned ominously that if the Supreme Court endorsed this statute, federal authorities would employ it against 500,000 Americans. Crockett argued that Medina's failure to submit the clear-and-present-danger issue to the jury violated the Eleven's Sixth Amendment rights. The heart of the Communists' case, however, was Sacher's summation, rated "excellent" by Justice Burton. The meaning of the clear-and-present-danger test, he argued, was that only an immediately threatening emergency could justify the government in abridging freedom of speech.[33]

Sacher's chances of prevailing with this argument were slight, for in Korea Chinese "volunteers" had crossed the Yalu River in strength, smashing General MacArthur's Home-by-Christmas Offensive and sending American troops streaming south in disordered retreat. At home hysteria ran high. Senator Joe McCarthy, the anti-Communist demagogue, was a national hero. When Elizabeth Gurley Flynn's defense committee attempted to buy advertising space for an attack on the Smith Act, even such liberal organs as the *New York Post*, *New York Times*, and *New Republic* turned it down.[34] This was a bad time to ask the Supreme Court for a dispassionate application of the clear-and-present-danger rule.

On 4 June 1951 the justices announced their decision. The CPUSA had lost badly, beaten by a vote of six to two. Vinson read the official opinion of the Court, a plurality one in which he spoke only for Burton, Minton, Reed, and himself. Although the case apparently had given his clerks some problems, the Chief Justice had not found it a difficult one to decide. To Vinson's way of thinking, "The government had to protect itself against communism. . . ." Consequently, as his former clerk, Howard Trienens, recalls, "if these guys were communists . . . those were not tough decisions for him." "This was the height of the Cold War," and Vinson, who had come to the Court from a wartime administration, still thought like a man mobilizing America for a struggle against the nation's enemies. Decisions involving Communists were for him "Foregone conclusions."[35]

In justifying his disposition of the *Dennis* case, the Chief Justice followed the lead of Learned Hand.[36] Like the court of appeals judge, he approved Medina's instruction that the defendants' conduct was punishable only if they had intended to bring about the violent overthrow of the government as speedily as circumstances would permit. The structure and purpose of the Smith Act, he said, demanded the inclusion of such intent as an element of the crime.

Vinson agreed with Hand that, as interpreted by Medina, the Smith Act was constitutional. Congress, he argued, had an undoubted right to prevent overthrow of the government by violent revolution. The only question was whether the means it had selected—the Smith Act—violated the First and Fifth Amendments. Vinson acknowledged that the statute punished communication but maintained that in previous cases neither the majority nor the dissenters had ever classified free speech as an unlimited and unqualified right. All justices had regarded it as sometimes subordinate to other societal values and considerations. Saving the government from violent overthrow, Vinson believed, was an interest substantial enough to warrant limiting expression. Had the Chief Justice been willing to rely on *Gitlow* and *Whitney*, he could simply have ruled that in passing the Smith Act Congress had recognized this fact and proscribed those utterances which would produce that result, but, like Hand, he felt compelled by recent decisions to employ the clear-and-present-danger rule.

As far as Vinson was concerned, the Holmes test could not mean that before the government might act, it had to wait "until the *putsch* is about to be executed, the plans have been laid and the signal is awaited."[37] If legitimate authority was aware that a group aiming at its destruction was indoctrinating members and committing them to act when the leaders felt circumstances were right, surely the time to deal with the situation had arrived. Whether the proposed rebellion had any chance of success was irrelevant, Vinson said, for an attempt to overthrow the government by force, even if doomed to failure from the outset, was, because of the physical and political danger it would cause, an evil great enough for Congress to combat. The Chief Justice quoted and endorsed as "succinct and inclusive" the words of Learned Hand: "In each case [courts] must ask whether the gravity of the 'evil' discounted by its improbability, justifies such invasion of free speech as is necessary to avoid the danger."[38] Vinson agreed with the courts below that during the period 1945-1948 a situation had existed which met the requirements of the rule. Like Hand, he found the danger in the conspiratorial nature of the Communist Party and the existence of the Cold War. These factors, he felt, had created a situation quite different from anything Holmes and Brandeis had ever confronted.

> The formation by petitioners of such a highly organized conspiracy, with rigidly disciplined members subject to call when the leaders, these petitioners, felt that the time had come for action, coupled with the inflammable nature of world conditions, similar uprisings in other countries, and the touch-and-go nature of our relations with countries with whom petitioners were in the very least ideologically attuned, convince us that their convictions were justified on this score.[39]

Or, as Justice Reed, who endorsed Vinson's opinion, put it, "a teaching of force and violence by such a group as this, . . . is enough at this period of the world's history to make the protection of the First Amendment inapplicable."[40] In other words, it was not so much *what* the Communist leaders planned to say that created a clear and present danger, as it was *who* they were.

Because the conspiracy itself created the threat, the Chief Justice added, there could be no merit in the petitioners' contention that conspiring to advocate, as distinguished from advocacy itself, was constitutionally protected. He then upheld Medina's refusal to refer the clear-and-present-danger question to the jury. As the Chief Justice saw it, whether activities that constituted a violation of the Smith Act fell within an area protected by the Constitution, as opposed to whether the defendants had broken the law or not, was an issue for a judge to decide. Because that was what determining whether a clear and present danger existed involved, the job was obviously a judicial one.

While Frankfurter agreed with Vinson's conclusion that the Communist leaders had been "properly and constitutionally convicted for violation of the Smith Act,"[41] he did not wish to associate himself with his colleague's reasoning. Frankfurter disagreed strongly with the policy decisions embodied in the Smith Act, fearing that such a law would silence critics of the government who did not advocate violent revolution but who feared authorities might misinterpret their remarks. Only his rigid devotion to judicial restraint enabled him to uphold the statute. In a concurring opinion Frankfurter proclaimed: "Free speech cases are not an exception to the principle that we are not legislators, that direct policymaking is not our province."[42] He did not like the Smith Act, but that law was within the bounds of reason, and therefore, in his eyes, constitutional.

By acknowledging that a statute, even if valid on its face, might be applied in such a way as to violate the First Amendment, Frankfurter kept the door to judicial review open, but only at the cost of making his deference to legislative policy making look a little threadbare. Like Hand and Vinson, he took judicial notice of the Cold War and concluded that it could "amply justify a legislature in concluding that recruitment of additional members for the Party would create a substantial danger to national security."[43] Perhaps the conspiratorial nature of the CPUSA and the Soviet-American conflict constituted a clear and present peril which could furnish constitutional justification for passage of a law punishing the solicitation of new members for such an organization. But it is hard to see how Frankfurter could rationalize as deference to the legislative will a decision upholding the application of the Smith Act to the Party's activities of the period 1945-48, in view of the fact that the statute did not explicitly mention recruitment and that it had been passed by Congress at a time when both world conditions and Communist policies differed considerably from those of the years covered by the indictment. Another problem with Frankfurter's restraint was that it ignored the great prestige of the Supreme Court and the power of that body to influence the thinking of a nation which worshiped its fundamental charter. By declaring the Smith Act constitutional, he and his colleagues had given that law a prestigious stamp of approval, which could not fail to hinder any legislative efforts to remove it from the statute books.[44]

Jackson, like Frankfurter, filed a concurring opinion. Unable to accept what Vinson had done to the clear-and-present-danger rule, he advocated dismissing Holmes's test as inapplicable and upholding the convictions as though they were not for a speech offense at all, but for conspiring to overthrow the government. Jackson began with the proposition that the clear-and-present-danger test did not apply to conspiracies such as communism. Because Stalinists regarded force as only one of many means to the end they sought, laws that dealt with violent overthrow and were designed to combat anarchists could not, if prosecutors had to establish the existence of a clear and present danger, ever reach them. Holmes's rule, Jackson argued, should be preserved pure and unmodified for the kind of situations, involving isolated actions by a few individuals, that had inspired it. Meanwhile, authorities could punish Communists for conspiring against the government. Although Jackson's opinion possessed a certain refreshing candor, his contention that the clear-and-present-danger test had developed out of cases which did not involve conspiracy was demonstrably incorrect. Also, the kind of law he endorsed for use against the CPUSA had a long and an inglorious history as an instrument for the oppression of unpopular groups.[45] Even the justice himself, although convinced it was constitutional, acknowledged that this was an awkward and inept remedy for communism.

Besides the concurring opinions of Jackson and Frankfurter, the *Dennis* case produced two dissents. One, by Justice Black, contended that, in order to uphold the Smith Act and the convictions of eleven radicals, the majority had distorted the clear-and-present-danger test, thus constricting the First Amendment. Far from being too restrictive of governmental power, Black thought, Holmes's test did not go far enough. The Supreme Court, he asserted, had no more right to use its own notions of reasonableness to sustain laws suppressing freedom of speech than to employ those of Congress for that purpose.

Black's fellow libertarian, William O. Douglas, complained that although this case had been argued as though it involved the teaching of sabotage, espionage, street warfare, and the like, the prosecution had neither introduced evidence of such advocacy nor prosecuted the defendants for seditious conspiracy. Douglas was sharply critical of the majority for rendering freedom of speech dependent, not on what was said, but on the identity of the speaker, and for making intent, rather than content, the crucial element in determining guilt. He found Jackson's opinion even more horrifying than Vinson's, observing that never until today had anyone seriously thought that the law of conspiracy could be used to turn speech into seditious conduct. Freedom of expression was the rule, he said, and only the likelihood of immediate injury to society could justify its restriction. Whether such a clear and present danger existed was obviously a matter for a jury to decide, but regardless of who made the determination, there should be evidence in the record. There was none here. Of Vinson's efforts to establish the existence of a clear and present danger by taking judicial notice of the Cold War, Douglas remarked acidly that the Court might as well say the petitioners' speech was illegal because the USSR and its army were a threat to world peace. What really mattered was the strength and tactical position of the Communists in this country. After recent assaults on them by everyone from labor unions to the attorney general, it was hard for him to see how they could now be so potent and strategically deployed as to necessitate suppressing them for their speech. The CPUSA constituted in his opinion "the most beset, and the least thriving of any fifth column in history."[46]

IV

The decision from which Douglas dissented so vigorously produced conflicting reactions. While Attorney General McGrath gloated, the Communists, continuing to deny their guilt, blamed the ruling on Cold War hysteria. Although aware that the decision represented a serious setback, the Party refused to accept defeat. The *People's World* headlined its editorial reaction to *Dennis* "THE FIGHT GOES ON." Both that paper and the National Committee talked of "popular resistance" and of the masses nullifying the ruling, but it quickly became apparent that labor defense had yielded preeminence to legalism. "Let us all sit down and write to President Truman protesting this injustice, [and] urging a rehearing of this shameful and tragic decision . . . ," the *Daily Worker* editorialized on 5 June. The next day its West Coast counterpart adopted the same line. Fighting back would take a form no more revolutionary than asking the capitalists' Court to reverse itself.[47]

The reason for the Party's conservatism was probably the precariously narrow base of its support. Numerous individuals spoke out against the decision, but too many were old and close friends of the CPUSA, such as Congressman Marcantonio, Elmer Benson and C. B. Baldwin of the Progressive Party, and William Patterson of the Civil Rights Congress. Outside the tiny solar system that revolved around the CPUSA, overwhelming approval greeted the *Dennis* decision. In the entire country only five major newspapers   the *New York Post*, the *Louisville Courier-Journal*, the *Madison* (Wisconsin) *Capital Times*, the *New York World*, and the *St. Louis Post-Dispatch*—expressed opposition. Protesting periodicals were equally rare. *The Nation* criticized Vinson for narrowly construing and perversely applying the clear-and-present-danger doctrine, and *Commonweal*, although observing that the CPUSA was a threat to national security which ought to be punished for something, did say it could not regard the Party's advocacy as placing the country in any immediate peril. A columnist for a black weekly, the *Amsterdam News*, also criticized the *Dennis* ruling. But the only significant groups to express opposition were the ACLU, the Socialist Workers Party, and the CIO, the last not until November.[48]

The rest of the country applauded loudly. "The Supreme Court decision upholding the conviction of the 11 Communist leaders is the most important reconciliation of liberty and security in our time," the *Washington Post* proclaimed. "The American people in overwhelming majority will rejoice in this judicial affirmation of the nation's right and power," cheered the *New Orleans Times-Picayune*. *Newsweek* and the *New York Times* were equally enthusiastic, as was the *Chicago Tribune*, which scolded Douglas for his dissent, insisting that "because the Communist Party in the United States is as much an instrument of Russian policy as is the Red army. . . rigorous measures in repressing it are warranted."[49]

What the American press found most heartening about the *Dennis* decision was the fact that it seemed to pave the way for total destruction of the CPUSA. "We are fighting Communism with blood and money on both sides of the world; now the Supreme Court permits us to fight it at home," the *Los Angeles Times* observed. The *Denver Post* agreed. "The Communist party, we would judge, is having its last breath in the United States," said the *San Francisco Chronicle*. Joy over the impending ruin of a hapless radical faction, important only as a symbol of the Cold War enemy, blinded a cheering throng to the real significance of the *Dennis* decision. Few editorial writers seemed aware that freedom of speech had been an issue in the case.[50]

Among legal commentators, who better understood all of its implications, *Dennis* did not fare so well. The ACLU published a pamphlet attacking the decision, and Howard Meyer, a former special assistant to the attorney general, called for its reversal. Writing in the *Virginia Law Review*, Louis Boudin pointed out that although the Justice Department had argued this case and judges at three levels had decided it, as if it involved a conspiracy to overthrow the government, the indictment made no such charge and the prosecution had offered no evidence to prove it. He argued that clear and present danger was a matter of fact which depended on particular circumstances. In view of the Communists' ideology, Boudin contended, such a threat could have existed between 1945 and 1948 only if the defendants had believed there was a revolutionary upsurge in the United States and one had in fact existed. Yet the government had attempted to establish neither of these things. Another critic of the decision was Harvard's Robert McCloskey, who took Vinson, as well as Hand and Medina, to task for amending the time element out of the clear-and-present-danger test. Criticism came also from Charles James Antieau of Washburn University and John A. Gorfinkel and Julian Mack II of the Golden Gate College of Law. Later Eugene V. Rostow of the Yale Law School and Francis D. Wormuth of the University of Utah joined in the assault on *Dennis*. In Rostow's opinion the fact that the Supreme Court had abandoned the doctrines of Holmes and Brandeis in order to uphold the Smith Act indicated that America was in the midst of a grave civil liberties crisis.[51]

While the *Dennis* ruling drew fire from many knowledgeable commentators, there were also respected individuals within the legal and scholarly communities who endorsed it. One of these was Princeton's renowned constitutional scholar, Edward S. Corwin. Wallace Mendelson of the Uni-

versity of Tennessee also commended the direction the Supreme Court
had taken. There was, he felt, a constitutionally significant difference
between clandestine speech and other kinds of talk. The clear-and-present-
danger test afforded protection to utterances so that they might compete
for acceptance in the marketplace of ideas, but Communists did their
teaching in secret, rather than under conditions which allowed free play
to the democratic corrective of counterdiscussion. It was their widespread
sub rosa activities which "constituted the danger." Elliot Richardson, a
future attorney general, also supported the revised version of the clear-
and-present-danger test and endorsed the way judges had applied it in the
Dennis case. Like Corwin and Mendelson, he made the conspiratorial nature of the Communist Party a crucial link in his argument.[52]

So did Sidney Hook, a professor of philosophy at New York University,
whose 1953 book *Heresy Yes—Conspiracy No!* set forth explicitly what
was a common assumption at the time: that, given the existing world situation, a conspiratorial movement with ties to Moscow necessarily threatened the survival of the United States. It was not their speech which made
this country's Stalinists dangerous, he argued, but their organizational ties,
which, "in effect [make] them a para-military fifth column. . . ." That assumption underlay not only the commentaries of Corwin, Mendelson, and
Richardson but also the opinions of Learned Hand and Fred Vinson. Here
was the flaw in *Dennis*. If the Communists were dangerous, it was because
of the nature of their organization, its ties with the Soviet Union, and
what the CPUSA might do, not because of the ideas they taught. The Cold
War might make these marginally more dangerous by encouraging a few
thoroughly indoctrinated comrades to practice what their leaders preached,
but the causal cord connecting Marxist-Leninist theory and revolutionary
action was long and tenuous. With anyone else but Communists, few lawyers or laymen would have found constitutionally sufficient justification
for cutting it at the point of mere preparation to teach. By making the
scope of First Amendment rights dependent not on *how* they were exer-
cized but *by whom, Dennis* created a dangerous precedent.[53]

V

Although there was little likelihood the high tribunal would change
its mind, the Communists nevertheless sought a rehearing. While lawyers
prepared the required motions, Elizabeth Gurley Flynn promoted a correspondence campaign aimed at Truman and intended to pressure the
President into persuading the Court to place rehearing on the agenda for

its October session. Liberal editor Aubrey Williams joined the Communists in urging the Court to reconsider its decision, but his support was exceptional. Few but weary fellow travelers came to the aid of the Party. On 18 June, backed by considerably less than a massive movement, the lawyers filed their petitions. One was a simple request for rehearing, whose strongest argument was that the lack of agreement among the six justices comprising the majority in *Dennis* had left the bounds of constitutionally protected speech in doubt. The Communists also asked for a rehearing on the order limiting the writ of certiorari.[54]

The Court accepted the petitions, but on 22 June, despite a barrage of Communist-inspired telegrams, it rejected a request to let the Eleven remain free on bail. Six days later, in New York, Judge Ryan, anticipating an order to put their sentences into effect, issued instructions to Harry Sacher for the Communist leaders to report to him on 2 July. When the Eleven appeared that day, they were only seven in number. Henry Winston, Gil Green, Robert Thompson, and Gus Hall had fled, forfeiting a total of $80,000 in bail.[55]

Their flight was no spur-of-the-moment action, for the Party leadership had debated at length whether some or all of the Eleven should go underground. Flynn and Winter argued that the CPUSA had other leaders capable of replacing the Smith Act victims and that for them to jump bail would only hurt the Party. Foster, Davis, and Thompson, however, convinced that the United States was entering a long Fascist-like period and that if the defendants entered prison, they would never emerge, insisted all of the Eleven should flee. Others, believing that the future held only reaction, not fascism, argued that in the days to come the CPUSA would have to function both legally and illegally and that the leadership should set an example for the entire organization to follow in this period of mixed operations, by having some of its members serve their sentences while the rest went underground. Finally, a majority voted for this compromise position. Thompson insisted on disappearing, and the group selected Winston, Green, Hall, and Dennis to join him. The General Secretary, never enthusiastic about going underground, failed to make his escape, because of what John Gates later called a "snafu." Gates himself was among those selected to go to prison, for, were he to flee it might endanger the legality of the Party newspaper. Because of his political prominence, Davis also stayed behind. These two, along with Dennis, Stachel, Potash, Williamson, and Winter, were soon on their way from New York to federal prisons around the country.[56]

Meanwhile, efforts continued to persuade the Supreme Court to reconsider its decision against them. Late in the afternoon of 18 June, after the filing of the motions for rehearing, Gates, in an apparently contrived move, had dismissed his counsel and retained John Raeburn Green, an anti-Communist lawyer seemingly interested only in the civil liberties aspects of the case. Green, an attorney with no use for labor defense, agreed to serve without fee, provided his client would give him a completely free hand. On 9 July he filed a petition for rehearing. All but one of the eight grounds on which Green based his request for reconsideration were objections to the Court's handling of the constitutional question. He went beyond the First Amendment issue only in contending that Gates deserved another hearing, because his former attorneys, burdened with contempt sentences and appeals of their own, had perhaps not been able to provide him with adequate and dispassionate representation.[57]

About two months later the Communists and their allies filed two documents embodying just the kind of matter with which Green did not wish to associate himself. In a supplemental petition for rehearing, the Foley Square defense lawyers, dismissing the legal issues as already adequately covered, urged a rehearing because the *Dennis* decision had denied the inalienable right of the people to organize a working-class party advocating scientific socialism and had given impetus to McCarthyism. Equally polemic was a petition from two black Illinois lawyers seeking permission to file a friend-of-the court memorandum.[58]

Neither such political appeals nor strictly legal ones did any good. On 8 October 1951, the Supreme Court denied the motions for rehearing. Speaking on behalf of the National Committee, Foster, Flynn, and Pettis Perry issued a statement condemning the actions of the justices. The CPUSA could do nothing more. Its fight was over.[59]

The Party had suffered a crushing defeat, and so had the First Amendment. The Supreme Court's "revolutionary departure from all previous interpretations of freedom of speech" had created what Aubrey Williams recognized as "a situation fraught with great danger and hazard. . . ." The possibilities for politically motivated abuse of *Dennis* were immense, and as Frankfurter realized, the Hand-Vinson modification of the clear-and-present-danger test could produce harmful results in future cases which had nothing to do with communism. In 1951 the First Amendment no longer meant what it once had. Because of judicial deliberations conducted in a Cold War climate, the right of each American to express his political beliefs now depended rather largely on who he was. As long as the emotions unleashed by Truman's crusade against international communism gripped the country, the legal principle which *Dennis* had established would threaten the liberties of all citizens. Those who realized that communism did not endanger freedom half so much as overreaction to it could only hope with Justice Black "that in calmer times, when present pressures, passions and fears subside, this or some later Court will restore the First Amendment liberties to the high preferred place where they belong in a free society."[60]

NOTES

1. Application of People *ex rel.* Rollins, *In re* Gates, 196 Misc. 770, 93 N.Y.S. 2d 147 (Sup. Ct. 1949); Davis V. Impelliteri, 197 Misc. 162, 94 N.Y.S. 2d 159 (Sup. Ct. 1950); "Communists: Bail and Bedlam," *Newsweek,* 14 November 1949, p. 25.

2. *DW,* 17 October 1949; Alexander Bittleman, "Reverse Wall Street's Verdict and Prevent the Outlawing of a Working-Class Political Party," *PA* 28 (November 1949): 1-2, 6-7; Gilbert Green, "For Communist Vigilance," *PA* 29 (May 1950): 115; Eugene Dennis, "For Communist Clarity and Resoluteness to Forge Working-Class and People's Unity," *PA* 29 (May 1950): 41-58; Elizabeth G. Flynn, "Mass Action Can Free the Eleven," *PA* 29 (May 1950): 150-52; Special Message to Congress, 8 August 1950, in U.S., Presidents, *Public Papers of the Presidents of the United States: Harry S. Truman,* 8 vols. (Washington, D.C.: GPO, 1961-66), 6: 207.

3. Eugene Dennis, "Let Us March Forward with Superior Confidence," *PA* 29 (July 1950): 10; "Communists on Appeal," *The Nation,* 1 July 1950, pp. 4-5.

4. Brief for Appellants on Jury Challenge, at 10-90, United States v. Dennis, 183 F. 2d 201 (2d Cir. 1950).

5. Brief for Appellants, at 6-403, United States v. Dennis, 183 F. 2d 201 (2d Cir. 1950).

6. *NYT,* 22 June 1950, p. 4; ACLU Weekly Bulletin no. 1443, 26 June 1950, pp. 1-2.

7. Marvin Shick, *Learned Hand's Court* (Baltimore and London: The Johns Hopkins Press, 1970), pp. 14-18, 19-21, 27-28; Irving Dillard's introduction to Learned Hand's *The Spirit of Liberty: Papers and Addresses of Learned Hand,* ed. Irving Dillard (New York: Alfred A. Knopf, 1952), pp. vii-xxii. Dillard quotes Frankfurter on p. xxii.

8. Memoranda by Thomas W. Swan, 6 June 1950, and Memorandum by Harrie Brigham Chase, 6 June 1950, all on United States v. Dennis, and all in Box 212, Learned Hand Papers, HLS; *NYT,* 22 June 1950, p. 4.

9. *NYT,* 22 June 1950, p. 4, and 23 June 1950, p. 5.

10. Ibid., 24 June 1950, p. 2.

11. Chase, Memorandum on United States v. Dennis, 30 June 1950, and Swan Memorandum on United States v. Dennis, 4 July 1950, Box 212, Hand Papers.

12. Masses Publishing Company v. Patton, 244 Fed. 535 (S.D.N.Y. 1917); Francis Biddle, *In Brief Authority* (Garden City, N.Y.: Doubleday & Co., 1962), p. 94; Gerald Gunther, "Learned Hand and the Ori-

gins of Modern First Amendment Doctrine: Some Fragments of History," *Stanford Law Review* 27 (February 1975): 721-28; Hand to Frankfurter, 8 June 1951, Box 64, Felix Frankfurter Papers, LC; Robert Samuel Lancaster, "The Jurisprudence and Political Thought of Learned Hand," (Ph.D. diss., University of Michigan, 1954), pp. 187-93, 199-201; Kathryn Griffith, *Judge Learned Hand and the Role of the Federal Judiciary* (Norman: University of Oklahoma Press, 1973), pp. 134-52; Elliot Richardson to Frankfurter, 27 August 1951, Box 40, Felix Frankfurter Papers, HLS. Hand did later point to "the Communist cases" as evidence of the beneficial results which judicial restraint had produced in the McCarthy era. "The Reminiscences of Judge Learned Hand," The Oral History Collection of Columbia University (1953), p. 159.

13. Shick, *Learned Hand's Court*, pp. 177-80; American Communications Association v. Douds, 339 U.S. 382 (1950); United States v. Dennis, 183 F. 2d 201 (2d Cir. 1950), at 211. Shick's discussion is not entirely satisfactory because, by failing to mention Hand's explicit statement that Douds was "not . . . authoritative here," he evades a hard question: whether the judge was following precedent or merely attempting to anticipate the political attitudes of his superiors.

14. United States v. Dennis, 183 F. 2d 201 (2d Cir. 1950).

15. Ibid., at 226.

16. Ibid., at 212.

17. Schenck v. United States, 249 U.S. 47 (1919); Whitney v. California, 274 U.S. 357 (1927), at 376; Hugh Calkins, "Memorandum on Dennis," Box 40, Frankfurter Papers, HLS.

18. United States v. Dennis, 183 F. 2d 201 (2d Cir. 1950), at 213.

19. Hand to Richardson, 29 February 1952, Box 64, Frankfurter Papers, LC.

20. Francis Wormuth, "Learned Legerdemain: A Grave But Implausible Hand," *Western Political Science Quarterly* 6 (September 1953): 550.

21. United States v. Dennis, 183 F. 2d 201 (2d Cir. 1950), at 236.

22. "Communism and Conspiracy," *New Republic*, 14 August 1950, p. 16; "Clear and Present Danger Re-examined," *Columbia Law Review* 51 (January 1951): 105-06; Memorandum, 17 August 1950, OF, HTL; "The Backdrop Changes," *Christian Science Monitor Magazine*, 19 August 1950, p. 3.

23. *DW*, 2 August 1950 and 25 October 1950; Alexander Bittleman, "We Are the Vanguard Party of Peace," *PA* 29 (September 1950): 14; Williamson v. United States, 184 F. 2d 280 (2d Cir. 1950); Petition for Writ of Certiorari, at 10-12, Dennis v. United States, 341 U.S. 494 (1951); Memorandum by Mr. Justice Frankfurter on Motion to Postpone Argument, Box 40, Frankfurter Papers, HLS; Dennis v. United States, 340 U.S. 863 (1950) and 340 U.S. 887 (1950).

24. Felix Frankfurter, "Memorandum for the Conference," 27 Feb-

ruary 1951, Hugo L. Black Papers, LC; Dennis v. United States, 339 U. S. 162 (1950); Harold W. Chase, *Security and Liberty: The Problem of Native Communists 1947-1955* (Garden City, N.Y.: Doubleday & Co., 1955), p. 15; C. Herman Pritchett, *Civil Liberties and the Vinson Court* (Chicago: University of Chicago Press, 1954), pp. 19-20; Walter F. Murphy, *Congress and the Court: A Case Study in the American Political Process* (Chicago: University of Chicago Press, 1962), pp. 72-73; Richard Kirkendall, "Tom Clark" and "Sherman Minton," in *The Justices of the United States Supreme Court 1789-1969: Their Lives and Major Opinions,* eds. Leon Friedman and Fred L. Israel, 4 vols. (New York and London: Chelsea House and R. R. Bowker, 1969), 4: 2665-68, 2699-703.

25. Pritchett, *Civil Liberties,* pp. 2, 20; Murphy, *Congress and the Court,* p. 73; Richard Kirkendall, "Harold Burton" and "Fred Vinson," in Friedman and Israel, *Justices of the Supreme Court,* 4: 2617-21, 2639-47.

26. Pritchett, *Civil Liberties,* pp. 17-18; John P. Frank, *Mr. Justice Black: The Man and His Opinions* (New York: Alfred A. Knopf, 1949), pp. 118-21, and "William O. Douglas" and "Hugo L. Black," in Friedman and Israel, *Justices of the Supreme Court,* 4: 2324-36, 2463-65; William O. Douglas, *Being an American* (New York: John Day Co., 1948), pp. 188-202, and *An Almanac of Liberty* (Garden City, N.Y.: Doubleday, 1954), p. 284.

27. Pritchett, *Civil Liberties,* pp. 17-18 and "Stanley Reed," in Friedman and Israel, *Justices of the Supreme Court,* 4: 2374-81.

28. Liva Baker, *Felix Frankfurter* (New York: Coward-McCann, 1969), pp. 94-95, 103, 119; Helen Shirley Thomas, *Felix Frankfurter, Scholar on the Bench* (Baltimore: Johns Hopkins Press, 1960), pp. 20-21.

29. Pritchett, *Civil Liberties,* p. 18. Hand believed Jackson "wrote the best opinions on the Court." "Learned Hand Reminisences," p. 87.

30. Frankfurter to Reed, 15 March 1951, Box 40, Frankfurter Papers, HLS; Brief for Petitioners, at 5-45 (quote on p. 45), Motion of National Lawyers Guild to File Brief as Amicus Curiae, and Motion of American Civil Liberties Union to File Brief as Amicus Curiae, Dennis v. United States, 341 U.S. 494 (1951).

31. Brief for the United States, at 157-63, Dennis v. United States, 341 U.S. 494 (1951) (quote on pp. 158-59).

32. Reply Brief for Petitioners, at 2-17, 27-28, Dennis v. United States, 341 U.S. 494 (1951).

33. *NYT,* 5 December 1950, p. 20; *DW,* 4 December 1950; "Argument by George Crockett, Jr., on the Constitutionality of the Smith Act in the Case of United States v. Dennis et al., United States Supreme Court, December 4, 1950," Meiklejohn Civil Liberties Library, Berkeley, California; "Diary for 1950," Box 2, Harold Burton Papers, LC.

34. *DW,* 5 December 1950.

35. Dennis v. United States, 341 U.S. 494 (1951); Interview with Howard J. Trienens and Newton N. Minow, 27 February 1975, Fred M. Vinson Oral History Project, University of Kentucky. All quotes are from Trienens.

36. Dennis v. United States, 341 U.S. 494 (1951). Shick's contention (*Learned Hand's Court*, p. 181) that Hand's opinion proved useful to Vinson, but did not influence the Supreme Court's decision, is clearly correct. In my analysis of the majority opinion in *Dennis* I have drawn insights from Milton R. Konvitz, *Fundamental Liberties of a Free People: Religion, Speech, Press, Assembly* (Ithaca, N.Y.: Cornell University Press, 1957), pp. 317-18; Pritchett, *Civil Liberties*, p. 73; Walter Berns, *Freedom, Virtue and the First Amendment* (Baton Rouge: Louisiana State University Press, 1957), pp. 205-06, 225; Eugene V. Rostow, "The Democratic Character of Judicial Review," *Harvard Law Review* 56 (December 1952): 218-20; and Louis Boudin, " 'Seditious Doctrines' and the 'Clear and Present Danger' Rule," *Virginia Law Review* 38 (February 1952): 155-56, 182-86, and (April 1952): 324-34. See also Marvin Shapiro, *Freedom of Speech: The Supreme Court and Judicial Review* (Englewood Cliffs, N.J.: Prentice-Hall, 1966), pp. 64-66.

37. Dennis v. United States, at 509.

38. Ibid., at 510.

39. Ibid., at 510-11.

40. Reed to Frankfurter, 13 March 1951, Box 40, Frankfurter Papers, HLS.

41. Dennis v. United States, at 517.

42. Ibid., at 539.

43. Ibid., at 547.

44. For critical analysis of Frankfurter's opinion see Konvitz, *Fundamental Liberties*, pp. 332-33.

45. Ibid.

46. Dennis v. United States, at 589. For a celebration of the Douglas dissent see Alan Barth, *Prophets with Honor: Great Dissents and Great Dissenters in the Supreme Court* (New York: Vintage Books, 1975), pp. 155-83.

47. "Communists: Worse Days Coming," *Newsweek*, 18 June 1951, p. 24; *DW*, 5 June 1951; *PW*, 5 June 1951 and 6 June 1951; National Committee, CPUSA, "America's Hour of Peril—Unite! Save Democracy and Peace!" *PA* 30 (July 1951): 2.

48. *DW*, 5 June 1951, 6 June 1951, 8 June 1951, and 11 June 1951; "Strait-jacketing Free Speech," *The Nation*, 16 June 1951, pp. 552-53; "The Nature of the Danger," *Commonweal*, 22 June 1951, p. 252; *Militant*, 11 June 1951, p. 3; ACLU Weekly Bulletin no. 1496, 2 July 1951, p. 1, and no. 1517, 26 November 1951, p. 1. The Eleven quoted from four of the five major newspapers in their Petition for Rehearing, at 3-5, Dennis v. United States, 341 U.S. 494 (1951), omitting only the

World. Its support was noted by *DW,* 6 June 1951. *Newsweek* ("Communists: Worse Days Coming," p. 24) had earlier said there were only two.

49. *Washington Post,* 6 June 1951; *New Orleans Times-Picayune,* 5 June 1951; "Communists: Worse Days Coming," p. 25; *NYT,* 10 June 1951, sec. 4, p. 8; *Chicago Tribune,* 6 June 1951.

50. *Los Angeles Times,* 6 June 1951; *Denver Post,* 5 June 1951; *San Francisco Chronicle,* 5 June 1951.

51. Charles Lam Markmann, *The Noblest Cry: A History of the American Civil Liberties Union* (New York: St. Martins Press, 1965), p. 176; *NYT,* 1 July 1951, sec. 4, p. 6; Boudin, "Seditious Doctrines" (February), pp. 155-56, 180-81, 186, and (April), pp. 324-34; Robert McCloskey, "Free Speech, Sedition and the Constitution," *American Political Science Review* 45 (September 1951): 168; John A. Gorfinkel and Julian W. Mack II, *"Dennis v. United States* and the Clear and Present Danger Rule," *California Law Review* 39 (December 1951): 495-500; Chester James Antieau, "Dennis v. United States—Precedent, Principle, or Perversion?" *Vanderbilt Law Review* 5 (February 1952): 143-46; Wormuth, "Learned Legerdemain," p. 555; Rostow, "Democratic Character," pp. 222-24.

52. Edward S. Corwin, "Bowing Out 'Clear and Present Danger,' " *Notre Dame Lawyer* 27 (Spring 1952): 358; Wallace Mendelson, "Clandestine Speech and the First Amendment—A Reappraisal of the Dennis Case," *Michigan Law Review* 51 (February 1953): 554-58 and "Clear and Present Danger—From Schenck to Dennis," *Columbia Law Review* 52 (March 1952): 330-31; Elliot L. Richardson, "Freedom of Expression and the Function of Courts," *Harvard Law Review* 65 (November 1951): 11-12, 18.

53. Sidney Hook, *Heresy, Yes—Conspiracy No!* (Garden City, N.Y.: Doubleday, 1953), pp. 105-06. In 1969 the Supreme Court would overturn the conviction of a Ku Klux Klan member who during a rally advocated the desirability of revolution under certain circumstances, holding that even this actual speech was too far removed from the ultimate evil of violent revolution to be constitutionally punishable (Brandenburg v. Ohio, 395 U.S. 444 [1969]).

54. *DW,* 11 June 1951, 14 June 1951, and 15 June 1951; *PW,* 15 June 1951; Williams to Chief Justice Fred Vinson, 13 June 1951, Box 308, Black Papers; Petition for Rehearing, at 2-13, and Motion for Leave to File Petition for Rehearing of Order Limiting Certiorari, Dennis v. United States, 341 U.S. 494 (1951).

55. *NYT,* 22 June 1951, p. 10, 23 June 1951, p. 6, and 3 July 1951, p. 5; United States v. Thompson, 177 F. Supp., 685 (S.D.N.Y. 1953); Testimony by Kevin T. Maroney, Internal Security Section, Criminal Division, Department of Justice, in HJC, *Hearings . . . on H.R. 3, Bill to Amend Title 18 United States Code to Provide Punishment for Persons Who Jump Bail,* 83rd Cong., 2d sess., 1954, p. 6.

56. Joseph R. Starobin, *American Communism in Crisis 1943-1957* (Cambridge, Mass.: Harvard University Press, 1972), p. 306, n. 10.

57. Petition for Rehearing of Gates, at 1-5, Dennis v. United States, 341 U.S. 494 (1951).

58. Supplemental Petition for Rehearing, at 1-4, and Petition for Leave to File Memorandum of Amici Curiae in Support of Petition for Rehearing, Dennis v. United States, 341 U.S. 494 (1951).

59. Dennis v. United States, 342 U.S. 842 (1951); National Committee, CPUSA, "The Court of Last Appeal Is the American People," *PA* 30 (October 1951): 1-3.

60. Williams to Vinson, 13 June 1951, Box 308, Black Papers; Frankfurter to Reed, 15 March 1951, Box 40, Frankfurter Papers, HLS; Dennis v. United States, 341 U.S. 494 (1951), at 581.

6
Repeat Performances

[The Dennis *case] was like the national company and the rest were the road shows.*
—Ann Fagan Ginger, interviewing Mary Kaufman
in *The Relevant Lawyers*

As the first light of dawn colored the Manhattan sky, a hundred FBI agents streamed out of the Foley Square Federal Building and piled into a fleet of waiting Buicks. While most of New York still slept, they rolled unnoticed through its streets. At 7:30 a.m. the wife of Simon Gerson heard a knock at the door of their Brooklyn apartment, and when she opened it, two agents barged in, awakened her sleeping husband, and dragged him away to Foley Square. At nineteen other homes around the city there were similar knocks that morning. Some of the intended victims were not at home, but the FBI managed to snare sixteen Communists in New York and another in Pittsburgh. It was 20 June 1951, and although the Eleven were not yet in prison, the all-out attack on the CPUSA made possible by the *Dennis* decision had begun. A nationwide assault, it would produce repeat performances of the Foley Square trial in cities from New Haven to Honolulu, staged not only to destroy the Party but also to educate the public about the menace of communism and to advance the interests of politicians and internal security bureaucrats.[1]

I

Preparations for this expanded war against the Party had begun long before June 1951. Apparently soon after the court of appeals upheld the Foley Square convictions, Attorney General McGrath summoned U.S. attorneys from across the country to Washington, where he laid before them plans to prosecute the regional leaders of the CPUSA. Public statements by McGrath and his subordinates made it clear that the Justice

Department was waiting only for a green light from the Supreme Court, and the Party had no illusions about what the future held. "[W]e don't doubt . . . ," wrote the *People's World* on 18 June 1951, "that the conviction of the 11 was only a beginning."[2]

It was indeed, as events two days later demonstrated. The FBI's targets on 20 June included most of the top national and New York Communists not previously prosecuted. The leading figure in the group was Elizabeth Gurley Flynn. Five alternate members of the National Committee—Pettis Perry, Claudia Jones, Sidney Steinberg, Fred Fine, and James Jackson— were also indicted, although the last three managed to slip through the fingers of the FBI. The others charged were all members of the National Education Commission, and many had other responsibilities as well. Alexander Trachtenberg, for example, headed the dummy corporation which published the *Daily Worker*, and V. J. Jerome, in addition to editing *Political Affairs*, was the chairman of the Party's Cultural Commission.[3]

"The new batch of indictments demonstrate [sic] that the government intends to follow up the Supreme Court decision by beheading the Communist Party of its leadership throughout the country," California organizational secretary Oleta Yates told a West Coast audience a few days later. On 26 July Yates herself was arrested. The government also indicted fourteen other California Communists, including Los Angeles leader Dorothy Healy, who had refused an offer of immunity if she would testify against the rest. The preeminent figure in the group was William Schneiderman, state chairman, American representative to the Comintern, alternate member of the National Committee, and long one of the leading figures in the CPUSA. Also arrested were two *People's World* officials, several members of the state board, five Los Angeles County functionaries, and a local organizer from San Francisco.[4]

Next came an assault on the past and present leadership of the Maryland Party. On 7 August the FBI arrested the head of District Four, George Myers, in Baltimore, and his predecessor, Philip Frankfeld, in New York. When Myers asked to consult with counsel, an FBI agent told him, "Don't worry. You'll see a lawyer soon enough." The next day his attorney, Maurice Braverman, arrived at the jail—in handcuffs. He too had been arrested. So had Frankfeld's wife, Washington, D.C., chairman Roy Wood, and Dorothy Blumberg, a former District Four secretary-treasurer, now residing in Brooklyn.[5]

Two days later the FBI struck again, taking into custody in Philadelphia Steve Mesarosh, chairman of the Western Pennsylvania Party. This Moscow-trained Communist, generally known as Steve Nelson, had long been one of the top figures in the American Stalinist movement. The

same day, authorities also arrested a former head of the Communist organization in West Virginia, now employed at national headquarters, two district officials, a steel industry organizer, and the Western Pennsylvania
representative of the *Daily Worker.*[6]

The next attack came in Hawaii, where the FBI took seven persons into
custody on 28 August. The best-known figure in the group was Jack Hall,
local leader of Harry Bridges's International Longshoreman's and Warehouseman's Union (ILWU). Also arrested were Charles Fujimoto, chairman
of the local Communist organization, his wife, and four other men who had
served on the territorial board. The Hawaiian Party was tiny, but McGrath
announced that he considered this blow at it extremely important—because
of the strategic significance of the islands in the fight against communism in
the Pacific.[7]

Having secured the nation's western defense frontier, the Justice Department rested. Not until the height of the 1952 presidential campaign,
amid Republican charges that the Truman administration was soft on communism, did the department resume its attack on the CPUSA. On 17 September 1952, the FBI seized leaders of the Michigan, Missouri, and Washington Parties. The group arrested in Detroit included two organizational secretaries (one of them Carl Winter's wife), two Communists specializing in
auto industry work, and a *Daily Worker* correspondent. Among the Missouri leaders taken into custody were state chairman James Forest and
United Electrical, Radio, and Machine Workers' official William Sentner, a
one-time member of the federal government's Seventh Regional War Labor
Board. The FBI also apprehended three of their associates and Forest's
wife. Arrests in Oregon, Washington, and Illinois netted six Pacific Northwest functionaries, including District Twelve Chairman Henry Huff and
Terry Pettus, a regional editor of the *People's World.* While this roundup
was in progress, President Truman stood before a Washington audience
describing his administration's drive against the Communists as a major
feature of the national campaign to eliminate subversion.[8]

The government's attack on the CPUSA temporarily lost momentum
after Truman turned over the White House to his Republican successor,
Dwight Eisenhower. But the new Attorney General, Herbert Brownell,
regarded domestic communism as a menace and supported the Smith
Act. Under his leadership the Justice Department "focused on those areas
where the Party's numerical concentration [was] well organized and disciplined," especially heavy industrial centers and ports. On 27 July 1953,
the FBI struck again, this time in the Philadelphia area, taking into custody three Eastern Pennsylvania District officials, the former editor of a
regional *Daily Worker* edition, and a one-time Party organizer. The FBI

also seized David Dubensky, once a member of the National Committee.[9]

After Philadelphia came Cleveland, where, on 9 October, government attorneys obtained indictments against eleven Communists, the most prominent of whom were Joseph Dougher, a former member of the National Committee, and George Watt, secretary of the National Review Commission. While this group consisted mainly of Party officials, from local through state level, it also included Elvidore Greenfield, an officer of the CRC. Eight of the indicted radicals were already in custody, and on 4 November Hoover announced that FBI agents in Pittsburgh had arrested the others, among them Foley Square witness Anthony Krechmarek.[10]

By the end of 1953, the Eisenhower administration, its right flank under fire from Senator McCarthy, had decided to emphasize domestic subversion in the following year's congressional campaign. No other issue seemed capable of unifying the badly factionalized Republican Party and carrying it to victory. During his early years in the White House, Eisenhower had taken a moderate position on the Communist issue, refusing to denounce McCarthy, but at the same time pursuing what he characterized as a "steady, positive policy. . . ." Now he took a hard line. In his January 1954 State of the Union Message the President requested passage of a law stripping convicted Smith Act violators of their citizenship. The Republican leadership expedited the proposed legislation, and on 30 August, two days after signing the Expatriation Act of 1954, Ike boasted that working together he and Congress would "blot out the Communist conspiracy." August saw Vice-President Richard Nixon on the campaign trail, charging that there were sinister ties between the Democrats and the CPUSA.[11]

With the administration determined to reap political profit from the Communist issue, and with the Justice Department under the leadership of the most politically minded member of the cabinet, additional Smith Act prosecutions were inevitable. On 4 June the government secured indictments against eight Connecticut functionaries, including state chairman Sid Taylor and his predecessor, Simon Silverman. Most of those taken into custody had worked at the state level, but one was a veteran section organizer. Two months later the FBI announced the arrest of five Rocky Mountain Communists, three of whom were members of the Party's expanding underground apparatus. The biggest catch was Arthur Bary, who, as a specialist in combating FBI penetration of the CPUSA, had worked closely with the top leaders of the organization. The Bureau also arrested his wife, Anita, ranking officials of the Colorado and Utah Parties, and Patricia Blau, a contact with the underground. Near the end of October the administration moved to shore up another of the island links in the nation's defense perimeter, indicting eleven Puerto Rican Communists

for conspiracy to violate the Smith Act. The 1954 campaign also produced six prosecutions under the membership clause of the act. All of
these arrests provided ideal support for the President's 8 October boast
that "There is no vacillation nor inaction on the part of this Administration in dealing with those who, by force or violence, would overthrow
the government of the United States."[12]

Soon after the election, the Justice Department stopped initiating
new cases. Hoover was becoming concerned about the number of "valuable current confidential informants" the trials were unmasking, and the
extent to which this was reducing "the highly essential intelligence coverage which this Bureau must maintain in the internal security field." He
urged that in the future only "top leaders," not "lesser functionaries,"
be tried, and that, "before prosecution is initiated, a most careful evalu-
ation . . . be made of the FBI informants who are to be used as witnesses
in order that it can be determined whether a greater benefit will result to
the security of the country through prosecution or through preservation
of our informants." Hoover's restraining influence kept the department
from seeking further indictments until the presidential election year of
1956 when Deputy Attorney General William Rogers recommended that
Republicans include in their platform both an assurance that "All laws regarding subversion and disloyalty have been vigorously enforced so as to protect our country," and a report on the exact number of convictions obtained since 1953. The Justice Department launched three more membership prosecutions and also secured a conspiracy indictment against seven
Massachusetts Communists, including present and past state chairpersons
Otis Hood and Ann Burlak Timpson. This Boston group was the last ever
prosecuted for conspiring to violate the Smith Act.[13]

Since 4 June 1951 the government had charged 126 Communists with
that offense. The media commonly referred to them as the "second-string"
leadership of the Party, but that description was not entirely accurate.
Elizabeth Gurley Flynn, a full member of the National Committee, was as
much a member of the "first string" as any of the Foley Square defendants,
and men like William Schneiderman, Steve Nelson, and Pettis Perry ranked
close behind her in status and influence. On the other hand, some of those
indicted were only county- or section-level functionaries. Probably because of the heavy emphasis on literary evidence in Smith Act cases, a
large number of the defendants were journalists writing for Stalinist publications. Some of those prosecuted, such as Maryland attorney Maurice
Braverman, who had often defended other Communists in court, and
Hawaiian labor leader Jack Hall, whose position with the left-wing ILWU
made him one of the most hated men in the islands, seem to have been

indicted less because of their standing in the CPUSA than because of the extensive publicity which their connections with radical activity had received. The only things common to all 126 were membership in the CPUSA and indictment for conspiracy to violate the Smith Act.[14]

II

The Party waged a futile fight to save these comrades from conviction, setting up new front groups and defense committees to mobilize moral and financial support for them. Among the groups created was the Committee to Defend V. J. Jerome, which enlisted well over a hundred artists and intellectuals, among them Paul Robeson and William E. B. Du Bois. Communist defense campaigns emphasized amnesty, a theme that the Party leadership hoped would have widespread appeal and could be exploited to halt the prosecutions. Some Stalinists, among them Elizabeth Gurley Flynn, felt sure that the CPUSA could build up a tremendous mass movement around its demands, but, as Eugene Dennis feared, progressive and democratic elements failed to get the Party's message, and most of the defense campaigns floundered. About the only significant support for amnesty came from a group headed by Eleanor Roosevelt, Norman Thomas, Lewis Mumford, and Henry Steele Commager, which did not speak up until the end of 1955. "Even at this late date, only a small minority of Americans grasp the national and world significance of the Smith Act outrages," Dennis complained to his wife in July 1953. The situation never improved, and in September 1955 Illinois Party leader Claude Lightfoot had to concede: "In almost all instances the mass fight failed to substantially get off the ground."[15]

While the CPUSA struggled unsuccessfully to arouse the public, juries ground out Smith Act convictions with monotonous regularity. Of the 126 Communists indicated after 4 June 1951, only ten won acquittal. One case ended in a hung jury, three Communists were severed from their codefendants because of ill health, and one died while awaiting trial. After the Supreme Court's 1957 decision in the *Yates* case, the government decided not to try eighteen of those against whom it had obtained indictments, but of the 105 Party leaders who stood trial and lived to see a judge and jury determine their fate, 93, or just under 89 percent, suffered conviction.[16]

The reason, charged William Z. Foster, was "the present war hysteria." Like the Eleven, later Smith Act defendants were casualties of the Soviet-American confrontation. Certainly, it was not the evidence that convicted

them. Not even Tom Clark, who had supervised early planning for the attack on the second-string Communists, considered the cases against them
strong. Yet the Detroit jury needed only six hours and twenty-three minutes to return guilty verdicts, despite the fact that there were a half dozen
defendants and presentation of the evidence had required fourteen weeks;
and the Baltimore jury spent less time deliberating than the judge had
charging it. One juror in the Honolulu case reported later that it had taken
his fellows less than an hour to decide that the Communist Party was a
conspiracy; many had made up their minds before the trial began.[17]

Judges actually treated Smith Act defendants better than did juries.
Courts consistently refused to set aside guilty verdicts or grant new trials,
but in imposing sentence most did not go nearly as far as the law allowed.
The 1948 revision of the *United States Code* provided a penalty of up to
five years in prison and a $10,000 fine for conspiracy to violate the Smith
Act, but only Judge William Mathes in Los Angeles imposed the maximum
sentence on all defendants. The six Communists tried in Detroit were the
only others assessed $10,000 fines, whereas thirty-six of those found guilty
elsewhere had to pay none at all. Judges also imposed only thirty-nine
five-year prison sentences, against fifty-five of less than maximum duration.[18]

While trial jurists frequently showed some mercy toward Smith Act
defendants, their colleagues on the appellate bench displayed almost none.
Courts of appeals affirmed every conviction that came before them during
the six years after the *Dennis* decision. None seriously questioned a district
judge's handling of First Amendment claims nor his conduct of a trial. The
Supreme Court did little more for convicted Communists. In 1953 it refused to hear the Baltimore case and two years later rejected a petition
for a writ of certiorari from Flynn and the other members of the second
New York group. Only the Pittsburgh defendants benefited from Supreme
Court action, gaining a new trial because of a ruling that their convictions
might have resulted from perjured testimony.[19]

Although the appellate road generally led to jail, Smith Act victims
continued to take it, bypassing other routes which they might have followed to freedom. One of these was flight. Of the eight Smith Act victims
who chose to flee, five succeeded. To be sure, the failures were spectacular
and no doubt unsettled other Communists contemplating similar action.
Gus Hall, ignoring a warning from the California Party that Mexico was
unsafe for Yankee radicals, tried to hide south of the border, and by October 1951 Mexican authorities had turned him over to the FBI. The flight
of Robert Thompson and Sidney Steinberg, a fugitive from the second
New York roundup, also ended in failure when, on 27 August 1952, fifteen FBI agents, disguised as fishermen, surprised them at a remote cabin

near Twain Hart, California. But the overall record of the Bureau in apprehending Smith Act fugitives was unimpressive. The others (Henry Winston, Gil Green, Fred Fine, James Jackson, and William Marron) remained at large until 1955-1956, when they surrendered voluntarily. Clearly, flight offered Smith Act victims an alternative to appellate litigation which was far more likely to keep them out of prison. Yet few attempted it.[20]

Another option, at least for some, was exile to Russia. In February 1952 Judge Edward Dimock gave the thirteen Communists convicted in New York's second trial a choice between jail and banishment to the USSR, and a year later Frank Picard made a similar offer to six Michigan Communists. Both groups refused to go, New York defendant Flynn telling Dimock, "We feel we belong here and have a political responsibility here. We feel we would be traitors to the American people if we turned our backs on them just to escape jail."[21]

Her words explain not only the refusal of Smith Act defendants to accept exile but also why so few fled from prosecution. The Party regarded itself as a political force, not a criminal conspiracy. Indicted members could not run without admitting that their organization was what its enemies charged. Nor could they, merely to stay out of jail, abandon that leadership of the American working class assigned to them by Marxism-Leninism. Most prosecuted Stalinists had to stand and fight, for in no other way could the Party prove to the masses that the government was framing it. Unable to recognize the hopelessness of their situation, Communists eschewed the alternatives to litigation and accepted continuing courtroom combat with the Smith Act.[22]

III

Again and again that law defeated them. A kind of grinding monotony characterized these trials, for although there was some variation between individual Smith Act cases, on the whole they were extremely repetitious, both of *Dennis* and of each other. To be sure, the passage of time did produce certain surface changes. Whereas the conspiracy charged against the Foley Square defendants had supposedly been conceived during the period of preparation and planning prior to the reconstitution convention of July 1945, by the time the Supreme Court decided *Dennis*, the events of those days were already six years in the past. Defendants in the later cases regularly insisted that the three-year statute of limitations barred those parts of the indictments against them that charged conspiracy to organize the CPUSA. Although often raised, this contention seldom prevailed. Trial judges in New York and Pittsburgh did sustain it, but others in

Los Angeles, Seattle, Honolulu, Baltimore, Detroit, Cleveland, and Puerto
Rico, refused to do so. Their reason was that under settled principles of
conspiracy law the statute of limitations ran only from the commission
of the last overt act, not from the date when the schemers entered into
their illegal concert.[23]

The enactment of new federal legislation also produced changes, although these were more apparent than real. The provision of the revised
United States Code covering conspiracy to violate any and all federal
laws, unlike the separate conspiracy section of the Smith Act, required
proof that defendants had committed an overt act in furtherance of their
agreement. Thus in all of the post-*Dennis* cases it was necessary both to
allege and to prove the commission of such acts. Because these deeds
did not have to be themselves unlawful, prosecutors usually satisfied
this requirement with evidence of such relatively innocuous actions as
attendance at meetings. Against Pettis Perry it alleged only that he "did
leave thirty-five East Twelfth Street, New York, N.Y.," the national
headquarters of the CPUSA.[24]

Like the new conspiracy section, the Internal Security Act of 1950
somewhat altered the structural design of Smith Act cases without changing their essential nature. Section 4(f) of that law declared that neither
holding office in nor belonging to a Communist organization should constitute per se violation of any federal law. Congress seems to have framed
the language of this provision in response to fears that the new statute,
which required Communist organizations and individuals to register with
the government, might compel self-incrimination with respect to the
Smith Act, thus violating the Fifth Amendment. The adoption of section
4(f) appeared to constitute a legislative policy decision favoring registration over prosecution as a method of protecting national security. With
this provision on the books, the Justice Department seemingly could no
longer equate the CPUSA with a conspiracy to violate the Smith Act
and in order to obtain a conviction would have to offer proof of something more than a defendant's activities as an officer and a member of the
Party. Trial courts regularly instructed juries that mere membership, or
even the holding of an office, in the radical organization was not sufficient evidence from which to infer guilt of conspiracy. But these judges
also charged that many kinds of normal Party activity might justify an
inference of intent to accomplish unlawful objectives, and thus support
a conviction. Such evidence was, of course, the same sort presented at
Foley Square.[25]

The effect of the Communist Control Act of 1954 was similar. It contained a "Findings of Fact" section which branded the CPUSA a conspiracy to overthrow the government of the United States and announced

that the Party's existence constituted a clear and present danger to national security. In passing this law, Congress had provided answers to the major questions confronting a Smith Act jury and judge respectively, and defendant members of the CPUSA naturally objected. The Cleveland group contended that the new statute had amended or repealed the old one, making it an ex post facto law, a bill of attainder, and a violation of due process. The Connecticut defendants also argued that the 1954 law had repealed the 1940 one, but the trial courts rejected both of these claims. In Connecticut Judge Robert Anderson concluded that Congress had made its findings of fact only for and in connection with the new law. "In the present case," he wrote, "the Government has the burden of proving all of the essential elements of the offense charged, just as if the Communist Control Act had never been passed. . . . "[26]

Despite enactment of several statutes bearing in one way or another on the Smith Act, cases tried under that law actually changed very little. They remained in fact, if not in theory, simply prosecutions of the CPUSA. The government generally disclaimed any intent to try the Party, but the indictments charged conspiracy, and, despite their denials, prosecutors usually equated the radical organization with the alleged illegal concert. They presented extensive evidence about underground operations and clandestine activity, which could serve no other purpose than to characterize the CPUSA as conspiratorial. Furthermore, given the fact that in Smith Act cases much of the most damaging evidence offered by the government always consisted of testimony about things said by Communists other than the defendants, the tendency to equate the Party with the conspiracy mentioned in the indictments was more or less inevitable. Unless made by co-conspirators, these third-party statements were inadmissible hearsay, but because the major, if not the only, connection between the person making them and the defendants was the Party, the government was in effect treating the CPUSA as the conspiracy.[27] In New York, defense attorney John McTernan observed:

> There was . . . supposed to be some other conspiracy hidden
> away somewhere below or alongside of or underneath some-
> thing in the Communist Party. . . . As the evidence unfolds,
> and the Government gets into greater and greater difficulty
> establishing a basis for the admission of these declarations,
> we find them closer and closer to saying the Communist Party
> is the conspiracy.[28]

Judges handled this issue in much the same way as did prosecutors. Although denying that the nature of the Party was an issue in the California case, William Mathes left little doubt that he equated the CPUSA with the alleged illegal concert, and the U.S. Fourth Circuit Court of Appeals talked freely about "the conspiracy in which the Communist Party was engaged." In the Third Circuit, judges resorted to sarcasm to brush aside complaints about the use of participation and office holding in the CPUSA to link defendants to a supposed plot. The legal commentator who remarked that in post-*Dennis* cases "the prosecution has treated the Communist Party itself as the conspiracy against which the [Smith Act] is directed" might well have extended his observation to embrace the federal judiciary.[29]

Actually, the numerous proceedings that followed *Dennis* were but variations of a single trial, with the CPUSA as the defendant. The indictments in these cases were nearly identical, and the courtroom proceedings were, like the endurance contest at Foley Square, agonizingly long; the seven-month Honolulu trial, for example, ended as the lengthiest in the history of Hawaii. A number of actors appeared in more than one performance of the Smith Act drama. The Justice Department sent out specialists from Washington to prosecute such cases, and several defense lawyers—among them Richard Gladstein, George Crockett, and Mary Kaufman—also participated in more than one. Some prosecution witnesses moved from trial to trial, and numerous Communists also took part in two or more trials, with the same person often appearing first as a witness and then later as a defendant.

The most obvious and fundamental similarity among the trials was their central issue: the meaning of Marxism-Leninism. Prosecutors contended that Communist dogma dictated the forceful overthrow of American governmental institutions and argued that juries might infer the intent of individual defendants to bring about violent revolution from their advocacy of that creed. The evidence they presented supported their contentions, but many of the quotations used by Justice Department lawyers were quite dated, and defendants disputed the applicability of these to current American conditions. The picture of Marxism-Leninism sketched by prosecution witnesses who had served as FBI informants was the slanted product of biased examination. One of these plants, Charles Litt, admitted that, prior to inserting him into the Party, the Bureau had affirmed that the CPUSA advocated violent overthrow of the government and then asked him to verify this proposition.[30]

The defense, of course, disputed such characterizations of Marxism-Leninism. As a witness in her own case, California Communist Oleta Yates presented a comprehensive statement of the Party position on the meaning of that philosophy, in which she maintained that the CPUSA had never taught the violent overthrow of the government. Yates sketched a picture of the Stalinist creed quite similar to that which Foster had presented at Foley Square. Armed conflict would accompany revolution, she explained, only if the ruling classes used force to block social change. "[S]o long as the democratic channels" were open and "democracy [was] continued and even expanded, . . . there [was] no need for fearing strife or violence. . . ." In any event, socialism was not an immediate issue in the United States, as the people here were not yet ready for it, Yates said. Until the masses reached a more advanced state of political awareness, the mission of the CPUSA would be simply to improve bourgeois democracy.[31]

A similar picture of Marxism-Leninism emerged from the testimony of Dr. John Somerville, a non-Communist academic who appeared as an expert witness in Philadelphia, Cleveland, and New York. Somerville, who was accustomed to classroom lecturing, found his role in Smith Act cases frustrating, because of the artificial impediments which the legal process placed in the way of an orderly and comprehensive presentation of his subject matter. Also distressing was the fact that no one seemed to pay much attention to him. Although Somerville was convinced that the ideas contained in Communist teaching did not make necessary an attempt, or even a conspiracy to attempt, to overthrow the U.S. government by force and violence, the belief that they did was so widespread that it made attempting to convince his listeners otherwise an exercise in futility.[32]

Nothing better demonstrated the hopelessness of Somerville's undertaking than the readiness with which juries accepted the concept of Aesopian language. When it suited their purposes, government attorneys would assert that Communists disdained to hide their views and would offer quotations as proof that they advocated violent overthrow of the government. When confronted with literature that failed to support their thesis, prosecutors would suddenly point to Aesopian language, contending that the document in question was just double-talk, designed to hide the real intentions of crafty conspirators. This was "Sort of a 'heads I win, tails you lose' proposition," Los Angeles defense attorney Ben Margolis lamented. "You can't beat it."[33]

Yet despite the futility of the undertaking, the Communists continued to engage the government in literary debates. The result was trials that were, like the original one at Foley Square, essentially battles of quotations. The government's selections invariably bristled with dangerous-sounding phrases such as "turn the imperialist war into civil war" and "smash the state machinery." The defense, contending that the prosecution had ripped the damning passages out of context, would counter with extended quotations intended to put them into what Communists regarded as the proper perspective. The result was 15,000-page transcripts which owed almost half of their bulk to a mishmash of disjointed literary excerpts. In the second New York trial, the reading of quotations became so tiresome that one juror fell asleep.[34]

Prosecutors seldom made any attempt to prove that individual defendants understood or interpreted all this Marxist-Leninist material as demanding forcible overthrow of the U. S. government. They simply loosed a literary avalanche upon the jurors and let them draw their own conclusions. As Somerville pointed out, under such conditions not even a qualified scholar could have formed accurate opinions and arrived at balanced judgments. "And among the jurors who sat in . . . Smith Act trials, there was probably not a single professional scholar. Yet they were expected to decide intricate issues of ideological doctrine."[35]

To help the jurors arrive at what they considered correct conclusions prosecutors supplied witnesses who not only identified literary evidence but also testified about the meaning placed on it by Communists and explained how Party teaching had manifested itself in the activities of the CPUSA. Those who took the stand for the prosecution also identified the defendants and told about offices those individuals had held and meetings in which they had seen them participate. Such witnesses almost all fell into one of two categories: FBI plant or disillusioned ex-Communist.[36]

Something more than patriotism motivated most of them. Barbara Hartle, a defendant in the Seattle trial and a prosecution witness in the Cleveland one, received a parole as her reward for assisting the government, while others worked for money. Until sometime in 1954, the Department of Justice maintained a stable of full-time paid "consultants," whose main function was to travel around the country providing expert testimony on the Communist Party at Smith Act trials and other proceedings. The Justice Department then switched to paying its witnesses on a per diem basis, giving them money only when they worked. Between 1 July 1953 and 15 April 1955, it doled out $43,000 to forty-seven self-styled authorities on the CPUSA. Some of these made only very small amounts. For example, between 1946 and 1952 two witnesses at the Los Angeles trial had received $144.50 and $212.50 respectively. On the other hand, Lloyd Hamlin, who also testified there, had earned $13,182.00 during the same period, and for seven years his only consistent source of income had been the FBI. A number of these professional witnesses represented rather dubious investments. Stephen Wereb, recipient of $3,254 of the taxpayers' money, admitted on the stand that he "never knew and . . . still [did not] know a darn thing about Marxism and Leninism. . . ." Paul Crouch was caught giving contradictory testimony in the various proceedings at which he appeared, and Harvey Matusow badly embarrassed his employers by committing perjury at the second New York trial. Though the money that went to witnesses such as these was not well spent, the same was not true of that paid to John Lautner, who received $32,000 between 1950 and 1955 and from 1951 on earned his entire living by supplying information on the CPUSA. So valuable were Lautner's services that, even after the consultant system was eliminated, he remained a federal employee in everything but name, working regularly and maintaining his own desk at the Justice Department.[37]

His background made his services well worth what the government paid for them. A native of Hungary, where he had fought for Bela Kun after World War I, Lautner drifted into the American Communist movement in 1929 and rose through the ranks as a functionary specializing in work with other members of his own ethnic group. Drafted during World War II, he received a commission in military intelligence and served overseas with a psychological-warfare unit. After his discharge, Lautner resumed his climb up the Communist ladder, and in May 1947 Robert Thompson appointed him to the New York Review Commission, the body responsible for discipline, security, and ideological conformity within the state Party. Lautner eventually became chairman of that unit and a member of the National Review Commission as well.

Then things began to go wrong. He investigated and cleared Angela Calomiris just before she testified as a government witness at Foley Square, and a number of other security lapses were also attributed to him. To make matters worse, at the 1949 trial of Hungarian Communist leader Laszlo Rajk, a man he had met in Europe during the war identified him as a Titoist. In January 1950 the Party sent Lautner to Cleveland, supposedly to take up a new assignment. There several comrades lured him into a cellar, stripped him naked, subjected him to a third degree interrogation, and threatened him with death. Only because he had by chance left the name of one of his assailants at his hotel did Lautner manage to escape alive. A few days later the *Daily Worker* announced his expulsion from the Party.

Expelling Lautner was a real blunder, because the former security officer soon went to the FBI, which recognized as a real prize a man who knew the innermost secrets of the CPUSA and had enjoyed a close working relationship with its top officials. Unlike Louis Budenz, Lautner could speak with authority about Party activities after 1945. Consequently he quickly displaced the Fordham professor as the government's chief witness in Smith Act trials, eventually testifying in more of them than any other person.[38]

His oft-repeated testimony was tremendously effective, for Lautner had supervised the creation of a large segment of the Party's underground apparatus and could discuss the clandestine activity of the CPUSA with great authority. On the basis of his experience as a teacher in Communist schools, he also offered convincing testimony that indoctrination, rather than discussion, characterized Stalinist pedagogy. Most devastating of all was the story of his interrogation in the Cleveland cellar, which was just the kind of thing that could ignite the passions of a jury. Although two judges excluded it as irrelevant, most overruled objections to the tale. Particularly in the first few trials at which he testified, defense counsel subjected him to rigorous cross-examination, emphasizing his pay and/or Communist ideology. Lautner sometimes displayed a rather weak understanding of Marxism-Leninism, but on the whole he held up well under this questioning. As he repeated his story again and again, inconsistencies appeared, but these were relatively minor. Though clearly biased, his testimony was relevant, fact-filled, nearly unshakable, and utterly devastating to defendant members of the CPUSA.[39]

Several other professional witnesses also offered damaging information, but much of their testimony was of extremely dubious value as evidence because it concerned statements allegedly made by other Party members outside the presence of the defendants and without their authorization. Although defense lawyers regularly objected to this kind of testimony, because of a well-established exception to the hearsay rule, they were generally unsuccessful. As Judge Charles McNamee explained, "If it is established by the requisite degree of proof that a defendant was a member of a conspiracy, then any act or declaration of any other co-conspirator, whether named as a defendant or not, which was . . . in the furtherance thereof, would be binding on all the members of the conspiracy. . . ." This was true even if it was "made or done in the absence of any particular defendant and without previous authorization or subsequent ratification by him."[40]

This ready judicial acceptance of third-party declarations was only one aspect of a much larger problem. Because the real defendant in these trials was the CPUSA, much of the evidence had little or nothing to do with the particular men and women in the dock. In addition, it was often chronologically remote, dating from well before the 1945 reconstitution convention. The only grounds for admitting such aged evidence was that it bore on the nature and objectives of the CPUSA. These were in issue, courts ruled, and, according to most, what the Party advocated before its dissolution in 1944 had an important bearing on its present character and goals. Few judges seemed aware of how illogical this theory sounded when applied to a conspiracy that had supposedly begun in 1945. Only because they, like everyone else, viewed these proceedings as essentially trials of the Communist Party, could they give it any credence.[41]

In order to discredit the CPUSA, government attorneys introduced a great deal of evidence which was, in a purely legal sense, irrelevant, much of it relating to Communist positions on American foreign policy. In Los Angeles a government attorney seriously cited as proof that the Party advocated the violent overthrow of the U.S. government the fact that it opposed aid to Chiang Kai-shek. Another prosecution tactic was filling the indictments with aliases (including maiden names) in the apparent hope that jurors would interpret the defendants' use of these as evidence of criminality. When counsel for the government complained that an aspect of Margolis's cross-examination had nothing to do with proving or disproving the Communist Party's advocacy of the violent overthrow of the government, the defense lawyer shot back: ". . . very little has been introduced in this case that has anything to do with that subject."[42]

The Communist side also injected irrelevancies, but the nature of the Smith Act and the kind of case presented by the government were at least partially responsible. The Party continued to preach and practice labor defense but with far less vigor and determination than in the past. The Philadelphia defendants responded to their indictment in traditional fashion, boldly announcing: "In the coming days and weeks, we intend speaking out in the most positive and forthright manner, in the courtroom as well as before the bar of public opinion, not alone to prove our innocence, but to help expose, as we have in the past, the true conspirators against the best interests of our nation and its people." Particularly in California, the supporters of Smith Act prisoners staged demonstrations and mass meetings, and there was picketing of courthouses and jails in some cities. At several trials backers of the accused maintained a visible presence in the courtroom, and now and then the Party press called upon readers to bombard government officials with cards and letters. But exhortations for correspondence blitzes now urged only demands that the government grant bail or amnesty, not attempts to "smash" Smith Act cases with a deluge of mail. Most rallies and demonstrations were small, and Communist witnesses were not as consistently propagandistic as in the past. Foster insisted upon classic political defenses of the Party's creed and actions, but the California group openly defied his instructions, and a Seattle defendant, unable to comply with the wishes of the National Secretary, committed suicide during his trial.[43]

Partly because the Communists made less determined use of labor defense, there were far fewer disturbances associated with the later Smith Act trials than with the original one at Foley Square. Another reason for the calmer atmosphere surrounding these proceedings was the fact that most of the judges who presided over them displayed far more restraint and far less partiality for the prosecution than had Harold Medina. W. Calvin Chestnut, who drove the Baltimore trial forward at a furious pace to produce swift convictions of all defendants, was an exception, as were

James M. Carter, an outspoken anti-Communist who handled some early phases of the Los Angeles case, and Frank McLaughlin, who harassed the Party members indicted in Honolulu. For the most part, though, fairness and balance characterized the performance of Smith Act judges. In none of the later cases did the appellate litigation involve the extensive charges of judicial misconduct which occupied the attention of the court of appeals in *Dennis*. Even individuals sent to jail by Judge Edward Dimock later commended him for the manner in which he had conducted the second New York trial. While some other jurists, such as Mathes, received a great deal of criticism from the Communists, their unemotional and generally impartial performances helped make these trials far more dignified than the chaotic spectacle on which they were modeled.[44]

The attorneys who represented the Communist defendants in the later cases also acted much more like lawyers and much less like instruments of a propaganda campaign than had their predecessors at Foley Square. Perhaps Medina's contempt sentences had intimidated radical advocates, for although some of those who had defended the Eleven and at least four other lawyers who were probably Communists participated in the later trials, there was no repetition of what had happened in 1949. Another reason for the change was the attitude of Mary Kaufman, leader of the defense teams in four of these proceedings, who believed that it was "not productive to use the courtroom as a political forum." Also important was a new willingness on the part of defendants to defer to the knowledge of their lawyers on legal questions. Those on trial continued to bind counsel to their interpretations of Party doctrine, but rather than treating attorneys as second-class citizens, to be ordered about but never consulted, they allowed them to make most decisions concerning courtroom tactics and some relating to broad trial and appellate strategy. Perhaps most important of all was the increasing participation of attorneys whose interest in the Smith Act cases arose not from sympathy for the ideology of the defendants but from concern for the civil liberties issues involved. After Foley Square, Communists, while still employing some advocates from the Left, made a deliberate effort to retain lawyers who could provide them with symbolic links to other segments of the community. The Los Angeles defendants, for example, engaged Leo Branton, a black, Alexander Schulman, attorney for several AFL unions, and A. L. Wirin, chief counsel for the Southern California ACLU. Thomas I. Emerson of the Yale Law School represented members of the second New York group, and in that city's third Smith Act trial a professor from Florida's Rollins College, a former associate of Clarence Darrow, and an NAACP lawyer all participated. Emerson got Flynn to agree that there would be no picketing of the courthouse and that the lawyers would be allowed to use their own judgment in building a case. There were examples of traditional labor defense in the post-*Dennis* proceedings, but those who supplied them were generally Party members acting as their own attorneys.[45]

While the conduct of the Communist side changed after Foley Square, that of federal prosecutors did not. They continued to ask for names, and defendants, joined occasionally by other witnesses, continued to go to jail for not supplying them. Both Elizabeth Gurley Flynn in New York and George Myers in Baltimore drew thirty-day contempt sentences. Judges in Seattle and Detroit each jailed two defendants, and the Washington jurist also locked up a third Communist who refused to testify fully. In Pittsburgh every major defense witness received a contempt sentence, and Art Shields, who covered that and several other trials for the *Daily Worker*, became convinced that the government was deliberately exploiting contempt law to subject Smith Act defendants to double punishment. St. Louis, where the judge consistently resisted the names tactic, was quite exceptional. In both Los Angeles and New Haven the defense planned to call several Communist witnesses but rested after the first one received a contempt sentence. On the positive side, by silencing Party members who might otherwise have talked for days, the names tactic at least did reduce somewhat the hideous length of Smith Act proceedings.[46]

Although the later trials were not exact replicas of the prototype, the differences were mainly ones of emphasis and degree. Consequently, these proceedings generated legal controversies similar to those that had arisen at Foley Square. The outcome of these disputes was also repetitious of what the *Dennis* case had produced, in that almost always the Communists lost. Certainly this was true of the constitutional issue. Despite the Supreme Court's ruling, defendants continued to challenge the validity of the Smith Act, sometimes on its face, but more often as applied in particular cases. The lower federal courts handled the free-speech issue in a host of ways, producing what one commentator called a "bewildering variety" of interpretations of *Dennis*. But not one of them upheld a First Amendment challenge to an indictment or conviction.[47]

Only one trial judge even evidenced substantial concern about the constitutional implications of Smith Act charges. Mathes dismissed the original Los Angeles indictment, requiring the prosecution to redraw it so as to allege intent to overthrow the government as speedily as circumstances would permit. On its face the statute demanded only establishment of intent to teach and advocate, but, he reasoned, the Supreme Court's interpretation made proof of the additional element mandatory. The government responded to Mathes's ruling by redrawing both the Los Angeles and Baltimore indictments and by including an allegation of intent to overthrow in the one it obtained in Pittsburgh. The indictments in Honolulu and New York, however, did not contain this element, and the district courts in those cities refused to regard that fact as significant.[48]

Although differing on this issue, judges were unanimous in their conviction that the Communists constituted a clear and present danger. Whether they did or not remained a matter for determination by judicial notice, with only Mathes seeming to think otherwise. Most judges, both trial and appellate, followed the lead of Medina, Hand, and Vinson, deciding for themselves that there was a clear and present danger and basing their finding on the international situation. Dimock's opinion in the second New York case discussed the Communist takeover of China, tensions in Berlin, and the problems of the French and British with Soviet-supported insurgencies in Indochina and Malaya. Upholding those convictions, Judge John Marshall Harlan referred to *Dennis* and added that "if the danger was clear and present in 1948, it can hardly be thought to have been less in 1951, when the Korean conflict was raging and our relations with the Communist world had moved from cold to hot war."[49]

Communists also met defeat when they attacked the indictments on nonconstitutional grounds. Their most frequent contention was that the government had failed to allege all the necessary elements of the offense as the Supreme Court had defined them in *Dennis*. Another common claim was that the indicting grand jury had not had before it sufficient evidence to justify its action. Neither of these complaints impressed trial judges.[50]

Defendants faired only slightly better when they tried to gain advance knowledge of the government's case against them. They repeatedly asked for bills of particulars and sometimes for discovery and lists of prospective prosecution witnesses. Despite numerous demonstrations that it was nearly impossible to prepare an adequate defense against a case which might include testimony by persons from all over the country and out of any period in the Party's past, as well as hundreds of pieces of literary evidence, district courts almost always rejected such requests, with only two trials breaking the pattern.[51]

Even more overwhelmingly negative was the judicial response to defense claims that the Cold War attitudes pervading the country made it impossible for Communists to receive a fair trial. This proposition was the basis for a number of motions for mistrial, continuance, change of venue, and the like, all of which failed. While some of these simply cited

the general climate of opinion in the country, others pointed to specific
actions by governmental agencies which, they alleged, had prejudiced the
rights of defendants. One complained that during the time when a Los
Angeles jury was attempting to decide whether an objective of the CPUSA
was the overthrow of the U.S. government by force and violence, the
FBI had issued a report saying that it was. Another source of complaint was
the fact that while the second New York trial was in progress, the Senate
Internal Security Subcommittee not only disseminated a pamphlet which
undertook to document the same conclusion but also held hearings on
Communist infiltration of the United Nations in the same building where
Dimock's courtroom was located. Also questioned was the highly publicized appearance of a Pittsburgh witness before Senator McCarthy's Permanent Investigations Subcommittee while that trial was in temporary
recess. In these and numerous similar instances, courts refused to grant
relief.[52]

Judges proved equally oblivious to the effect on potential jurors of
anti-Communist literature and radio and television broadcasts. Mathes,
for example, refused to grant a continuance, despite the fact that ten
days before the Los Angeles trial commenced, local newspapers had begun publishing a serialized version of Herbert Philbrick's *I Led 3 Lives*.
What generally convicted Smith Act defendants, John Somerville believed,
was a notion that Communist teachings necessitated the violent overthrow
of the American government, which was "driven home by constant repetition, in all manner of exaggerated, emotionally powerful, and psychologically effective forms in the daily and weekly press, the picture magazines, on the screen, radio, television and in a hundred other places." The
judiciary did nothing to prevent this.[53]

Nor did it respond favorably to requests from Communists not to be
tried with one another. Judges did grant some motions for severance, but
all involved defendants who were seriously ill. They turned a deaf ear to
pleas such as those of lawyer Maurice Braverman, who claimed that, having
often appeared as counsel for the Communist Party, he could not get a
fair trial if forced to face a jury alongside its leaders; of Alexander Trachtenberg and George Charney, who protested the linking of their fates with
that of captured fugitive Sidney Steinberg; and of Benjamin Careathers
and Irving Weisman, who claimed that they would suffer from association
with fellow Pittsburgh Communists James Dolson, Steve Nelson, and Andrew Onda, all of whom had recently been convicted under a Pennsylvania
law similar to the Smith Act.[54]

Judges also lacked sympathy for Communist claims that the federal
jury system was stacked against them, so that although the later Smith

Act cases produced a bevy of challenges to grand and petit arrays, all of these proved unsuccessful. In Connecticut Judge Robert Anderson did throw out one indictment, because the jury commissioners of his district had failed to perform their duties in the manner required by law. But he upheld another, handed down by a new grand jury, despite claims that the body which returned it, although selected according to correct procedures, was nevertheless improperly constituted. The other challenges, most of them nearly identical to the one made by the Eleven at Foley Square, all met immediate and unqualified defeat.[55]

Indicted leaders of the CPUSA were more successful in their fights for reasonable bail. This subject was, with the possible exception of the constitutional question, the major source of controversy in the post-*Dennis* cases. The flight of Winston, Hall, Green, and Thompson resulted in the crippling of the Civil Rights Congress Bail Fund, for when a grand jury investigating their disappearance asked fund trustees Frederick Vanderbilt Field, W. Alpheous Hunton, Dashiell Hammett, and Abner Green to identify those who had lent it money, they refused, with the result that Judge Ryan jailed them for contempt and the court revoked the bond which the CRC had already posted for members of the Flynn group. By becoming fugitives, the four Foley Square defendants also pushed bail in some later Smith Act cases to incredible heights. For example, a U.S. commissioner, Martin Epstein, set bond for two Baltimore defendants at $75,000 and $100,000, and the California Communists faced initial demands for bail ranging from $2,500 to $100,000, with the district court eventually settling on a uniform figure of $50,000. In Pittsburgh the sums required were smaller, but at $15,000 to $20,000 they were still substantial.[56]

Although pretrial bail was high, it was even more difficult for Communists to gain release while appealing. Judge Mathes, convinced that no amount of money could ensure that members of a highly disciplined organization which had already sent Smith Act violators into hiding would appear to serve their sentences, refused to free any of the California defendants on appeal bond. The district court in Honolulu adopted a similar position, and, after the Pittsburgh trial, Rabe Marsh, believing erroneously that Smith Act defendants could draw on the resources of the CPUSA, doubled the bond of the defendants in that case, despite a previous ruling that they were paupers.[57]

Only when the court of appeals, under pressure from the Supreme Court, ordered him to do so did Mathes lower his $50,000 pretrial bond to $5,000 for some defendants and $10,000 for the rest. He then tried to make some new defendants post the old amount, only to have his judicial superiors again overrule him. His efforts to deny the convicted

California Communists release on appeal bond also brought intervention from above. After considerable haggling with Mathes, the U.S. Court of Appeals for the Ninth Circuit itself granted bail in the amount of $20,000 per person. It also ordered the release of the Honolulu defendants on $15,000 appeal bond. Despite their desire to keep Communists locked in jail, most district courts eventually yielded to pressure from above and contented themselves with asking for an average of $10,000 per defendant during the pre-conviction period and $20,000 while a case was on appeal. Even these amounts, though low by previous standards, were high in relation to the means of really poor defendants, and the Denver group spent several months in jail, unable to raise the money needed to obtain release on bond.[58]

IV

The Justice Department shed no tears for Communists left to languish in prison cells, for that agency was profiting from its war on the CPUSA, and it was determined to press the attack until the enemy was reduced to impotency. Just after the California arrests U.S. Attorney Ernest Tolin announced: "This is the first move in a program to destroy the Communist Party in the west." True, political factors determined the timing of a number of prosecutions, as evidenced by the initiation of four new cases during the 1952 campaign and three more while the 1954 one was in progress, and there seems to have been some relationship between the San Juan indictments and the shooting up of the House of Representatives by Puerto Rican nationalists. The Pittsburgh arrests netted two men, Andy Onda and Jim Dolson, who were at the time on trial for violation of a state version of the Smith Act, so that the *Daily Worker* may have been right when it accused the government of attempting to influence their jury. The FBI struck the Hawaiian Party the day before a contract involving 18,500 sugar workers represented by Jack Hall's ILWU was scheduled to expire, and the district court had to call the grand jury there into special session after the arrests were made in order to obtain indictments; hence charges that authorities in the islands were attempting to behead the union at a crucial moment may have had some basis in fact. But even though other factors apparently influenced the timing of particular prosecutions, the Justice Department's primary motivation was a desire to cripple the CPUSA.[59]

Soon after *Dennis*, *Newsweek* reported that the FBI would follow a strategy of repeatedly lopping off the leadership of the Party while leaving the rank and file alone. Although this analysis was essentially correct, Attorney General McGrath did not wish ordinary members to realize that they were safe. Two weeks later, in an interview with Ernest Lindley, *Newsweek*'s Washington bureau chief, he warned that any member with knowledge of the organization's unlawful purposes was liable to prosecution. When asked how far his department planned to cast its Smith Act net, the Attorney General refused "to tip our hand." McGrath's Republican successor, Herbert Brownell, who considered mass prosecutions impractical and regarded selective attacks on the Party's leadership as the most effective method of employing the Smith Act, adopted the same policy. In a 9 April 1954 radio broadcast, Brownell assured the public that this program would destroy the viability of the CPUSA. Three days later he told a House Committee that his agency hoped "to cripple the domestic leadership of the Communist Party . . . on the simple ground that the best way to go after a conspiracy . . . is to get the leaders of that conspiracy."[60]

The Justice Department hoped to achieve something more—publicity. Departmental spokesmen explained this objective as though it were an aspect of the effort to destroy the Party. In a 1954 interview with *U.S. News & World Report* Brownell attributed a drop in CPUSA membership to the publicity generated by the trials, and Hoover endeavored to convince Congress that:

> A wider public knowledge of the aims, plans, and purposes of the Party has resulted from the continuing arrests and convictions of Communist leaders for conspiring to teach and advocate the violent overthrow of the government; and an enlightened public is one of the most potent weapons against the nation's internal enemy.[61]

Contrary to the claims of Hoover and Brownell, if a Red threat really existed, these highly publicized trials only interfered with serious efforts to combat it, for they misdirected the public's attention. Those Americans who worried most about communism did so, according to a 1954 opinion poll, because they feared a third world war between the United States and the Soviet Union. Consequently, one would have expected them to view the CPUSA as dangerous primarily because of its potential to engage in fifth-column activities. Such was not the case. Instead, the survey revealed, Americans considered Communists a menace primarily because they believed these radicals might convert others to their way of thinking. As an

Illinois grill man put it, "There's always a danger to have someone preaching against our form of government. Eventually someone's going to believe
him." Actually, in the early 1950s few Americans were likely to accept
anything they heard from a Communist, so that the Party's chances of
taking over the country by teaching and advocacy were nonexistent. But
it was on this impossibility that the Smith Act prosecutions focused public attention.[62]

The government's legal attack on the CPUSA also hampered FBI efforts
to investigate Communist activity, for, as Hoover pointed out, putting informants on a witness stand ruined them for further investigative work.
Alerted by the Foley Square trial to the presence of spies in their midst,
the Communists dived underground and adopted security measures designed to screen out government sources, thus making the FBI's job even
more difficult. Coverage of an underground organization required more
personnel than checking on an open one, and sometimes the Bureau lacked
the necessary manpower. The FBI had to resort to selective investigation and to rely more heavily on informants than it considered desirable.
The inability of the Bureau to capture more than three of the eight Smith
Act fugitives indicates how difficult it found the task of covering the underground Party.[63]

Although aware that the original Smith Act prosecution had pushed
the CPUSA below the surface and that more would only drive it deeper,
the Department of Justice pressed on with its trials. The publicity these
proceedings generated did not facilitate the destruction of the CPUSA,
but it did serve the interests of empire-building bureaucrats. In a candid
moment J. Edgar Hoover's one-time assistant William Sullivan admitted
that, although the FBI chief knew "the Party didn't amount to a damn,"
he used it as "an instrument to get appropriations from Congress." The
Smith Act prosecutions and the investigative problems which they created
for the Bureau provided its director with reasons to request extra money
and manpower. In 1951, Hoover told the Senate Appropriations Committee that he needed an additional $467,000 and 187 new employees, point-
ing out in support of this request how much more difficult checking on
the Communist Party had become since the Foley Square trial. In 1953
he told the same body that during the previous year his agency had concentrated on the maintenance of internal security, and that to keep up with
its increased workload in this area, it needed fourteen new supervisory positions in Washington and a 10 percent increase in its $70 million budget.
The committee gave him what he wanted.[64]

How could Congress refuse an agency that repeatedly advertised in Smith

Act trials around the country how it was saving the nation from communism?
Brownell provided the best of all possible arguments for Hoover's expensive
requests when he told Congress in 1956:

> The success of the Department's program against subversives,
> which during the period October 1949 to June 30, 1956, has
> resulted in the conviction of 102 Communists under the
> Smith Act and the proposed or pending trial of 28 others, is
> due in large part to the careful and painstaking investigative
> efforts of the FBI.[65]

Hoover was not the only man in the Justice Department who used the
Smith Act to justify empire building. By September 1953, according to
Deputy Attorney General William Rogers, the prosecutions had badly
overtaxed the department's manpower. In order to handle them more
effectively the Criminal Division combined a number of smaller offices
into a Subversive Activities Unit. Then on 9 July 1954 the department
created a separate Internal Security Division "to concentrate on antisubversive activities." By May the new organization had one-fourth of
its ninety-member legal staff committed to trying leaders of the CPUSA,
yet its chief, Assistant Attorney General William F. Tompkins, was complaining that "the personnel of the Smith Act unit is scarcely adequate
in numbers to cope with the cases ahead of us." After 1957, as the government wound down its war on the Party, the need for this anti-Communist empire disappeared, and in a confidential memorandum written
in 1959, the assistant attorney general in charge of civil litigation, George
C. Doub, recommended abolition of the organization which the Smith
Act had kept so busy. "The Internal Security Division does not have sufficient work for division status and substantial economies can be effect-
ed as a result of the change," he said.[66]
Small wonder that in 1957, when Tompkins's organization was still
on the make, a commentator, struck by the high cost of the legal war
against the CPUSA, mused: "Can it be that the party harasses the Government even as the Government harasses the party . . . ?"[67] The answer
was no. While the Department of Justice, with its repeated and repetitious Smith Act trials, did indeed seek to harass, cripple, and destroy the
CPUSA, the harassment was all in one direction. For the Party's enemies
the prosecutions were a boon rather than a burden. What was bad for the
Communists was simultaneously good for the Department of Justice and
the FBI.

NOTES

1. "Communism: Second Echelon Roundup," *Newsweek*, 2 July 1951, p. 18; "Communists: Roundup No. 2," *Time*, 2 July 1951, p. 15; *NYT*, 21 June 1951, p. 16.

2. Thomas Michael Holmes, "The Spectre of Communism in Hawaii, 1947-1953" (Ph.D. diss., University of Hawaii, 1975), pp. 294-95; Justice, *Annual Report for 1949*, p. 4; ACLU Weekly Bulletin no. 1444, 3 July 1950, p. 1; Max Lowenthal, *The Federal Bureau of Investigation* (New York: William Sloan Associates, 1950), p. 461; "McGrath: U.S. Plans New War on Reds and Travelers," *Newsweek*, 16 July 1951, p. 5, *PW*, 18 June 1951.

3. *NYT*, 21 June 1951, pp. 1, 16.

4. "The Supreme Court Decision: *Clear and Present Danger*," Oleta Yates Papers, Bancroft Library, University of California at Berkeley; Justice, "List of Smith Act Cases Involving Communist Party Leaders," photocopy (undated) (hereinafter cited as Justice, "List"); *NYT*, 27 July 1951, p. 1, and 1 September 1951, p. 5; *Yates Transcript*, pp. 290-382; Dorothy Healy, personal interview with the Author at her home in Los Angeles, 31 December 1973.

5. *NYT*, 8 August 1951, pp. 1, 5; George Myers, personal interview with the Author at CPUSA National Headquarters, New York City, 8 August 1973.

6. *NYT*, 18 August 1951, pp. 1, 6; "Communists: FBI Roundup No. 4," *Newsweek*, 27 August 1951, p. 27.

7. *NYT*, 29 August 1951, pp. 1, 10; Appellee's Brief, at 215-57, Fujimoto v. United States, 251 F. 2d 342 (9th Cir. 1958) and United States v. Fujimoto, no. 10495, Crim. (D. Hawaii 1952), Transcript of Proceedings, pp. 8323-25, opinion report in 102 F. Supp. 890 (D. Hawaii 1952) (hereinafter cited as *Fujimoto Transcript*); Holmes, "Communism in Hawaii," pp. 287-88.

8. *NYT*, 18 September 1952, pp. 1, 14; *DW*, 5 October 1953 and 11 May 1954.

9. Charles Goodell, personal interview with the Author at Old Executive Office Building, Washington, D.C., 29 May 1975; *NYT*, 30 July 1953, p. 24. The quote is from Herbert Brownell, Jr., Memorandum for the President, 6 October 1956, Whitman File, Box 8, Administration Series, DEL.

10. Justice, "List"; *NYT*, 7 October 1953, p. 20.

11. Herbert Parmet, *Eisenhower and the American Crusades* (New York and London: Macmillan Co., 1972), pp. 338, 382; Eisenhower to Harry Bullis, 18 May 1953, CF, OF 133E-1, DEL; Eisenhower to William E. Robinson, 12 March 1954, Whitman File, Box 3, DDE Diaries, 1953, DEL; Memorandum for Mr. Hughes, Box 1, Whitman File, Legislative Meetings Series, DEL; U.S., Presidents, *Public Papers of the Presidents of the United States: Dwight D. Eisenhower*, 8 vols. (Washington, D.C.:

National Archives and Records Service, 1960-61), 2: 13, 781; 68 Stat.
1146 (1954).

12. Goodell interview; Justice, "List"; *NYT*, 30 May 1954, pp. 1,
25, and 2 August 1954, p. 18; Robert Mollan, "The Smith Act Prosecutions: The Effect of the Dennis and Yates Decisions," *University of Pittsburgh Law Review* 26 (June 1965): 719, n. 62; *DW*, 31 May 1953; A.
L. Wirin and Samuel Rosenwein, "The Smith Act Score," *The Nation*,
26 February 1955, p. 180. Eisenhower made his statement to a Republican group in Denver (Presidents, *Public Papers: Eisenhower*, 2: 896).

13. FBI Director to Attorney General, 13 June 1955 and FBI Direc-
tor to Assistant Attorney General William F. Tompkins, 29 June 1955,
files of the Federal Bureau of Investigation, Washington, D.C.; *NYT*, 30
May 1956, p. 8, and 12 September 1957, p. 34; Justice, "List"; "First
Draft: Suggestions for 1956 Republican Platform," William P. Rogers
Papers, DEL.

14. A. L. Wirin and Samuel Rosenwein, "The Smith Act Prosecutions,"
The Nation, 12 December 1953, p. 486; Myers interview; Maurice Braverman, telephonic interview with the Author, 18 August 1976.

15. Justice, *Annual Report for 1952*, p. 387; Elizabeth G. Flynn,
"Freedom for the Communist Leaders," *PA* 31 (July 1952): 61-65;
National Committee, CPUSA, "Free Gene Dennis and All Political Prison-
ers," *PA* 33 (June 1954): 2; Arnold Johnson, "Amnesty and the Struggle
Against McCarthyism," *PA* 33 (June 1954): 61; Eugene Dennis to Peggy
Dennis, 16 September 1952, in Eugene Dennis, *Letters from Prison* (New
York: International Publishers, 1956), p. 49; *DW*, 5 July 1953, 15 Octo-
ber 1953, and 3 January 1956; Dalton Trumbo, *The Time of the Toad:
A Study of Inquisition in America* (New York: Harper & Row, 1972),
p. 130. For Dennis's comment see his letter to Peggy, 2 July 1953 (Den-
nis, *Letters*, p. 89). For Lightfoot's see his "The Struggle to End the Cold
War at Home," *PA* 34 (September 1955): 42. For lists of those who joined
the Committee to Defend V. J. Jerome see Box 4, Victor J. Jerome Papers,
Sterling Library, Yale University.

16. Justice, "List." The figures include only conspiracy cases. The
membership ones are treated in Chapter 10. The defendant who died was
William J. Pennock, one of the Communists tried in Seattle (Justice,
Annual Report for 1953, p. 178). Computation is complicated by the
third New York trial, held from 9 April to 31 July 1956. All of the defendants in that case were part of the Flynn group. Four had been fugitives at the time of the second New York trial and one, Marion Bachrach,
was severed from it because of illness. Two others, Alexander Trachtenberg and George B. Charney, were convicted along with Flynn but were
subsequently granted new trials by an appellate court (see United States
v. Stein, 140 F. Supp. 761 [S.D.N.Y. 1956]). Bachrach was acquitted in
the third New York trial and Trachtenberg and Charney convicted. For

statistical purposes I have counted those verdicts and ignored the results
of their first trial.

17. National Committee, CPUSA, "On Conviction of the Thirteen
Communist Leaders," *PA* 32 (January 1953): 1 (this statement was signed
by Foster) and "On the Michigan Smith Act Convictions," *PA* 33 (March
1954): 1; Braverman interview; *In re* Bouslog-Sawyer, 41 Hawaii 403 (1956);
Ovid Demaris, *The Director: An Oral Biography of J. Edgar Hoover* (New
York: Harpers, 1975), p. 128.

18. Justice, "List."

19. Yates v. United States, 225 F. 2d 146 (9th Cir. 1955); Wellman
v. United States, 227 F. 2d 757 (6th Cir. 1955); United States v. Mesarosh,
223 F. 2d 449 (3rd Cir. 1955); Frankfeld v. United States, 198 F. 2d 679
(4th Cir. 1952), *cert. denied*, 344 U.S. 922 (1953); United States v. Flynn,
216 F. 2d 354 (2d Cir. 1954), *cert. denied*, 348 U.S. 909 (1955); Mollan,
"Smith Act Prosecutions," pp. 712-13; Mesarosh v. United States, 352 U.S.
1 (1956).

20. Don Whitehead, *The FBI Story: A Report to the People* (New
York: Random House, 1956), p. 297; Mollan, "Smith Act Prosecutions,"
p. 719, n. 62; Kremen v. United States, 231 F. 2d 155 (9th Cir. 1956);
NYT, 6 December 1955, p. 30; United States v. Green, 140 F. Supp.
117 (S.D.N.Y. 1956); Healy interview; *DW*, 29 September 1953.

21. *NYT*, 3 February 1953, p. 1, 20 February 1954, p. 7. The quote
is from the 1953 article.

22. Myers interview; Arnold Johnson, personal interview with the
Author at CPUSA National Headquarters, New York City, 8 August 1973.

23. United States v. Frankfeld, 101 F. Supp. 449 (D. Md. 1951);
United States v. Fujimoto, 102 F. Supp. 890 (D. Hawaii 1952); United
States v. Schneiderman, 106 F. Supp. 892 (S.D. Cal. 1952); United States
v. Flynn, 216 F. 2d 354 (2d Cir. 1954); United States v. Mesarosh, 13
F.R.D. 180 (W.D. Pa. 1952); United States v. Marabal Carrion, 140 F.
Supp. 226 (D. Puerto Rico 1956). The trial court rulings on this mat-
ter in the Seattle and Detroit cases are unreported, but both are discussed
by the court of appeals in Wellman v. United States, 227 F. 2d 757 (6th
Cir. 1955).

24. Osmond K. Fraenkel, "The Smith Act Reconsidered," *Lawyers
Guild Review* 16 (1956): 153; *DW*, 22 June 1951.

25. 64 Stat. 987 (1950); Wirin and Rosenwein, "The Smith Act Score," p.
178. On the issue of congressional intent see *Cong. Record*, 81st Cong.,
2d sess., 5 September 1950, p. 14190, and 20 September 1950, pp.
15198-99. For examples of judicial treatment of section 4(f) see United
States v. Kuzma, 141 F. Supp. 91 (E. D. Pa. 1954); United States v.
Schneiderman, 106 F. Supp. 906 (S.D. Cal. 1952); United States v.
Mesarosh, 223 F. 2d 449 (3rd Cir. 1955); Wellman v. United States, 227
F. 2d 757 (6th Cir. 1955); and United States v. Brandt, no. 21076—Crim.

(N.D. Ohio 1955), Transcript of Proceedings, at 1144-45, opinion report
in 139 F. Supp. 367 (N.D. Ohio 1955) (hereinafter cited as *Brandt Transcript*).

26. 68 Stat. 775 (1954); United States v. Brandt, 139 F. Supp. 367
(N.D. Ohio 1955); United States v. Silverman, 132 F. Supp. 820 (D. Conn.
1955) (quote on p. 831).

27. Interview with Mary Kaufman, in *The Relevant Lawyers: Conversations Out of Court on Their Clients, Their Practice, Their Life Style*,
ed. Ann Fagan Ginger (New York: Simon & Schuster, 1972), p. 205.

28. United States v. Flynn, Record of Trial Proceedings, page 8841,
opinion report in 106 F. Supp. 966 (S.D.N.Y. 1952).

29. *Yates Transcript*, pp. 2087, 3394-402; United States v. Schneiderman, 106 F. Supp. 906 (S.D. Cal. 1952); Frankfeld v. United States,
198 F. 2d 679 (4th Cir. 1952), at 686; United States v. Mesarosh, 223
F. 2d 449 (3rd Cir. 1955); "Post-Dennis Prosecutions Under the Smith
Act," *Indiana Law Journal* 31 (Fall 1955): 114-15.

30. Wirin and Rosenwein, "Smith Act Prosecutions," pp. 485-88;
"Post-Dennis Prosecutions," pp. 113, 116; *NYT*, 20 June 1953, p. 5, 1
August 1956, p. 1; *Yates Transcript*, pp. 5071 and 10114; Ginger, *Relevant Lawyers*, pp. 208-09.

31. *Yates Transcript*, pp. 10400-1159 (quote on p. 10574).

32. John Somerville, *The Communist Trials and the American Tradition: Expert Testimony on Force and Violence* (New York: Cameron
Associates, 1956), book jacket, pp. 7-9, 29-31, 162, 226; Royal France,
My Native Grounds (New York: Cameron Associates, 1957), p. 241.

33. *Yates Transcript*, p. 393.

34. Wirin and Rosenwein, "Smith Act Prosecutions," p. 487; *DW*,
9 January 1952.

35. Wirin and Rosenwein, "Smith Act Prosecutions," p. 487; Somerville, *Communist Trials*, p. 173.

36. Wirin and Rosenwein, "Smith Act Prosecutions," p. 487; Herbert
L. Packer, *Ex-Communist Witness: Four Studies in Fact Finding* (Stanford,
Calif.: Stanford University Press, 1962), pp. 11-12.

37. *NYT*, 24 August 1955, p. 23; Richard H. Rovere, "The Kept
Witnesses," *Harpers* 210 (May 1955): 25-34; *Yates Transcript*, pp. 1832-
39, 2513, 4188, 12156-61 (quote on p. 4188); Record vol., at 196-97,
Noto v. United States, 367 U.S. 290 (1961); *DW*, 28 May 1954; Harvey
Matusow, *False Witness* (New York: Cameron & Kahn, 1955), pp. 60-62.

38. Packer, *Ex-Communist Witness*, pp. 6, 178-86; Record, at 9307-
316, McGrath v. Communist Party of the United States of America, 1
S.A.C.B. 1 (1952) (hereinafter cited as *Record*); *Yates Transcript*, pp. 1929-
2677; John Gates interviewed on NBC news special "American Communism Today," 26 August 1973.

39. Packer, *Ex-Communist Witness*, pp. 185-225.

40. Wirin and Rosenwein, "Smith Act Prosecutions," pp. 487-88;

United States v. Schneiderman, 106 F. Supp. 892 (S.D. Cal. 1952); United
States v. Flynn, 216 F. 2d 354 (2d Cir. 1954); United States v. Mesarosh,
223 F. 2d 449 (3rd Cir. 1955); Wellman v. United States, 227 F. 2d 757
(6th Cir. 1955); *Yates Transcript,* pp. 3771-73. For McNamee's comment
see *Brandt Transcript,* p. 1379.
    41. *Yates Transcript,* pp. 5486-99, 7683-84; "Post-Dennis Prosecu-
tions," p. 115; United States v. Mesarosh, 223 F. 2d 449 (3rd Cir. 1955);
Wellman v. United States, 227 F. 2d 757 (6th Cir. 1955).
    42. *Yates Transcript,* pp. 235, 3027-28, 3972-74a (quote on pp. 3027-
28); *Brandt Transcript,* pp. 801-07, 1360-79.
    43. Joseph R. Starobin, *American Communism in Crisis 1943-1957*
(Cambridge, Mass.: Harvard University Press, 1972), pp. 208, 302, n. 30;
Al Richmond, *A Long View from the Left: Memoirs of an American Revolutionary* (Boston: Houghton Mifflin, 1973), pp. 322, 329-30; Healy
interview; *DW,* 15 August 1951, 10 July 1952, 3 November 1952, and
26 November 1952; *Worker* (Nat. Ed.), 8 February 1953 and (New York
—Harlem Ed.), 6 December 1953; Appendix to Brief for Appellee, at 373,
Scales v. United States, 367 U.S. 203 (1961). For the statement of Philadelphia defendants see *DW,* 21 September 1953. The *DW* reported attendance at two New York rallies in early 1952 as 5,000 and 2,200, but these
figures were probably somewhat inflated, and most seem to have drawn
no more than a few hundred (7 January 1952 and 2 May 1952).
    44. Myers interview; Wirin and Rosenwein, "Smith Act Prosecutions,"
p. 488; Vern Countryman, "The Bigots and the Professionals," *The Nation,*
28 June 1952, p. 642; National Committee, CPUSA, "On Conviction of the
Thirteen Communist Leaders," pp. 3-4; *DW,* 25 April 1952; Connelly v.
United States Dist. Court, 191 F. 2d 692 (9th Cir. 1951); *Yates Transcript,*
pp. 5023-27, 10031, 10069, 12531-64; George B. Charney, *A Long Journey* (Chicago: Quadrangle Books, 1968), p. 217; Richmond, *Long View,*
pp. 316-18; Healy interview; United States v. Fujimoto, 101 F. Supp. 293
(D. Hawaii,.1951); France, *My Native Grounds,* p. 238.
    45. Charney, *A Long Journey,* pp. 227, 240-41; Healy and Johnson
interviews; interview with Kaufman, in Ginger, *The Relevant Lawyers,* pp.
214-15; Richmond, *Long View,* p. 324; *DW,* 21 November 1951, 12 March
1952, 10 December 1952, 1 February 1954, and 6 April 1956; *Brandt Transcript,* p. 98; "The Reminiscences of Thomas I. Emerson," Part 2 (1953):
2276-77, The Oral History Collection of Columbia University; HUAC
(Communist Legal Subversion: The Role of the Communist Lawyer, 86th
Cong., 1st sess., H. Rept. 41, pp. 30-60) identified Harriet Bouslog-Sawyer
(Honolulu), Ben Margolis (Los Angeles), and Hyman Schlessinger (Pittsburgh) as members of the Party. Yetta Land, who represented Cleveland
defendants, was also a Communist, according to *Worker* (New York—Harlem Ed.), 18 March 1956.
    46. *DW,* 26 March 1952, 3 April 1952, 20 November 1952, 4 Decem-
ber 1952, 1 January 1953, 28 July 1953, 4 August 1953, 10 August 1953,

1 February 1954, 2 February 1954, 29 April 1954, 30 April 1954, 21
February 1956, 28 February 1956, 4 April 1956, 28 May 1956; Yates
v. United States, 355 U.S. 66 (1957); Dasbach v. United States, 254 F.
2d 687 (9th Cir. 1958); Healy interview; Thomas Arthur Shields, personal interview with the Author at CPUSA National Headquarters, New
York City, 8 August 1973.
    47. Mollan, "Smith Act Prosecutions," pp. 706, 711; "Post-Dennis
Prosecutions," p. 107.
    48. *Yates Transcript*, pp. 3373-74; "Post-Dennis Prosecutions," pp.
109-10; United States v. Flynn, 216 F. 2d 354 (2d Cir. 1954); United
States v. Fujimoto, 107 F. Supp. 865 (D. Hawaii 1952); United States
v. Frankfeld, 103 F. Supp. 48 (D. Md. 1952).
    49. United States v. Schneiderman, 106 F. Supp. 906 (S.D. Cal. 1952);
Wellman v. United States, 227 F. 2d 757 (6th Cir. 1955); United States
v. Flynn, 216 F. 2d 354 (2d Cir. 1954) (quote on p. 367); United States
v. Silverman, 129 F. Supp. 496 (D. Conn. 1955); Yates v. United States,
225 F. 2d 146 (9th Cir. 1955); United States v. Mesarosh, 13 F.R.D. 180
(W.D. Pa. 1952), 223 F. 2d 449 (3rd Cir. 1955); Frankfeld v. United States,
Pa. 1952), 223 F. 2d 449 (3rd Cir. 1955); Frankfeld v. United States,
198 F. 2d 679 (4th Cir. 1952).
    50. "Post-Dennis Prosecutions," p. 107; United States v. Frankfeld,
101 F. Supp. 449 (D. Md. 1951), 102 F. Supp. 422 (D. Md. 1952), and
103 F. Supp. 48 (D. Md. 1952); United States v. Fujimoto, 107 F. Supp.
865 (D. Hawaii 1952) and 102 F. Supp. 890 (D. Hawaii 1952); United
States v. Silverman, 129 F. Supp. 496 (D. Conn. 1955), 132 F. Supp.
820 (D. Conn. 1955); United States v. Kuzma, 141 F. Supp. 91 (E.D. Pa.
1954); United States v. Mirabal Carrion, 140 F. Supp. 226 (D. Puerto
Rico 1956); United States v. Mesarosh, 13 F.R.D. 180 (W.D. Pa. 1952);
United States v. Stein, 140 F. Supp. 761 (S.D.N.Y. 1956).
    51. United States v. Frankfeld, 101 F. Supp. 449 (D. Md. 1951), 103
F. Supp. 51 (D. Md. 1952); United States v. Schneiderman, 104 F. Supp.
405 (S.D. Cal. 1952); United States v. Fujimoto, 102 F. Supp. 890 (D.
Hawaii 1952); United States v. Brandt, 139 F. Supp. 349 (N.D. Ohio 1955);
United States v. Mesarosh, 13 F.R.D. 180 (W.D. Pa. 1952); United States
v. Silverman, 129 F. Supp. 496 (D. Conn. 1955), 132 F. Supp. 820 (D.
Conn. 1955); United States v. Stein, 18 F.R.D. 17 (S.D.N.Y. 1955), 140
F. Supp. 761 (S.D.N.Y. 1956); United States v. Mirabal Carrion, 140 F.
Supp. 226 (D. Puerto Rico 1956).
    52. United States v. Flynn, 216 F. 2d 354 (2d Cir. 1954); United
States v. Mesarosh, 13 F.R.D. 180 (W.D. Pa. 1952), 223 F. 2d 449 (3rd
Cir. 1955); Wellman v. United States, 227 F. 2d 757 (6th Cir. 1955);
United States v. Schneiderman, 106 F. Supp. 906 (S.D. Cal. 1952).
    53. Wirin and Rosenwein, "Smith Act Prosecutions," p. 489; Somer-
ville, *Communist Trials*, p. 199.
    54. Justice, "List"; United States v. Frankfeld, 103 F. Supp. 48 (D.

Md. 1952); United States v. Fujimoto, 102 F. Supp. 890 (D. Hawaii 1952); United States v. Mesarosh, 13 F.R.D. 180 (W.D. Pa. 1952); Wellman v. United States, 227 F. 2d 757 (6th Cir. 1955); United States v. Brandt, 139 F. Supp. 367 (N.D. Ohio 1955); United States v. Stein, 140 F. Supp. 761 (S.D.N.Y. 1956); United States v. Silverman, 129 F. Supp. 496 (D. Conn. 1955), 132 F. Supp. 820 (D. Conn. 1955).

55. United States v. Silverman, 129 F. Supp. 496 (D. Conn. 1955) and 132 F. Supp. 820 (D. Conn. 1955); United States v. Frankfeld, 101 F. Supp. 449 (D. Md. 1951); United States v. Fujimoto, 102 F. Supp. 890 (D. Hawaii 1952), 105 F. Supp. 727 (D. Hawaii 1952), 107 F. Supp. 865 (D. Hawaii 1952); Fujimoto v. U.S. District Court, 199 F. 2d 27 (9th Cir. 1952); United States v. Flynn, 106 F. Supp. 966 (S.D.N.Y. 1952); United States v. Mesarosh, 13 F.R.D. 180 (W.D. Pa. 1952); United States v. Brandt, 139 F. Supp. 349 (N.D. Ohio 1955); United States v. Mirabal Carrion, 140 F. Supp. 226 (D. Puerto Rico 1956); *DW*, 21 January 1954 and 8 February 1955.

56. United States v. Field, 193 F. 2d 92 (2d Cir. 1951); United States v. Field, 193 F. 2d 109 (2d Cir. 1951); Green v. United States, 193 F. 2d 111 (2d Cir. 1951); United States v. Flynn, 190 F. 2d 672 (2d Cir. 1951); *NYT*, 18 August 1951, p. 1; United States v. Schneiderman, 102 F. Supp. 52 (S.D. Cal. 1951); Stack v. Boyle, 342 U.S. 1 (1951); Wirin and Rosenwein, "Smith Act Prosecutions," p. 488.

57. United States v. Schneiderman, 106 F. Supp. 941 (S.D. Cal. 1952); Wirin and Rosenwein, "Smith Act Prosecutions," pp. 488-89; United States v. Mesarosh, 115 F. Supp. 332 (W.D. Pa. 1953).

58. Stack v. Boyle, 342 U.S. 1 (1951); United States v. Spector, 193 F. 2d 1002 (9th Cir. 1952); Wirin and Rosenwein, "Smith Act Prosecutions," pp. 488-89, and "The Smith Act Score," p. 179.

59. *DW*, 29 August 1951, 21 October 1954, 25 October 1954, 10 January 1955; *NYT*, 29 August 1951, pp. 1, 10, 1 September 1951, p. 5, and 20 June 1953, p. 1. Tolin is quoted in Richmond, *Long View*, on pp. 307-08. Holmes denies that the Hawaiian prosecution was part of a union-busting plot, but his own evidence casts grave doubts on this conclusion ("Communism in Hawaii," pp. 290-312).

60. "Communism: Second Echelon Roundup," p. 18; "U.S. Plans New War," p. 23; Goodell interview; "Attorney General Brownell Says: 'Success of FBI Is Outstanding,' " *U.S. News & World Report*, 16 April 1954, pp. 112-13; testimony by Brownell in HJC, *Hearings . . . on H.R. 226 . . .*, 83rd Cong., 2d sess., 1954, p. 137; untitled speech by Herbert Brownell, Rogers Papers.

61. SApp, *Hearings . . . Departments of State, Justice and Commerce, Appropriations for 1954: Department of Justice*, 83rd Cong., 1st sess., 1953, p. 195; "Interview with Herbert Brownell, Jr.," *U.S. News & World Report*, 4 September 1953, pp. 40-41. Hoover is quoted in Justice, *Annual Report for 1953*, p. 401.

62. Samuel Stouffer, *Communism, Conformity and Civil Liberties* (Garden City, N.Y.: Doubleday & Co., 1955), pp. 76, 157-58, and 164 (quote on p. 164).

63. Justice, *Annual Report for 1952*, p. 14, and *Annual Report for 1952*, p. 18; SApp, *Hearings . . . Making Appropriations for the Departments of State, Justice, and Commerce and the Judiciary for the Fiscal Year Ending June 30, 1952*, 82d Cong., 1st sess., 1951, 1: 42; HApp, *Hearings . . . Departments of State, Justice, Commerce and the Judiciary Appropriations for 1953*, 82d Cong., 2d sess., 1952, 4: 174; "Communism: Second Echelon Roundup," p. 18; "Reds: Jail for Fourteen," *Newsweek*, 18 August 1952, p. 23.

64. SApp, *State, Justice, and Commerce 1952*, 1: 38-52, and *State, Justice and Commerce for 1954*, pp. 159-67. Sullivan is quoted in Demaris, *The Director*, p. 167.

65. Justice, *Annual Report for 1956*, p. 5.

66. Rogers to J. Edward Lumbard, 28 September 1953, Rogers Papers; Justice, *Annual Report for 1955*, pp. 44-66; Herbert Brownell, Jr., Memorandum for the President, 6 October 1956, Whitman File, Box 8, Administration Series, DEL; testimony by Tompkins, SApp, *Hearings . . . Making Appropriations for the Departments of State, Justice, Commerce, the Judiciary and Related Agencies for the Fiscal Year Ending June 30, 1956*, 84th Cong., 1st sess., 1955, p. 708; Memorandum to Attorney General by George C. Doub, 4 February 1959, Rogers Papers.

67. Milton R. Konvitz, *Fundamental Liberties of a Free People: Religion, Speech, Press, Assembly* (Ithaca, N.Y.: Cornell University Press, 1957), p. 336.

7
The Collapse of
the Communist Party

> The Communist Party, we would judge, is having its last
> breath in the United States.
>
> —San Francisco Chronicle
> 5 July 1951

The Smith Act prosecutions fatally wounded the CPUSA. Certainly they were not the only reason for the dramatic decline of American communism, during little more than a decade after World War II, from the status of a potent radical movement to that of a moribund sect. Events abroad, hostility at home, and the foolishness of the Party's own leadership all contributed to its downfall, but the role of the prosecutions was crucial. Although failing to behead the CPUSA, the Justice Department's legal attack did produce a substantial reduction in its size and did induce Communists to adopt security measures detrimental to their movement. Even more important was what the prosecutions did to the Party's organizational cohesion. So badly did they weaken the bonds holding the CPUSA together that, when pressured by foreign events in 1956, American communism collapsed under the strain.

I

Students of the Party's decline have generally failed to grasp the importance of the Smith Act prosecutions. Joseph Starobin, a prominent Communist during the late 1940s and early 1950s who, after leaving the movement, subjected it to scholarly analysis, attributes the waning of the CPUSA to its own mistakes. In his opinion, although gradual achievement of radical reform was possible in the postwar United States, the Party frequently adopted policies based on the assumption that it must engage in a protracted struggle for total change. Among the errors in judgment resulting from its faulty analysis of the situation were a commitment to continually discerning and doing what the Russians desired and a decision to send part of the organization underground. Most unfortunate of all, in Starobin's opinion, was the all-out support which the CPUSA gave to Henry Wallace's third-party presidential bid in 1948. This, he feels, destroyed communism's position in the CIO and exploded the reputation for political expertise which had once made it a valued ally of non-radical office seekers. The Wallace campaign opened the way for a vicious attack on the movement by liberals and labor, which negated all the opportunities for advance that were inherent in postwar conditions and staggered what had been a thriving organization.[1]

Starobin's analysis differs considerably from that of David Shannon, an academic whose lack of personal involvement with the CPUSA perhaps gives him a bit more objectivity. Shannon agrees that the Party made mistakes, and he too sees the Wallace campaign as an unwise adventure which caused anti-Stalinist reactions in both the liberal community and the CIO. He even emphasizes the disastrous consequences of Communist obeisance to the Soviet Union and criticizes the Party's cultural, religious, and racial policies. But, unlike Starobin, Shannon assigns primary responsibility for the failure of the CPUSA to external conditions, rather than to the follies of the Stalinists themselves. Prosperity, the Cold War, and popular anti-communism put the Party in a difficult position, he says, and then developments abroad destroyed it. The most important of these were two foreign events that occurred in 1956: Nikita Khrushchev's speech to the Twentieth Congress of the Soviet Communist Party, during which he revealed some of the atrocities committed by the late Joseph Stalin; and Russia's brutal repression of the Hungarian Revolution. Jolted by these and related incidents, the CPUSA collapsed completely. As far as Shannon is concerned, its "final crisis" was entirely the result of "the Russian denunciation of Stalin and the crushing of the Hungarian revolution."[2]

The divergent arguments of Starobin and Shannon highlight two of the major reasons for the decline of the CPUSA. The environment in Cold War America was extremely hostile for a group that preached Stalinism and supported the policies of the Soviet Union. In November 1945 the CPUSA was able to elect two of its own to the New York City Council; yet within a dozen years the Party had become so distasteful to Americans, even in its Gotham stronghold, that a Stalinist running for a seat on that same body could poll only 1 percent of the vote. Liberal hostility toward the CPUSA began to develop before the 1948 campaign, and the Taft-Hartley Act of 1947, with its anti-Communist oath provision, would have weakened the Party's hold on the CIO, even if Stalinists had not supported Henry Wallace. But policies adopted by Stalinists themselves did make a bad situation much worse, increasing the isolation of their organization and alienating former friends, whose support, or at least toleration, the Party needed to retain any measure of legitimacy until the Cold War climate moderated sufficiently for communism to regain some of its appeal. Nor is there any doubt that the international events of 1956 precipitated the collapse of the CPUSA. Within a little more than two years after Khrushchev's speech, the Party lost up to 85 percent of its membership.[3]

While Starobin and Shannon do elucidate factors that contributed to the decline of American communism, neither provides an entirely satisfactory explanation for that phenomenon. Although purporting to trace the history of the movement from 1943 to 1957, Starobin devotes over 80 percent of his book to the first six years of this period. Consequently, what he offers his reader is really more a commentary on the Party's loss of influence and growing isolation than an explanation for its organizational collapse, something that clearly occurred during the years 1956-1958. Shannon focuses on this crucial period, but his analysis is flawed by his insistence that events abroad were sufficient to wreck the CPUSA. Memoranda unearthed by the Church Committee during its 1975 probe of U.S. intelligence agencies clearly establish that the FBI, through covert intervention in intra-Party debates, promoted the factionalism that tore the CPUSA apart after Khrushchev's 1956 speech. Even if one assumes that the Bureau's efforts only hastened a disintegration which would have occurred even in their absence, Shannon's thesis remains inadequate, because it fails to explain why the Party could not weather the 1956 crisis as it had a similar one on the eve of World War II. No foreign event ever shocked the CPUSA more than did the 1939 signing of a nonaggression pact between the Soviet Union and Hitler's Germany, for militant opposition to fascism had been the Party's motive force during the Popular Front era. Disgusted by what the Russians had done, as many as 20,000 American comrades abandoned communism forever. But more than twice that many stuck with the Party, and, despite its reduced size, the CPUSA remained structurally sound. Responding readily to direction, the organization executed the total reversal of its line which the new Soviet foreign policy required. Why the Party could not ride out the 1956 crisis, as it had this earlier one, Shannon does not explain.[4]

The explanation that he fails to seek is the Smith Act prosecutions and what they had done to the organization. Shannon acknowledges that the Justice Department's legal offensive was one of several factors which adversely affected the Party's fortunes during the early 1950s, but he eschews any attempt to assess the nature or extent of the damage it inflicted, justifying his refusal by pointing to the alleged impracticability of determining "that this or that causal factor was responsible for x percentage of the party's deterioration."[5] For the period prior to 1956, Shannon is correct; although one can identify the effects of the Smith Act, it is impossible to measure precisely the relative significance of these and the other afflictions from which the Party suffered. The years of crisis and collapse are another matter, for then the effects of the prosecutions were crucial. Because of them an organization that had weathered the storms of 1939-1940 collapsed before the winds which blew against it from abroad in 1956.

II

The Smith Act prosecutions undermined, and thus helped to topple, the CPUSA, but they did so in a manner quite different from that contemplated by the Department of Justice. Federal prosecutors, it is true, did accomplish one of their objectives, which was to drain off a substantial portion of the Party's limited financial resources. The cost of defending the Eleven was at least $5,847 a week, and the final bill for their trial may have run as high as $500,000. Appealing the *Dennis* verdict required $18,000 a week for preparation of the brief and $40,000 for printing the record, and the unfavorable decision of the Supreme Court meant having to pay fines that totaled $110,000. The later prosecutions proved expensive too. Despite the numerous reductions ordered by appellate courts, bond in sixteen post-*Dennis* cases averaged $9,000 per person, and although the CRC maintained a bail fund to which Smith Act victims could turn for help, its resources were insufficient to aid them all. Trial expenses were high in the later cases, and despite the fact that the Party and the Civil Rights Congress mounted numerous fund-raising drives in connection with them, for which Henry Winston claimed great success, these do not seem to have produced nearly enough money. The Michigan trial ended with the defendants $10,000 in debt, and five years after their day in court, Flynn and her comrades still owed a lawyer $5,712.98.[6]

Although the creation of ad hoc defense organizations may have spared the CPUSA some of the direct costs of resisting legal attack, these expenses did impose upon the Party a heavier financial burden than it could afford, for they forced the organization to terminate the salaries of some paid functionaries. Communists had always considered it vital to have the largest possible number of people laboring full time for the movement. The Party's many paid employees—perhaps 800 or more—gave it the capacity to mobilize a much higher proportion of its membership than more conventional political groups, but, while the weekly salaries of these functionaries were quite modest, even at $50-$75 apiece they cost the CPUSA a great deal of money. By November 1948, the burden of defending individuals subjected to prosecution by the Justice Department had become so great that the CPUSA no longer could afford all its paid employees and had to drop some from the payroll. Most of these functionaries probably remained loyal to the organization, but, like Matt Cvetic, an undercover informant who had to take a job selling life insurance, they had less time than before to devote to Party work. The turnover among cadre required to earn their own livings had always been high, because of the killing workload involved in trying to handle two jobs at once, and, after their removal from the payroll, some probably ceased doing much for the movement.[7]

But even though a shortage of money caused by the Smith Act prosecutions probably deprived the Party of some paid functionaries, the Justice Department failed to achieve its principal objective: the decapitation of the CPUSA. The government managed to force John Williamson, Jack Stachel, and Irving Potash to accept voluntary deportation after they emerged from prison, but by 1960 seven of the Eleven had again participated in a CPUSA convention. Elizabeth Gurley Flynn also returned to an active role in the Communist movement, as did eight of nine alternate members of the 1950 national committee. Nor were the prosecutions successful in permanently depriving the Party of lower-level leadership. In 1957, when the CPUSA held its first national convention in a number of years, fifty Smith Act victims participated. Ten of those who failed to do so were still in prison, and a few others had been deported. A number who did not come were unable to travel freely because of restrictions imposed on them by trial or appellate courts as conditions of release on bail, but their absence from the councils of the Party was involuntary and temporary. The proceedings of the convention (a rather unsatisfactory source because they do not contain a complete roster of delegates) seem to indicate that a number of prosecuted Communists from western Pennsylvania, Ohio, Maryland, Hawaii, and the Pacific Northwest dropped out of active leadership as a result of their encounters with the Smith Act, but men who held top-level posts in the CPUSA during the late 1950s insist this was not so, attributing any otherwise inexplicable absences to a reorgani-

zation carried out in 1956 when the CPUSA dissolved its underground apparatus. As John Williamson insists, "Of the many Party leaders arrested,
tried, and sentenced under the Smith Act. . . . the overwhelming majority
stood the test of battle. . . ."[8]

III

Although the prosecutions failed to decapitate the Party, they did reduce its size dramatically. During the four years after January 1946, despite
the increasing intensity of the Cold War, the CPUSA actually grew slightly.
Although its strength, which leaped from 52,500 to around 73,000 as the
result of a 1946 recruiting drive, declined thereafter, reaching 60,000 by
the summer of 1948, it still had 54,174 members as late as the end of 1949.
Then Party membership plummeted, dropping by about one-fifth during
1950 and plunging another 6,812 the following year. By early 1953 the
strength of the CPUSA stood at 24,796, down more than 50 percent in a little
over three years. Thereafter, although the Party continued to shrink, the rate
of decline dropped off, so that as late as the end of 1955, it still had
22,663 members.[9]
     Because this loss of numbers occurred while American soldiers were
fighting Communist armies in Korea, it seems probable that some of those
who left the CPUSA did so because of displeasure over its opposition to
the war, and that others quit because of fear that identification with the
enemy might wreck their reputations. But neither the FBI nor the Party
offered these explanations for the membership decline. Instead, available
evidence indicates, that the major reason for that phenomenon was the
Smith Act prosecutions. J. Edgar Hoover long recognized the existence
of a causal connection between these and the drastic drop in Party strength,
but at first he failed to understand its complexity. His surmise was that arrests and convictions frightened Communists into quitting. In early 1950,
the FBI informed the White House that the major reason for the shrinking of the CPUSA was the intimidating effect of prosecutions and deportations, and, as late as February 1953, the director continued to offer
such an explanation. But John Gates, George Charney, George Myers,
Arnold Johnson, and Dorothy Healy—all Smith Act defendants and Party
leaders at the time of the prosecutions—reject this thesis, and the timing
of the massive drop in membership supports their position. This decline
began in 1950, while the Eleven were still appealing their convictions. As Communists anticipated no further arrests until the Supreme Court decided the
Dennis case, they had no reason to desert the CPUSA until the high tribunal ruled in June 1951.[10]

Although fear of the Smith Act did not inspire the mass exodus that occurred between 1950 and 1953, there was a causal connection between the prosecutions and the Party's membership losses. The Foley Square trial was a frightening experience for Communists. The undercover informants who testified in Harold Medina's courtroom horrified their former comrades, convincing most of them that the Party had been thoroughly infiltrated by the FBI. In a May 1950 *Political Affairs* article Gil Green summed up the conclusion which shaken radicals drew from what they had seen:

> At Foley Square we witnessed a number of scummy stool pigeons take the stand and lie themselves blue in the face about our Party. But we knew then, and we know even more so today, that J. Edgar Hoover exposed only those of his Gestapo agents that were either in secondary positions, had already outlived their usefulness or had doubles in the organization into which they had bored. He certainly did not expose his main agents and his network of brother rats.

Speaking for the National Committee, Green went on to scourge his comrades for their lack of vigilance and their failure to scrutinize adequately the records of suspect members. Whenever an individual acted in an "undisciplined, irresponsible, careless, factional, or anti-Party manner," he said, it was the duty of the leadership to call him to task, criticize him, and demand that he explain his actions. "We should of course not make the charge that a given individual is a stool pigeon unless we know that to be the case," Green observed, "but neither can we permit people who by their actions create suspicion in the minds of the Party to continue to do damage merely because we are not certain as to whether they are conscious enemies or not."[11]

Hoover describes what followed Green's call to action: "Member after member completely innocent of the Party's charges [was] expelled."[12] The CPUSA carried on an internal witch hunt which at least equaled in intensity the worst excesses of McCarthyism. Like their opponents, Communists set up loyalty boards, called review commissions, to screen out unreliables, and, convinced that "the enemy" was trying to foment opposition to the "political line" of the Party, made ideological conformity a litmus test for the detection of traitors. Communists developed a long list of banned ideas and, distrusting almost everyone, hastily threw out any comrade whose behavior seemed at all suspicious. One man was ejected solely for opening a door on a hot night, thus accidentally allowing the FBI to photograph a meeting he was attending.[13]

In addition to those members formally expelled, there were doubtless many others, regarded as unenthusiastic or suspected of disloyalty by someone in authority, who simply found themselves gradually excluded from participation in Party activities. In July 1951 the organizational department of the CPUSA announced that all Communists who had not reregistered would be dropped from the rolls, a move that had the effect of eliminating many loyal, but inactive, comrades. The "lopping off approach" took many forms, and the exact number of victims claimed by each is not, and probably never will be, known, but the overall impact of this policy is clear: It was the major cause of the sharp decline in membership which marked the period 1950-1952. Eventually, this fact became so obvious that even Hoover accepted it. On 23 February 1953, informing a House subcommittee about the recent decline in Party membership, he explained, "This drop has been due largely to a housecleaning by the Communists. . . ."[14]

Besides throwing out old members, the Party also became extremely reluctant to recruit new ones. Many Communists seem to have felt that halting enlistments was the best way of keeping informers from penetrating the organization. As early as February 1951 Henry Winston spoke out against this attitude, but his words had little effect. Two years later, there still existed "strong currents of resistance to Party recruiting."[15]

Reluctance to take in new members, coupled with expulsions, produced changes in the composition of the CPUSA which were, from the Stalinist point of view, highly undesirable. Because the curtailment of recruiting stopped the infusion of young people into the Party, the membership grew steadily older. At the same time, the proportion of blacks and industrial workers declined. For ideological reasons Communists had always put great emphasis on building their strength among blacks and laboring people, and consequently the CPUSA had held out incentives to entice members of these groups into the Party and had elevated them rapidly into leadership positions. Because they were so vigorously solicited, these comrades often lacked the motivation and commitment of other recruits, a fact that made them prime targets for "lopping off." Henry Winston warned his fellow Communists that their quest for absolute security would reduce the Party's "working class composition and our Negro workers in particular," but they were too fearful of informers to listen. The middle-class element also shrank, so that increasingly the CPUSA became an organization composed of aging foreign-born radicals who had been active in the Communist movement since its earliest days. These veterans were totally reliable, but most of them lived in isolation from the mainstream of American society, and their growing strength relative to that of other segments of the membership was not a healthy thing for the CPUSA.[16]

IV

The Party's suicidal reaction to the Smith Act prosecutions cost it more than members. Bent on protecting their organization against legal attack, Communists adopted security measures that greatly reduced the efficiency of the CPUSA, while at the same time increasing its isolation from the general public. The immediate cause of the resulting problems was the factor Starobin emphasizes: the mistakes of the Party's own leaders. But Communists did not reason in a vacuum, and the Smith Act was one of the most important considerations shaping some of their more disastrous decisions.

Among these errors in judgment none had more serious consequences than the resolution to send much of the Party underground. Even before the indictment of the Twelve, leaders of the CPUSA, convinced that the United States was becoming Fascist, began to plan a dive for cover. As early as 1946, Eugene Dennis issued a vague warning that the CPUSA might have to submerge in order to survive, and in June 1947, after returning from a trip to Europe, Foster presented the National Committee with a detailed plan for underground operations. Communists were at the time worried about Secretary of Labor Lewis Schwellenbach's call for the outlawing of their organization. This threat passed, and the Party did not implement Foster's scheme, but in November, after O. John Rogge predicted Justice Department raids against the CPUSA, the FBI received "information reflecting definite underground preparations on the part of certain Communist Party districts," and Massachusetts Stalinist leaders briefly went into hiding. Later the Mundt-Nixon bill, an ancestor of the McCarren Internal Security Act, shot fear through Communist ranks, and in the spring of 1948 word came down from the leadership that the Party was about to submerge. Local clubs drew up detailed organizational plans, then waited for a signal to put them into effect.[17]

The indictment of the Twelve in July 1948 caused Communists to become more diligent in their preparations. Robert Thompson instructed John Lautner to concentrate on readying the New York state organization for underground operations, and by December 1949 Lautner had created a seven-level structure including over 3,000 members. In Massachusetts the Party drew up a mobilization plan, and, in July and August of 1948, units in the Boston area staged full-scale practices. After the

Foley Square jury returned its verdict in October, word went out from
national headquarters to commence underground operations, and by
1949 some Communists, already withdrawn from their branches, were
beginning to set up hiding places and telephone contacts for others who
would drop out of sight later. The submersion process picked up speed
when the Eleven met their first appellate defeat and reached maximum
velocity after the Supreme Court upheld the Foley Square convictions.
Expecting the wave of additional arrests which followed the *Dennis* decision, national headquarters ordered local units to send one-third of
their best personnel into hiding. By the time the Court ruled, the operative leadership of the Party, at least in California, was already underground. Soon other key functionaries also became "unavailable."[18]

The Communists who entered the underground were among the Party's
most dedicated and trusted members. The case histories of twenty-five of
them reveal that all had been in the movement for more than two decades.
Those who became unavailable fell into one of three categories. The "deep
freeze" group included Thompson, Winston, Hall, and Green, the fugitives
from the second New York trial, and several hundred other knowledgeable
and experienced functionaries whose eventual prosecution the Party expected. These men and women went into prolonged hiding. The CPUSA
put into a "deep, deep freeze" (often abroad) other trusted cadre, not
necessarily prominent in the past, who were to assume leadership and
responsibility should the authorities manage to smash the rest of the Communist command structure. Finally, there were those members whose status was operative but unavailable (OBU). They moved about the country,
often in disguise, attempting to maintain liaison between the concealed
and public hierarchies of the CPUSA. The Party sought to integrate only
10 percent of its membership into the underground structure, resolving
that, if declared illegal, it would sacrifice the rest.[19]

Those who entered the underground found themselves involved in the
type of life usually reserved for the heroes and villains of grade-B spy thrill-
ers. They employed fictitious names, passwords, and secret contacts, carried false identification, altered their appearances, held furtive meetings
in the middle of the night, and in general behaved in a thoroughly clandestine manner. The Party brought Andrew Remes, former Wisconsin state
chairman, into the national office and gave him the assignment of procur-
ing a string of meeting places, telephone contact points, and hideouts for
use by the unavailables. Other functionaries attempted to mount a coun-
terintelligence operation against the FBI agents assigned to investigate
the underground.[20]

The unavailables stayed out of sight until 1955, when the CPUSA, persuaded that the political climate had changed, dissolved its underground

apparatus. In September of that year Max Weiss, wanted for violation of
the Smith Act, openly visited a Party headquarters in Harlem. Two months
later second-string fugitives William Marron, Fred Fine, and James Jackson
surrendered to authorities, and in 1956, with their fellow Foley Square
defendants now out of prison, Green and Winston also turned themselves
in.[21]

By the time of its dissolution the underground had done the CPUSA
immense harm, for besides costing Communists millions of dollars, the
system had badly damaged Party morale. Unavailables endured many
hardships, perhaps the worst of which was prolonged separation from
their families. Those members left behind in the open organization led
easier lives but resented being told what to do by unseen leaders whose
decisions they felt powerless to influence. Particularly damaging to the
political effectiveness of the Party was the internal orientation to which
it succumbed during the underground era. The functionaries who dominated affairs during the early 1950s were an "inner type," more concerned with administration and security than with expanding Communist influence among trade unionists, blacks, and progressives. At the
very time when the "objective situation" was most unfavorable and a
major effort was needed just to keep from losing ground, the CPUSA
abandoned the struggle for popular acceptance and support. By 1953
it had virtually given up sending spokesmen before legislative bodies and
no longer sought to purchase radio time and newspaper advertising space.
Mass leaflet distribution had virtually ceased, and many Communist offices
and headquarters were closed. Public meetings and even efforts to rent
halls in which to hold them were just fading memories. Wise old Alexander
Bittleman warned his comrades that, "The class struggle and the political
life of the country cannot be stopped at will, and a political party cannot
stop functioning among the masses for a time and then pick up where it
left off," but they would not listen. For too long, Communists, fearing
the Smith Act, isolated themselves from the public whose support they
badly needed.[22]

Although the underground was the most disastrous of the Party's security measures, others were also harmful. In the late summer and early autumn of 1948 the CPUSA reduced the size of its basic unit, breaking up
the large clubs which had developed during World War II and reviving three-
to-five-member cells, now called squads. The objective was to limit the number of comrades an informant who managed to penetrate the Party could
identify, but because their members knew other Communists from the days
of the large clubs and continued to see them socially, the squads failed to
accomplish the desired compartmentalization. The creation of numerous
small units so badly overtaxed the leadership resources of the CPUSA that

the new groups tended to be run badly. Their meetings, irregular and poorly planned, often provided inadequate opportunity for political discussion and yielded few positive results, so that many Communists quit their squads in disgust while others, lost in the reorganizational shuffle, simply never joined one.[23]

Restrictions on meetings, imposed to protect leaders from arrest, also impaired the efficiency of the CPUSA, by limiting contact among key functionaries. "Conventions and all large gatherings of the Communist Party were abolished during this period as a security measure," an investigator reported later. Although its constitution provided for biannual national conventions, the organization, after ordering some key personnel to remain away from the one that assembled just after the indictment of the Twelve, held none at all between 1950 and 1957. Even the National Committee did not meet for five years. Rules forbade the congregation of all members of any one leadership group. A rotating system, put into effect at national headquarters in early 1949, permitted only a portion of the Party's top officials to be in the building at any one time; others hid out, telephoning the office periodically for messages. As the Foley Square trial neared its conclusion, and fear of raids increased, the rotating system was also put into effect at the state level, and even some section organizers received instructions to stay away from their offices for a time.[24]

The CPUSA went to as much trouble to protect its secrets as to save its functionaries, sharply restricting the use of telephones and the mails and requiring members to pass along notifications of meetings by word of mouth. With increasing frequency it resorted to couriers for confidential communication. Information formerly distributed in mimeographed documents was now chalked on blackboards, from which it could be erased quickly, and any message put in written form had to be destroyed immediately after reading. Pittsburgh Communists were under orders not to call one another by name in their headquarters, because the building might be bugged. The CPUSA ceased issuing membership cards and, while collecting extensive information about each comrade, recorded no names, simply depending on the memories of subordinate leaders to match individuals with their numbered dossiers. The Party kept no minutes of meetings and maintained all financial records in code.[25]

Whatever their contribution to security, such measures clearly reduced efficiency. It was extremely difficult for various organizational levels to maintain contact with one another (assembling twenty leaders for a conference once took six weeks). Messages sent through the clandestine communication system often became garbled in transmission. Dispersed, unable to communicate effectively, and hamstrung by security procedures, national and district leaders found it impossible to organize necessary work adequately. The Party's checkup and control system broke down, and its fundamental procedural principle, democratic centralism, became badly distorted.[26]

In short, the CPUSA lost the capacity to act. As a result of the way the Party responded to legal attack, it became isolated, slow moving, bureaucratic, and inefficient. The Smith Act prosecutions were not the direct cause of its infirmity, but they had inspired the Communist decisions that debilitated the organization. Because of them, the Party staggered toward its climactic crisis as a helpless cripple.

V

Neither ruinous security measures nor the loss of two-thirds of its members killed the CPUSA. Indeed, by the time disaster overtook the Party in 1956, its internal purges had long since ended, and Communists were dissolving the underground. But prosecution had inflicted other, even more serious, wounds. The Smith Act attack had destroyed the organizational cohesion of the CPUSA, disrupting its leadership and internal discipline and softening the iron ideological conformity which had always been its greatest strength. Consequently, by 1956 the Communist Party was, like a house undermined by termites, ready to fall before the first strong wind that blew against it.

Nothing did more to weaken the CPUSA than the disruption of its leadership. While only twenty-nine convicted conspirators served time in prison, this group included most top officials of the Party, among them every regular member of the 1948 National Committee except William Z. Foster. Seven of the Eleven spent nearly four years behind bars, and the others even longer, because of contempt sentences imposed as punishments for their flights from justice. Both the Party's principal newspaper and its monthly journal lost their editors to penal institutions, and the Communist educational apparatus was without its ranking personnel for periods of one to two years, as was the large and important New York state organization. Because of the high bail demanded in Smith Act cases, even those defendants who avoided prison sentences generally spent some time in a cell. In Denver it took six months for all of the accused to gain release on bond.[27]

While a Smith Act victim languished in jail, the CPUSA was deprived of his leadership. In July 1954 Flynn reminded her comrades of what had happened to Eugene Dennis: "He is a political prisoner . . . his voice silenced, his pen stilled, his reading matter censored, his letters limited to his family, with punishment threatened if any portion of them is published or read at a public gathering." Prison officials did not want the General Secretary to continue running the Party from the Atlanta penitentiary, and, though Dennis attempted to do so, by passing instructions to his wife in correspondence and during prison visits, he was generally unsuccessful. The authorities subjected his mail to rigorous censorship, with the aim of deleting all "directives." When they prevented the General Secretary from commenting on domestic and international events, Congressman Vito Marcantonio led a delegation to see James V. Bennett, head of the federal prison system. This protest won Dennis the right to discuss matters reported in the press, but the ban on directives remained in force. Censorship of his letters was strangely erratic, and sometimes messages that violated the proscription did get through, but to a large extent the government managed to isolate the General Secretary from his subordinates on the outside. Authorities at the Lewisburg, Pennsylvania, penitentiary allowed John Williamson to correspond only with his wife, mother, and eldest son and returned a number of letters to Maurice Braverman as "unacceptable." How strictly the mail of a Communist prisoner was screened depended rather largely on the attitude of the associate warden at the particular institution where he was confined; thus some National Committee members did succeed in sending their comrades a few instructions. Visitors also maintained a kind of liaison between the prisoners and the Party. Although the Smith Act did not completely isolate and silence the top officials of the CPUSA, the prosecutions did make it impossible for them to provide their organization with the sort of day-to-day direction they had given it in the past.[28]

While the Eleven were on trial, high-ranking Communists, such as Steve Nelson, endeavored to impress upon their subordinates the importance of preparing themselves to take over vacant leadership positions. The New York Party attempted to create a horizontal structure, which would give it two reserves for every important official, and similar planning went on throughout the CPUSA. In order to have an alternative system of command and control, the Party sent hundreds of functionaries underground. Yet it was so unsuccessful in replacing what the prosecutions took away that by 1953, according to J. Edgar Hoover, the National Committee was "more or less inoperative. . . ." A similar paralysis of leadership extended throughout the Party.[29]

Communists tried to prevent the development of this situation by creating a reserve system and designating certain individuals to fill particular positions if the need arose, but for security reasons it kept those selected completely isolated from the jobs they might one day have to fill. Untrained reservists found themselves called upon to handle assignments for which their only preparation was the reading of a few reports, and performed accordingly. Creation of the underground only made a bad situation worse. Probably because most Communists assumed that those officers who remained "available" would soon go to prison, the CPUSA never clearly defined the relationship between, and the respective responsibilities of, its public and secret leadership groups, nor clarified lines of authority sufficiently to establish who was running the organization. In California, for example, the state board, which headed the open Party, developed an analysis of the political situation which directly contradicted the position of the unavailables; neither group would accept the views of the other, and the two marched smartly off in different directions.[30]

The disruption produced by the jailing of key cadre, whom the Party could not effectively replace, was only one of many ways in which the prosecutions interfered with the efficient management and administration of CPUSA affairs. Even when not confined, a Smith Act victim often found it impossible to devote himself fully to the business of the Party. He had to spend a great deal of time raising funds or be left without sufficient money to meet the legal and other expenses connected with his trial and also, of course, had to waste endless hours in court. The Baltimore defendants worked seven days a week on their case and often had to devote more than sixteen hours out of twenty-four to it. The National Committee continued to meet during the Foley Square trial, but only on open dates and long weekends in gatherings surrounded by tight security, and its members had to relegate important work to the few hours available after daily court sessions. While his case was on appeal, a Smith Act defendant had more time, but the legal system might restrict his use of it. A federal district court, for example, imposed limitations on travel by the Eleven which interfered with Party plans to have them speak at May Day rallies around the country.[31]

Even after serving his sentence, a prosecuted Communist was not a truly free person. In accordance with statutory requirements the government granted Gates and Dennis sixteen months time off for good behavior, but the terms of their paroles forbade participation in any CPUSA activities. Gates could not return to his position at the *Daily Worker* and had to take a job in a plastics plant. Although friends briefed him on the affairs of the Party, he could do no political work until his five-year sentence ended.[32]

Such deprivation of leadership caused discipline to deteriorate within the CPUSA. After the Eleven went to prison, Phillip Frankfeld, then a district organizer in Maryland, attempted to exploit the confusion in Communist ranks and propel himself into an important national office by publicly advocating an unauthorized alteration of the Party "line." Still capable of slapping down a lone deviant, his superiors expelled Frankfeld, but the national leadership became too impotent to maintain control over the two most important components of the CPUSA. While Robert Thompson, chairman of the New York Party, was absent, a "young Turk" movement, led by county organizers, battled against his policies, and a bitter conflict developed between the Empire State organization, to which approximately half the membership of the CPUSA belonged, and the national office. Across the continent, California Communists also shook off their traces and moved out on an independent course. Theirs became "the only section of the Party where the 'unavailable' madness [did not go] to such extraordinary lengths as elsewhere. . . . " The Californians strove "and with success, to maintain the Party's legal status and to defend it ably." In addition, they bluntly rejected orders from William Z. Foster concerning the conduct of their Smith Act case. Party operations had become so decentralized that even the strongest leadership might have been unable to control these rebels, and at that time strength was hardly the striking characteristic of the Communist high command. By either imprisoning or driving underground almost all of the top officers of the CPUSA, the Smith Act prosecutions had left the organization excessively dependent for direction on the ailing Foster. He was utterly incapable of controlling his willful subordinates on the West Coast, and, with the Californians joining the New Yorkers in revolt, the national office found itself without any real control over more than 60 percent of the movement.[33]

Besides weakening leadership and discipline, the Smith Act prosecutions also undermined Party unity by eating away at the blind acceptance of dogma which had long been the strongest bond holding the CPUSA together. The government's legal attack had little effect on the content of the Communist creed. The CPUSA continued to take as its guiding principle the policies of the Soviet Union. Likewise, the Smith Act produced no real change in the Party's attitude toward violence and revolution, although the prosecutions did cause the CPUSA to be extremely careful about what it said on these subjects. According to FBI informants, after the first trials Communists hastily destroyed all literature containing the word "force," and sometime around 1950 the National Education Commission issued a statement disclaiming certain study outlines, texts, and publications, while instructors began to teach from bare written frameworks, around which they filled in violent revolutionary material orally or with reading assignments given aloud. Whether or not such stories are true, it is certain that in 1948 the Party altered its constitution in a deliberate, but belated, attempt to establish that Communists could not possibly be guilty of advocating the overthrow of the government by force and violence. Leaders of the CPUSA who testified on this subject at Smith Act trials were less than totally candid. Those who took the stand at Foley Square gave so many Party members the impression that they had renounced the right of revolution that by the spring of 1950 both Eugene Dennis and William Z. Foster felt compelled to reassure their comrades publicly that this was not the case, and Elizabeth Gurley Flynn's obfuscations during the second New York trial evoked considerable criticism from one of her co-defendants. Although reluctant to acknowledge the fact in court, Communists, remaining committed to a socialist revolution, continued to believe that violence would probably accompany it. The Smith Act prosecutions did not change their thinking on this subject, and only in the field of intra-Party race relations, where the crusade against "white chauvinism" died out almost immediately after its principal proponent, Pettis Perry, went to prison, did they have any real impact on the line of the CPUSA.[34]

While doing little to change the content of Communist dogma, the prosecutions did affect the attitude of many Party members toward their ideology. Prior to the government's Cold War assault on the CPUSA, almost all Communists had accepted on blind faith the doctrines handed down to them from above, but by the time the Smith Act prosecutions ended, many no longer would. Legal attack put some Communists behind bars and drove others into the underground. In both places cadre found themselves, suddenly, perhaps for the first time in years, physically cut off from the hectic routine of the open Party. By themselves, alone in their cells or in hiding, they had little to occupy their minds and plenty of time to think. This was a dangerous situation for the CPUSA. As the Senate Judiciary Committee once explained, a Communist normally "lives in a world which is hermetically sealed off from the outside by a more and more impenetrable iron curtain of continuous indoctrination to which he has become addicted to the exclusion of all other outside sources of information and thought." As long as members remained caught up in the feverish activity of routine Party business, it was impossible for them to accept any reality counter to the Communist outlook. Psychological independence became possible only when they experienced a period of physical or emotional separation. After service in World War II detached thousands of young men from the CPUSA and surrounded them with non-Communists, a substantial proportion decided not to return to the Party. The separation from the organization which the Smith Act imposed on hundreds of key cadre proved equally subversive of its control over them.[35]

No one knows how all reacted to the various types of isolation into which legal pressure forced them, but the case of Northwest District official Barbara Hartle, once regarded as the outstanding woman Communist on the Pacific Coast, is suggestive. In the summer of 1950, Party superiors ordered Hartle underground, and for the next two years, using assumed names, she moved from city to city in Washington and Oregon. This is how hiding out affected her:

> I wasn't able to associate closely with Communists. I wasn't in just daily morning, noon, and night contact with other Communists. Thousands of meetings and many, many books to read and reports to make and people to teach, and demonstrations to hold, and picket lines and signs to make, and all these millions of things that just practically swallow up an individual in the Communist movement.
>
> I did have a chance to read, again, some literature which I had been much interested in in the past, before I joined the Communist Party, and some histories that were not on the good list of the Communist Party.
>
> I think I loosened the bonds a little bit, the discipline a little bit, at that time, because it was then that I decided that I was just—well, I was disgusted with the Communist Party.

In 1953 a federal court convicted Hartle of conspiring to violate the Smith Act, and while free on bond, she revealed her doubts to a reporter, who persuaded her to go to the FBI. A short time later she deserted the Communist movement.[36]

In leaving the Party so soon after her doubts arose, Hartle was probably not typical of those who experienced similar misgivings. Most remained in the CPUSA until at least 1956 or 1957. A prominent example is John Gates, who describes his stay in the Atlanta penitentiary as "a period of intense re-examination of ideas." Gates found particularly disturbing the absence of a mass movement for the liberation of the Smith Act victims. Why had one failed to develop, he asked himself? The more he looked at the civil liberties record of the CPUSA, the more Gates wondered whether there was not something wrong with its attitude toward democracy. He also began to question the undeviating identity between the Party's positions and those of the USSR. Gates now realized that "it was simply not human to have no differences" and that Soviet policy could not possibly have "always been right and not mistaken even once. I could not help feeling finally that there must be something wrong in our relations with

the Soviet Union," he says. Now a doubter, Gates found it impossible to
accept Russian explanations for suspicious events in the Soviet Union
and the satellite countries. In this state of mind he decided to read George
Orwell's *1984*, a book that the Party long ago had condemned as Trotskyite heresy. Actually, Gates did not particularly like it, but his decision
to look at such a work was the significant thing. As he himself says, "Reading Orwell did not open my eyes: rather it was the fact that events had
opened my eyes and this caused me to read Orwell." The more Gates pon-
dered, the more the closed system of thought in which he had lived since
becoming a Communist cracked and crumbled. "All this self-probing was
carrying me beyond a mere questioning of our former tactics and policies,"
he says, "and into an examination of fundamental propositions." Like
Gates in his cell, those Communists hiding out in the United States and
abroad also used their free time to take a hard look at basic Party policy.[37]

Such an examination was precisely what American communism could
not endure. The Party line had always served as an ideological glue, holding the pieces of the CPUSA together. Communists might not always see
eye to eye with one another, but once the Party spoke, disagreement in-
evitably ceased. Individuals might err, but the organization, which received
the line from Moscow, was always correct. Communists blindly accepted
dogma handed down from above, because to challenge Marxist-Leninist
doctrine was to call truth a lie. To quit the movement was as unthinkable
as renouncing salvation. This unthinking ideological conformity made it
easy for leaders to control the membership and gave the Party a cohesion
which no political group that tolerated internal disagreement over fundamental questions could match.

Gates, with his now-questioning intellect, represented a threat to the
organizational stability of the CPUSA, as did anyone who had developed
a similar frame of mind. How many of these there were, no one knows,
but the Smith Act prosecutions had caused a great many Communist
functionaries to undergo the kind of isolation experienced by Gates and
Hartle. It did not affect all of them in the same way. Atlanta made a rebel
of Dennis, but unlike Gates, the General Secretary never challenged the
really fundamental principles of the Party. Sid Stein and Fred Fine emerged
from hiding to become advocates of change; Robert Thompson did not. In
the turmoil that eventually wracked the Party there were activists on both
sides who had experienced isolation and others in each camp who had not.
Nevertheless, the separation phenomenon clearly played a role. It is worth
noting that, while Gates, who had been to prison, headed the faction advocating change, Foster, who had experienced neither jail nor the underground,
led the opposition. Also suggestive is the fact that Foster drew his most in-

transigent support from among professionals—the lawyers, doctors, and businessmen classified as members-at-large—whose Party lives had been least affected by the organization's recent problems. On the other hand, as Starobin points out, almost all of those who had been underground rebelled. They and functionaries who had served prison sentences had far more reason to doubt the wisdom of their Party.[38]

The questioning outlooks that many cadre brought back from their periods of isolation undermined the unity and strength of the CPUSA, for these were the men and women who comprised much of the permanent skeleton which an unstable membership with a high turnover rate fleshed out to form the Party. By 1956, both ideologically and organizationally, the CPUSA was on the verge of collapse. "It was," as Robert Bendiner observed at the time, "already far gone when events in Moscow, Poznan, and Budapest came to shake the whole Communist world. . . ."[39] The Smith Act prosecutions had so weakened the Party that any substantial stress could bring it crashing down, and all the Russians did was supply the strain which an already rotten structure could not endure. First came Khrushchev's speech at the Twentieth Party Congress in February 1956 and close on its heels revelations about anti-Semitism in the Soviet Union, which had a strong emotional impact on the heavily Jewish American party. Before this country's Communists could recover from those shocks, they learned of the uprisings in Poland and Hungary and of Russia's brutal repression of them.

Assaulted by wave after wave of profoundly disturbing news from abroad, the Communist Party disintegrated into squabbling factions. Doubters like Gates saw in the news from Eastern Europe proof of the fallibility of the Soviet Union and, joining with comrades concerned about authoritarianism in the Party, they demanded a more democratic and American form of Communist organization consistent with a peaceful transition to socialism. *Party Voice* printed denunciations of the Foster-Dennis leadership and appeared to endorse that heretical Titoist notion, national communism. The leaders of the New York organization supported Gates, whereas Dennis, who for a time backed reform, eventually aligned himself with Foster's conservative Stalinist forces. The California organization went its own unique way, and the long-repressed rank and file, invited by the *Daily Worker* to express itself, did so with a vengeance. The FBI, anxious to capitalize upon and augment the mounting turmoil within the Party, urged its informants "to engage in controversial discussions around such issues as Soviet intervention in the Hungarian revolution and the cult of Stalin, as well as to be critical of certain leadership factions . . . ," and sent anonymous mailings "to those [Communists] who had serious doubts regarding the competence of Party leaders. . . .''[40]

At first it appeared the squabbling within the CPUSA would end in victory for Gates and his reform-minded followers, but they failed to sustain their momentum. In February 1957 the American Communist Party held its sixteenth national convention. Although the dissidents had a clear majority, they feared the consequences of a split, and in their eagerness to avoid one determined not to mention Poland, Hungary, or Russian anti-Semitism. They settled for lukewarm compromises on most other matters, and the convention ended, in effect, as a victory for Foster and his orthodox supporters. Certainly, that is the way many of the dissidents interpreted the outcome. Disgusted and under increasing pressure from the Fosterites, who steadily tightened their control over the organization, more and more dissenters departed. By the summer of 1958 the Party's crisis was over. The conservatives had triumphed, but their prize was a nearly dead Party of only 3,000 to 6,000 members.[41]

As a political force American communism had for all practical purposes ceased to exist. Because it was the period 1956-1958 that witnessed the final great decline of the CPUSA, it is easy to overemphasize the importance of the dramatic events of those years. The news out of Eastern Europe hit the American Party with the force of a tidal wave. In explaining the collapse of the CPUSA, though, the important question is not what made the wave but why the organization which it struck could not stand the strain. If the discipline and ideological conformity which had bound the CPUSA together in the past had still existed, the organization might have weathered the storm, but by 1956 both had deteriorated under the pressure of legal attack. The Russians tried, by endorsing the views of Foster and Dennis, to settle the controversy over Stalin which Khrushchev's speech had initiated within the American Party, but their intervention failed to silence Gates and his fellow dissenters. Even the National Committee of the CPUSA, although accepting the essence of the Soviets' position, insisted upon expressing certain reservations. Because of these, Foster opposed its statement on the subject, but, when a vote was taken, the titular head of the Party found himself a minority of one. Things had changed a great deal since 1945, when the mere publication of an article by a spokesman for the world Communist movement could topple Earl Browder and elevate Foster to command of the CPUSA. The aging chairman eventually regained control of his organization, but only because the opposition departed. Once, even defections on the scale of those which occurred during the years 1956 through 1958, particularly by hard-core cadre, would have been unthinkable. Although every bit as disturbed by the Hitler-Stalin pact as Gates and his supporters were by

Khrushchev's speech and the Soviet attack on Hungary, Barbara Hartle had remained loyal to the CPUSA, but during the crisis of the 1950s her counterparts left the organization in droves. By that time most American Communists would no longer accept whatever Russia did, and the top officials of the CPUSA could no longer control them.[42]

The Smith Act prosecutions had fundamentally changed the Party, so badly undermining it that the organization could no longer endure the kind of crises which it had lived through in the past. The government's legal attack did not prove sufficient by itself to destroy the CPUSA. The Party managed to survive both the drastic decline in membership and the ill-advised security measures which prosecution inspired, and even the loss of organizational cohesion, although a grievous injury, was not necessarily a fatal one. But, just as a major illness often leaves the human body too weak to survive minor infections which it could otherwise resist , so the Smith Act left the CPUSA in such a weakened condition that it could not cope with the problems that beset it in 1956. Although the Russians struck the fatal blow, it was the U.S. Department of Justice that was ultimately responsible for the collapse of the Communist Party.

NOTES

1. Joseph R. Starobin, *American Communism in Crisis, 1943-1957* (Cambridge, Mass.: Harvard University Press, 1972), pp. 108-14, 186-91, 195, 214-23.

2. Shannon, *Decline*, pp. 155-57, 181, 364-71 (quote on p. 371).

3. Shannon, *Decline*, pp. 4, 360; Alonzo Hamby, *Beyond the New Deal: Harry S. Truman and American Liberalism* (New York and London: Columbia University Press, 1973), pp. 151-54; Starobin, *American Communism in Crisis*, p. 202; Louis Jay Herman, "Turmoil in U.S. Communism," *The New Leader*, 21 January 1957, pp. 7-10.

4. U.S., Congress, Senate, Select Committee to Study Governmental Operations with Respect to Intelligence Activities, *Hearings . . . Federal Bureau of Investigation*, 94th Cong., 1st sess., 1975, pt. 6: 372-73, 819-20. On the drop in Party membership after the Hitler-Stalin pact see Nathan Glazer, *The Social Basis of American Communism* (New York: Harcourt, Brace & World, 1961), p. 92, and J. Edgar Hoover, *Masters of Deceit: The Story of Communism in America and How to Fight It* (New York: Henry Holt & Co., 1958), pp. 4-5, 119.

5. Shannon, *Decline*, p. 202.

6. *Cleveland Press*, 14 March 1956; *DW*, 4 April 1949, 17 January 1952, 29 January 1952, and 19 June 1955; Elizabeth G. Flynn, "Mass Action Can Free the Eleven," *PA* 29 (May 1950): 151-53, and "The Militant Traditions of Labor Defense Inspire Our Fight Today," *PA* 30 (Feb-

ruary 1951): 124; Justice, "List"; United States v. Weiss, 233 F. 2d 463 (7th Cir. 1956); Field v. United States, 193 F. 2d 86 (2d Cir. 1951); testimony by J. Edgar Hoover in SApp, *Hearings . . . Departments of State, Justice and Commerce and the Judiciary for the Fiscal Year Ending June 30, 1952,* 82nd Cong., 1st sess., 1951, pt. 1: 71; Henry Winston, "Building the Party— Key to Building the United Front Struggle," *PA* 29 (May 1950): 64; Shannon, *Decline,* p. 199; Justice, *Annual Report for 1954,* p. 384; Arnold Johnson and George Myers, personal interviews with the Author at National Headquarters, CPUSA, 8 August 1973; John T. McTernan to Elizabeth G. Flynn, Box 5, Victor J. Jerome Papers, Sterling Memorial Library, Yale University, New Haven, Conn.

7. Glazer, *Social Basis,* p. 72; Claire Neikind, "U.S. Communism: Its Underground Plans and Its Secret Business Empire," *The Reporter,* 23 January 1951, p. 8; Hoover, *Masters of Deceit,* pp. 110, 148-49; Matt Cvetic, *The Big Decision* (Hollywood: Matt Cvetic, 1959), pp. 146-48.

8. Robert Mollan, "Smith Act Prosecutions: The Effect of the Dennis and Yates Decisions," *University of Pittsburgh Law Review* 26 (June 1965): 716-20; Justice, "List"; CPUSA, *Proceedings (Abridged) of the 16th National Convention of the Communist Party, U.S.A.* (New York: New Century Publishers, 1957), pp. 16-252; HUAC, *Hearings . . . Northern California District of the Communist Party: Structure, Objectives, Leadership,* 86th Cong., 2d sess., 1955, pt. 4: 2383-84; list of National Committee members from February 1951 issue of *PA; DW,* 13 February 1957; Myers and Johnson interviews; John Williamson, *Dangerous Scot: The Life and Work of an American Undesirable* (New York: International Publishers, 1969), p. 172. Potash reentered the country illegally. He was jailed for a year and a half and then released on bond pending deportation.

9. Shannon, *Decline,* pp. 92, 202, 364-69; Glazer, *Social Basis,* pp. 92-93; Record, at 9648, McGrath v. Communist Party of the United States of America, 1 S.A.C.B. 1 (1952) (hereinafter cited as *Record*); HApp, *Hearings . . . Department of Justice Appropriations for 1952,* 82d Cong., 1st sess., 1951, p. 336, *Hearings . . . Departments of State, Justice, Commerce and Judiciary Appropriations for 1953,* 82d Cong., 1st sess., 1952, pt. 4: 174, and *Hearings . . . Appropriations for the Departments of State, Justice and Commerce for the Fiscal Year Ending June 30, 1954: Department of Justice,* 83rd Cong., 1st sess., 1953, p. 137; SApp, *Hearings . . . Making Appropriations for the Departments of State, Justice, Commerce and the Judiciary for the Fiscal Year Ending June 30, 1952,* 82d Cong., 1st sess., 1951, pt. 1: 82; Justice, *Annual Report for 1954,* p. 383.

10. Testimony by Hoover in HApp, *State, Justice for 1953,* p. 174; Gates, *The Story,* p. 157; George B. Charney, *A Long Journey* (Chicago: Quadrangle, 1968), p. 202; Johnson and Myers interviews; Dorothy Healy, personal interview with the Author at her home in Los Angeles, 31 December 1973; Stephen J. Spingarn, Memorandum for Mr. Hopkins, Box 31, Stephen J. Spingarn Papers, HTL.

11. "For Communist Vigilance," *PA* 29 (May 1950): 117-18.

12. Hoover, *Masters of Deceit*, p. 178.

13. Ibid., p. 182; Shannon, *Decline*, pp. 227-29, 239-41, 369; Starobin, *American Communism in Crisis*, pp. 196-98; Charney, *A Long Journey*, p. 207; Elmer Larson, "On Guard Against Enemy Infiltration," *PA* 31 (October 1952): 28; HUAC, *Hearings . . . Investigation of Communist Activities in the Albany, N.Y. Area*, 83rd Cong., 2d sess., 1954, pt. 3; 4327.

14. Starobin, *American Communism in Crisis*, pp. 220-21; testimony by Hoover, HApp, *State, Justice for 1954*, p. 137. The phrase "lopping off approach" is used by Henry Winston in "Gear the Party for Its Great Tasks," *PA* 30 (February 1951): 52.

15. Winston, "Gear the Party," p. 52; Alex Parker, *Organizing the Party for Victory over Reaction: Report Delivered at the National Conference of the Communist Party* (New York: New Century Publishers, 1953), pp. 42-43. "Alex Parker" was a pen name used by someone in the Party's underground (Shannon, *Decline*, p. 231).

16. Glazer, *Social Basis*, pp. 121-28, 151, 163-64; Parker, *Organizing the Party*, p. 23; Gates, *The Story*, p. 193; Winston, "Gear the Party," p. 52.

17. Neikind, "Secret Business Empire," p. 6; Eugene Dennis, "American Democracy Must Not Commit Suicide," *PA* 26 (April 1947): 291-92; testimony by Lautner in ISC, *Hearings . . . Subversive Influences in the Educational Process*, 82d Cong., 2d sess., 1952, p. 250; testimony by Barbara Hartle in Appendix to Brief for Appellee, at 221-22, Scales v. United States, 367 U.S. 203 (1961); J. Edgar Hoover to Harry Hawkins Vaughn, 12 November 1947, Box 167, President's Secretaries' Files, Papers of H.S. Truman, HTL; Herbert A. Philbrick, *I Led 3 Lives: Citizen, "Communist," Counterspy* (New York: McGraw-Hill Book Co., 1952), pp. 252-53, 257; Julia Brown, *I Testify: My Years as an Undercover Agent for the FBI* (Boston and Los Angeles: Western Islands Publishers, 1966), p. 27; Starobin, *American Communism in Crisis*, pp. 172-73.

18. Testimony by Lautner in *Record*, pp. 9359-63; Don Whitehead, *The F.B.I. Story: A Report to the People* (New York: Random House, 1956), pp. 135, 298-99; *Yates Transcript*, pp. 5030-32; Philbrick, *I Led 3 Lives*, pp. 259-60; Irving Howe and Lewis Coser, *The American Communist Party: A Critical History (1919-1957)* (Boston: Beacon Press, 1957), p. 478; Flynn, "Militant Traditions," pp. 124-32; Healy interview; Al Richmond, *A Long View from the Left: Memoirs of an American Revolutionary* (Boston: Houghton Mifflin, 1973), p. 299.

19. Hoover, *Masters of Deceit*, p. 276; testimony by Hoover in HApp, *State, Justice for 1953*, pt. 4: 175; Shannon, *Decline*, p. 230; Starobin, *American Communism in Crisis*, pp. 221-22; testimony by Lautner in *Record*, pp. 9363-84.

20. HJC, *Hearings . . . on H.R. 3, A Bill to Amend Title 18 United States Code to Provide Punishment of Persons Who Jump Bail*, 83rd Cong.,

2d sess., 1954, p. 6; *Public Record*, p. 656; Shannon, *Decline*, pp. 232-33; testimony by Lautner in *Record*, pp. 9410-11; Starobin, *American Communism in Crisis*, p. 222.

21. Shannon, *Decline*, pp. 251-72; Justice, *Annual Report for 1956*, p. 211; Charney, *Journey*, p. 239; Williamson, *Dangerous Scot*, p. 202.

22. Hoover, *Masters of Deceit*, pp. 275-77, 285-87; Larson, "On Guard," p. 20; Charney, *A Long Journey*, p. 210; Starobin, *American Communism in Crisis*, pp. 221-22; Parker, *Organizing the Party*, pp. 7-10; Flynn, "Militant Traditions," p. 128; Alexander Bittleman, "Mass Tasks Facing the Party Today," *PA* 30 (September 1951): 17.

23. ISC, *The Communist Party of the United States of America: What It Is and How It Works: A Handbook for Americans*, 84th Cong., 1st sess., 1955, Committee Print, p. 50; HUAC, *Hearings . . . Investigation of Communist Activities in the San Francisco Area*, 83rd Cong., 1st sess., 1953, pt. 3: 3309, 3409-10; Shannon, *Decline*, p. 229; Parker, *Organizing the Party*, pp. 14-17.

24. HUAC, *Hearings . . . Structure and Organization of the Communist Party of the United States*, 87th Cong., 1st sess., 1961, pt. 1; 569-70 (quote on p. 570); Gates, *The Story*, p. 164; testimony by Lautner in *Record*, pp. 9414-16; FBI, "Communist Party, USA (Action of CP re Arrest of National Board Members), Internal Security (C)," typescript, 26 July 1948, Box 167, President's Secretaries' Files, HTL.

25. Testimony by Hoover in SApp, *State, Justice for 1952*, pt. 1: 85; Cvetic, *Big Decision*, p. 116; Shannon, *Decline*, pp. 228-29; *Yates Transcript*, p. 5169; Hoover, *Masters of Deceit*, p. 156; testimony by Lautner in *Record*, pp. 9332-41; testimony by Cvetic in HUAC, *Hearings . . . Exposé of Communist Party of Western Pennsylvania Based upon Testimony of Mathew Cvetic*, 81st Cong., 2d sess., 1950, pp. 1235-36; ISC, *Communist Party of the United States*, pp. 23, 53.

26. Shannon, *Decline*, p. 229; Parker, *Organizing the Party*, pp. 14-17; Myers and Johnson interviews.

27. Justice, "List"; *DW*, 28 December 1955.

28. Elizabeth G. Flynn, "Freedom for Eugene Dennis and the Battle for Democracy," *PA* 33 (July 1954): 5; Starobin, *American Communism in Crisis*, pp. 5, 221; Gates, *The Story*, p. 140; Eugene Dennis to Peggy Dennis, 20 September and 18 October 1951, 27 January, 3 February, 13 November, and 24 November 1953, and 7 March, 14 March, 24 May, and 19 July 1954, Eugene Dennis, *Letters from Prison* (New York: International Publishers, 1956), pp. 14-15, 17-18, 64-66, 68, 99, 114-15, 122-23, 127; Williamson, *Dangerous Scot*, p. 194; Myers and Johnson interviews; Maurice Braverman, telephonic interview with the Author, 18 August 1976.

29. Testimony by Matt Cvetic in HUAC, *Communist Party of Western Pennsylvania*, p. 1341; testimony by Lautner in *Record*, pp. 9364-80; Hoover, *Masters of Deceit*, p. 280; testimony by Hoover in HApp, *State, Justice for 1954*, p. 138.

30. Testimony by Lautner in *Record*, pp. 9386-87; Starobin, *American Communism in Crisis*, pp. 4-5; Healy interview; Richmond, *Long View*, pp. 312-14.

31. *DW*, 10 December 1948; testimony by Lautner in *Record*, pp. 9425-31; Braverman interview; Bettv Gannett, *The Communist Program and the Struggle for Jobs, Peace, Equal Rights and Democracy* (New York: New Century Publishers, 1954), p. 2.

32. Gates, *The Story*, pp. 155-57.

33. Ibid., pp. 158-59 (quote on p. 158); Charney, *A Long Journey*, pp. 226, 232-33; Healy interview; ISC, *Communist Party of the United States*, p. 34.

34. ISC, *Communist Party of the United States*, p. 1; Gates, *The Story*, p. 78; Hoover, *Masters of Deceit*, p. 7; Shannon, *Decline*, pp. 264, 271; testimony by Emanuel Richardson in HUAC, *Activities in the Albany Area*, pt. 4: 4361; testimony by Ralph Clontz in Appendix to Brief, at 1274-85, Scales v. United States, 360 U.S. 926 (1959); testimony by Dennis Lancaster in *Yates Transcript*, pp. 6696-97; Eugene Dennis, "For Communist Clarity and Resoluteness to Forge Working-Class and People's Unity," *PA* 29 (May 1950): 41-58; William Z. Foster, "People's Front and People's Democracy," *PA* 29 (June 1950): 29; V. J. Jerome to National Committee, 6 December 1952, Box 2, Jerome Papers.

35. ISC, *Communist Party of the United States*, pp. 47-48; Frank S. Meyer, *The Moulding of Communists: The Training of the Communist Cadre* (New York: Harcourt, Brace & Co., 1961), p. 157; Howe and Coser, *American Communist Party*, p. 422; Shannon (*Decline*, p. 109) and Starobin (*American Communism in Crisis*, p. 35) both point to prolonged separation from Party life as the reason why the CPUSA retained so few of its veterans.

36. Hoover, *Masters of Deceit*, pp. 121-22; testimony by Hartle in HUAC, *Northern California District*, pt. 1: 1976.

37. Gates, *The Story*, pp. 141-55 (quotes on pp. 141, 145, 155); Starobin, *American Communism in Crisis*, pp. 6, 307, n. 13.

38. Charney, *A Long Journey*, pp. 261, 264, 284; Starobin, *American Communism in Crisis*, p. 223; Myers and Johnson interviews.

39. Robert Bendiner, "The U.S. Communists—Rebellion in Microcosm," *The Reporter*, 13 December 1956, p. 20.

40. Shannon, *Decline*, pp. 272-347; Howe and Coser, *American Communist Party*, pp. 493-97; Starobin, *American Communism in Crisis*, pp. 225-27; Select Committee to Study Intelligence Activities, *Federal Bureau of Investigation*, pt. 6: 819.

41. Shannon, *Decline*, pp. 318-64.

42. Ibid., pp. 297-301; Hoover, *Masters of Deceit*, p. 119.

8

Return to Reason

> *The greatest danger to this country is not Communism. The greatest danger is that we might adopt the tactics that the Communists employ, at least in other countries. Once we do that . . . we then go down the road to tyranny and degradation of human spirits.*
>
> —Judge Charles J. McNamee
> 10 February 1956

The Communist Party was not the only victim of the Smith Act prosecutions. Civil liberties suffered too. At first, few Americans seemed concerned about what the government's war on the CPUSA might do to constitutional rights, and even the ACLU, intimidated by public opinion, shrank from defending victims of the Smith Act. But after international tensions began to ease in 1953, many people grew worried about what the methods used to combat domestic communism were doing to civil liberties. Shocking revelations concerning professional witnesses on whom the government had relied to obtain Smith Act convictions directed a portion of this anxiety toward the prosecutions, and so did the efforts of several local bar associations to preserve the right to counsel for Communist defendants. Both served to undermine support for the government's attack on the Party by reminding Americans that preservation of their country's traditional constitutional guarantees was far more important than successful prosecution of the CPUSA.

I

When the Smith Act attack began in 1948, the constitutional rights of Communists had few defenders. So pervasive was public hostility in this country toward Russia and its allies that even the ACLU was intimidated. A week after the government moved against the Twelve, ACLU director Roger Baldwin, and three members of the board, Arthur Garfield Hays, Raymond Wise, and John Finerty, wrote to the attorney general, vowing to defend the Communist leaders. During an August 1948 speech, Hays vigorously condemned the prosecution, and in October the ACLU submitted to the district court a brief attacking the constitutionality of the indictments. Soon, though, concerned about the damage to its reputation which might result from close association with symbols of the Cold War enemy, the ACLU drew back from the Communist case, announcing, on the day the trial began, that it would take no part in the proceedings and that even it the Twelve were convicted, it would assist them before higher courts only in challenging the constitutionality of the Smith Act. Baldwin took care to emphasize his organization's lack of sympathy for the CPUSA. After the Foley Square jury returned its verdicts, the ACLU did support the convicted radicals in their appeal, but it remained cautious, filing friend-of-the-court briefs but taking care to dissociate itself as much as possible from the defendants.[1]

The *Dennis* decision, regarded by the union's executive director, Patrick Murphy Malin, as of "transcendent importance," jolted the ACLU into adopting a more activist posture. Malin prepared a lengthy analysis of the various opinions in the case, which he circulated to other officers, including, interestingly enough, the one responsible for public relations. A revised version went to the board of directors, which, on 25 June 1951, adopted a statement condemning the Supreme Court's decision and expressing a determination to see it overruled. Although Malin insisted that the ACLU was making "no change in policy," it certainly appeared to be doing so, for the statement promised that the organization would not only continue to participate in appellate litigation and work to secure repeal of the Smith Act but that it would also intervene in future Communist cases at the trial level.[2]

Although playing a more active role than in the past, the ACLU did not entirely overcome its caution. It published a pamphlet attacking the Supreme Court's ruling, and during 1952 civil liberties union representatives intervened in both the Baltimore and Los Angeles cases. But the national leadership did not believe that the Justice Department, at least as long as it remained within the bounds of the *Dennis* decision, should refrain from prosecuting members of the CPUSA, and it insisted, despite objections from a number of local affiliates, on publicly expressing opposition to communism. Even at the trial level, ACLU involvement in Smith Act litigation continued to consist mainly of filing friend-of-the-court briefs. Hays declined an offer to serve as trial counsel for the Flynn group, and although

A. L. Wirin of the union's southern California affiliate joined the Los Angeles and Honolulu defense teams, he did so as a private attorney rather than as a representative of his organization.[3]

The reluctance of the ACLU to endanger its standing with the public by becoming too deeply involved in the defense of Stalinists is understandable, for with the world frozen into hostile blocs, and Red soldiers killing American boys in Korea, the idea of civil liberties for Communists was anathema to most people. As late as the fall of 1953, two-thirds of those interviewed by the Gallup poll opposed even allowing a Party member to make a speech. As far as the overwhelming majority of Americans was concerned, the Cold War enemy had no rights.[4]

II

By late 1953, though, global tensions had begun to ease somewhat. Eisenhower, a former soldier who understood better than Harry Truman the limitations of military power, proved considerably less bellicose than his predecessor. Although the frightening noises associated with the brinksmanship diplomacy of Secretary of State John Foster Dulles tended to obscure the fact, the new administration was more willing than the old to accept the mere amelioration of international difficulties. Ike, who entered office with a political commitment to end the war in Korea, settled for a negotiated peace there, agreeing to an amistice, signed on 27 July 1953, which simply confirmed the existing battlefield stalemate. Termination of the Korean conflict encouraged a new spirit of accommodation. On the Soviet side of the Iron Curtain, where Joseph Stalin had died a few months earlier, the new Russian leadership evidenced a belief in the possibility of peacefully resolving that country's differences with the United States, and the truce, by halting a war which had threatened to expand into Manchuria, and perhaps even the USSR itself, reinforced its cooperative tendencies. The Soviet Union's successful testing of a hydrogen bomb in August 1953 also promoted accommodation, for now that Russia had broken the American monopoly on the most awesome weapon known to man, its leaders had less reason to fear that the United States might launch a preventive war. They felt self-confident enough to enter into peaceful give and take with the West, and in May 1955, by signing a long-delayed Austrian peace treaty, indicated their willingness to negotiate a resolution of Cold War controversies.

Two months later, Eisenhower and the prime ministers of Britain and France met with the Russians at Geneva in a summit conference, which, although it produced few substantive agreements, was nevertheless of considerable significance. By sitting down together, the United States and the Soviet Union, as a practical matter, abandoned the pursuit of military victory in the Cold War and accepted the status quo in Europe and China. Although the conference did not end the conflict between the two superpowers, it did alter the nature of their struggle. Geneva took the Soviet-American contest out of the realm of moral absolutes and returned it to the status of an international conflict of interest in which something less than total victory could be tolerated. In the years that followed, the United States and Russia concentrated on competing for prestige and allies in the underdeveloped areas of the world, thereby introducing into global politics a new spirit, if not of peace, at least of coexistence.[5]

III

At home too the mood was changing. Through the early 1950s the Communist issue had dominated domestic politics, making the man who had become the symbol of the national crusade against subversion, Senator Joseph McCarthy, such a potent figure that few dared to challenge him or the principles for which he stood. By the winter of 1953-1954, anti-radical and anti-libertarian attitudes, commonly referred to as McCarthyism, had permeated every aspect of American life. But while the night was black, dawn was imminent, for the 1952 elections had brought to power McCarthy's own Republican Party.

Eisenhower did not effect all of the changes which the Wisconsin senator and his backers desired, and, driven by consistency and political ambition, the anti-Communist demagogue pressed on with the attack on the Washington bureaucracy which he had begun while Truman occupied the White House. Eventually, he met resistence. During the Truman years, tensions created by an unnaturally long exclusion from presidential and administrative power had agitated conservatives, prompting their congressional spokesmen to direct ever more strident charges of subversion at the liberal-dominated executive branch. The Republican victory in 1952 relieved the frustrations long felt by these opponents of reform and forced upon them the restraint and responsibility which the exercise of power demands.[6] McCarthy, useful for both partisan and psychological reasons while the GOP was in opposition, now became an annoyance to many in his own party. Soon after taking office, Eisenhower found it necessary to oppose the Wisconsin anti-Communist on a number of issues and to insist that fellow Republican senators restrain his reckless behavior.

Besides arousing the opposition of others in the GOP, McCarthy lost influence with the country. His popularity peaked in December 1953 and started a downward slide. The senator's televised confrontation with the Department of the Army in the spring of 1954, which exposed him before the public as a crude and vicious demagogue, further eroded an already crumbling power base. By 10 April, a Cleveland area minister had become convinced the McCarthy personified "the demagogic ideology that represents a greater threat to American freedom than Communism." Finally, even the Wisconsinite's Senate colleagues, long irritated by his persistent disregard of accepted rules and standards of behavior and his frequent attacks on fellow members, reached the point where they too had had enough. On 2 December 1954, they voted to censure Joe McCarthy. Thereafter, the politician whose name had become synonymous with hysterical anti-communism declined rapidly into insignificance, dying a little more than two years later an almost forgotten man.[7]

The fall of McCarthy did not put an end to everything connoted by the term "McCarthyism," but it did indicate that the times were changing. Congressional committees now began to probe critically into injustices perpetrated against public employees under the government's loyalty-security program, and the federal courts displayed a new willingness to protect the rights of those accused of Communist connections, more and more demanding that legislative investigations and administrative proceedings accord alleged subversives some measure of due process. The ACLU, growing braver as the years passed, became somewhat more active and outspoken in defense of the rights of Communists. Perhaps most dramatic of all was the emergence of Harry Cain, a conservative former Republican senator from the state of Washington, as an outspoken critic of federal efforts in the loyalty-security field. By February 1955, the *Washington Post* was convinced that the country had reversed direction and was now moving away from hysteria toward a sober reevaluation of its fight against subversion.[8]

IV

At about this time, Harvey Matusow, a professional witness, who had helped send Elizabeth Gurley Flynn and other members of the second New York group to prison, admitted committing perjury, with the result that the public also began to question the way in which the government had obtained its Smith Act convictions. Matusow's shocking revelation marked only the latest change of course in an erratic life. He had drifted into

the Communist movement after his discharge from the Army at the end
of World War II. Then, in February 1950, having become disillusioned
with the CPUSA—in part because of the government's prosecution of the
Eleven—he went to the FBI. For about half a year, the Bureau paid him
$70-$75 a month for regular written reports on the Party. Despite his
service as an informant, when Matusow returned to active duty with the
Air Force in 1951, he found himself under constant scrutiny by counter-
intelligence agents. In an unsuccessful attempt to put an end to this annoyance, he arranged to testify before the House Un-American Activities Committee.

This appearance launched him on a new career as an ex-Communist
witness. After his release from the Air Force in December 1951, he testified before HUAC and the Senate Internal Security Subcommittee and
sold his story to the Hearst press. The New York Board of Education hired
Matusow as a special consultant and the Ohio Un-American Activities Committee put him on its payroll as an investigator. He served for a time as
assistant editor of the anti-Communist periodical *Counterattack* and even
became an intimate of Joe McCarthy. In an attempt, he later said, to remove all doubts about his loyalty, Matusow agreed to testify against Flynn
and her associates. Justice Department attorneys coached him carefully,
and, as preparations for the trial progressed, the witness continually em-
bellished his story, to make it more to their liking. On the stand Matusow
twisted and distorted the truth and even volunteered an outright lie in order to persuade Judge Dimock to admit into evidence the damning *Law
of the Soviet State.*

After sending several Communists to prison and wrecking many reputations, the man suddenly decided to tell the truth. Matusow suffered from
a compulsive need constantly to enhance his own importance, and because
repetition had deprived his stories of their news value, he felt the need to
make a dramatic gesture which would enable him to regain the spotlight.
Then too, the professional ex-Communist needed money. Before announcing he would no longer testify for the government, Matusow had tried
without success to interest several publishers in his story, and confessing
perjury was bound to make it more marketable.

The first hint that the informer had lied came in comments to the press
by a man in whom he had confided, Bishop G. Bromley Oxnam. These remarks aroused the interest of Albert Kahn and Angus Cameron, partners
in a fledgling publishing concern. Not only had Matusow accused both of
Communist connections, but his stories had cost Cameron a job and also
convicted Kahn's friend, union leader Clinton Jencks, in a Taft-Hartley
oath case. Jencks too found the news about Matusow exciting. Anxious

to have the perjurer admit that his testimony against him had been false, he suggested that Cameron & Kahn do the book which the recanting liar wished to write. When Jencks guaranteed that his Mine, Mill, and Smelter Workers Union would purchase at least 2,000 copies, the publishers made contact with Matusow at a vacation retreat in Taos, New Mexico, and arranged for him to fly to New York.

By January 1955, the perjurer had a manuscript ready for printing, but a problem had developed. When Kahn talked to Harry Sacher, the lawyer informed him that any motion for a new trial in the Flynn case would have to be filed by 2 February and that to support one he needed an affidavit from Matusow. The publisher hesitated, for he feared that if his author confessed prematurely, it might jeopardize the book. Matusow had slipped out of Taos just before federal agents arrived to caution him about indiscreet talking, and there was cause for concern about what the government might do if it learned of his writing venture. But, finally, the perjurer did draft an affidavit. Meanwhile, his worried publishers accelerated their production schedule, and Kahn informed Stewart Alsop about the book. On 28 January the nationally syndicated columnist broke the news of *False Witness* to his readers. Radio commentators immediately picked up the story, and the next day the newspapers were full of it. As Kahn wrote later, "Overnight the affair of Harvey Matusow had become a *cause célèbre.*"

On 2 February an FBI agent served the former witness with a subpoena ordering him to appear before a federal grand jury in New York. Judge Dimock ruled that Matusow could not testify until after a retrial hearing in the Flynn case; thus the investigation targeted his publishers. The grand jury ordered Cameron and Kahn to appear with copies of all correspondence and records relating to the book, as well as all drafts, manuscripts, and galley proofs, and Assistant Attorney General William F. Tompkins came up from Washington to take personal charge of the probe. Invoking the First Amendment, the publishers refused to produce any of the subpoenaed material, and, after two days, Judge John Clancey cited Kahn for contempt. Worried above all else that the government might suppress the book, he and his partner then decided to make such action pointless by releasing to the press everything they had been withholding from the grand jury. Having taken this step, Cameron and Kahn, now in a position to cooperate with the investigation, negotiated an agreement with Tompkins which allowed them to turn over the subpoenaed material twenty-four hours after making it public.[9]

Although his publishers were now out from under the threat of jail, Matusow still had to explain his perjury to Judge Dimock. During seven days of testimony the false witness attempted to blame Assistant U.S. Attorney Roy Cohn for his lying, but the government produced briefs which disproved his charges of subornation. Lying about his own lying earned Matusow a perjury conviction, which the Court of Appeals subsequently affirmed.

Although able to discredit thoroughly the compulsive falsifier, the government still suffered from his revelations. Dimock rejected the demands of most defendants for new trials, because the only Matusow testimony which had contributed to their convictions concerned statements made in the presence of third parties, and the judge did not feel they had made sufficient effort to refute it with testimony from those persons. But the major proof that Alexander Trachtenberg and George Charney had intended to bring about the violent overthrow of the government was Matusow's accounts of remarks they allegedly had made to him in private. Because the only way those defendants could have met his evidence was by taking the stand themselves, thus giving up their constitutional right to remain silent, Dimock set aside the verdicts against them and granted each a new trial.[10]

His order was only a small part of the problem which Matusow's revelations created for the Department of Justice. Even before *False Witness* rolled off the presses, that agency had found it necessary to fire professional witnesses Paul Crouch and Manning Johnson for unreliability. Now there arose, in the words of the *Portland Oregonian*, "a groundswell of revulsion" against the government's maintenance of a stable of hired informers. Although the conservative *Chicago Tribune* attempted to explain away Matusow as a tool of those who wished to discredit the exposure of communism, papers as diverse in political orientation as the *United Automobile Worker*, the *New York Times*, and Joe McCarthy's hometown *Appleton Post-Crescent* strongly denounced him. The *Washington Post* ripped into the Justice Department for its carelessness, and the *St. Louis Post-Dispatch* demanded from the attorney general what it considered a long overdue explanation of the government's use of hired informers. Chester Davis of the *Winston-Salem* (North Carolina) *Journal and Sentinel* observed that, "Although McCarthyism has been attacked many times and for many reasons, no one has struck at it harder or with more telling effect than this opportunistic, calculating, psychopathic liar. . . ." Matusow's perjuries could benefit the health of the American political and judicial system, wrote the *San Francisco Chronicle*, if they taught certain "Federal officials" to be more critical of "the glib, recanting, ex-Communist who is ready to tell all. . . ."[11]

From the *Washington Post* came questions that government prosecutors could not avoid pondering if they had any concern for either their integrity or their image. "How many Americans have been unjustly convicted on the basis of Matusow's perjured testimony?" that paper asked. "How many others have been sent to prison or condemned before Congressional investigating committees by other former Communist perjurers who, like Matusow, decided to make witnessing a lucrative career?" These were, the *Post* observed, "questions which the Department of Justice, in all conscience, needs to ask itself." Apparently that agency did do some soul searching, for not until March 1956 did it initiate another Smith Act prosecution, and when an International News Service reporter asked for an explanation of this inactivity, the department admitted that the Matusow incident was one of the principal reasons.[12]

The furor that resulted from this affair reduced the political appeal of the Smith Act prosecutions, for it heightened growing fears that the methods employed by the government to combat communism were threatening civil liberties. During the summer of 1955, a man in Detroit told Albert Kahn: "Since Matusow's confession things have changed quite a bit here. For one thing, you read a lot more in the papers about constitutional rights. . . ."[13]

V

Of even greater importance in stimulating awareness of these privileges and their importance was the fight waged by a number of bar associations to preserve the right to counsel for Communist defendants. The legal profession entered this struggle rather late, for its initial reaction to the Smith Act prosecutions was one of revulsion, inspired not by what the government was doing, but by the conduct of the defendants, their supporters, and their lawyers. As early as February 1949, the House of Delegates of the American Bar Association (ABA) passed a resolution condemning the picketing of courts as a threat to the integrity and independence of the judiciary. In June three representatives of that organization appeared before a congressional subcommittee to urge passage of legislation outlawing such activity. Angered by the courtroom conduct of the barristers defending the Eleven, Emanuel Celler, now chairman of the House Judiciary Committee, called for disciplinary action against them, as did prominent criminal lawyer Newman Levy. Most attorneys seemed to share the concern of the New York County Bar about Communists' lack of respect for the courts and their interference with the orderly administration of justice.[14]

After the Foley Square trial, numerous lawyers and judges joined in efforts to punish those attorneys who had disrupted it. Both the Second

Circuit Court of Appeals and the Supreme Court upheld the contempt
convictions which Medina had imposed upon the rowdy advocates. These
attorneys also came under hostile scrutiny by professional associations in
their home states. After an investigation by the Essex County (New Jersey)
Bar Association, both the state and federal supreme courts disbarred Abraham Isserman, who did not fully regain the right to practice his profession
until 1961. At the urging of the Association of the Bar of the City of New
York and the New York County Lawyers Association, Chief Judge Carrol
C. Hincks of the U.S. District Court for the Southern District of New York
disbarred Harry Sacher, necessitating that the Supreme Court restore
to him the right to follow his profession. Richard Gladstein avoided punishment in his native California, but when he went to Hawaii, intending
to participate in another Smith Act defense, he had to fight off efforts
by a territorial judge to suspend him from practice there. George Crockett
drew fire from the grievance committee of the Michigan State Bar Association for his conduct at Foley Square, and, on its recommendation,
in November 1954, three judges of a state circuit court publicly repri-
manded him.[15]

The professional reaction against the attorneys who defended the Eleven
arose not only out of horror at what had taken place in and around Medina's
courtroom but also from hostility toward communism, a virus that had
infected the American Bar Association even before the Foley Square trial
began. By 22 September 1950 the ABA had become sufficiently agitated
for its House of Delegates to adopt a resolution urging that all attorneys
be required to file affidavits declaring whether they were, or ever had
been, members of the CPUSA. Although this resolution evoked sharp criticism from a committee of the Association of the Bar of the City of New
York and from a group of twenty-seven prominent attorneys—which included, in addition to such well-known civil libertarians as Zechariah Chafee,
Jr., three former ABA presidents, among them the conservative John W.
Davis—anti-Communist sentiment continued to dominate the councils of
the national lawyers' organization. On 24 February 1951, after a three-
month investigation, an ABA committee, headed by the former president
of the District of Columbia Bar Association, Austin F. Canfield, recommended that all Communists and advocates of Marxism-Leninism be expelled from legal practice. Two days later, the House of Delegates voted
unanimously to urge that lawyers' groups throughout the country take
such action. In 1953 it added to this proposal a call for the investigation
of those attorneys who invoked the Fifth Amendment when questioned
about possible affiliation with the CPUSA "to determine [their] fitness
to continue to practice. . . ."[16]

By then, "While bar associations and legislatures [had] not followed the leadership of the ABA along the precise road suggested, they [had] to a disquieting degree moved in the same direction." In states such as Maryland and New Jersey the legislatures imposed loyalty tests for admission to the bar, while in Colorado, Washington, and Oklahoma applicants had to make unqualified denials of past as well as present involvement in subversive activities. California passed laws designed both to prevent Communists from becoming lawyers and to force out of the legal profession any advocates of violent revolution who had already gained entry. In Michigan and Louisiana bar associations encouraged state supreme courts to adopt loyalty tests for those who wished to practice law. The disbarment of attorneys such as Hyman Schlessinger in Pennsylvania and the rejection of applicants such as George Anastaplo in Illinois demonstrate that such laws and court rules were not merely idle threats. A minority of states stood firm against proposals to subject present and prospective members of the bar to political inquisition, but in most of the country there was an increasing tendency, supported by the legal profession itself, to probe the "political activity, belief and association" of those who would practice law, "as a test of loyalty."[17]

Among the attorneys found wanting were Maurice Braverman and George Blake Charney, two Smith Act defendants who were disbarred. In theory, Braverman lost the right to practice in Maryland, and Charney suffered expulsion in New York, because the federal courts had found them guilty of a felony, but the fate of Schlessinger, a Communist who served as defense counsel in two Smith Act trials, suggests that the intolerance of the legal profession toward their radicalism was also a factor. Clearly, it was the politics and associations of controversial attorney Harriet Bouslog-Sawyer which aroused the ire of the Hawaii bar and earned her a one-year suspension for conduct during the Honolulu trial which, in the opinion of the Supreme Court, did not warrant such harsh punishment.[18]

Although concern about courtroom disruption and hostility toward communism shaped the bar's initial reaction to the Smith Act cases, eventually many lawyers grew more concerned about the inability of the defendants to obtain competent legal representation. During the early 1950s, as Justice William O. Douglas observed at the time, "Those accused of illegal Communist activity . . . [had] difficulty getting reputable lawyers to defend them." The timidity of the ACLU, the intimidating effect of the contempt sentences imposed on the Foley Square defense staff, and the assault by the legal profession upon its radical wing combined with the attacks of the Justice Department and the Un-American Activities

Committee on the National Lawyers Guild (an organization to which all
of the attorneys who had defended the Eleven belonged) to restrict sharply the number of advocates willing to take such cases for ideological reasons. Those who might have represented Party members simply for the
fee shrank from doing so because, as University of Minnesota law professor Charles Alan Wright observed, "the public attitude toward lawyers
who represent unpopular defendants, and particularly those accused of
disloyalty, is so hostile. . . ." The bar, as Douglas noted, was afraid. Some
lawyers "could not volunteer their services, for if they did they would
lose clients and their firms would suffer." Others feared "they would be
dubbed as 'subversive' by their community and put in the same category
as those they . . . defend." Perhaps the fears of the bar were exaggerated,
but the fate of Alexander Schullman, whose law practice vanished after
he agreed to participate in the Los Angeles Smith Act case, was not a happy one for the profession to contemplate. So reluctant did attorneys become to represent Communist defendants that, after talking to well over
a hundred without finding one willing to take his case, Pennsylvania
Party leader Steve Nelson had to defend himself during a Pittsburgh sedition trial.[19]

No group found it more difficult to obtain competent counsel than
the victims of the Smith Act. The Baltimore group interviewed over
thirty lawyers, all of whom expressed unwillingness to appear on behalf
of politically unpopular defendants. After making twelve to fifteen unsuccessful attempts to hire an attorney, Maurice Braverman finally gave
up and defended himself. In New York Elizabeth Gurley Flynn and her
comrades approached about 200 attorneys, who refused to take their
case, most because of the possible economic and social consequences of
involvement with it. The New Yorkers found it equally difficult to obtain appellate counsel, and one attorney, Mary Kaufman, was left to prepare their appeal alone. In St. Louis the story was much the same.[20]

By early 1952 Justice Douglas had expressed concern about the problems Communist defendants encountered in seeking counsel, and so had
the President. In September 1951 Harry Truman reminded the bar of its
obligation to protect the rights of the accused. "It seems to me that if
this tradition is to be meaningful today, it must extend to all defendants,
including persons accused of such abhorrent crimes as conspiracy to overthrow the government by force . . .," he said. By July 1953 an ABA committee was prepared to acknowledge that the bar had a "duty . . . to see
that all defendants, however unpopular, have the benefit of counsel for
their defense. This is not," it took care to emphasize, "because lawyers
will agree with the views of such clients. . . ." The anti-communism that

had victimized radical attorneys remained strong in the legal profession, but, recognizing "that there can be no fair trial without aid of counsel and that the cornerstone of our system of justice is a fair trial for all," many attorneys came to the conclusion that they must do something to prevent the further erosion of a fundamental right supposedly guaranteed to all Americans by the Sixth Amendment.[21]

That lawyers should have risen to the defense of constitutional rights is understandable, for, as available evidence indicates, although hostile to the radicals in their own ranks, attorneys were less worried about communism than the public as a whole and more concerned about the preservation of traditional civil liberties. A 1954 survey disclosed that, among local community leaders, bar association presidents exhibited a higher degree of willingness to give members of the CPUSA the right to speak than did any other group except newspaper publishers. They displayed considerable concern about civil liberties and were more tolerant of nonconformists than almost any other persons in the towns and cities studied. Although unwilling to tolerate the presence of Communists within their own fraternity, lawyers felt bound, probably because of respect for the legal order inculcated by their training and professional experiences, to accord members of the CPUSA those rights which the law of the land guaranteed to every citizen.[22]

Although committed to civil liberties generally, the bar felt a special devotion to the Sixth Amendment. The right to counsel, viewed from a slightly different perspective, was the right to hire an attorney, and anything that endangered this privilege threatened also the economic foundation of the bar. Consequently, lawyers defended this civil liberty more vigorously than any other. Whatever their personal views about communism, attorneys dared not let the attack upon it destroy the market for their services. They had to defend the right to counsel—even if that meant aiding the CPUSA.

Thus it was that in September 1952 the New York and Maryland Bar Associations took steps toward making the Sixth Amendment something more than an empty promise for Communist defendants. The Committee on Civil Rights of the Empire State group informed the public that it had "always been recognized in the profession that it is the duty of the bar to see to it that even the most unpopular defendants and those charged with the most repellent of crimes can obtain counsel who will do what is possible and proper in their defense." New York lawyers pledged to support, against all criticism and attack, any attorney who offered his services to a Communist and to strive to educate the profession and the public about the rights and duties of those representing clients associated with distasteful causes. The Maryland Bar Association went even further, resolving that, at the request of any person charged with being a Communist or subversive person, it would appoint one or more lawyers to represent him. This procedure, the committee drafting the resolution hoped, would shield individual attorneys from public censure.[23]

A year after the Maryland and New York bars expressed themselves on the subject, a group of lawyers, by coming to the aid of Smith Act defendants, put into practice the principle which those organizations had enunciated. Despite diligent effort, the wives of the Communists indicted in Philadelphia had little luck in finding counsel for their husbands. Many prominent lawyers refused to take the case, and one firm, after accepting a retainer, returned it within twenty-four hours. The women appealed to Bernard G. Segal, chancellor of the Philadelphia Bar Association, but even he could find no attorney willing to risk defending Communists. On 5 August 1953, one of the wives reported to Judge Alan K. Grim that seven of the eight defendants had failed to obtain lawyers, thus forcing him to postpone arraignment. In the meantime, the bar association had passed a resolution proclaiming that the right to counsel was dependent upon public acceptance of a correlative right of attorneys to defend any clients they chose, without having the reputation of those they represented imputed to them. The organization pledged to support any advocate who used his skills on behalf of an unpopular individual, as long as the attorney conducted himself with dignity. Thomas D. McBride, chairman of the bar's Civil Rights Committee, finally agreed to take the Smith Act case and assembled a team of topflight young lawyers, which included a former city solicitor and a one-time investigator for the state attorney general's office. These men, who worked without pay, provided the Communists with an able defense. The judge praised them as the "unsung heroes" of the trial, and the press, convinced that what they had done demonstrated the excellence of the American system of justice, also offered its congratulations.[24]

The bar played an even bigger role in Cleveland, where, by the summer of 1955, Smith Act defendants, indicted nearly two years earlier, still had managed to retain only three lawyers. Two of the Communists elected to defend themselves, but five others finally informed Judge Charles J. McNamee that they were financially unable to employ counsel, thus compelling him to assign lawyers to the case. Because Smith Act trials were so long, and appointed attorneys still served without pay in federal courts, McNamee realized that participation in this case would probably work a financial hardship on any lawyer he assigned to it. Therefore, he turned to the Cleveland Bar, which promptly followed the path blazed by its counterpart in Philadelphia. As it reported later: "For the purpose of upholding the right to counsel, the Association agreed to assist the court."[25]

No member expressed any objection to participating in the defense
of Communists, a task which the organization undertook, as its president,
Eugene Freedheim, emphasized, out of a sense of public duty. The motivation of the assigned attorneys was the same. No one should attribute
to them any Communist beliefs or opinions, Freedheim insisted. "They
only believe that every man accused of crime is entitled to a defense presented by competent counsel as provided in the United States Constitution," he told readers of the *Cleveland News.*[26]

After consultation with the association, Judge McNamee appointed one
attorney from each of the six leading trial law firms in the city. The em-
ployers of these men agreed to donate their services for the duration of
the trial, while the Cleveland Bar volunteered to compensate an additional attorney and to pay the expenses of all seven appointed lawyers. The
association requested that local firms not providing attorneys donate
$100 per member and asked lawyers' groups in other northern Ohio cities
to contribute also. This fund drive, which received the endorsement of
the executive committee of the state bar, eventually raised $25,870.[27]

Judge McNamee commended the association for its "magnificent response" to a " most unusual challenge," and most of the public apparently shared his enthusiasm for its efforts on behalf of the indicted Communists. Although one of the defense attorneys received some abuse in the
form of anonymous letters, telegrams, and phone calls, Freedheim heard
no criticism of what his organization was doing, and the local press heap-
ed praise upon the bar. Even the strongly anti-Communist *Catholic Universe Bulletin* praised the seven attorneys assigned to the case for "performing the highest duty of the legal profession—giving their services to
uphold the principle that any person accused of crime receive equal justice before the law."[28]

Cleveland and Philadelphia were not the only cities in which professional associations came to the aid of Smith Act defendants. When the Denver group, indicted in August 1954, found it impossible to obtain attorneys because of the "political dangers" connected with their case, the trial
judge designated eleven leading lawyers—including a past president of the
local bar, a former Republican Party treasurer, and the mayor's brother-
in-law—to represent them. Aware that the trial would likely be a long one
and that working free might impose a financial burden on the lawyers, he
appealed to the Denver Bar Association for help, and it responded by taking up a collection to support them. At about the same time, when a federal district court in New Haven designated several attorneys to represent
Smith Act defendants, the Connecticut Bar Association, pointing to constitutional guarantees of the right to counsel, urged the public to support
these lawyers and called upon its own membership to provide financial as-

sistance. In a little over a year it managed to raise $15,000.[29]

While the efforts of these bar associations made a number of highly skilled attorneys available to Smith Act defendants, at first those advocates achieved no better results than the lawyers who had preceded them. The Philadelphia trial ended in August 1954 with the conviction of all defendants; and in Denver bar-backed lawyers won the appreciation of their clients, but no acquittals.[30]

In Cleveland the results were different. Because of the impressive array of legal talent representing the defendants there, Communists were optimistic about the trial. In a total break with Party tradition, the *Worker* conceded that, "Should the defense succeed in wresting even partial victory, it will be due to the competency and ability of these lawyers as well as to the prevailing political climate of lessening tensions abroad and at home." Even before the jury began its deliberations, the defendants wrote to thank the Cleveland Bar Association for the performance of the attorneys that organization had supplied.[31]

As the Party hoped, the gradual relaxation of Cold War tensions combined with high-quality legal talent to produce favorable results. The first hint that Cleveland might be different came on 5 January 1956, when, after the prosecution rested its case, McNamee directed a verdict of acquittal for defendant David Katz. Although Katz had a long history of involvement in the Communist movement, the evidence that the government had presented against him consisted mainly of material relating to the activities of his wife, in which he had participated only as her companion. McNamee considered such proof insufficient to provide any reasonable basis for a finding of involvement in the alleged conspiracy. As the *Cleveland Plain Dealer* was quick to point out, in eleven earlier Smith Act trials around the country, judges had seen fit to free only two of more than a hundred defendants. The action of the Cleveland jury was even more unprecedented. Its deliberations, which lasted from 31 January to 10 February 1956, were the longest in any Smith Act trial, and its members took several dozen ballots. In the end, while finding six defendants guilty, they acquitted four others.[32]

Those they freed were indistinguishable from the Communists convicted in earlier Smith Act trials. All had long records as Party activists. Joseph Dougher admitted past service on the National Committee and extensive recruiting activities. Michael Campbell had been a member of the state committee and the man in charge of Stalinist education and "Negro work" in Ohio. Frieda Katz was one of the leading Communists in the Cleveland area, and the prosecution felt it had established that Elvidore Greenfield was a Party public relations director. Much of the evidence against these four involved activities a number of years in the past, but that had long been standard in Smith Act cases. Because Judge McNamee considered the proof against Greenfield and Campbell, although not strong, entirely sufficient to present a jury question, and regarded that against Dougher and Frieda Katz as ample to support any verdict, the acquittal of these four defendants was obviously due less to the weakness of the prosecution's case than to changing times and the skill of their lawyers.[33]

After the jury returned its verdict, McNamee publicly commended the performance of the appointed attorneys. "I am proud of the way in which they represented these clients . . . ," he said. As far as the judge was concerned, communism was not the preeminent threat to the United States. "The greatest danger is that we might adopt the tactics that the Communists employ. . . ." But that would never happen, he felt sure, as long as there were jurors and lawyers who would perform as those in this case had.[34]

Many people apparently shared the judge's feelings, for public reaction to the surprise outcome of the trial was generally favorable. Communists, of course, were pleased, although the six convictions tempered their joy somewhat. The Party press represented the Cleveland verdicts as a breakthrough, and Frieda Katz agreed, pointing out that the acquittals interrupted the regular pattern of Smith Act trials. The defendants, the *Daily Worker*, and the *People's World* all felt certain that the outcome of this case, indicating as it did that Cold War emotions were subsiding, represented a setback for McCarthyism and an important advance in the struggle against the Smith Act. The partial success in Cleveland so buoyed the hopes of the Party and its friends that on 25 March the Emergency Civil Liberties Committee staged in Carnegie Hall the first major meeting protesting the prosecutions which New York had seen in years.[35]

Others without the personal interest in the verdicts felt by Communists and their close allies also praised the outcome of the trial, for it proved, they felt, the superiority of this country's judicial system. "American justice has served to its highest degree in this case," the *Cleveland News* editorialized, adding that a completely opposite outcome would have resulted in Russia or any other Iron Curtain country. The *Press* echoed these sentiments, as did the *Plain Dealer*, which praised the self-sacrificing attorneys who had represented the Communist defendants. Municipal Judge Perry Jackson wrote to the Cleveland Bar Association to commend the efforts of the organization and the lawyers it had provided.[36]

Whereas the general public looked with favor upon the work of these attorneys and the outcome of the trial, the Justice Department did not.

Asked to comment on the acquittals, a government lawyer replied, "I think the verdict stinks." Assistant Attorney General William F. Tompkins was equally outspoken. On 5 March he told United Press reporter Robert Coll that the volunteer defense of Communist leaders by local bar associations was helping the CPUSA and undermining the Smith Act. Tompkins sharply criticized the Cleveland and Cuyahoga County bars, insisting that lawyers who did what the members of those organizations had were dupes of the Communists.[37]

Although it was the acquittals that triggered Tompkins's outburst, other factors lay in the background, among them the fact that local bar associations were foiling the Justice Department's plan to bankrupt the Communist Party. On 14 March, spokesmen for Attorney General Brownell admitted that one of the government's objectives in trying leaders of the CPUSA was to force the Party to expend its limited resources on legal defense. Also, Tompkins, who had political ambitions, was angling for the Republican gubernatorial nomination in New Jersey, and his principal opponent in a fight for control of the GOP organization in Essex County was the liberal Senator Clifford Case, whom Joe McCarthy had attacked during the 1954 campaign. Thus Tompkins may well have viewed an assault on the Cleveland Bar Association as a means of rallying anti-Communists to his candidacy.[38]

Whatever the motivation behind his attack, that organization was not about to sit quietly by while anyone, even an assistant attorney general, slandered it. Eugene Freedheim promptly released a statement branding Tompkins's remarks "unfair." "The community here in Cleveland know that we are not dupes of the Communist Party," he declared. At the next regular luncheon meeting of the association, Judge McNamee and the seven appointed attorneys sat at the head table as honored guests, while Freedheim informed the membership that a special meeting of the executive committee had authorized the filing of a complaint with the Grievance Committee of the ABA, charging the Assistant Attorney General with violation of the Canons of Professional Ethics.[39]

Present to hear these fighting words was the scheduled speaker, American Bar Association President E. Smythe Gambrell. When his turn came to address the assembled lawyers, he reminded them that the ABA had always taken a firm stand against communism. But, Gambrell added, it also believed that members of the CPUSA were entitled to a fair trial. He vigorously defended those local bar groups which had provided counsel for accused Communists.[40]

The American Civil Liberties Union also leaped to the defense of the Cleveland organization. On 7 March, Patrick Malin dispatched a telegram to Tompkins, expressing shock at his statement. It represented, Malin said, an attack, not only on local bar associations and individual attorneys, but also on the constitutional rights of everyone accused of a crime. The seriousness of the situation was aggravated, he pointed out, by the fact that several Smith Act cases were still before the courts. Malin reminded Tompkins that in a 1953 speech, his superior, Attorney General Brownell, had contrasted this country's system of justice with the Soviet Union's, citing as proof of the American one's superiority the right of defendants here to the protection of the Sixth Amendment. The ACLU's Ohio affiliate wrote Brownell to remind him that all the Cleveland Bar Association had done was help shoulder the burden of assuring Communists the representation to which the Constitution entitled them. "If the Smith Act is undermined by the right to counsel," it declared, "then its foundation must be weak."[41]

Spokesmen for other bar associations joined the ACLU in condemning Tompkins and expressing support for the Cleveland organization. Thomas D. McBride, head of the Philadelphia defense team, told the press that his group intended to demand a public apology from the Assistant Attorney General and a disavowal of his remarks from Brownell. Spokesmen for the Denver and Connecticut Bar Associations announced that their groups felt no shame about defending Communists and did not believe anyone had duped them. The Cuyahoga County (Ohio) Bar Association wrote the Attorney General urging him to give Tompkins's statements his personal attention, and Gambrell again publicly endorsed the action of Freedheim and his colleagues.[42]

The press also rallied behind the Cleveland Bar Association. "Many newspapers jumped into this issue," Freedheim reported later, "and none of them, so far as I know, sided with the Assistant Attorney General's statement." The *Cleveland Plain Dealer* questioned Tompkins's value to the Eisenhower administration, and the *New York Post* his fitness to retain office. The *Washington Post* and *Cleveland Press* were also highly critical. The *Akron Beacon Journal* expressed the sentiment of many newspapers when it declared: "Judge McNamee and the lawyers who responded to his appeal were not 'dupes'; they were simply more sensitive than Tompkins to a fundamental tradition of American justice—that every accused person is entitled to a proper defense."[43]

Supported by the press and much of the legal prefession, the Cleveland Bar Association launched a counterattack. Regarding the matter as too important to settle in any other way, Freedheim and defense attorney George Farr flew to Washington on 15 March, hoping for a face-to-face showdown with the Attorney General. They did not get one. By now the

Justice Department had become quite sensitive about the Tompkins incident, imposing a tight ban on comments to the press about it, and Brownell, although in Washington and apparently in the building, would not see
the visitors from Cleveland. Freedheim and Farr did manage, though, to
obtain a meeting with Tompkins, his assistant Thomas Hall, and Deputy
Attorney General William Rogers.

Although Justice attempted to camouflage a retreat under fire, the
outcome of this six-hour conference was clearly a victory for the Cleveland Bar Association. Rogers contended that it was politically impossible
for the department to give Freedheim and Farr the retraction they wanted but indicated a willingness to accept some formula which would allow
his agency to back off without embarrassment. In the end, Tompkins issued a statement in which he denied ever challenging the right of any defendant, however unpopular, to an attorney, or criticizing the Cleveland
Bar Association, either directly or indirectly.[44]

Freedheim and Farr expressed willingness to terminate the dispute on
this basis, and the executive committee of their organization subsequently
voted to do so, although the Cleveland Bar received some criticism for
ending the fight by accepting Tompkins's implausible denial. Coll, unwilling to have his own veracity questioned in order that the Justice Department might slither out of a difficult position, produced handwritten notes
which rather solidly established that Tompkins had called lawyers who
defended Communists "dupes," and also "suckers." While the *Cleveland
Press* criticized the lawyers for not continuing the fight, they took the
position that the issue was now one between the Justice Department and
the media. The bar had achieved its objective: vindication of the right
to counsel.[45]

For their vigorous defense of that constitutional principle Freedheim
and his colleagues received numerous plaudits. The *Nation* and the *St.
Louis Post-Dispatch* praised the president of the Cleveland Bar Association, and Dean Erwin Griswold of the Harvard Law School wrote him
to express appreciation for the way his group had responded to remarks
which could not have passed unchallenged. Quite different was the effect of the incident on Tompkins's reputation. The ABA openly questioned his honesty, and charges of smear and attempting to intimidate lawyers continued to echo through the pages of the *Cleveland Press.* The
New York Post editorialized with acid sarcasm: "We welcome Tompkins'
belated announcement that he is reconciled to that provision of the Bill
of Rights guaranteeing the right to counsel." The assistant attorney general's political star fell to earth and no more was heard of his bid for
the governorship of New Jersey. In March 1958, citing "personal reasons,"

he resigned from the Justice Department to return to private law practice.[46] Tompkins was the victim of changing times. Had he launched his attack on the Cleveland Bar five years earlier, the outcome might have been far different, but by 1956, with the intensity of the Cold War much diminished, many Americans cared more about constitutional rights than communism. Incidents such as the Matusow scandal had awakened them to the danger which the government's attack on the CPUSA posed to civil liberties and had forced them to ponder the relative value of the two. Tompkins insisted that successful Smith Act prosecutions were more important than the preservation of a fundamental constitutional right, but the country decided otherwise. Clearly, its priorities were changing, and reason rather than blind passion now governed its response to domestic communism. For the Smith Act the environment had become a most unhealthy one.

NOTES

1. ACLU Weekly Bulletins no. 1344, 26 July 1948, p. 1, no. 1355, 11 October 1948, p. 1, and no. 1369, 17 January 1949, p. 1; *PW*, 11 August 1948; Motion of the American Civil Liberties Union for Leave to File Brief in Amicus Curiae, at 2-3, Dennis v. United States, 341 U.S. 494 (1951).

2. Memorandum from the Executive Director to the Board of Directors on the Smith Act Decision and the Future, 20 June 1951, General Correspondence, 1951, vols. 1-5, ACLU Papers, Seeley G. Mudd Library, Princeton University; ACLU Weekly Bulletin no. 1496, 12 July 1951, p. 1.

3. Memorandum from Executive Director to Board of Directors; Charles L. Markmann, *The Noblest Cry: A History of the American Civil Liberties Union* (New York: St. Martins Press, 1965), p. 176; ACLU Weekly Bulletins no. 1525, 21 January 1952, p. 3, no. 1529, 18 February 1952, p. 1, no. 1556, 25 August 1952, p. 2; *Yates Transcript*, pp. 12572-74; *DW*, 31 January 1951; Mary S. McAuliffe, "The American Civil Liberties Union During the McCarthy Years," in *The Specter*, ed. Robert Griffith and Athan Theoharis (New York: New Viewpoints, 1974), pp. 154-69; United States v. Fujimoto, 107 F. Supp. 865 (D. Hawaii, 1952).

4. George Gallup, *The Gallup Poll: Public Opinion 1935-1971*, 3 vols. (New York: Random House, 1972), 2:1191.

5. D. F. Fleming, *The Cold War and Its Origins, 1917-1960*, 2 vols. (Garden City, N.Y.: Doubleday, 1961), 2: 1053-54; Walter La Feber, *America, Russia, and the Cold War* (New York: John Wiley and Sons, 1967), pp. 136-88; Stephen Ambrose, *Rise to Globalism: American Foreign Policy 1938-1970*, (Baltimore: Penguin Books, 1971), pp. 217-45.

6. Earl Latham, *The Communist Controversy in Washington: From*

the *New Deal to McCarthy* (Cambridge, Mass.: Harvard University Press, 1966), pp. 400-01, 423.

7. On the decline of McCarthy's popularity see Gallup, *The Gallup Poll*, 2: 1003, 1135, 1201, 1220, 1225, 1237, 1241, 1263. The minister, Harry B. Taylor of the Church of the Covenant, is quoted by the *Cleveland Plain Dealer*, 10 April 1954.

8. *Washington Post*, 12 February 1955; ACLU, *Clearing the Main Channels: 35th Annual Report of the American Civil Liberties Union, July 1, 1954 to June 31, 1955* (New York: ACLU [?], 1955 [?]), p. 27, and *Liberty Is Always Unfinished Business: 36th Annual Report of the American Civil Liberties Union, July 1, 1955 to June 30, 1956* (New York: ACLU [?], 1956 [?]), p. 27.

9. The best accounts of Matusow's activities are found in his own book *False Witness* (New York: Cameron & Kahn, 1955), and in the opinion of Judge Dimock in United States v. Flynn, 130 F. Supp. 413 (S.D.N.Y. 1955). Where there is a conflict between the two, I have relied on Dimock. Material from *False Witness* is taken from pp. 26-54 and 126-34, from Albert Kahn's introduction, pp. 8-14, and from the cover. On Matusow's dealings with the FBI, see Louis B. Nichols to Morris Ernst, 20 October 1955, Morris L. Ernst Papers, Harry Ransom Center, University of Texas at Austin. Material on the activities and legal problems of Matusow's publishers is from the introduction and from Albert Kahn's unpublished book (presently in proof), "National Scandal: A Warning from the McCarthy Era," pp. 1-2, 11-13, 22, 48-55, 67-69, 74-75, and 83-103. Kahn's statement appears on p. 67 of the latter.

10. Matusow, *False Witness*, p. 132; United States v. Flynn, 130 F. Supp. 413 (S.D.N.Y. 1955).

11. For 4 February 1955, see the *Chicago Tribune*, the *Appleton* (Wis.) *Post-Crescent*, the *St. Louis Post-Dispatch*, and the *San Francisco Chronicle*; see also the *United Automobile Worker*, February 1955. Editorials from the *New York Times* and *Portland Oregonian* on Matusow are reprinted in Motion for Leave to File Brief Amicus Curiae and Brief of International Longshoreman's and Warehouseman's Union, at Appendix B., Yates v. United States, 354 U.S. 298 (1957). Davis's comments are quoted by Kahn ("National Scandal," p. 153).

12. *Washington Post*, 2 February 1955; Justice, "List"; "Prosecuting Communists," *America*, 10 September 1955, p. 556.

13. Quoted in Kahn, "National Scandal," p. 185.

14. *NYT*, 2 February 1949, p. 14, 20 June 1949, p. 7, and 7 September 1949, p. 22; *DW*, 12 May 1949 and 16 June 1949.

15. United States v. Sacher, 182 F. 2d 416 (2d Cir. 1950), aff'd., 343 U.S. 1 (1952); *NYT*, 18 October 1949, p. 21; *In re* Isserman, 9 N.J. 269, 87 A. 2d 903 (1952), r'hrng denied, 9 N.J. 316, 88 A. 2d 199 (1952); *In re* Isserman, 345 U.S. 286 (1953); *In re* Disbarment of Isserman, 348 U.S. 1 (1954); Isserman v. Ethics Committee, 345 U.S. 927 (1953); As-

sociation of the Bar of the City of New York v. Isserman, 271 F. 2d 784
(2d Cir. 1959); *In re* Isserman, 35 N.J. 197, 172 A. 2d 425 (1961); *In re*
Sacher, 206 F. 2d 358 (2d Cir. 1953), *r'hrng denied*, 206 F. 2d 358; Sacher
v. Association of the Bar of the City of New York, 347 U.S. 388 (1954);
Gladstein v. McLaughlin, 230 F. 2d 762 (9th Cir. 1955); *DW*, 25 March
1952 and 17 November 1954; Jerold S. Auerbach, *Unequal Justice: Lawyers and Social Change in Modern America* (New York: Oxford University
Press, 1976), pp. 240-46. Auerbach's Chapter 8 is by far the best survey
of attacks on left-wing lawyers by courts and professional associations
during the Cold War era. Its only flaw is a rather one-sided condemnation
of the bar, which details the many occasions when the legal profession
failed to meet its obligation to represent radical defendants but ignores
those when it did.

    16. *NYT*, 28 November 1950, p. 14, 25 February 1951, p. 44,
27 February 1951, p. 14; "The Independence of the Bar," *Lawyers Guild
Review* 13 (Winter 1953): 166-67; Auerbach, *Unequal Justice*, pp. 233-
39. The ABA is quoted by "Independence of the Bar" on p. 167.

    17. "Independence of the Bar," p. 168; *In re* Schlessinger, 404 Pa.
584, 172 A. 2d 835 (1961); *In re* Anastaplo, 3 Ill. 2d 471, 121 N.E. 2d
826 (1954); *In re* Anastaplo, 366 U.S. 82 (1961).

    18. Braverman v. Bar Association of Baltimore City, 209 Md. 328,
121 A. 2d 473 (1956), *cert. denied*, 352 U.S. 830 (1956); *In re* Braverman, 148 F. Supp. 56 (D. Md. 1957); *In re* Bouslog-Sawyer, 41 Hawaii
403 (1956); *In re* Sawyer, 260 F. 2d 189 (9th Cir. 1958); *In re* Sawyer,
360 U.S. 622 (1959); *NYT*, 14 January 1955, p. 9.

    19. Auerbach, *Unequal Justice*, pp. 234-35, 248-49; HUAC, *Report
on the National Lawyers Guild: Legal Bulwark of the Communist Party*,
81st Cong., 2d sess., 1950, H. Rept. 3123, p. 5; Charles Alan Wright, "The
Right to Counsel and Counsel's Rights," *The Nation*, 21 November 1953,
p. 426; "Independence of the Bar," p. 165; Steve Nelson, *The Thirteenth
Juror: The Inside Story of My Trial* (New York: Masses and Mainstream,
1955), pp. 118-19, 131; Fowler Harper, "Loyalty and Lawyers," *Lawyers
Guild Review* 11 (Fall 1951): 205; Hannah Bloom, "The Laws Diminish-
ing Return," *The Nation*, 29 December 1951, p. 556; Milnor Alexander,
"The Right to Counsel for the Politically Unpopular," *Law in Transition*
22 (Spring 1962): 19, 22. Douglas is quoted by Alexander on p. 22.

    20. "Independence of the Bar," pp. 164-65; Maurice Braverman, tele-
phonic interview with the Author, 18 August 1976; *DW*, 31 January
1952.

    21. Truman and the ABA Committee are quoted in "Independence of
the Bar," on pp. 163 and 158 respectively.

    22. Samuel Stouffer, *Communism, Conformity, and Civil Liberties*
(Garden City, N.Y.: Doubleday & Co., 1955), pp. 42, 52, 233. Auerbach
errs when he states (*Unequal Justice*, p. 240) that lawyers were neither more
nor less hysterical than other Americans.

23. The New York resolution is quoted in ACLU Weekly Bulletin no. 1561, 29 September 1952, p. 1. On the action of the Maryland Bar Association see that bulletin and William O. Douglas, *An Almanac of Liberty* (Garden City, N.Y.: Doubleday, 1954), p. 286.

24. *Philadelphia Inquirer*, 23 March 1953, 6 August 1953, 13 August 1953, and 14 August 1954; *Worker* (Nat. Ed.), 5 July 1953.

25. Cleveland Bar Association, "The Right to Counsel: Report," typescript, p. 1, RTC.

26. Eugene Freedheim, personal interview with the Author at his office in Cleveland, 4 June 1971; "Federal Judge Charles J. McNamee Names 7 Attorneys to Defend Communists," *The Cleveland Bar Association Journal* (September 1955), and *Cleveland News*, 2 November 1955, RTC.

27. Cleveland Bar Association, "The Right to Counsel," p. 2; "Cleveland Bar Praised in Smith Act Case," *The Ohio Bar*, 7 November 1953, pp. 1091-92, RTC.

28. McNamee to Freedheim, 17 August 1955, *Cleveland Press*, 13 August 1955, *Catholic Universe Bulletin* article by James T. Flannery, 28 October 1955, RTC; Freedheim interview; Alexander, "Counsel for the Politically Unpopular," p. 33.

29. *Cleveland Press*, 14 March 1956; *Denver Post*, 26 May 1955; *DW*, 20 October 1954, 16 May 1955, 24 October 1955, and 7 December 1956; *Worker* (Nat. Ed.), 2 October 1955.

30. Justice, "List"; *Denver Post*, 26 May 1955.

31. Julia Brown, *I Testify: My Years as An Undercover Informant for the FBI* (Boston and Los Angeles: Western Islands Publishers, 1966), pp. 83-84; *Worker* (New York—Harlem Ed.), 15 January 1956, p. 6; Lucille Bethancourt et al., to the Cleveland Bar Association, 30 January 1956, RTC.

32. Transcript Ordered by the Court of Appeals, at 1097-98, 1422-46, Brandt v. United States, 256 F. 2d 79 (6th Cir. 1958) (cited hereinafter as *Brandt Transcript*); *Cleveland Plain Dealer*, 6 January 1956, *Cleveland News*, 10 February 1956, RTC.

33. *Brandt Transcript*, pp. 1094-98, 1118-23, 1133-55, 1253-56, 13935-89; Brandt v. United States, 256 F. 2d 79 (6th Cir. 1958).

34. Address of Judge McNamee to the Jury, RTC.

35. *Cleveland News*, 10 February 1956, RTC; *DW*, 13 February 1956; *PW*, 14 February 1956; *Worker* (New Jersey Ed.), 25 March 1956.

36. *Cleveland Press*, 14 February 1956; *Cleveland Plain Dealer*, 11 February 1956; Jackson to Freedheim, 2 March 1956, and *Cleveland News*, 13 February 1956, RTC.

37. *Cleveland Press*, 10 February and 6 March 1956. The lawyer's comment appears in the 10 February edition.

38. Freedheim regards the acquittals as Tompkins's primary motivation. For the others see *Cleveland Press*, 14 March 1956.

39. Cleveland Bar Association, "The Right to Counsel," pp. 2-5. A copy of Freedheim's statement is to be found in RTC.

40. *Cleveland Press*, 8 March 1956.

41. ACLU Weekly Bulletin no. 1741, 12 March 1956, pp. 1-2; *Cleveland Press*, 7 March 1956. The Weekly Bulletin (p. 2) quotes the Ohio Civil Liberties Union.

42. *Cleveland Press*, 8 March 1956 and 15 March 1956; *Cleveland News*, 8 March 1956, RTC.

43. Freedheim interview; *Cleveland Plain Dealer*, 8 March 1956; *Cleveland Press*, 7 March 1956, *New York Post*, 8 March 1956, and *Akron Beacon-Journal*, 7 March 1956, RTC; *Washington Post*, 11 March 1956.

44. The account of the confrontation between the Cleveland lawyers and the Department of Justice is based heavily on the Freedheim interview and also on *NYT*, 16 March 1956, p. 8, *Cleveland Plain Dealer*, 16 March 1956, and Cleveland Bar Association, "The Right to Counsel," pp. 4-5, RTC. For information on the press blackout see ACLU Weekly Bulletin no. 1743, 26 March 1956, p. 1.

45. Freedheim interview; *NYT*, 16 March 1956, p. 8; *Cleveland Press*, 17 March 1956; *New York Post*, 18 March 1956, RTC.

46. "The Nation Applauds," *The Nation*, 7 April 1956, p. 271; *St. Louis Post-Dispatch*, 23 March 1956; *Cleveland Press*, 11 April 1956; Griswold to Freedheim, 21 March 1956; "The Press Is Saying," *American Bar Association Co-ordinator and Public Relations Bulletin*, 15 June 1956, and *New York Post*, 18 March 1956, RTC; Tompkins to Attorney General William Rogers, 12 March 1958, William P. Rogers Papers, DEL.

9
The Supreme
Court Reconsiders

> There is hope . . . that in calmer times, when present pres-
> sures, passions and fears subside, this or some later Court
> will restore the First Amendment liberties to the high pre-
> ferred place where they belong in a free society.
> —Justice Hugo Black
> *Dennis* v. *United States* (1951)

With the arrival of the calmer times on which Justice Black had, in 1951, pinned his hopes for the future, judges, like other citizens, grew more concerned about civil liberties. Regaining its sense of proportion, the Supreme Court came to realize that unrestrained attacks on the CPUSA, which ignored and even trampled upon fundamental freedoms, threatened American democracy far more than did communism. In 1957, the high tribunal spoke again on the subject of the Smith Act, and this time there was a vast difference in what it had to say.

I

By then the Court was no longer the same body that had decided *Dennis*. With *Brown* v. *Board of Education*, a landmark 1954 ruling against school segregation, the high tribunal had embarked upon a drive to bring the operation of American institutions into line with professed American ideals that would drastically alter constitutional law. The leader of this judicial revolution was Earl Warren, named by Eisenhower to replace Fred Vinson as Chief Justice, after the author of the *Dennis* opinion died in 1953. The appointment of Warren, the Republican vice-presidential nominee in 1948 and one of several unsuccessful aspirants for the top spot on the ticket in 1952, was a political payoff to liberal elements in the President's party, but the new head of the Court was a leftist only by conservative GOP standards. A favorite of Red-baiting publisher William Randolph Hearst, he had, just before World War II, denied that civil rights afforded any protection to members of the CPUSA. In 1942, as attorney general of California, Warren challenged incumbent Culbert Olson for the governorship, using anti-radicalism as a weapon against his progressive rival. Later, during the 1952 campaign, although more restrained than some of his GOP colleagues, he joined in the Republican attack on the Truman administration for allowing Reds to gain a foothold in the federal government and, while campaigning in Wisconsin, was decidedly evasive on the subject of Joe McCarthy.[1]

In his early days as Chief Justice, Warren stood about in the middle of the Court on Cold War issues, but, during the 1955 term, he moved to the left, joining forces with Black and Douglas. His reason was concern about the excesses of McCarthyism. In November 1955 the Chief Justice warned readers of *Fortune* magazine that, "In the present struggle between our world and Communism, the temptation to imitate totalitarian security methods is a subtle temptation that must be resisted day by day. . . ." Warren believed that in a Cold War which was becoming increasingly a contest for the minds and hearts of the unaligned masses of the globe, the United States could succeed only by demonstrating through positive action that its institutions were superior to those of the USSR. Addressing a convention of the American Bar Association at Philadelphia in August 1955, he declared, "If the world is made to see that the provisions of our constitution guaranteeing human rights are living things, enjoyed by all Americans, and enforceable in our courts everywhere, it will do much to turn the tide in our favor and therefore toward peace."[2]

Eisenhower's second Supreme Court nominee reached similar conclusions. In November 1954 John Marshall Harlan, grandson of a famous turn-of-the-century justice by the same name, came to the high tribunal as a replacement for the recently deceased Robert Jackson. After a career spent mainly with a Wall Street law firm, but interspersed with periods of public service as a prosecuting attorney, Harlan had received an appointment to the Second Circuit Court of Appeals in February 1954. During his brief tenure on that bench, he wrote a lengthy opinion upholding the Smith Act convictions of the Flynn group, which bore the unmistakable stamp of Cold War thinking. But, as a true conservative, Harlan found profoundly disturbing the reactionary hysteria associated with the recent anti-Communist crusade. "No thoughtful observer of the American scene since the fighting of World War II ended can fail to be concerned about some of the excesses of thought, utterance, and action that have too frequently characterized our outlooks in this perplexing period of history," he told an audience at Brandeis University on 30 October 1955. Although some endeavored to justify these excesses as useful to preserve freedom, Harlan considered their character decidedly un-American.[3]

While the new justice had faith that the country could overcome McCarthyism, that phenomenon worried him. As far as Harlan was concerned, this nation's heritage of freedom was in no danger from the alien ideology of communism, nor from the Soviet Union.

> The dangers of which we must really beware are, I think, of a quite different character. They are that we shall fall prey to the idea that in order to preserve our free society some of the liberties of the individual must be curtailed, at least temporarily. . . . I have no doubt that the apostles of communism would like nothing better than to see us follow such shallow and unwise counsel, for just as surely as the relaxation of curbs on individual freedoms would be fatal to communism, so the imposition of such curbs in this country would divide and frustrate us, leading inevitably to the impairment of the strength of our society. Curbs on freedom are not always easy to discern. And we must be careful that measures designed for legitimate ends are not made instruments of oppression.[4]

Obviously, a judge with such ideas was a threat to the Smith Act. So was the third of Eisenhower's Supreme Court nominees, William Brennan. A man with a background considerably more liberal than Harlan's, Brennan was the son of a Newark union official and politician, who had raised him to be a good, although not especially active, Democrat. After graduating near the top of his class at Harvard Law School, the future justice had returned home to practice labor law, ironically as a representative of management. In 1948 a Republican governor asked him to serve as a trial judge. Two years later, Brennan moved up a notch in the New Jersey judicial hierarchy, and in 1952 he became a member of the state supreme court. His rise beyond that level was due not only to judicial experience but also to the friendship of Attorney General Brownell, the backing of Secretary of Labor James Mitchell, and the enthusiastic support of New Jersey Chief Justice Arthur T. Vanderbilt, a political ally of Thomas Dewey. But the most important reason why Eisenhower named him to replace Sherman Minton in 1956 was his religion; Cardinal Spellman had pressured the White House to appoint a Catholic.

Brennan shared the Roman faith and Irish ancestry with Joe McCarthy—but nothing else. In 1954, he gave two speeches criticizing abuses associated with recent anti-Communist hearings and comparing those proceedings to the Salem witch hunts. While the Senate was considering his nomination, McCarthy cross-examined Brennan for a full day about these remarks, and the Wisconsin demagogue then cast the only vote against his confirmation. The reason, McCarthy said, was that the nominee's opinions were likely to hinder the nation's efforts to combat communism.[5]

II

Within two years right-wing politicians, such as Senator James Eastland (D., Miss.), were complaining that not only Brennan, but all of Eisenhower's appointees, were insufficiently anti-Communist. A major reason was the fate of the Smith Act. For more than four years after *Dennis* the Supreme Court had refused to review any cases arising under that law. Then the California group asked for a writ of certiorari, and a number of organizations supported its request with petitions for leave to file friend-of-the-court briefs. One of these was the ILWU, a decidedly left-leaning labor union, and another was the ACLU, but a group of California citizens, headed by Nobel Prize-winning chemist Linus Pauling, which was concerned about the use of paid informers, and numerous members of the Southern California-Arizona Conference of the Methodist Church, joined these organizations in requesting a review of the convictions. The Methodists struck a note which must have produced sympathetic vibrations throughout the Court. "In this area [sic] of relaxed international tensions, when an attempt is being made in a peaceful world atmosphere to foster a true appreciation of American ideals, it would be anomalous and harmful for this court to place its stamp of approval upon constitutional encroachments in the area of human rights," they said. On 17 October 1955, the Court granted certiorari. Communists saw its action as a reflection of the spirit of Geneva and a sign that it was now "possible to end the cold war against . . . Constitutional liberties. . . ." They soon had more reason to rejoice, for the justices also granted certiorari in the Pittsburgh case. With both the western Pennsylvania and Los Angeles convictions under review, hopes rose that the time for reversal of *Dennis* had arrived, and the ACLU and TRB, Washington correspondent for the *New Republic*, joined in urging the Court to overturn its 1951 ruling.[6]

There were hints that it might do so. One was the Court's 1956 decision in *Pennsylvania* v. *Nelson*. Finding a libertarian use for the Smith

Act, Warren ruled that, in passing that law, Congress had preempted the
field of sedition against the federal government and that states were,
therefore, barred from punishing such conduct.[7] Just as discomforting
to proponents of legal warfare on the CPUSA was *Communist Party* v.
Subversive Activities Control Board, in which the justices threw out an
order requiring the Stalinist organization to register with the agency responsible for enforcing the Internal Security Act. Because of the government's reliance on what Justice Frankfurter considered the untrustworthy
testimony of professional informants and admitted perjurers, the Court
granted the radical group a new hearing.[8]

Concern about perjured testimony also produced an order remanding
the Pittsburgh Smith Act case. Appearing as a friend of the court, the
ACLU argued that the evidence adduced against the defendants was insufficient to sustain the convictions and that the rapidly shrinking CPUSA
could not possibly constitute a clear and present danger. The petitioning
Communists themselves contended among other things that the prosecution should have established, not only that they had taught and advocated
the overthrow of the government, but also that they had used "language
inciting or inflaming persons to act rather than study or think things over."
The Court did not have to deal with these issues, for, on 27 September,
Solicitor General J. Lee Rankin and Assistant Attorney General William
Tompkins filed a motion to remand. Since the trial, they reported, Joseph
Massei, a witness against two of the defendants, had given other sworn
testimony which the government had reason to question. Though convinced
that their man had told the truth in Pittsburgh, Rankin and Tompkins believed it would serve the interests of justice to return the case to the district court for a hearing on the credibility of his testimony. The Court
went even further than they requested, reversing the judgments against
the defendants and granting them a new trial.[9]

III

That left only the California case before it. In that one, Communists
convicted in Los Angeles had appealed the outcome of a trial which was
in almost all respects a happy contrast to the riotous monstrosity at
Foley Square. It had generated no warfare between court and counsel,
and, at least until after the jury returned a verdict, Judge Mathes had
treated the defendants quite fairly. After reviewing his conduct of the
trial, the Ninth Circuit Court of Appeals pronounced it impeccable and
upheld the convictions in almost mechanical fashion.[10]

According to that tribunal's Judge James Alger Fee, whose disposition of the case ignited Communist protests in Berkeley, San Francisco, and Los Angeles, the most impressive thing about *Yates* v. *United States* was the fact that the Supreme Court had already ruled on almost all of the assignments of error presented by appellants. The principles that the main and concurring opinions in *Dennis* had laid down were, he felt, virtually conclusive in this case. Although the court of appeals saw no new issues in *Yates*, the Supreme Court nevertheless agreed to review the case, largely because it offered a way for justices concerned about the excesses of the anti-Communist crusade to limit the Smith Act prosecutions without having to take the embarrassing step of directly overruling *Dennis*.[11]

In a brief supporting the Communists' petition for a writ of certiorari, the ACLU urged forthright reversal, on grounds that the Smith Act was and always had been unconstitutional, but the Court evidenced no desire to take such a bold step. With *Yates* it did not have to, for petitioners pointed out numerous ways in which the justices might distinguish this case from the earlier one. As defendant Al Richmond remembers it, the Californians and their lawyers, although convinced that political considerations would decide the contest, based their appellate strategy on the assumption that "the skill of legal gamesmanship lies in devising a splendid variety of technical pegs on which the court can hang its decision." Thus, some of the arguments they advanced were quite narrow and in fact did not even apply to all of the defendants. In a petition applicable only to himself, William Schneiderman contended that the judgment against him was invalid because essentially the same issues and evidence had already been adjudicated in his 1943 citizenship case. Attorney Augustin Donovan, participating at the request of the California bar, filed a brief arguing that the convictions of Richmond and Philip "Slim" Connelly, both editors of the *People's World*, raised special questions of freedom of the press. The problem with the arguments advanced on behalf of these men, from the point of view of justices concerned about recent anti-Communist excesses, was that they afforded no means of limiting the Smith Act.[12]

But the petition filed by Norman Leonard, Ben Margolis, Alexander Schulman, and A. L. Wirin for all of the defendants did. Of the eight questions these attorneys raised, two involved issues that the Court had not previously considered and which afforded particularly fine avenues of approach for a judicial assault on the Smith Act. One was whether the courts below had erred in their construction of the term "organize." Lawyers for the Communist petitioners contended that the definition of that word used by Fee and Mathes, who described organization as a

continuing process embracing such activities as recruitment, was contrary
to law, and also to the First and Fifth Amendments. The Court had not
previously considered this question, because the trial judge in Pittsburgh
had ruled favorably on a defense motion contending that the statute of
limitations barred prosecution for conspiracy to organize the CPUSA,
thus making it impossible for those convicted there to raise that issue
on appeal. The other significant question was whether Mathes's refusal
to give that part of the *Dennis* charge which stated that the Smith Act
punished only advocacy employing language reasonably and ordinarily
calculated to incite those hearing it to action constituted an erroneous
construction of the statute that violated the First Amendment. The failure of the trial judge to adopt Medina's language is inexplicable, for even
the prosecution had urged him to do so. Certainly, it made *Yates* unique.
As Schneiderman's attorney, Robert Kenny, pointed out, this was the
first case presented to the Court "where there was a refusal to give such
instruction." Although the government opposed review, the justices
seized upon the opportunity to consider these issues.[13]

In August 1956 lawyers for the West Coast radicals filed three briefs
with the Court. In one of these Donovan questioned the sufficiency of
the evidence against Richmond and Connelly and argued that, given the
nature of the government's case against these two defendants, their convictions violated the First Amendment. Kenny argued that the 1943
deportation proceeding barred the entire prosecution, at least as to Schneiderman, and also criticized the quality and strength of the government's
proof.[14]

The third brief, submitted for all of the defendants by Leonard, Schulman, and Wirin, contended that the court below had sustained the convictions in plain disregard of the standards set down in Dennis.[15] They
could stand, it argued, only if proof of long-time membership and officer-
ship in the Communist Party and participation in its legal activities were
held sufficient to justify a finding of guilt on charges of conspiracy to violate the Smith Act, for, as to five of the petitioners, that was all the evidence established. There was nothing in the few utterances attributed to
the others which in any way substantiated their connection with the alleged conspiracy or their possession of the required specific intent. The
government had simply piled one inference on top of another, lawyers
for the Communists charged. The prosecution had alleged and proved only
two overt acts, and both of those were innocuous public meetings protected by the First Amendment. The attorneys castigated the government for employing the discredited doctrine of guilt by association and
also criticized Mathes for several of his rulings. In addition, they accused

the trial judge of mishandling the clear-and-present-danger issue by failing to determine whether the defendants had possessed, either independently or jointly, the power to bring about the overthrow of the government.

These lawyers also condemned Mathes for his failure to charge that the Smith Act punished only advocacy and teaching in the language of incitement to action. Their brief pointed out that both sides had requested this instruction and reminded the Court that in the *Dennis* case not a single jurist had construed the statute as proscribing any other kind of speech. "This Court has uniformly held, in the light of law and history, that in our constitutional system the line must be drawn between the advocacy of ideas and doctrines, no matter how unpalatable, and the advocacy of ideas in language of direct incitement to unlawful action," counsel maintained, adding, "The construction of the Smith Act by the courts below was a palpable violation of the First Amendment."[16]

These lawyers also contended that the definition of "organize" employed by Mathes and Fee could find no support in the dictionary, legal precedents, or legislative history. If one properly construed the word, they maintained, the statute of limitations barred the present prosecution, insofar as the case involved conspiracy to organize the CPUSA. Because the jury had returned a general verdict, there was no way of telling whether it might have based its finding entirely on that aspect of the charge; consequently the convictions had to fall.

In requesting reversal of the judgments against them, the Californians had the support of other Communists convicted under the Smith Act, as well as the backing of the American Civil Liberties Union, which also filed a friend-of-the-court brief. The ACLU argued that the type of evidence the government had presented in this case was insufficient to sustain the convictions and that, if the Court upheld them anyhow, the result would be contraction of the freedom to exchange political opinions. It disputed the notion that the Party posed a threat to national security and pointed out that the Smith Act prosecutions, rather than eliminating whatever danger existed, only made the task of investigative agencies more difficult.[17]

On 24 September the Department of Justice responded to the Communists and their backers. It defended the trial judge's interpretation of the word "organize" and contended that, even if the part of the indictment alleging organization were invalid, it would not matter, because, by its verdict, the jury had found conspiracy not only to organize but also to teach and advocate and either alone was enough to convict. The government also argued that the Smith Act, as construed and applied in this case, did not violate the First Amendment. Mathes's charge to the jury had correctly explained advocacy of violence, it contended, because there had been no need for him to delineate the meaning of that concept in terms of "incitement"—a word that, according to the Justice Department, had an "inappropriate" connotation of immediacy.[18]

Not long after filing this brief, the government again confronted its Communist adversaries before the Supreme Court. On 8 October the lawyers for the California radicals presented their case, and the next day Phillip Monahan replied for the Justice Department. Whereas counsel for the Communists impressed Justice Burton, the government attorney did not, and Monahan had to field some tough questions from his auditors. Douglas asked what specific deeds the defendants had performed in advocating violence, and Reed wanted to know whether the government attorney thought mere membership in the Party constituted an overt act. Harlan inquired about the links between these petitioners and the alleged conspiracy. Replying to this last question, Monahan argued, rather lamely in view of the supposed magnitude of the Communist menace, that because the charge was conspiracy, the government did not even need to prove that the defendants had "urge[d] violence with their own lips."[19]

IV

The Court's decision did not come until the following spring. On 17 June, "Red Monday" to some, the justices electrified the country with a cluster of opinions striking hard at McCarthyism. In *Watkins* v. *United States* the Court by a six-to-one vote overturned a contempt conviction against a man who had refused to answer certain questions before the House Un-American Activities Committee, declaring that the First Amendment limited the investigative powers of Congress and that questions posed by bodies like HUAC had to meet the test of pertinency to legitimate legislative purposes.[20] The six-to-two decision in *Sweezy* v. *New Hampshire* imposed similar standards on investigations conducted under the authority of state legislatures.[21] In *Service* v. *Dulles* the Court ordered the federal government to reinstate an alleged security risk.[22] As if these three were not enough, the Court also produced a libertarian decision in the Smith Act case.[23] By a six-to-one vote, it freed five of the California Communists and ordered new trials for the rest. Justice Brennan and an even more recent Eisenhower appointee, Charles E. Whittaker, both of whom had ascended to the high bench too late to participate in all stages of the case, took no part in the decision. Only Justice Clark dissented.

The official opinion of the Court, written by Harlan, had the complete support of only two other justices, Earl Warren and Felix Frankfurter. The votes of Harlan and the Chief Justice were predictable products of their growing personal reaction against McCarthyism. That of Frankfurter was more surprising, for he had, of course, been part of the majority in *Dennis*. But, while voting with Vinson in the earlier case, Frankfurter had not considered his opinion a binding precedent for the future. By 1957 the excesses of the anti-Communist crusade, so disturbing to Warren and Harlan, had shaken him too, converting his reluctant support for the Smith Act into quiet opposition. In an early 1955 exchange of letters with Erwin Griswold, Frankfurter revealed how upsetting he found the activities of Senator McCarthy. The fact that the rest of the federal judiciary had responded to *Dennis* by enlisting in the Justice Department's war on the CPUSA also disturbed him. By the fall of 1951, Frankfurter had become convinced of the need to impress upon the lower courts the fact that they "must not treat defendants even under the Smith Act prosecutions as though they were an indiscriminate lump, and especially as though their guilt were already assumed." Although he apparently agreed with his colleagues' refusal to grant certiorari in the *Flynn* and Baltimore cases, by the time the Pittsburgh and Los Angeles defendants requested review, his attitude had changed. The Pennsylvania record struck him as completely inadequate to justify conviction, particularly as it gave little indication that the Party had any immediate plans to overthrow the government by force and violence; thus Frankfurter decided that reversal was in order. The problem was singling out "any specific point" that would justify it. He set his clerks to work on this problem, and, after examining several possibilities, they and the justice apparently decided that the admission of certain statements by alleged co-conspirators offered the most plausible basis for the decision he wished to make. When the government raised the issue of possible perjury, it became possible to dispose of the case without reaching its merits. While welcoming this opportunity, Frankfurter, along with Burton and Harlan, opposed granting the defendants a new trial. What they wanted was a district court investigation of the perjury allegations. Frankfurter remained deeply concerned about the type of evidence the Justice Department was using in Smith Act cases and wanted stiffer standards imposed upon it.[24]

In *Yates* Harlan produced an opinion that satisfied his desires. Long, complex, and painfully dull, it made difficult reading, even for a lawyer, but it was a model of scholarship and technical precision. With this opinion, Harlan managed to erect new safeguards for freedom of expression, while avoiding a wrenching reversal of *Dennis*. He and Frankfurter were judicial conservatives who earlier had defended the Smith Act; therefore, although they wished to reverse the convictions and check abusive use of that law, they could not employ short simple constitutional arguments to accomplish their objectives. Frankfurter and his clerks had discussed the possibility of reversing the Pittsburgh convictions because of the absence of an immediate revolutionary threat, but they had to reject the idea, because such a decision would have involved a retreat from *Dennis*. Just as Frankfurter's earlier insistence that the Smith Act represented a permissible congressional policy choice limited what he could do now, Harlan, as the author of the Second Circuit's *Flynn* decision, also worked in the shadow of his past professions. Whatever its stylistic weaknesses, his *Yates* cpinion was a masterful piece of reasoning, admirably suited to disguise a change in outlook and allow its author and Frankfurter to maintain at least the illusion of consistency.[25]

Harlan began his discussion with the organization issue and determined that "since the Communist Party came into being in 1945, and the indictment was not returned until 1951, the three-year statute of limitations had run on the 'organizing' charge and required the withdrawal of that part of the indictment from the jury's consideration."[26] Under this interpretation, at the time of its adoption a key provision of the Smith Act would not have applied to the CPUSA, but Harlan insisted that the legislative history of the statute did not indicate that Congress had written the clause in question with particular reference to the Party. The justice rejected the contention that Mathes's misinterpretation of "organize" was a harmless error, because the trial judge's charge was not, in his opinion, clear and specific enough to support the conclusion that the jury had found the defendants guilty of conspiring to teach and advocate, as well as to organize. There was no way to determine, Harlan said, whether the jurors had believed the overt act which they were legally required to find was in furtherance of one objective or the other. Hence the Court had to set aside the verdict.

Harlan found another reason for reversal in Mathes's failure to instruct the jury that in order to convict it must find the defendants had conspired to promote advocacy aimed at producing conduct rather than commitment. The question was, he said, "whether the Smith Act prohibits advocacy and teaching of forcible overthrow as an abstract principle, divorced from any effort to instigate action to that end, so long as such advocacy or teaching is engaged in with evil intent. We hold," he announced for the Court, "that it does not."[27] Although the government claimed to have relied on *Dennis*, Harlan contended that it had misinterpreted the 1951 decision, for although Vinson had said the Smith Act was directed at advocacy, rather than discussion, "it is clear that the reference was to advocacy of action, not ideas. . . ."[28] A speaker might violate that law by urging his listeners to act at some distant time, Harlan said, but, while immediacy was not a necessary element of the crime, incitement was. "The essential distinction is that those to whom the advocacy is addressed must be urged to *do* something, now or in the future, rather than merely to *believe* in something."[29] In the massive record before him, he found few instances of speech which would amount to advocacy of action.

Having made two determinations, each of which required reversal, the Supreme Court could simply have remanded the case for a new trial. Instead, the justices scrutinized the record to determine whether they should leave the way open for the government to retry some or all of the defendants. The result of this examination was a conclusion that against Richmond, Connelly, Rose Chernin Kusnitz, Frank Spector, and Henry Steinberg the evidence was clearly insufficient. The Smith Act prosecutions had always depended upon an equation between the teaching of Marxism-Leninism and advocacy of violent overthrow of the government as a principle of action, but, in Harlan's opinion, the evidence here proved only that the CPUSA taught abstract doctrine. The government had established nothing about these five defendants other than that they were officers and members of the Communist Party. Given the terms of section 4(f) of the Internal Security Act, there was simply no legal proof that could link them to a conspiracy to teach and advocate revolution as a rule of action. The Court, therefore, ordered their acquittal. According to Harlan, the record did contain evidence of incidents involving the other nine defendants which might be shown to constitute such teaching and advocacy. While doubtful that this could be done, he was not prepared to say at this stage of the case that it was impossible, nor to forbid the retrial of those Communists under proper legal standards. Clearly, though, his expectation was that the Justice Department would not again obtain convictions.

Although joining Harlan in voting to reverse, Harold Burton and Hugo Black filed separate opinions. Burton, like Frankfurter, had moved from the *Dennis* majority to the *Yates* one, but he had done so only because of his exasperation with Mathes's charge, and he wanted to make it clear that in his view the Court had misinterpreted "organize."[30] Black, speaking also for Douglas, agreed with Harlan's treatment of that issue, but not with his handling of the advocacy problem. As far as the Alabama libertarian was concerned, any conviction for agreeing to advocate, as distinguished from agreeing to act, violated the First Amendment, even if the conspirators planned to urge action, rather than merely belief. In Black's opinion, the Court should have freed all fourteen defendants.

The only dissenter, Tom Clark, argued that the evidence in this case paralleled and was just as strong as that in *Dennis* and—doubtless a reminder to Justice Harlan—*Flynn* as well. He believed the Court should affirm the convictions, but if his colleagues insisted upon reversing them, Clark contended, they ought not arrogate to themselves the responsibility for acquitting defendants. That was a jury's job. Although convinced that the government should have another chance to make a case against the California Communists, the former attorney general conceded that, under the theories which the Court had announced, it was doubtful whether on remand the prosecution could muster sufficient evidence to obtain new convictions.

It was clear to the man who had launched the Smith Act prosecutions nine years earlier that his colleagues had dealt a devastating blow to the Justice Department's war on the Communist Party. In 1951 the Supreme Court had given federal prosecutors a green light; now the high tribunal had changed the color to red. "It is difficult," wrote University of Illinois political scientist Jack Peltason, "not to agree with Justice Clark's intimation that in fact the decision reverses, or at least severely restricts the sweep of, the *Dennis* Doctrine." This was something of an overstatement, for the new opinion was not legally inconsistent with the old, and, had the Court applied its 1957 standards to the 1951 case, the result could still have been affirmance. Yet history would validate the judgment of the student commentator for the *University of Minnesota Law Review*, who concluded after *Yates* that "little remains of the Smith Act with reference to Communists."[31]

The Supreme Court had wrecked the instrument which six years earlier it had honed into a potent weapon for war against the CPUSA. The reason for its change of outlook was readily apparent at that time. The Sunday after Harlan read his opinion, E. W. Kenworthy of the *New York Times* reported from Washington that observers there agreed the decision reflected "the great changes in political climate at home and abroad, since Chief Justice Vinson wrote the Dennis opinion."[32] To most of those who sat on the Supreme Court, methods used to attack domestic communism, which were regarded as appropriate and even necessary at a time when the Cold War between the United States and Russia was at its most frigid, now seemed far more menacing to American democracy than did the CPUSA. Even those justices committed to judicial restraint felt compelled to resist such tactics. By relying upon statutory interpretation, the Court avoided an open constitutional attack upon the Smith Act, but Harlan's subtleties were nearly as lethal as outright invalidation. The Smith Act still lived, but it was now a helpless cripple.

NOTES

1. 347 U.S. 483 (1954); Paul L. Murphy, *The Constitution in Crisis Times 1918-1969* (New York: Harper & Row, 1972), p. 320; Walter F. Murphy, *Congress and the Court: A Case Study in the American Political Process* (Chicago: University of Chicago Press, 1962), pp. 132, 154-55, 264-65, and 282; Luther A. Huston, *Pathway to Judgment: A Study of Earl Warren* (Philadelphia and New York: Chilton Books, 1966), pp. 124-25; Anthony Lewis, "Earl Warren," in *The Justices of the United States Supreme Court 1789-1969: Their Lives and Major Opinions*, ed. Leon Friedman and Fred L. Israel, 4 vols. (New York and London: Chelsea House and R. R. Bowker, 1969), 4: 2724-28.

2. Murphy, *Congress and the Court*, p. 86; Norman Dorsen, "John Marshall Harlan," in *The Justices of the Supreme Court*, 4: 2804-05. The *Fortune* article is reprinted in Henry M. Christman, ed., *The Public Papers of Chief Justice Earl Warren* (New York: Simon & Schuster, 1959), pp. 236-37, and the Philadelphia speech is quoted in *NYT*, 25 August 1955, p. 10.

3. David L. Shapiro, ed., *The Evolution of a Judicial Philosophy: Selected Opinions and Papers of Justice John M. Harlan* (Cambridge, Mass.: Harvard University Press, 1969), p. 285.

4. Ibid., pp. 286-88 (quote on p. 288).

5. John P. Frank, *The Warren Court* (New York: Macmillan Co., 1964), pp. 115-23.

6. "Communism and the Supreme Court—A Growing Debate," *U.S. News & World Report*, 18 July 1958, pp. 81-82; Amicus Curiae Brief of ILWU, Motion by American Civil Liberties Union, Southern California Branch, for Leave to File Brief Amicus Curiae, Motion for Leave to File Brief Amicus Curiae [by a group of Concerned California Citizens], and Motion for Leave to File a Brief Amicus Curiae and Brief of Members of the Southern California-Arizona Conference of the Methodist Church, at 4-5, Yates v. United States, 354 U.S. 298 (1957); Yates v. United States, Schneiderman v. United States, and Richmond v. United States, 350 U.S. 860 (1955); Mesarosh v. United States, 350 U.S. 922 (1955); *PW*, 18 October 1955; ACLU Weekly Bulletin no. 1773, 22 October 1956, p. 2; TRB, "Smith Act Reconsidered," *New Republic*, 17 September 1956, p. 2.

7. 350 U.S. 497 (1956).

8. 351 U.S. 115 (1956).

9. Mesarosh v. United States, 352 U.S. 1 (1956); Brief for American Civil Liberties Union as Amicus Curiae, at 2-26, Mesarosh v. United States and Yates v. United States, 354, U.S. 298 (1957); Brief for Petitioner, at 14, and Motion to Remand, at 1-6, Mesarosh v. United States.

10. Yates v. United States, 225 F. 2d 146 (9th Cir. 1955).

11. Ibid.; *PW*, 21 March 1955.

12. Motion by American Civil Liberties Union, Southern California Branch, for Leave to File Brief Amicus Curiae, at 1-2, Yates v. United States, 354 U.S. 298 (1957); Al Richmond, *A Long View from the Left: Memoirs of an American Revolutionary* (Boston: Houghton Mifflin, 1973), p. 358; Petition of William Schneiderman for Writ of Certiorari, at 27-40, and Petition of Al Richmond and Philip Marshall Connelly for Writ of Certiorari, at 2, Yates v. United States, 354 U.S. 298 (1957).

13. Petition for Writ of Certiorari, at 1-6, and Brief in Opposition, Yates v. United States, 354 U.S. 298 (1957); Brief for Petitioners, at 115, Mesarosh v. United States, 352 U.S. 1 (1956); *Yates Transcript,* p. 1382. For Kenny's comment see Reply of Petitioner William Schneiderman to Brief for the United States, at 2, Yates v. United States. According to Associate Justice Tom Clark (personal interview with the Author at the Supreme Court Building, Washington, D.C., 17 August 1976), Mathes, a fraternity brother of his, told him he considered the Medina charge "insufficient" and felt an obligation to "do more."

14. Reply Brief for the United States, Brief for Petitioners Richmond and Connelly, at 81-104, and Brief for Petitioner Schneiderman, at 26-45, Yates v. United States, 354 U.S. 298 (1957).

15. For a summary of their arguments see Brief for Petitioners, at 116-23, Yates v. United States, 354 U.S. 298 (1957).

16. Ibid., at 121.

17. Brief for Jack Hall, Joseph Kuzma, et al., as Amici Curiae, at 2-51, Yates v. United States, 354 U.S. 298 (1957); ACLU Brief, *Yates and Mesarosh,* at 2-26.

18. Brief for the United States, at 70-136, Yates v. United States, 354 U.S. 298 (1957).

19. *NYT,* 10 October 1956, p. 21; "Diary for 1956," Box 3, Harold Burton Papers, LC.

20. 354 U.S. 178 (1957).

21. 354 U.S. 234 (1957).

22. 354 U.S. 363 (1957).

23. 354 U.S. 298 (1957).

24. Frankfurter to Irving Brandt, 11 October 1951, Box 52, Frankfurter to Griswold, 31 March 1955 and 11 April 1955, Griswold to Frankfurter, 7 April 1955, Box 59, Frankfurter to Chief Justice Vinson, 24 October 1951 (unsent letter), Box 109, and 1956 memorandum entitled, "Nelson v. United States," untitled and undated memorandum on the Nelson Case, and "Notes Concerning Nelson" (prepared on an unspecified date by one of Frankfurter's clerks), Box 220, Felix Frankfurter Papers, LC; dissenting opinions of Frankfurter and Harlan, Mesarosh v. United States, 352 U.S. 1 (1956). When interviewed, Justice Clark said he thought Frankfurter was looking for an excuse to reverse in *Yates* and simply seized on the specific issues raised by counsel as justification for doing so.

25. Murphy, *Congress and the Court*, p. 122; "Notes Concerning Nelson."

26. Yates v. United States, 354 U.S. 298 (1957), at 312.

27. Ibid., at 318.

28. Ibid., at 320.

29. Ibid., at 324-25.

30. Clark interview.

31. Jack W. Peltason, "Constitutional Liberty and the Communist Problem," in *Foundations of Freedom in the American Constitution*, ed. Alfred H. Kelly (New York: Harper & Brothers, 1958), p. 120; "Recent Cases: Criminal Law—Smith Act—Interpretation of 'Organize' and 'Advocate,' " *Minnesota Law Review* 2 (December 1957): 305.

32. *NYT*, 23 June 1957, sec. 4, p. 5.

10
Winding Down a War

---

*... the Yates decision leaves the Smith Act, as to any fur-
ther prosecution under it, a virtual shambles. ...*
—Judge Richard Chambers
Fujimoto v. United States (1958)

Yates was the beginning of the end. The decision evoked a mixed reaction, but applause exceeded condemnation, and the congressional Cold
Warriors who attempted to reverse the Supreme Court through legislation achieved only meager results after long delay. The Department of
Justice was forced to give up on its conspiracy cases, and when federal
prosecutors attempted to develop the membership clause of the Smith
Act into a tool for carrying on their courtroom crusade against the
CPUSA, the Supreme Court again intervened, validating that provision,
but rendering it almost impossible to use.

I

The Court's *Yates* decision inspired a variety of comments. The defendants, who had expected to go to prison, were overjoyed. "Victory
is indeed sweet," sighed the *People's World.* Government lawyers, realizing that the Supreme Court had made the job of convicting Stalinists
vastly more complicated, complained bitterly, as did the outspokenly
anti-Communist American Legion, which passed a resolution condemning *Yates.* The popular press was neither as ecstatic as the Party nor as
outraged as the Justice Department and the Legion. The *New York Times,*
which itself praised the decision, surveyed the views of other New York
dailies and a variety of papers across the country and found eight supporting the Supreme Court, seven opposing it, and one adopting an essential-

ly neutral position. Division on this issue cut across party and even philosophical lines. The Republican *New York Herald-Tribune* called *Yates*
"an important further reenforcement for traditional rights of free speech,"
while the *Chicago Tribune*, also a frequent backer of the GOP, charged
the Court with taking "an unduly fastidious approach to the motivation
of Communists." The Democratic press was also divided, with the *Philadelphia Inquirer* and the *Cleveland Plain-Dealer* assaulting the decision,
while the *St. Louis Post-Dispatch* praised the justices for strengthening
the Bill of Rights. The Trotskyist *Militant* endorsed *Yates*, and at the
conservative end of the political spectrum *Life*, the *Saturday Evening
Post*, the *Dallas Morning News*, and the *Los Angeles Times* all criticized
it. But the *Appleton* (Wis.) *Post-Crescent*, while indicating mild displeasure, expressed a tolerant attitude toward the Court, and the *Denver
Post* commended this libertarian ruling. The *New Orleans Times-Picayune*
expressed pessimism about the future, but the *Hartford Courant*, convinced that America's ultimate security lay in maximizing freedom, except when there was an imminent threat of hostile action, was happy
that "The Supreme Court has now once more made history by choosing
liberty," and proclaimed, "We need not be afraid." Obviously, the *Yates*
decision had badly divided the press, but the balance, though close, did
seem to tilt slightly in favor of the Court.[1]

Lawyers and legal commentators disagreed quite as much as writers
for lay newspapers and magazines. The *Yates* decision won the endorsement of the *West Virginia Law Review*, which lauded the Court for assuring the country "that one of our most cherished freedoms, the right to
express one's views without fear of censure, has not been encroached
upon." Legal journals at UCLA and the University of Minnesota also supported the decision, although the latter publication expressed some concern about the capacity of government to combat communism in the
future.[2]

No law review opposed *Yates*, but some older members of the legal
fraternity liked that decision a great deal less than did the editors of these
student-run journals. Addressing a conference of the National Association
of Attorneys General, which met a week after the high tribunal acted,
New Hampshire's chief legal officer, Lewis C. Wyman, urged passage of
legislation to undo *Yates* and other recent Supreme Court rulings on communism. Two months later Wyman appeared before a congressional committee to express amazement at Harlan's interpretation of advocacy and
ask that the "organizing" section again be made applicable to the CPUSA.
The following January, Frank Ober, a well-known Maryland anti-Communist, attacked the Court in the pages of the *American Bar Association*

Journal, and in a 1958 lecture Learned Hand, who considered *Yates* inconsistent with *Dennis,* argued that there were occasions when a speaker might lose the right to talk, even though he dealt only with principles divorced from action.[3]

The American Bar Association offered hints that it agreed with the critics. In the summer of 1957 the ABA held a two-stage annual meeting, with successive sessions in New York and London. At the first gathering the delegates voted down a resolution by Judge Palmer Hutchinson of Dallas, which expressed support for the Supreme Court and condemned attacks upon it. In London former Maryland state senator Herbert O'Connor, chairman of the Committee on Communist Strategy and Tactics, delivered a report sharply critical of the high tribunal's recent rulings and recommended a six-point legislative program to reverse them. Among his proposals was one for correction of the notion that Congress had not intended the Smith Act to prohibit advocacy and teaching of forcible overthrow as an abstract principle. The report requested no action by the House of Delegates and was simply accepted and filed, so that it did not constitute an ABA policy statement. But the obvious implication of the events which had transpired at the two sessions was that the bar opposed *Yates.*[4]

There was no doubt at all that some members of the House and Senate did, as Congressman Francis Walter (D., Pa.) demonstrated two days after the decision, when he warned Communists: ". . . we have accepted the challenge and we are going to pass the type of legislation that even the Supreme Court will understand." Walter received the support of the Senate Internal Security Subcommittee, and the Justice Department also studied "the faint possibility of securing appropriate new legislation. . . ." Between 23 July 1957 and 22 July 1958, Walter and Congressmen Kenneth Keating (R., N.Y.), William C. Cramer (R., Fla.), and William Colmer (D., Miss.) all introduced bills designed to "correct" the judicial interpretation of "organize," and Keating tried unsuccessfully to obtain administration backing for such measures.[5] Angered by *Yates* and other recent rulings which interfered with the crusade against domestic communism, Senator William Jenner of Indiana offered a comprehensive bill to take away the Court's appellate jurisdiction in five types of loyalty and subversion cases. His measure, while anathema to Deputy Attorney General William Rogers, appealed not only to national security alarmists but also to Southern racists, who had nursed a smoldering animosity toward Earl Warren and his colleagues since their 1954 school segregation decision.

Although attractive to some members of Congress, Jenner's proposal did not appeal to the public, a fact dramatically demonstrated during hearings held by a Senate Judiciary subcommittee in February 1958. Witnesses supporting the bill substantially outnumbered those opposing it, but the only really important organization which they represented was the Veterans of Foreign Wars. The American Legion declined to take a stand on the measure, and large and conservative groups such as the American Farm Bureau Federation, the U.S. Chamber of Commerce, and the National Association of Manufacturers were conspicuous for their silence. Some of the witnesses were persons of stature, but their testimony was suspect, because they were either, like Senator Strom Thurmond of South Carolina, notorious segregationists, or, like *National Review* editor L. Brent Brozell, identified with a long list of right-wing causes. Only Edward S. Corwin, Princeton's renowned constitutional scholar, was both prominent and disinterested enough to make a truly effective witness. Those who opposed the bill, though outnumbered, represented larger and more influential organizations, such as the ACLU, the NAACP, the American Jewish Congress, the AFL-CIO, and the Bar of the City of New York.

The two sides submitted correspondence and newspaper editorials supporting their positions, and again those urging defeat of the Jenner bill had an obvious edge. The leader of the opposition, Senator Thomas Hennings (D., Mo.), had written to the deans of almost all the large law schools in the country, and also to partners in some of the nation's leading law firms. Every practicing attorney who replied opposed the bill, and the sentiment of the law schools was nearly as one-sided. Only three deans and two professors favored it, and most of these endorsements were qualified. The Duke and Southern Methodist faculties unanimously opposed the measure, and even the University of Alabama Law School labeled it unwise. Jenner's editorial support came from three papers in his home state, two in middle-sized Southern cities, two in California, and one in New Bedford, Massachusetts. The most important of the lot was the not very influential *Los Angeles Examiner*. Opponents of the proposed legislation, on the other hand, included the *St. Louis Post-Dispatch*, the *Washington Post*, the *Chicago Tribune*, the *New York Times*, and the *Milwaukee Journal*.

Those seeking to defeat the Jenner bill had two other potent allies. One of them was the House of Delegates of the American Bar Association, which passed a resolution attacking the measure. Although many ABA members were unhappy about recent decisions, they believed their organization had a duty to defend the Supreme Court. Also opposing the bill was Rogers, who had by now become attorney general. He wrote to Senator James Eastland, branding the bill a threat to the independence of the judiciary, which, if passed, would impair the proper administration of justice and harm America's balanced system of government.

Confronted with overwhelming opposition, Jenner hinted that he was willing to compromise. His friend Senator John Marshall Butler (R., Md.) worked out a series of amendments to the bill, eliminating all but one of the provisions for withdrawal of Supreme Court jurisdiction and proposing to deal with particular decisions in a variety of other ways. To overcome the *Yates* distinction between incitement and advocating abstract doctrine, Butler suggested inserting into the Smith Act a qualifying phrase that would explicitly make teaching and advocacy punishable, regardless of their immediate probable effect. The proposed new section would also include a definition of "organize," embracing the recruitment of additional members and the forming, regrouping, or expansion of new and existing units, clubs, and classes.

After adopting these amendments, on 30 April, the Judiciary Committee voted ten to five to recommend passage of the renamed Jenner-Butler bill. That measure, however, still faced potent opposition. In a 17 April letter to Senator Alexander Wiley, Deputy Attorney General Lawrence Walsh had made it clear that the Justice Department remained hostile. In addition, the five liberals on the committee filed a puissant minority report. Wiley (R., Wis.), Hennings (D., Mo.), William Langer (R., N.D.), John Carroll (D., Col.), and Estes Kefauver (D., Tenn.), subjected the bill to a scorching critique, pointing out, among other things, that because of the changes made by Butler, most of the present proposal had never been the subject of hearings or investigation by the committee. To make up for this omission the liberal minority included critical correspondence from the Justice Department, many law school deans, and numerous bar associations and other organizations. Finally, the Jenner-Butler bill faced the opposition of Majority Leader Lyndon Johnson (D., Tex.), who feared this measure might cause a breach in the Democratic Party, damaging to his personal prestige and presidential ambitions, and that its enactment would reflect adversely on the wisdom of the Senate. Consequently, despite its favorable recommendation, the Jenner-Butler bill failed on the floor. Johnson helped the liberals round up votes against it and, when he was sure they had enough, he allowed proponents of the measure to introduce it as an amendment to some noncontroversial legislation on appellate procedure. Hennings promptly offered a motion to table, and it carried forty-nine to forty-one. The majority consisted mainly of western and northern Democrats, with most of the nays coming from Republicans and Southerners, but four Democrats from Texas and Tennessee and a small group of GOP senators, most of them liberal, but including conservative Everett Dirkson of Illinois, provided the margin of victory.[6]

While attention focused on the Jenner-Butler bill, legislation to reverse one aspect of the *Yates* decision slipped quietly through the House. On 6 August 1958, after holding hearings on several similar proposals, the Judiciary Committee recommended passage of a measure to redefine "organization," submitted by Congressman Walter. Its report asserted that Congress had intended "organize" to denote a continuous process and indicated that this effort to restore that meaning had the support of the Justice Department. When the Walter bill came before the full House on 12 August, its only critics were members who thought the measure did not go far enough. William Cramer, sponsor of a similar bill, informed his colleagues that it was essential "to plug the gaping holes in the dike that Congress erected by the Smith Act to outlaw communism in this country, the dike erected by Congress to prevent this floodtide of insidious, atheistic communism from inundating our free society." He accused the Supreme Court of sacrificing security "on the altar of so-called individual rights." The father of the Smith Act, John McCormack, now majority leader, also spoke in favor of the bill, which he considered necessary to make the law operate as those who enacted it had intended. Walter's measure passed the House on a voice vote but died in the Judiciary Committee of the more liberal Senate.[7]

The following year the lower chamber tried again. On 15 January Walter reintroduced his bill and on 18 February the Judiciary Committee endorsed it for the second time. On 24 February supporters of the measure received a powerful boost from the House of Delegates of the American Bar Association, which voted approval of a series of recommendations for legislative action to overcome recent Supreme Court decisions, submitted to it by the Committee on Communist Strategy, Tactics, and Objectives. The ABA called upon Congress to amend the Smith Act, so as to make illegal all intentional advocacy of violent overthrow of the government, and also urged passage of legislation redefining "organize" to include the recruitment of members, the formation of new units, and other activities of an organizational nature. On 2 March, the House repassed the Walter bill.[8]

Again it died in the Senate. While the action of the House of Delegates won the applause of Southern congressmen and newspapers, it drew fire from liberal quarters. The ACLU was highly critical; both the Philadelphia and New York City bars repudiated the resolutions; and former Justice Department official Warren Olney III protested them by resigning from ABA. The organization's president, Ross Malone, went on the defensive, insisting in a series of public appearances that the ABA had meant no disrespect to the Supreme Court. In August the group's Committee on Con-

stitutional Rights submitted a report, drafted by Arthur Sutherland of
the Harvard Law School, which examined the same decisions as had the
Committee on Communist Strategy and concluded that the justices had
done nothing which impaired the security of the nation. By 1959 seven
of the Republican senators who had earlier pushed legislation attacking
the Court were no longer in office, having either retired or lost their
seats. Observers generally interpreted the 1958 election results as proof
that the country had returned to liberalism, and few leaders of either
party wished to enter the 1960 canvass with a record of attempting to
curb the most liberal branch of the federal government. Again Walter's
bill died in the Senate Judiciary Committee.[9]

In January 1961, long after the controversy over *Yates* had subsided,
William Cramer introduced another bill to redefine "organize." Once
again the House Judiciary Committee recommended passage, offering
as argumentation only long quotations from its 1958 report. On 1 May
the Cramer bill encountered a minor roadblock when California Democrat James Roosevelt, unable to obtain what he regarded as a satisfactory explanation of the measure, insisted that the House postpone consideration. But on 15 May, amended to include some technical changes
in language suggested by Deputy Attorney General Byron White, it passed with little discussion and no opposition.[10]

White then wrote to the chairman of the Senate Judiciary Committee,
James O. Eastland (D., Miss.), urging favorable action on the proposal.
This time, although taking nearly a year to act, the committee sent the
bill to the floor with a recommendation for passage. When Majority Leader Mike Mansfield (D., Mont.) brought up the Cramer measure on 8 June
1962, he read a statement explaining it, and no one raised any objections.
The only man to speak was Keating (now a senator), who withheld his
remarks until after adoption of the bill. He insisted that, despite its dwin-
dling size, the Communist Party remained a threat to national security."I
am glad," Keating said, "that at long last we are about to close this gap
in our laws against subversion." The silence that answered him gave mute
testimony to how little his colleagues any longer cared, about either the
CPUSA or its nemesis, the Smith Act.[11]

II

The controversial statute with which the government had harassed
American communism almost out of existence was by that time practically a dead letter. The *Yates* decision did nothing for those Communists

who had already exhausted their appeals by the time it was rendered. When Henry Winston and Gil Green asked the Supreme Court for a rehearing, it rejected their petition, and they, the other nine Foley Square defendants, eleven of the Communists convicted in the second New York trial, and the members of the Baltimore group all had to serve their sentences. But *Yates* did save from prison all other Party members charged with conspiring to violate the Smith Act.[12]

Although given the opportunity to retry nine of the California defendants, the government decided not to do so. In a letter to the trial judge, the Justice Department admitted inability to satisfy the evidentiary requirements which the Supreme Court had laid down, and in December 1957, on motion of the prosecution, the district court dismissed the indictment.[13]

In other cases courts of appeals, deciding for themselves that the government could not meet the *Yates* standards, forced it to surrender by ordering acquittals. On 11 September 1957, three judges in the Second Circuit, finding the record of the Connecticut trial devoid of evidence establishing the necessary incitement, ordered the release of all defendants.[14] In his opinion Judge Charles Clark noted that, although government informers, who had operated at high levels within the Party, had testified at the trial, the 9,200 page transcript contained not a single example of revolutionary advocacy. His colleague, Carrol C. Hincks, convinced that the jury's verdict was in no way inconsistent with the *Yates* test, dissented, and, at his urging, a petition asking for review of the case by the entire court of appeals was submitted to its other judges. They turned Hincks down, with only Harold Medina supporting his request.

Soon after this defeat the government suffered another in the Philadelphia case. Candidly evaluating its own evidence, the Justice Department conceded that, with respect to two of the Eastern Pennsylvania District defendants, it simply could not meet the evidentiary requirements of *Yates*. The Third Circuit Court of Appeals found nothing in the record indicating that two others had done anything more than advocate Marxism-Leninism as an abstract doctrine, and consequently it ordered judgments of acquittal for them also. But the judges did think prosecutors might be able to make a case against the remaining defendants and gave them permission to try.[15]

In January 1958 the less cooperative Ninth Circuit Court of Appeals reversed the convictions against both the Seattle and Honolulu groups and ordered judgments of acquittal for all defendants. Judge Richard Chambers seemed to regret the decision which the Supreme Court's recent ruling had forced upon him. With a touch of bitterness he observed that *Yates* had left "the Smith Act, as to any further prosecution under it, a virtual shambles. . . ."[16]

A Second Circuit order dismissing the indictments against the Communists convicted at the third New York trial soon demonstrated the accuracy of his observation, as did the outcome of those cases in which courts of appeals, although overturning convictions, authorized new trials. On 24 June 1957, soon after deciding *Yates*, the Supreme Court reversed the judgments against the Detroit defendants and sent their case back to the Sixth Circuit for reconsideration. There a three-judge panel, speaking through Sheckelford Miller, overturned the convictions but concluded that "the evidence shows far more than mere advocacy of Communism as an abstract doctrine" and directed the district court to retry the defendants. Courts of appeals in the Sixth and Eighth Circuits reached similar conclusions with respect to the Cleveland and St. Louis groups, authorizing new trials for both. But in none of these cases could the government produce what *Yates* demanded. In the late summer of 1958 it moved for dismissal of the indictments in both Detroit and St. Louis, and a year later, when the U.S. attorney in Cleveland had to admit he could not meet the new evidentiary requirements, the district court dropped the charges in that case. The five Philadelphia defendants ordered retried by the court of appeals also gained their freedom in this way, as did the Pittsburgh Communists to whom the Supreme Court had granted a new trial.[17]

In both Boston and Puerto Rico the Justice Department gave up without a fight, moving for dismissal of the indictments against Communists who had not yet been tried when the Supreme Court decided *Yates*. In only one case did the government attempt a second trial. On 23 August 1957, because the judge below had failed to withdraw the organization portion of the charge from the consideration of the jury, the Tenth Circuit Court of Appeals reversed the judgments against the Denver group. Chief Judge Sam G. Bratton, although not uncritical of the prosecution, felt it deserved another chance, and the Supreme Court refused to review his decision. At a second trial in the winter of 1959 the judge withdrew that portion of the indictment charging conspiracy to organize, but the result was the same: the conviction of all defendants. The government's triumph proved only temporary, for, on 31 May 1961, the court of appeals again reversed. This time the decision, which turned on the failure of the prosecution to produce a large number of documents connected with witness John Lautner's service to the government and the refusal of the trial judge to order it to turn them over, had nothing to do with the Smith Act. Brattons's ruling left the way open for another trial, but, after considering the matter for several years, the Justice Department de-

cided to give up on the case, and in November 1964 it asked Judge Alfred
A. Arruj to drop all charges against the defendants. According to a spokesman for the department, the government had elected not to go to court
again, because "the currently available evidence is not such that this case
could be successfully retried."[18]

Thus ended the prosecution of Communists for conspiracy to violate
the Smith Act. Although there had been some delay, *Yates* had at last
written a conclusion to the story that began in July 1948. Evaluating the
impact of that decision, one commentator noted that it had "mainly
served to bar legal action against Communist leaders about whom there
was little real evidence of any activity presenting any immediately ob-
servable threat to the security of the United States." As the FBI saw it,
though, court decisions had thwarted the interests of justice. In his annual report for 1958, J. Edgar Hoover complained of "growing public
complacency toward the threat of subversion" and of the Communists'
new-found mastery of "the art of cloaking themselves in every right and
privilege enjoyed by the inhabitants of our democracy," which enabled
them "to scoff at America's laws while taking bold action to strengthen
their ties with Russia." The result, he remarked bitterly, was that "10
years after the original group of 11 Party leaders were indicted on charges
of conspiring to teach and advocate the overthrow of our government
by force and violence the Communists [have] succeeded in locating loop-
holes and technicalities which [have] nullified [most of] the convictions. . . ."[19]

III

Hoover insisted that the Justice Department must take "an aggressive
approach to problems of national security, designed effectively to counter-
act the current apathetic attitude inside and outside Government circles
toward this problem. . . ." Attorney General Rogers, though, did not
share his alarm, and J. Walter Yeagley, the man who had succeeded William F. Tompkins as head of the Internal Security Division, believed that
the prosecution of subversives should not be conducted like a crusade.
The government's legal attack on the CPUSA continued, but in a more
businesslike manner than once had been the case.[20]

Deprived by the courts of the weapon with which it had waged that
war, the Justice Department attempted to fashion a replacement from
the membership clause of the Smith Act. By June 1957 federal prosecutors had already conducted some preliminary experiments with that pro-

vision. The first Communists indicted for membership were the Foley
Square defendants, but the government chose to try them only for conspiracy. The indictments based on the other charge remained in effect,
and when the convicted radicals emerged from prison, authorities rear-
rested them. The Communists soon obtained release on bond, and the
Justice Department never brought them to trial for membership, probably because prosecutors decided to hold these cases in abeyance pending
the outcome of litigation intended to test the constitutionality of the
clause.[21]

Unlike the Twelve, those Communists indicted after *Dennis* were
charged only with conspiracy. Because of possible conflict between the
membership clause and the Internal Security Act, the Justice Department
refrained from further use of the Smith Act provision until a case arising
under the 1950 law had advanced far enough through the appellate courts
to provide some assurance that a prosecution for belonging to the CPUSA
would not encounter judicial opposition. But on 12 April 1954, Attorney
General Brownell assured a House Judiciary subcommittee that it could
"anticipate some rather interesting developments" in the near future. On
14 May, the government quietly secured a membership indictment against
Illinois Party Secretary Claude Lightfoot, and twelve days later federal
authorities took him into custody.[22]

By the end of 1954 prosecutors had charged six other Stalinists with
the same offense. Two of these were never tried. The case against Martha
Stone was dismissed, and she was prosecuted instead for participation in
the Connecticut conspiracy. It took more than a year after his indictment
for authorities to locate and arrest Max Weiss, so that by the time the government was ready to try him, other membership cases were already on
appeal. The judge elected to await a Supreme Court ruling on the constitutionality of the clause, and when the high tribunal's decision inspired
doubts about the advisability of trying Weiss at all, the government moved,
in January 1962, to dismiss the charges against him.[23]

Other Communists indicted in 1954 were less fortunate. Albert Blumberg, a former Johns Hopkins professor and now legislative director of
the CPUSA, was arrested on 3 September at the Party's New York City
headquarters and formally charged a week later in Philadelphia. On 8
November the government secured a secret indictment against John Noto
and, the following September, finally managed to apprehend this Buffalo
Communist, who had been underground since 1951. By then it had also
taken into custody the head of the Carolina Party, Junius Irving Scales,
an Air Force veteran and former history graduate student. By April 1956

the government had tried these three, and also Claude Lightfoot, for membership in the CPUSA.[24]

Although arising under a different provision of the Smith Act, their cases resembled the conspiracy ones in a number of ways, such as excessively high bail. The figures initially set for Noto and Lightfoot were $30,000 and for Weiss $35,000. The trials were similar too. Professor Somerville, who appeared as a defense witness in the *Blumberg* membership proceeding, found it logically identical to the Philadelphia conspiracy one in which he had testified earlier, because in both kinds of cases the real defendant was the Communist Party. The prosecution adduced the same Marxist-Leninist teaching "and the same battle of books was once more fought through." In the *Scales* case Judge Albert Bryan reminded jurors that the issue before them was not whether they agreed or disagreed with the objectives and policies of the CPUSA and, in deference to section 4(f) of the Internal Security Act, instructed: "You cannot convict the defendant merely because he was a member or an officer of the Communist Party, no matter what were the principles and teachings of the Party; for membership alone is not a crime." Nevertheless, the government conducted these proceedings as though the prisoner in the dock were an organization rather than an individual and, as in the conspiracy cases, offered irrelevant but inflammatory evidence, intended to discredit the CPUSA. During the *Scales* trial, for instance, the government had Barbara Hartle testify at length about Communist opposition to the American role in Korea.[25]

Most witnesses in membership cases, like so many in conspiracy trials, were ex-Communists, a substantial proportion of whom had supplied information to the FBI while still in the Party. Four of the nine persons who testified for the government in the *Blumberg* trial had been Bureau informants, and in the *Scales* case the figure was six out of eight. One change, indicative of attitudes inspired by the Matusow revelations, was Judge Bryan's instruction to the North Carolina jury "that the testimony of witnesses who were in the employ of the Department of Justice, or any of its agencies, must be examined with greater scrutiny and care than the testimony of an ordinary witness." But even in Bryan's courtroom one thing remained the same: the identity of the star witness—John Lautner.[26]

The most obvious similarity between the membership and conspiracy cases was their outcome. The trials of Lightfoot, Scales, Noto, and Blumberg all ended in conviction, although, at least in the first of these cases, that result was not achieved easily. It took seven ballots to produce a verdict against Lightfoot, and initially five jurors voted "innocent." The

Illinois Party leader regarded his conviction as a demonstration of the pervasive influence of McCarthyism, but the difficulty with which it was
achieved actually was a good indication of the extent to which emotional anti-communism was losing its grip on the country.[27]

After their convictions in early 1955 both Lightfoot and Scales appealed. Once again, Party spokesmen called for mass action to bring about
reversals, and Lightfoot urged Communists to persuade black leaders, trade
unionists, educators, students, scientists, and cultural figures to file friend-
of-the-court briefs on his behalf. The National Lawyers Guild responded
to this appeal, but the demonstration of popular support that he sought
did not materialize. The only other briefs came from the American Civil
Liberties Union and its Illinois division. The ACLU's national office also
kept an interested eye on the *Scales* litigation.[28]

On 7 November 1955, speaking for himself and two colleagues on the
U.S. Court of Appeals for the Fourth Circuit, Chief Judge John J. Parker
declared in that case that the evidence against Scales amply sustained the
charge in the indictment against him. He disposed of a constitutional challenge to the membership clause by quoting at length from *Dennis* and
from the opinion of the court of appeals in the Baltimore conspiracy case
and declaring that, in light of these two decisions, there could be no doubt
as to the validity of that provision. Section 4(f) of the Internal Security
Act constituted no barrier to the present prosecution, Parker determined,
because it provided only that mere membership in the Communist Party
might not constitute a violation of any federal criminal statute. "Membership with knowledge of the criminal purpose of the organization remains
a crime," said the judge. Besides rebuffing the appellant on these points,
he also rejected several lesser defense contentions, among them that the
trial court should have supplied Scales's attorney with copies of reports
concerning statements which prosecution witnesses had made to the FBI.[29]

Claude Lightfoot fared no better than his North Carolina comrade,
for in January 1956 the Court of Appeals for the Seventh Circuit upheld
his conviction. Chief Judge Ryan Duffy agreed with Parker about the constitutionality of the membership clause. Although Lightfoot's lawyers
had emphasized the ending of the Korean War and had stressed the Spirit
of Geneva, as far as Duffy was concerned, "whether a clear and present
danger existed cannot depend on whether the faces of Communist leaders
in Russia are suffused with smiles." The record before him, he felt, contained sufficient evidence to support the charge that the CPUSA was an
organization of the type the Smith Act denounced and to prove that
Lightfoot was a ranking member, familiar with and dedicated to Communist goals, who intended to help the Party accomplish its objectives.

Like Parker, Duffy brushed aside a claim that the court below had erred in refusing to order the prosecution to produce a report which one of its witnesses had submitted to the FBI.[30]

After winning appellate victories in *Scales* and *Lightfoot*, the Department of Justice sought, and on 23 March 1956 obtained, membership indictments against Emanuel Blum, former leader of the New England Communist movement, and Michael Russo, later a defendant in the Boston conspiracy case. Then, on 4 April, the government struck in the Far West, indicting John Cyril Hellman in Butte, Montana. Eventually it decided, on the basis of *Yates*, that the evidence against Blum would not meet the Supreme Court's standards and moved for dismissal of his indictment; and, after the Russo prosecution hung in limbo until 1962, the government dropped it also, because of the outcome of constitutional litigation in other cases. Only Hellman stood trial. After hearing evidence for a little less than three weeks during May 1958, a jury returned a guilty verdict against him, and he received a five-year prison sentence. Hellman appealed, but at the suggestion of both his counsel and attorneys for the government the Court of Appeals for the Ninth Circuit decided not to take the case under submission until the Supreme Court rendered a decision in *Scales*.[31]

In that case, and in *Lightfoot* as well, the Justice Department suffered a serious setback. In early 1956 the Supreme Court granted certiorari in both. They were argued that October and then in June 1957 restored to the docket for reargument. Initially, the Justice Department treated with disdain petitioners' contention that the government should have turned over to defense lawyers written statements furnished to the FBI by prosecution witnesses; but when the Court ruled in *Jencks* v. *United States* in May 1957 that a conviction obtained after failure to produce such material was unconstitutional, it was forced to reconsider its position. On 24 September 1957, Solicitor General Rankin filed a memorandum admitting that, in light of *Jencks*, *Lightfoot* and *Scales* ought to be remanded for further proceedings. On 14 October the high tribunal reversed the judgments in both cases.[32]

The government promptly moved to retry Scales, deferring additional action in *Lightfoot* until final determination of its companion case. That the North Carolina defendant should have been the one to face a judge and jury again was ironic, for during the intra-Party battling in 1957 he had sided with the Gates faction and, after its defeat, had withdrawn from the CPUSA. By the time his second trial for membership in that organization began in February 1958, he no longer belonged to it. Because the indictment covered a three-year period ending 15 November 1954, this fact was legally irrelevant, but it did give the proceedings somewhat the appearance of a bad joke.[33]

The second *Scales* trial differed considerably from the first, for by now the Supreme Court had decided *Yates*. The defense contended that the evidence in this case was substantially identical to what the government had presented in California, and the prosecution, apparently agreeing, sought to strengthen its hand by calling far more witnesses than in 1955. But despite its differing appearance, the second trial ended in the same way as the first, with the jury returning a verdict of guilty and the court sentencing Scales to six years in prison.[34]

The case then started its return journey to Washington. On 15 October 1958, the court of appeals affirmed the second conviction. Like Parker, Judge Morris Soper upheld the constitutionality of the membership clause and rejected the contention that section 4(f) barred prosecutions under it. None of the host of other arguments advanced by the appellant produced favorable rulings. Refusing to accept Soper's word as final, Scales carried his appeal on to the Supreme Court, which, on 15 December, despite government objections, granted an unrestricted writ of certiorari.[35]

Two weeks later the U.S. Second Circuit Court of Appeals upheld the membership conviction of John Noto. On the basis of a lengthy review of the proof adduced at his trial, three judges concluded that the government had "proved by sufficient evidence that the defendant was an active member in an organization teaching and advocating the violent overthrow of the Government well knowing the aim and purpose of the Party and with intent to achieve its illegal purpose." Noto had contended that the membership clause was invalid, because it failed to include intent as an element of the offense and imputed guilt only by association; but Judge Sylvester Ryan and his colleagues disagreed, holding that intent necessarily followed from the knowledge of purpose which the law demanded. Like other jurists who had considered the matter, they also decided that section 4(f) and the membership clause did not conflict.[36]

Four months after this ruling, Telford Taylor, once an American prosecutor at Nuremburg, argued Scales's case before the Supreme Court. The brief that he and North Carolina attorney McNeil Smith submitted contended that the membership clause violated the First and Fifth Amendments. In order to establish the constitutionality of that provision, they insisted, the government had to meet the "action inciting" test of *Yates*. It had tried to do this by introducing books and pamphlets attacking U.S. Korean policy, and although the court of appeals had approved the use of such material to prove advocacy of the type forbidden by the Smith Act, Taylor and Smith argued this was impermissible under the First Amendment. The two attorneys also contended that section 4(f) barred prosecution of any Communist for violation of the membership clause, a conclusion they considered inescapable in light of the legislative history of the Internal Security Act.[37]

The Justice Department's brief challenged all of these contentions. The government argued that the membership clause was valid, both on its face and as applied. Believing that provision would be unconstitutional unless it required proof of intent, government lawyers argued that such an element, although not explicitly mentioned in the statute, was nevertheless present. Justice Department attorneys dismissed *Yates* in two pages, only to have Taylor and Smith charge them with meeting that precedent chiefly by attempting to sweep it under the rug. Scales's counsel had the backing of the ACLU, which filed an amicus curiae brief.[38]

Although the Supreme Court had by now heard the case twice, it still could not arrive at a decision. Perhaps because of the recent congressional attacks upon the high tribunal, Justice Frankfurter wished to avoid deciding any Communist cases for a while, and his colleagues went along with him. On 29 June they ordered *Scales* reargued the following November, asking the two sides to address themselves to five specific issues. In a sharp dissent Tom Clark pointed out that all of these had been covered previously and chastised his brethren for their inordinate delay.[39]

Clark had more cause for complaint when, on 12 October, the Court granted certiorari in *Noto* and set argument in that case for 23 February, postponing *Scales* until the same date. On 5 February, it agreed to review *Communist Party of the United States* v. *Subversive Activities Control Board*, a case arising under the registration provisions of the Internal Security Act. Because some constitutional and statutory issues raised by the three cases were interrelated, the justices desired to hear and decide all of them together, and as the calendar for the remainder of the term was full, they set argument for 10 October. Clark was outraged. "I have found no appellate case in the history of the Court that has been carried on the active docket so many consecutive Terms or argued so often," he complained.[40]

Despite Clark's protests, the membership cases had to wait until October, and, in the meantime, counsel for Scales and Noto filed additional briefs. Although John Abt, representing the Buffalo Communist, joined Taylor and Smith in attacking the membership clause, he emphasized the weakness of the evidence against his client. It was, Abt contended, "devoid of any statement by petitioner, or by anyone in his presence, advocating violent action, present or future, for the overthrow of the Government." The evidence in this case was, he said, palpably insufficient to prove either that the CPUSA advocated forcible overthrow in the language of incitement or that Noto had any knowledge of its doing so. The Justice Department disagreed, contending that the Party's actions did demonstrate inculcation of revolutionary aims and purposes, intended as a call to violent action when the time was ripe. In reply Abt pointed to the conspiracy cases which the government had dropped and argued that they amounted to an admission of inability to meet the incitement-to-action test which *Yates* had established.[41]

Although the wide-ranging arguments of Smith and Taylor failed to free their client, Abt's more restricted approach produced results. In the face of the furor generated by the judicial assault on McCarthyism which culminated in the landmark decisions of 17 June 1957, the Supreme Court had done a great deal of backpeddling on Cold War issues. During the term beginning in October 1956, it had rejected civil liberties claims in only 26 percent of cases decided by full opinion, but in the two succeeding sessions that figure had risen to 41 and then to 48 percent. The Smith Act rulings of 5 June 1961 demonstrated that the Court's retreat had been only a tactical withdrawal. The high tribunal voted five to four to uphold the judgment against Scales and the validity of the membership clause, with both Frankfurter and Harlan members of the majority, and the author of the *Yates* opinion also writing this one. But the Court, with Harlan again acting as its spokesman, overturned the conviction of Noto on evidentiary grounds, and in this way deprived the *Scales* ruling of most of its value as a precedent. While appearing to give a great deal with his right hand, Harlan took most of it away with his left.[42]

His *Scales* opinion, like his *Yates* one, was long and dull but a masterpiece of scholarship and reasoning. Harlan decided that section 4(f) had not repealed the membership clause, because its purpose was simply to inform courts that they must avoid interpreting other parts of the Internal Security Act in such a way as to make mere membership in some Communist organization a violation. The legislative history of section 4(f) showed, Harlan believed, that Congress had elected *not* to pay the price of wiping out the Smith Act provision in order to safeguard the registration segment of the McCarran Act from possible Fifth Amendment attack.

Turning to constitutional issues, he again ruled against Scales, citing *Dennis* as authority for reading specific intent into the meaning of the membership clause. Harlan also announced that it was proper to interpret that provision as applying only to "active" members. As thus limited by the courts below, the clause did not deprive Scales of his rights. As applied to him, it violated neither the Fifth Amendment, by imputing guilt to an individual merely on the basis of his associations and sympathies, nor the First Amendment, by infringing freedoms of political expression and association. "We can discern," Harlan said, "no reason why membership, when it constitutes a purposeful form of complicity in a group engaging in this same forbidden advocacy, should receive any greater protection" than the combination involved in *Dennis.*[43]

Harlan next examined the evidence and adjudged it sufficient to sustain the conviction. Such a review was, he conceded, normally the function of a court of appeals, but as this was the first time membership convictions had come before the high tribunal, the justices felt compelled "to provide guidance for the future to the lower courts in an area which borders so closely upon constitutionally protected rights."[44] Required to meet the *Yates* evidentiary standards, Harlan said, the prosecution had done so. It had shown the teaching of forcible overthrow, accompanied by directions as to the type of illegal action to be taken when the time for revolution arrived, and had also demonstrated the existence of a contemporary, although legal, course of conduct intended to render effective the illegal undertaking advocated. Harlan regarded as particularly impressive the testimony of two witnesses who had provided a type of evidence notably lacking in the *Yates* record: statements by the defendant himself which supplied unequivocal evidence that Communists systematically preached violent revolution and also clearly established the nature of his own membership, knowledge, and intent. Scales could not be guilty unless this advocacy was broad based enough to be attributable to the CPUSA as an organization, but the testimony, which had described activities in various states, including the teaching at seven different schools, seemed to Harlan adequate for that purpose.

Four other justices did not share his views. Brennan, dissenting for himself, Warren, and Douglas, argued that in passing section 4(f) Congress had "legislated immunity from prosecution under the membership clause of the Smith Act."[45] He also scolded Harlan for sloppy reading of the statute, pointing out that his colleague had reversed the order of a key word and phrase, thus altering the meaning of the law he was evaluating. Black objected to the decision, because he believed the First Amendment absolutely forbade Congress to outlaw membership in any political party or similar association, and Douglas added a separate dissent, in which he charged that this ruling borrowed "from the totalitarian philosophy." It was, he felt, contrary to the theory of government expressed in the First Amendment. "When belief in an idea is punished as it is today," Douglas asserted, "we sacrifice those ideals and substitute an alien, totalitarian philosophy in their stead."[46]

The situation hardly warranted the gloom permeating his dissent, for although Harlan's *Scales* opinion was potentially dangerous, his *Noto* one drastically restricted its impact. In that case the crafty conservative, having made his bow to the legislature by validating the statute, focused on the evidence. The *Noto* record, he observed, suffered from many of the same infirmities as the *Yates* one. At the trial the government had amply demonstrated that the Party taught the abstract doctrine of inevitable revolution, but it had produced little evidence which would support an inference of advocacy of action. The small amount of testimony which pointed in the required direction was too narrowly based, relating only to Communist activity in western New York. In contrast to the *Scales* record, Harlan noted, this one contained no utterances by the petitioner himself capable of establishing the necessary incitement. Reversing the judgment against Noto, the justice laid down the following guidlines for future membership cases:

> There must be some substantial direct or circumstantial evidence of a call to violence now or in the future which is both sufficiently strong and sufficiently pervasive to lend color to the otherwise ambiguous theoretical material regarding Communist Party teaching, and to justify the inference that such a call to violence may fairly be imputed tó the Party as a whole, and not merely to some narrow segment of it.[47]

These words made future membership prosecutions, while theoretically possible, practically very difficult. Only if the government was willing, in order to convict a single Communist, to retry the entire CPUSA, utilizing informants from all over the country, and could also produce evidence of what amounted to unlawful advocacy by the defendant himself, did it have any hope of obtaining success.

The Court's severe limitation of its own decision was a shrewd move, for *Scales* elicited a less than favorable response. The general press was divided. Among magazines conservative *National Review* and Catholic *America* praised it, while liberal *New Republic* was sharply critical, and rightish *U.S. News & World Report* felt the Court had not gone far enough. Similar division characterized newspaper reaction. The radical *Militant* called *Scales* a dangerous legal blow to political freedom, and the liberal *St. Louis Post-Dispatch* was almost as hostile. In the opinion of the *New York Times*, this decision could "only serve again to divert public attention to the virtually nonexistent internal Communist threat." At the other end of the political spectrum the *Chicago Tribune* applauded the Court for dealing a body blow to the CPUSA, and the *Los Angeles Times* also expressed approval. The *Washington Post* did not like *Scales* but was more critical of Congress for passing bad laws than of the justices for up-

holding them. All in all, the division over *Scales* was close, but it did
seem to incline ever so slightly toward opposition.[48]

No such ambiguity characterized the reaction of legal commentators,
which was almost entirely negative. Five legal periodicals analyzed the
decision, and the only one that even hinted at sympathy for it was the
University of Florida Law Review. From Harvard, Notre Dame, and the
University of Cincinnati came sharp criticism. Writing for *New Republic*,
noted legal scholar Alexander Bickel also denounced the decision.[49]

The judiciary manifested a similar lack of enthusiasm for *Scales*. The
only judges called upon to apply the Supreme Court's ruling were Frederick G. Hamley and two colleagues on the Ninth Circuit Court of Appeals, who interpreted it narrowly and reversed the membership conviction of Cyril Hellman. In an opinion filed 14 February 1962, Hamley
picked up the cue which Harlan had offered with his emphasis on the
presence or absence of evidence showing personal advocacy by individual
defendants and used it as the departure point for a line of reasoning
which led him to the conclusion that the government had failed in this
case to establish the requisite illegal intent. Proving such intent required
more than a showing of active membership in the CPUSA, he said. The
appellant had served as a Party organizer, teacher, and recruiter. "But
nowhere in the evidence which the Government calls to our attention,
or in the entire record which we have independently examined, do we
find testimony that Hellman personally advocated violent overthrow of
the Government."[50]

As the *Ohio State Law Journal* pointed out, Hamley might have in-
ferred illegal advocacy from evidence of the teaching of forceful overthrow and a contemporary, although legal, course of action clearly undertaken for the purpose of promoting the objectives taught. But the
judge ignored this part of Harlan's opinion, because he did not want to
interpret the law in such a way as to necessitate declaring it unconstitutional. Doubtless as the justice had intended, Hamley took the narrow-
er of two roads opened by *Scales*. The probable effect of his decision was
not difficult for even a student commentator to discern. "Since activities
of this kind could probably be successfully prosecuted under other federal statutes which do not impose such a staggering burden of proof," he
wrote, "the courts may now have interpreted the membership clause of
the Smith Act so narrowly that it has lost its intended effect."[51]

Certainly they had interpreted it so narrowly that the government
could no longer utilize that provision against the Communist Party. After *Scales* the Department of Justice initiated a full-scale review of all
membership-clause cases for the purpose of ascertaining whether the gov-

ernment's evidence met the Supreme Court's standards. Even before
Hellman, federal prosecutors had decided not to retry Noto and Lightfoot and had called off the Weiss prosecution. In the wake of that decision the government moved for dismissal of the indictments against
both Hellman and Russo. On 29 June 1962 the district court in Philadelphia reversed the Blumberg conviction on *Jencks* grounds, and although
the judge denied a motion for acquittal and announced that he considered
the evidence sufficient, the government, after wrestling for more than
nine months with the problem of whether or not to retry him, moved
for dismissal in this case too.[52]

Nor did the Department of Justice initiate any new membership prosecutions. The government had by now about exhausted the supply of
important but untried Party leaders, and, besides, by 1959, the earliest
year for which the statute of limitiations would allow a post-*Scales* indictment, Communists had become so careful about what they said and
did that proving membership of the type required by that decision and
Noto was virtually impossible. As a weapon with which to wage war upon
the CPUSA, the Smith Act had lost its utility. *Yates* had made conspiracy
prosecutions impossible, and now the membership clause too was a spent
bullet. The battle that had begun in the long ago days of the Great Depression was over. The Smith Act had reached the end of its anti-Communist
career.[53]

NOTES

1. Dorothy Healy, personal interview with the Author at her home
in Los Angeles, 31 December 1973; *PW*, 22 June 1957; *NYT*, 23 June
1957, sec. 4, p. 5; Walter F. Murphy, *Congress and the Court: A Case
Study in the American Political Process* (Chicago: University of Chicago
Press, 1962), p. 120. See the *New York Times*, 18 June 1957, p. 32, for
its own editorial position. For that newspaper's summary of the editorial
reactions of other papers see its issue of 19 June 1957, p. 19. The views
of the *Courant*, the *Herald-Tribune*, the *Plain Dealer*, and the *Inquirer*
are quoted in the 19 June summary. See also *Chicago Tribune*, 19 June
1957; *St. Louis Post-Dispatch*, 18 June 1957; *Militant*, 24 June 1957;
"Editorial: The Supreme Court and Liberty," *Life*, 1 July 1957, p. 30;
"Its Up to Congress to Salvage Our Security System," *Saturday Evening
Post*, 20 July 1957, p. 10; *Los Angeles Times*, 19 June 1957; *Appleton*
(Wis.) *Post-Crescent*, 22 June 1957; *Denver Post*, 11 June 1957; *New
Orleans Times-Picayune*, 18 June 1957; *Dallas Morning News*, 19 June
1957, CF, GF, 4-A, DEL.

2. J. McD., "Case Comments: Constitutional Law—Smith Act—Requirement of Words of Incitement," *West Virginia Law Review* 60 (December 1957): 94; Robert W. Vidor, "Constitutional Law: Smith Act:

Meaning of 'Advocate' as Used in the Act and the Nature of Evidence Sufficient to Convict Under the Act," *U.C.L.A. Law Review* 5 (March 1958): 316-20; "Recent Cases: Criminal Law—Smith Act—Interpretation of Organize and Advocate," *Minnesota Law Review* 42 (December 1957): 305.

3. "What Two Critics Say About the Court's Rulings on Reds," *U.S. News & World Report*, 9 August 1957, p. 114; testimony by Wyman in HJC, *Supreme Court Decisions: Hearings Before the Special Subcommittee to Study Decisions of the Supreme Court of the United States . . . on the Decision in the Case of Mallory vs. the United States*, 85th Cong., 1st sess., 1957, pp. 205-06; Frank Ober, "Communism and the Court: An Examination of Recent Developments," *American Bar Association Journal* 44 (January 1958): 89; Learned Hand, *The Bill of Rights* (New York: Atheneum, 1964), pp. 59-60.

4. Murphy, *Congress and the Court*, pp. 118-19. The report submitted by O'Connor is reprinted in SJC, *Limitations of Appellate Jurisdiction of the United States Supreme Court: Hearings . . . on S2646*, 85th Cong., 1st sess., 1957, pp. 18-19.

5. SJC, *Internal Security Annual Report for 1957*, 85th Cong., 2d sess., 1958, S. Rept. 1472, pp. 211-17; "Minutes of Cabinet Meeting," 28 June 1957, Whitman File, Box 9, Cabinet Series, DEL; *Cong. Record*, 85th Cong., 1st sess., 23 July 1957, p. 12510, 29 July 1957, p. 12958, and 2d sess., 2 July 1958, p. 12944, and 22 July 1958, p. 14669; Notes on Legislative Meeting, 4 December 1957, Whitman File, Box 2, Legislative Meetings Series, DEL. Walter is quoted by *NYT*, 20 June 1957, p. 12.

6. For the history of the Jenner-Butler bill see Murphy, *Congress and the Court*, pp. 160-71, 196-208; Donald G. Morgan, *Congress and the Constitution: A Study of Responsibility* (Cambridge, Mass.: Belknap Press, 1966), pp. 270-91; and C. Herman Pritchett, *Congress Versus the Supreme Court 1957-1960* (Minneapolis: University of Minnesota Press, 1961), pp. 119-20. On support for and opposition to the original Jenner bill see SJC, *Limitations of Appellate Jurisdiction*. The views of senators and others urging defeat of the amended Jenner-Butler bill can be found in SJC, *Limitation of Supreme Court Jurisdiction and Strengthening of Antisubversive Laws*, 85th Cong., 2d sess., 1958, S. Rept. 1586, pp. 21-84, and the changes in the Smith Act proposed in that measure on p. 3 of the same document. Rogers also set forth his opinion of both the original bill and Butler's version in a 27 May 1958 letter to President Eisenhower (Whitman File, Box 35, Administration Series, DEL). For the decisive vote see *Cong. Record*, 85th Cong., 2d sess., 20 August 1958, p. 18687.

7. HJC, *Amendment of Section 2385 of Title 18, United States Code, to Define the Term "Organize" as Used in That Section*, 85th Cong., 2d sess., 1958, H. Rept. 2495, pp. 1-4; *Cong. Record*, 85th Cong., 2d sess., 2 July 1958, p. 12994, 12 August 1958, pp. 17169-71 (quotes on pp. 17169, 17170), and 13 August 1958, p. 17245.

8. *Cong. Record*, 86th Cong., 1st sess., 15 January 1959, p. 737; HJC,

Defining the Term "Organize" as Used in the Smith Act, 86th Cong., 1st sess., 1959, H. Rept. 39, pp. 1-4; "Resolutions of the Special Committee on Communist Tactics, Strategy and Objectives," William P. Rogers Papers, DEL; *Cong. Record*, 86th Cong. 1st sess., 2 March 1959, p. 3157.

9. Murphy, *Congress and the Court*, pp. 226-38; Pritchett, *Congress Versus the Supreme Court*, pp. 125-26; *Cong. Record*, 86th Cong., 1st sess., 5 March 1959, p. 3281.

10. *Cong. Record*, 87th Cong., 1st sess., 25 January 1961, p. 1245. and 1 May 1961, p. 6975; HJC, *Defining the Term "Organize" as Used in the Smith Act*, 87th Cong., 1st sess., 1961, H. Rept. 248, pp. 1-4.

11. *Cong. Record*, 87th Cong. 1st sess., 16 May 1961, p. 8018, and 2d sess., 8 June 1962, pp. 10012-14 (quote on p. 10014); SJC, *Defining the Term "Organize" as Used in the Smith Act*, 87th Cong., 2d sess., 1962, S. Rept. 1410, pp. 1-4. As finally passed, this measure read: "As used in this section, the terms 'organizes' and 'organize,' with respect to any society, group, or assembly of persons, include the recruiting of new members, the forming of new units, and the regrouping or expansion of existing clubs, classes, and other units of such society, group, or assembly of persons" (76 Stat. 103 [1962]).

12. Dennis v. United States, 355 U.S. 936 (1958); Justice, "List of Smith Cases, Involving Communist Party Leaders," photocopy (cited hereinafter as Justice, "List").

13. Justice, "List"; Robert Mollan, "Smith Act Prosecutions: The Effect of the Dennis and Yates Decisions," *University of Pittsburgh Law Review* 26 (June 1965): 732.

14. United States v. Silverman, 248 F. 2d 671 (2d Cir. 1957).

15. United States v. Kuzma, 249 F. 2d 619 (3rd Cir. 1957).

16. Fujimoto v. United States and Huff v. United States, 251 F. 2d 342 (9th Cir. 1958), at 342.

17. United States v. Jackson, 257 F. 2d 830 (2d Cir. 1958); Wellman v. United States, 354 U.S. 931 (1957), 253 F. 2d 601 (6th Cir. 1958), at 608; Sentner v. United States, 253 F. 2d 310 (8th Cir. 1958); Brandt v. United States, 256 F. 2d 79 (6th Cir. 1958); Justice, "List"; Mollan, "Smith Act Prosecutions," pp. 731-33; "Smith Act Conspiracy," *Civil Liberties Docket* 4 (August 1959): 93; Justice, *Annual Report for 1958*, p. 255. Miller's statement appears on p. 608 of the *Wellman* opinion.

18. Justice, "List"; Bary v. United States, 248 F. 2d 201 (10th Cir. 1957) and 292 F. 2d 53 (10th Cir. 1961); *NYT*, 14 November 1964, p. 8.

19. Mollan, "Smith Act Prosecutions," p. 735; Justice, *Annual Report for 1958*, pp. 334-35, 336.

20. William P. Rogers, telephonic interview with the Author, 17 August 1976; "Internal Security Division Goals—1959," Rogers Papers. Hoover's statement appears in a memorandum, entitled "Objectives of Department of Justice, 1959," in the Rogers Papers.

21. Mollan, "Smith Act Prosecutions," pp. 716-18; Justice, *Annual Report for 1957*, pp. 201-02, and "List."

22. HJC, *Hearings . . . on H.R. 226 . . . H.R. 9663*, 83rd Cong., 2d sess., 1954, p. 138; Justice, "List" and *Annual Report for 1954*, p. 113.

23. Justice, "List"; Mollan, "Smith Act Prosecutions," p. 720, n. 64.

24. *DW*, 7 October 1954; John Somerville, *The Communist Trials and the American Tradition: Expert Testimony on Force and Violence* (New York: Cameron Associates, 1956), p. 210; Justice, "List"; Mollan, "Smith Act Prosecutions," p. 720, n. 64; Lucius J. Barker and Twiley W. Barker. Jr.. *Freedoms, Courts, Politics: Studies in Civil Liberties* (Englewood Cliffs, N.J.: Prentice-Hall, 1965), p. 95; *NYT*, 18 September 1955, p. 37. Mollan errs in saying that Blumberg was the first Communist arrested on a membership charge.

25. ACLU Weekly Bulletin no. 1739, 27 February 1956, p. 2; *Worker* (Nat. Ed.), 25 July 1954, and 16 October 1955; *DW*, 17 October 1955; Somerville, *Communist Trials*, p. 202; Appendix to Brief for Appellant, at A-37, and Appendix to Brief for Appellee, at 144-45, 380-439, Scales v. United States, 367 U.S. 203 (1961). For Bryan's remark see Transcript of Record, at 110, Scales v. United States, 367 U.S. 203 (1961).

26. United States v. Blumberg, 207 F. Supp. 28 (E.D. Pa. 1962); Brief for Petitioner, at 5, Scales v. United States, 367 U.S. 203 (1961). Bryan's statement appears in Appendix to Brief for Appellant, at A-45, Scales v. United States, 367 U.S. 203 (1961).

27. Claude Lightfoot, *"Not Guilty"* (New York: New Century Publishers, 1955), p. 8; *DW*, 27 January 1955. The trials of Lightfoot, Scales, Blumberg, and Noto ended respectively on 26 January 1955, 21 April 1955, 7 March 1956, and 12 April 1956 (Justice, "List").

28. John Williamson, "To My Comrades," *PA* 34 (July 1955): 39; Claude Lightfoot, "The Struggle to End the Cold War at Home," *PA* 34 (September 1955): 45; Lightfoot v. United States, 228 F. 2d 861 (7th Cir. 1956); ACLU, *Clearing the Main Channels, 35th Annual Report of the American Civil Liberties Union, July 1, 1954 to June 30, 1955* (New York: American Civil Liberties Union [?], 1955 [?]), pp. 26-27; Scales v. United States, 227 F. 2d 581 (4th Cir. 1955).

29. Scales v. United States, 227 F. 2d 581 (4th Cir. 1955), at 589.

30. United States v. Lightfoot, 228 F. 2d 861 (7th Cir. 1956), at 870.

31. Justice, "List"; Herbert A. Philbrick, *I Led 3 Lives: Citizen, "Communist," Counterspy* (New York: McGraw-Hill, 1952), p. 123; Hellman v. United States, 298 F. 2d 810 (9th Cir. 1962).

32. Jencks v. United States, 353 U.S. 657 (1957); Barker and Barker, *Freedoms, Courts, Politics*, p. 96. The grant of certiorari in *Scales* is reported as 350 U.S. 992 (1956) and the decision reversing the Court of Appeals as 355 U.S. 1 (1957). The grant of certiorari and the final decision in Lightfoot are reported as 353 U.S. 979 (1955) and 355 U.S. 2 (1957), respectively. For a statement of the government's initial position on the production of statements see Brief for the United States, at 20, Scales v. United States, 367 U.S. 203 (1961). The Court discusses

the Justice Department's admission of error in the two 1957 decisions.

33. Justice, "List"; Barker and Barker, *Freedoms, Courts, Politics*, pp. 95-96; Laurent B. Frantz, "Junius Scales," *The Nation*, 30 December 1961, p. 529.

34. Justice, "List"; Brief for United States, at 52-53, Scales v. United States, 367 U.S. 203 (1961).

35. Scales v. United States, 260 F. 2d 21 (4th Cir. 1958), 360 U.S. 924 (1959); Memorandum for the United States, at 1-70, Scales v. United States, 367 U.S. 203 (1961).

36. United States v. Noto, 262 F. 2d 501 (2d Cir. 1958), at 506.

37. Brief for Petitioners, at 8-9, Scales v. United States, 367 U.S. 203 (1961).

38. Brief for the United States, at 23-38, Reply Brief for Petitioner, at 1-7, and Brief for American Civil Liberties Union as Amicus Curiae, Scales v. United States, 367 U.S. 203 (1961).

39. Justice Tom C. Clark, personal interview with the Author at the U.S. Supreme Court Building, Washington, D.C., 17 August 1976; Scales v. United States, 360 U.S. 924 (1959); Murphy, *Congress and the Court*, p. 229.

40. Noto v. United States, 361 U.S. 813 (1959); Scales v. United States and Noto v. United States, 361 U.S. 952 (1960), at 953.

41. Brief for Petitioner on Reargument, at 1-41, Scales v. United States, 367 U.S. 203 (1961); Brief for Petitioner, at 7, 22, Brief for the United States, at 27, and Reply Brief for Petitioner, at 2, Noto v. United States, 367 U.S. 290 (1961).

42. Murphy, *Congress and the Court*, p. 246; Scales v. United States, 367 U.S. 203 (1961); Noto v. United States, 367 U.S. 290 (1961).

43. Scales v. United States, 367 U.S. 203 (1961), at 229.

44. Ibid., at 230.

45. Ibid., at 278-79.

46. Ibid., at 263, 274.

47. Noto v. United States, 367 U.S. 290 (1961), at 298.

48. Barker and Barker, *Freedoms, Courts, Politics*, pp. 123-24; Alexander Bickel, "The Communist Cases," *New Republic*, 19 June 1961, pp. 15-16; "Court Ruling: Death Blow to Reds?" *U.S. News & World Report*, 19 June 1961, p. 44; *Militant*, 12 June 1961; *St. Louis Post-Dispatch*, 11 June 1961; *NYT*, 7 June 1961, p. 40; *Chicago Tribune*, 7 June 1961; *Los Angeles Times*, 7 June 1961; *Washington Post*, 7 June 1961.

49. Raymond L. Wise, "Is Dennis Really a Menace?" *University of Florida Law Review* 15 (Fall-Winter 1962): 375-76; "The Supreme Court 1960 Term," *Harvard Law Review* 75 (November 1961): 114-16; Paul J. Driscoll, "Constitutional Law—Due Process of Law—Self-Incrimination Privilege—Membership in the Communist Party Held to Be Criminal Offense—Communist Party Required to Register with Attorney General,"

Notre Dame Lawyer 37 (December 1962): 242-43; James R. Phelps, "Judicial Technique and the Communist Party; The Internal Security and Smith Acts Construed," *University of Cincinnati Law Review* 31 (Spring 1962): 155-62; "Criminal Law—Smith Act—Membership Clause Requiring Active Membership in Communist Party and Specific Intent to Use Violence Held Not to Violate the First or Fifth Amendments," *Vanderbilt Law Review* 15 (December 1961): 284; Bickel, "The Communist Cases," pp. 15-16.

    50. Hellman v. United States, 298 F. 2d 810 (9th Cir. 1962), at 813.

    51. "Membership Clause of the Smith Act Held to Carry Rigid Standards," *Ohio State Law Journal* 23 (Fall 1962): 764.

    52. Justice, *Annual Report for 1961*, pp. 7, 257, and "List"; United States v. Blumberg, 207 F. Supp. 28 (E.D. Pa. 1962).

    53. Kevin Maroney, personal interview with the Author at Internal Security Division, U.S. Department of Justice, 22 January 1971.

Conclusion

By the early 1960s the only reminder of the Smith Act's past successes was a tiny handful of radicals languishing in federal prisons. Even before the *Scales* decision, many of the sedition statute's victims (beginning with Regina Frankfeld in October 1954) had regained their liberty. In May 1955 three of the Eleven—Eugene Dennis, John Gates, and Carl Winter— were freed. Jack Stachel and John Williamson also received their releases, but the government soon deported both of them, and Irving Potash as well. Benjamin Davis, who had served extra time because of a contempt sentence received while testifying as a witness at the Pittsburgh trial, emerged from prison forty-four days after his codefendants. By the end of fiscal 1956 twenty-nine convicted Communists had finished serving their sentences, among them Gus Hall, whose flight to Mexico had earned him an extended stay behind bars. Twenty-four months later only two Smith Act defendants remained in prison.[1]

After a year and a half of resistance, on 7 July 1961, federal authorities responded to pleas for the release of one of these. Henry Winston had been suffering from a painful brain tumor, and although surgery in a New York hospital had saved his life, it left him unable to see. At the suggestion of the Justice Department, President John F. Kennedy commuted Winston's sentence to time served. "They took away my sight," the blinded radical announced upon regaining his liberty, "but not my vision." Exactly three weeks after Winston returned home, authorities liberated his comrade and one-time fellow fugitive, Gil Green. Appropriately, this last of the Eleven to return to freedom did so, after a handcuffed journey from the Leavenworth Penitentiary, at the Foley Square courthouse where it had all begun thirteen years earlier.[2]

That left only Junius Scales, an ex-Communist who had renounced the Party, still suffering for the Cold War heresies of the CPUSA. The *New York Times* urged his release, and on 2 February 1962 a group of prominent citizens—including Norman Thomas, head of the Socialist Party, Reinhold Niebuhr, a renowned philosopher-theologian, and Grenville

Clark, former chairman of the ABA's Bill of Rights Committee—organized to seek a presidential pardon for Scales. By 3 April their campaign,
which had received an endorsement from *The Reporter*, had attracted
550 signatures, among them those of two federal judges and five senior
partners in leading North Carolina law firms. Nine of the twelve jurors
who had voted to convict Scales also asked for his release. On Christmas
Eve, Kennedy responded, commuting the sentence of the last Smith Act
prisoner. In the opinion of the *New York Times*, the President had "acted with courage and wisdom as well as in the best American tradition. . . ."[3]

The *Times* editorial wrote a fitting conclusion to the Smith Act story,
for that law and the war on communism waged with it had never been
in the best American tradition. Political prosecutions have occurred
throughout this country's history, sometimes reaching epidemic proportions during periods of extreme social tension, but although the United
States has often deviated from the libertarian ideals embodied in the
Bill of Rights, it has never entirely forsaken them. During the early years
of the Cold War, the nation's devotion to civil liberties proved to be little more than theoretical. But as international tensions eased, a country
that had embarked upon an attempt to square its racial practices with
the tenets of the Constitution also sought to bring its treatment of dissenters into line with the libertarian ideals of the First Amendment.

The rulings of the Warren Court came too late to save the CPUSA from
serious harm. By the time the judiciary neutralized the Smith Act, that
law already had accomplished the objectives of its framers. In 1935, when
John McCormack began his drive for the adoption of an anti-Communist
sedition law, the Party had been a viable and growing organization. Twenty-seven years later, when Junius Scales walked out of prison, it was moribund. There is no denying that the CPUSA contributed greatly to its own
downfall. Labor defense proved a futile and self-defeating strategy, and
the Party's organizational response to legal attack was nothing short of
suicidal. Nor can one ignore the impact of the Cold War. Had the United
States not confronted Russia in what politicians chose to characterize as
an ideological struggle for control of the world, the government might
never have felt compelled to launch the Smith Act prosecutions, and certainly these would not have proved as devastating as they did. Nevertheless, while the Smith Act was not the only reason for the decline of the
CPUSA, it did trigger the organizational collapse of American communism.

That law also inflicted damage far beyond the Party's shrinking ranks.
The Supreme Court decision which made possible the Justice Department's nationwide attack on the CPUSA threatened the First Amend-

ment rights of all Americans and added its considerable weight to the repressive atmosphere associated with McCarthyism. In order to send Communists to jail, the Supreme Court lent its prestige to a hysterical crusade against political nonconformity, which ultimately stifled much legitimate dissent.

The Smith Act prosecutions had another unfortunate effect in that, while destroying the CPUSA, they simultaneously stimulated the growth of federal investigative and prosecuting agencies. The FBI and the Internal Security Division did not wither away as the Communist Party declined but, instead, simply selected new targets for their attention. During the 1960s and early 1970s, they spearheaded a massive attack on outspoken critics of American society and government, directed not only at gunwielding Panthers and fanatical Weathermen but also at peaceful dissenters such as Benjamin Spock and Martin Luther King. Organizations and individuals far less radical than the CPUSA endured investigation, harassment, and prosecution.

Like their Stalinist predecessors, many of these later dissidents ultimately found themselves in court. For newspaper readers old enough to remember what had happened in New York two decades earlier, many aspects of the 1969 Chicago 7 trial were distressingly familiar. Chaotic, and political in both inception and conduct, it was Foley Square all over again. The story of American political justice neither began nor ended with the prosecutions of the CPUSA, but the Communist cases contributed to the growth of the delusion that major issues of domestic and foreign policy can be settled by litigation and thus encouraged future generations to carry their political struggles into the courtroom.

Seldom has a model been less worthy of emulation, for there were few winners in the Smith Act war. The Communists, with their labor defense strategy, only rendered worse the already difficult position of their Party. Nor did the administration that initiated the prosecutions profit politically from them. When the Republicans drove the Democrats from power in 1952, one of their most effective campaign issues was domestic communism. The American people were losers too. By endangering some of their most fundamental rights, the Smith Act prosecutions threatened, in the name of saving democracy from communism, to subvert and destroy the very thing they were supposed to preserve. Only the government lawyers, bureaucrats, and FBI agents who made political justice their vocation really profited from the government's legal attack on the CPUSA.

Fortunately for the nation, despite the dangerous potential of the *Dennis* decision, American liberty managed to survive the challenge of a bad law. Even though the emotions generated by the Cold War were powerful and made the Smith Act for a time irresistible, in the end the nation's devotion to its fundamental values proved even stronger. The bar and the Supreme Court, official guardians of the Constitution, were slow to rise to its defense, but when they did, the public responded favorably, following their lead rather than that of the national security alarmists in Congress and the professional anti-Communists in the Department of Justice.

Although the Smith Act is still on the statute books, because of the *Yates* and *Noto* decisions there is little likelihood that the government will again employ its conspiracy, advocacy, or membership provisions against a dissident organization. But America has not renounced political justice, and the attitudes that produced this law and demanded its use against a hapless radical sect are fully capable of fashioning other instruments of repression. As long as the devotion to fundamental freedoms which thwarted the Smith Act remains strong, there is little cause for concern, but whenever it fades, other Americans will surely share the fate of the Cold War Communist Party.

NOTES

1. *PW*, 11 October 1954 and 2 March 1955; *DW*, 18 April 1955 and 12 April 1957; Justice, *Annual Report for 1957*, pp. 201-02, and *Annual Report for 1959*, p. 341.

2. *PW*, 8 July 1961 and 5 August 1961; Arnold Johnson, George Myers, and Thomas Arthur Shields, personal interviews with the Author at CPUSA National Headquarters, New York City, 6 August 1973.

3. Lucius J. Barker and Twiley W. Barker, Jr., *Freedoms, Courts, Politics: Studies in Civil Liberties* (Englewood Cliffs, N.J.: Prentice-Hall, 1965), pp. 124-25; "Junius Scales," *The Reporter*, 15 March 1962, p. 14; Justice, "List of Smith Act Cases Involving Communist Party Leaders," photocopy; *NYT*, 28 December 1962, p. 6.

Bibliographical Essay

Since the story of the Smith Act and the Communist Party is primarily a legal one, the richest veins from which to mine information about it are the reports and transcripts of the federal courts. Although scholars have devoted substantial attention to the Supreme Court's decision in *Dennis v. United States*, 341 U.S. 494 (1951), and lesser amounts to some of the high tribunal's other Smith Act rulings, most of the more than 200 printed decisions generated by the prosecutions and related litigation scattered through the pages of the *United States Reports*, the *Federal Reporter* (2d Series), and the *Federal Supplement* have been largely ignored. So, for the most part, have the *United States Supreme Court Records and Briefs*, useful sources of factual information as well as legal arguments. Transcripts of Smith Act trials are so long, dull, and repetitious that even participants in the cases find them boring, but because they reveal both the weakness of the government's evidence and the defense tactics of the Communist Party, these documents are essential to any real understanding of the prosecutions. Of particular importance is the transcript of the first Foley Square trial, availavle also as Joint Appendix to the Brief for Appellants and the Brief for the Appellee, *United States v. Dennis*, 183 F. 2d 210 (2d Cir. 1950). Although not itself a product of Smith Act litigation, Record, *McGrath, Attorney General v. Communist Party of the United States*, 1 S.A.C.B. 1 (1952), is also valuable, because of the information it contains on the CPUSA and particularly on the Party's underground operations.

Although not as enlightening as judicial records, a number of manuscript collections do offer important insights into why the prosecutions took place and why the courts responded to them as they did. Of particular significance, because of what they reveal about the political background of the *Dennis* case, are the papers of John F. X. McGohey, located at the Harry S. Truman Presidential Library in Independence, Missouri. Other useful collections at the Truman Library are the papers of Stephen J. Spingarn, J. Howard McGrath, Clark Clifford, and Charles Murphy, as well as the President's Secretaries' Files from the Papers of Harry S. Truman and the White House Official Files. The holdings of the Dwight D. Eisenhower Presidential Library in Abilene, Kansas, are less valuable, although the Ann Whitman File of the Papers of Dwight D. Eisenhower as President does contain some important material, particularly in its Administration Series, and the papers of William P. Rogers and the White House Central Files are also useful.

The relevant manuscripts of the justices who spoke for the Supreme Court in the principal Smith Act cases, Fred Vinson and John Marshall Harlan, are deposited at the University of Kentucky and Princeton University respectively, but, unfortunately, they remain closed to researchers. The papers of their colleagues Harold Burton, Hugo L. Black, and Felix Frankfurter, however, are available at the Manuscript Division of the Library of Congress, and, while the first of these collections is not particularly informative concerning the Smith Act cases, the second is helpful, and the third is quite valuable. There is also a great deal of significant material in the Felix Frankfurter papers at the Manuscript Division of the Harvard Law School Library. The Sherman Minton collection at the Truman Library, on the other hand, contains nothing on the Smith Act cases. Learned Hand's papers at the Manuscript Division of the Harvard Law School Library are useful, but, unfortunately, contain no memoranda by him on the *Dennis* case. The man who presided at the trial of the Eleven, Harold Medina, has deposited his papers at Princeton University.

Concerning the passage of the Smith Act, the manuscripts of members of Congress, such as John McCormack and Hatton Sumners, are uninformative, but there is a great deal of relevant correspondence from the public in the National Archives files of the House and Senate Judiciary Committees on Seventy-sixth Congress bill H.R. 5138 (in Record Groups 233 and 46 respectively). The House Judiciary Committee file on that measure's Seventy-fourth Congress ancestor, H.R. 4313 (in Record Group 233), contains similar material. Also useful is the Bureau of the Budget's 017 "Overthrow of Government—United States" (Record Group 51, Series 39.1, Box 125), also at the National Archives.

Of particular importance to students of the Smith Act are the clippings and correspondence collected by the Cleveland Bar Association in a scrapbook entitled "The Right to Counsel," maintained in the Cleveland home of that organization's former president, Eugene Freedheim. The library of the Meiklejohn Civil Liberties Institute in Berkeley, California, houses a large number of briefs and transcripts from Smith Act cases, while the American Civil Liberties Union Papers at the Seeley G. Mudd Manuscript Library, Princeton University, contain a limited amount of useful material.

More valuable than ACLU files are the weekly bulletins issued by the organization's Feature Press Service, which are available on microfilm. There
are also a few significant items in the Morris L. Ernst manuscripts at the
Humanities Research Center of the University of Texas at Austin.

Few Smith Act defendants have made their personal papers available
to researchers. One who has is Victor J. Jerome, and those that he deposited at the Yale University Library are a rich vein of material on campaigns to enlist support for prosecuted Communists. The Oleta Yates collection at the Bancroft Library of the University of California at Berkeley,
on the other hand, includes almost nothing of value.

I learned more about the defendants' side of the Smith Act story from
personal interviews than from manuscripts. Of greatest value was a discussion with Dorothy Healy (31 December 1973). Other Smith Act defendants with whom I spoke were Arnold Johnson and George Myers (both
on 8 August 1973) and Maurice Braverman (19 August 1976). Also useful was an interview with Thomas Arthur "Art" Shields (8 August 1973),
who covered several of the trials for the *Daily Worker*. On the government
side, I talked with former Second Assistant Deputy Attorney General
Charles Goodell (29 May 1975) and with Kevin T. Maroney (22 January
1971), who, at the time of the interview, was a deputy assistant attorney
general in the Internal Security Division, as well as with two former attorneys general, Tom C. Clark and William P. Rogers (both on 17 August
1976). Justice Clark also shared with me his somewhat hazy recollections
of Supreme Court deliberations on the *Yates* and *Scales* cases. Particularly
informative concerning bar association efforts to provide Communist defendants with counsel was a discussion with Eugene Freedheim (9 June
1971).

I found useful as supplements to my own interviews the memoirs of
Learned Hand and Thomas I. Emerson in the Columbia Oral History Collection, the reminiscences of Howard J. Trienens and Newton N. Minow
in the Fred M. Vinson Oral History Collection at the University of Kentucky, and an interview with John Gates which NBC news broadcast as
part of the program "American Communism Today" on 26 August 1973.
Also helpful was personal correspondence with Justice Clark and Abraham Isserman.

While personal recollections offer insights unavailable elsewhere, government documents are actually far more valuable sources of information on
the Smith Act and its employment against the Communist Party. Of special importance are the *Annual Reports of the Attorney General of the
United States* for the years 1941 through 1962. The Department of Justice suspended publication of these in 1942 and did not resume it until

1955. For the intervening years the report of the attorney general himself is available, often in mimeographed form, at most repositories, but those of subordinate divisions, including the FBI, must be consulted at the Justice Department library in Washington, D.C.

The *Congressional Record* yields a great deal of information on the passage of the Smith Act, but because efforts to amend that statute in the 1950s and 1960s excited little debate, it is far less helpful with respect to them. Any examination of the legislative history of the Smith Act should begin with the 1934 hearings and report of the House Special Committee on Un-American Activities. Of particular importance on the law's 1935 ancestors are the hearings and reports of the House Judiciary Committee on H.R. 6427 and those of the House Military Affairs Committee on H.R. 5845. The Senate Naval Affairs Committee also issued a report evaluating the latter measure. On the origins of the Smith Act itself, the reader should consult the publications of the House Committee on the Judiciary, especially *Crime to Promote Overthrow of the Government: Hearings . . . April 12 and 13, 1939*, 76th Cong., 1st sess., 1939. The Senate Committee on the Judiciary also generated a number of relevant documents, but the only one that includes a significant amount of information is *Crime to Promote Overthrow of the Government: Hearings . . . May 17, 1940*, 76th Cong., 3rd sess., 1940. Also informative is the House Conference Committee's *Alien Registration Act of 1940*, 76th Cong., 3rd sess., 1940, H. Rept. 2683. The best sources of information on amendments to the Smith Act are reports of the House and Senate Judiciary Committees, particularly the former. These bodies also published a number of other documents which shed light on various aspects of the Smith Act story. The House Judiciary Committee's *Hearings . . . on H.R. 226 . . .*, 83rd Cong., 2d sess., 1954, contains some important remarks by Attorney General Brownell explaining his department's motivation and timing in prosecuting the CPUSA, and its *Hearings . . . on H.R. 3, Bill to Amend Title 18, United States Code to Provide Punishment for Persons Who Jump Bail*, 83rd Cong., 2d sess., 1954, is also quite important. Among the most useful documents put out by the Senate Judiciary Committee are *Limitation of Supreme Court Jurisdiction and Strengthening of Antisubversive Laws*, 85th Cong., 2d sess., S. Rept. 1586, 1958, informative concerning the fate of congressional efforts to overturn *Yates*, and *Limitation of Appellate Jurisdiction of the United States Supreme Court: Hearings . . . on S. 2646*, 85th Cong., 1st sess., 1957, also good on that subject. The Internal Security Subcommittee of the Senate Judiciary Committee produced the useful *Hearings . . . Subversive Influences in the Educational Process*, 82d Cong., 2d sess.,

1952, and *The Communist Party of the United States of America: What It Is and How It Works: A Handbook for Americans*, 84th Cong., 1st sess., 1955, Committee Print.

Despite their witch hunt character, the many hearings of the House Committee on Un-American Activities between the late 1940s and the early 1960s did unearth substantial amounts of information about the Communist Party and the effect on that organization of the Smith Act prosecutions. Unfortunately for the historian, this useful wheat is buried amid mountains of worthless chaff, and even with the aid of the inadequate index prepared by the committee, locating it is at best difficult. A particularly important HUAC document is *Hearings on Proposed Legislation to Curb or Control the Communist Party of the United States*, 80th Cong., 2d sess., 1948, which reports Attorney General Clark's statement, six months before the indictment of the National Board, that prosecution of Communists for violation of the Smith Act was impractical. HUAC's *Communist Legal Subversion: The Role of the Communist Lawyer*, 86th Cong., 1st sess., 1959, H. Rept. 41, contains a great deal of data on some of the attorneys who defended victims of the Smith Act, but the reliability of this information is uncertain.

Those interested in the prosecutions, the Party, or both will find highly informative the annual hearings of the House and Senate appropriations committees on Department of Justice budgets for the years 1941-53, which include testimony by several attorneys general and by J. Edgar Hoover and other department officials that reveals a great deal about both the CPUSA and the attitudes and objectives of the individuals responsible for the legal attack on it. Particularly important on FBI harassment of the Party is the Senate Select Committee to Study Governmental Operations with Respect to Intelligence Activities' *Hearings . . . Federal Bureau of Investigation*, 94th Cong., 1st sess., 1975, pt. 6. The National Archives publication *Public Papers of the Presidents of the United States* (GPO, 1957-) and Samuel I. Rosenman, ed., *The Public Papers and Addresses of Franklin D. Roosevelt*, 9 vols. (New York: Macmillan Co., 1938-50) are valuable in assessing presidential views on the CPUSA.

The best sources of information on Communist attitudes toward the Smith Act and the nature of the Party's response to the prosecutions are the New York *Daily Worker*, which ceased publication in 1957, and the San Francisco Bay area *Daily People's World*, which eventually found it necessary to become a weekly. Although technically independent, both of these papers were for all practical purposes organs of the CPUSA. The weekend *Worker* is valuable also, because its regional editions sometimes published items about second-string cases that never appeared in either of the dailies. Articles in the Party's theoretical journal, *Political Affairs*,

often revealed a great deal about the organization's internal policy debates. The *Proceedings (Abridged) of the 16th National Convention of
the Communist Party U.S.A.* (New York: New Century Publishers, 1958
[?]) are informative concerning intra-Party controversy, but the extent
to which they have been edited raises doubts about their reliability. The
same is true of the correspondence in Eugene Dennis, *Letters from Prison*
(New York: International Publishers, 1956). Among the scores of pamphlets which the Party issued during the 1940s and early 1950s are several of considerable significance to students of the Smith Act. These include Eugene Dennis, *The Case for the Communist Party: Opening Statement to the Jury by Eugene Dennis* (New York: New Century Publishers,
1949), and *Ideas They Cannot Jail* (New York: International Publishers,
1950); Benjamin Davis, *Why I Am a Communist* (New York: New Century Publishers, 1947); Betty Gannett, *The Communist Program and the
Struggle for Jobs, Peace, Equal Rights and Democracy* (New York: New
Century Publishers, 1954); and Claude Lightfoot, *Not Guilty!* (New York:
New Century Publishers, 1955). Of special importance in assessing the
impact of prosecution on the CPUSA is Alex Parker (a pseudonym for an
unknown underground leader), *Organizing the Party for Victory over
Reaction: Report Delivered at the National Conference of the Communist Party* (New York: New Century Publishers, 1953). With respect to the
nature and development of the Party's labor defense strategy the *Labor
Defender*, published from 1926 to 1937 by the International Labor Defense, and its successor, *Equal Justice*, are particularly informative. Also
helpful on this subject are two radical publications from the early 1920s,
the *Labor Herald* and the *Workers Monthly*, as well as *The Communist*,
the journal that became *Political Affairs*.

Memoirs of persons active in the CPUSA before and during the period
of the prosecutions are another important source of information. The
most valuable of these are John Gates, *The Story of an American Communist* (Edinburgh: Thomas Nelson & Sons, 1958), Al Richmond, *A
Long View from the Left: Memoirs of an American Revolutionary* (Boston: Houghton Mifflin, 1973), and George B. Charney, *A Long Journey*
(Chicago: Quadrangle, 1968), all of them by Smith Act defendants. The
reader should keep in mind, however, that these men eventually left the
Party. For the views of two Smith Act defendants who did not, see John
Williamson, *Dangerous Scot: The Life and Work of an American Undesirable* (New York: International Publishers, 1969), and Benjamin J. Davis,
*Communist Councilman from Harlem: Autobiographical Notes Written
in a Federal Penitentiary* (New York: International Publishers, 1969),
books that unfortunately say surprisingly little about the Foley Square
trial. Similarly, William L. Patterson, *The Man Who Cried Genocide: An*

Autobiography (New York: International Publishers, 1971), although
devoting a chapter to the Civil Rights Congress, is silent concerning that
organization's activities during the trial of the Eleven. Of only slightly
greater value is Steve Nelson, *The 13th Juror: The Inside Story of My
Trial* (New York: Masses & Mainstream, 1955), which focuses on the
author's Pennsylvania sedition case rather than his Smith Act trial. Far
more useful is Royal France, *My Native Grounds* (New York: Cameron
& Associates, 1957), by a defense attorney. Herbert A. Philbrick, *I Led
3 Lives: Citizen, "Communist," Counterspy* (New York: McGraw-Hill
Book Co., 1952), and Angela Calomiris, *Red Masquerade: Undercover
for the FBI* (Philadelphia and New York: J. B. Lippincott Co., 1950),
both relate the experiences of FBI informants who testified at Foley
Square. Matt Cvetic's privately printed potboiler, *The Big Decision* (Hollywood, 1959), and Julia Brown's *I Testify: My Years as an Undercover
Agent for the FBI* (Boston and Los Angeles: Western Islands Publishers,
1966), are also by informants, but they are less valuable and less reliable.
Harvey Matusow's *False Witness* (New York: Cameron & Kahn, 1955)
makes fascinating reading, but one cannot depend on it either, because
the author was an admitted perjurer. Useful primarily for background are
Francis Biddle, *In Brief Authority* (Garden City, N.Y.: Doubleday & Co.,
1962), Benjamin Gitlow, *I Confess: The Truth About American Communism* (New York: E. P. Dutton & Co., 1940), James P. Cannon, *The First
Ten Years of American Communism: Report of a Participant* (New York:
Lyle Stuart, 1962), and Angelo Herndon, *Let Me Live* (New York: Arno
Press and New York Times, 1969). Harry S. Truman, *Memoirs by Harry
S. Truman*, 2 vols. (Garden City, N.Y.: Doubleday & Co., 1956), is of
extremely marginal utility.

Despite the limited nature of the role played by the American Civil
Liberties Union in the Smith Act cases, the separately titled annual reports of that organization are a valuable source of information about them.
So are a number of popular periodicals, particularly *Time, Newsweek,
New Republic*, and *The Nation*. *The Reporter* carried several relevant
stories, as did *U.S. News & World Report* and *American Mercury*, while
items of interest also appeared in *Harpers, Life, Look*, the *Saturday Evening Post, Readers' Digest, Christian Science Monitor Magazine, Fortune,
America, Commonweal*, and the *New Leader*. On the legislative process
which produced the Smith Act see *Christian Century, Current History,
Fortune, Forum, Congressional Digest, Publishers' Weekly, Saturday Review of Literature, National Republic*, and *Vital Speeches*. The *New York
Times* also published a substantial number of stories on this subject and
even more that dealt with the prosecutions and appellate court reaction

to them. Other non-Communist newspapers consulted in the preparation
of this study were the *Appleton* (Wis.) *Post-Crescent* (1948-62), *Chicago
Tribune* (1935-62), *Cleveland Plain Dealer* (1948-56), *Cleveland Press*
(1948-56), *Denver Post* (1948-61), *East Bay Labor Journal* (1936-45),
Los Angeles Times, (1948-61), *The Militant* (1948-62), *New Orleans Times-
Picayune* (1935-57), *Philadelphia Inquirer* (1953-54), *Pittsburgh Courier*
(1948-62), *St. Louis Post-Dispatch* (1948-61), *San Francisco Chronicle*
(1935-61), *U.A.W. Solidarity* (1957-61), *United Automobile Worker*
(1948-1957), *Washington Post* (1935-61), and *Wisconsin News* (1935).

In addition to such popular sources, there are also many scholarly articles and books, as well as several doctoral dissertations, which examine
various facets of the Smith Act attack on American communism. Although
its author underestimates the significance of the government's legal attack
on the CPUSA, David Shannon's *The Decline of American Communism:
A History of the Communist Party of the United States Since 1945* (New
York: Harcourt, Brace and Co., 1959), is still the best book on the Party
during the period of the prosecutions. Joseph R. Starobin, *American Communism in Crisis 1943-1957* (Cambridge, Mass.: Harvard University Press,
1972), is well researched and includes some information which Shannon's
book does not, but it devotes most of its attention to the years prior to
the Foley Square trial. Irving Howe and Lewis Coser, *The American Communist Party: A Critical History (1919-1957)* (Boston: Beacon Press,
1957), is useful, despite the anti-Communist orientation of its authors,
and so is the even more biased *Masters of Deceit: The Story of Communism in America and How to Fight It* (New York: Henry Holt and
Co., 1958), by J. Edgar Hoover, who employs sources unavailable to
writers not associated with the FBI. William Z. Foster's *History of the
Communist Party of the United States* (New York: International Publishers, 1952), based partly on personal recollections and partly on research,
is slanted too, but in the opposite direction. On the development of the
CPUSA prior to 1948 Theodore Draper, *American Communism and Soviet Russia: The Formative Period* (New York: The Viking Press, 1960),
is a solid piece of scholarship, whereas James Oneal and G. A. Werner,
*American Communism: A Critical Analysis of Its Origins, Development
and Programs* (New York: E. P. Dutton & Co., 1947), is less reliable.
Nathan Glazer, *The Social Basis of American Communism* (New York:
Harcourt, Brace & World, 1961), is excellent on the composition of
the CPUSA, and Clinton Rossiter, *Marxism: The View from America*
(New York: Harcourt, Brace & World, 1960), is good on the Party's ideology. Frank S. Meyer, *The Moulding of Communists: The Training of Com-*

munist Cadre (New York: Harcourt, Brace and Co., 1961), is helpful in understanding the thinking of Party functionaries. On relations between CPUSA and other organizations see Max A. Kampleman, *The Communist Party vs. the CIO: A Study in Power Politics* (New York: Frederick A. Praeger, 1957), and Wilson Record, *Race and Radicalism: The N.A.A.C.P. and the Communist Party in Conflict* (Ithaca, N.Y.: Cornell University Press, 1964). The *Digest of the Public Record of Communism in the United States* (New York: Fund for the Republic, 1955), is an excellent bibliography and collection of source material, but its value to one interested in the Smith Act is reduced considerably by the fact that it was published while the government was still prosecuting the CPUSA.

With respect to earlier legal attacks on the Party, this book is superb. Also essential to an understanding of those assaults are Robert K. Murray, *Red Scare: A Study in National Hysteria 1919-1920* (Minneapolis: University of Minnesota Press, 1955), and Stanley Coben, *A. Mitchell Palmer: Politician* (New York and London: Columbia University Press, 1963), the two best works on the anti-radical outburst which rocked the country just after World War I. William Preston, *Aliens and Dissenters: Federal Suppression of Radicals 1903-1933* (Cambridge, Mass.: Harvard University Press, 1963), is excellent too, but this book deals mainly with attacks on the Industrial Workers of the World, rather than the Communist Party, and it is thin on the last decade of the period the author purports to cover. Much better on the 1920s is Paul Murphy, *The Meaning of Freedom of Speech: The First Amendment Freedoms from Wilson to FDR* (Westport, Conn.: Greenwood Publishing Co., 1972). The most extensive discussions of the 1922-23 Michigan criminal syndicalism prosecution of the party's leaders, however, are in Donald M. Johnson, *The Challenge to American Freedoms: World War I and the Rise of the American Civil Liberties Union* (Lexington: University of Kentucky Press, 1963), and my own "The Smith Act and the Communist Party: A Study in Political Justice," Ph.D. dissertation, University of Wisconsin, 1973, and "The Mechanics of Repression: J. Edgar Hoover, the Bureau of Investigation and the Radicals, 1917-1925," *Crime and Social Justice* 7 (Winter/Spring 1977): 49-58. The classic study of the court decisions resulting from attacks on radicalism and dissent during these years is Zechariah Chafee, Jr., *Free Speech in the United States* (Cambridge, Mass.: Harvard University Press, 1941). Alan Reitman, ed., *The Pulse of Freedom: American Liberties 1920-1970s* (New York: W. W. Norton, 1975), contains good articles by Murphy and Jerold Auerbach on the 1920s and 1930s respectively but is less satisfactory on the period of the Smith Act prosecutions. Jane Perry Clark, *De-*

portation of Aliens from the United States to Europe (New York: Arno Press and the New York Times, 1969), Elridge Foster Dowell, *A History of Criminal Syndicalism Legislation in the United States*, Johns Hopkins University Studies in Historical and Political Science, series 57, no. 1 (Baltimore: The Johns Hopkins Press, 1939), and Walter Gelhorn, ed., *The States and Subversion* (Ithaca, N.Y.: Cornell University Press, 1952), are all worthwhile but of rather limited value to one primarily interested in federal prosecutions of the CPUSA.

The methods employed by the Party to turn prosecution to its own advantage are analyzed in my article "The Trials of Labor Defense: The Smith Act Cases and the Transformation of Communist Party Litigation Strategy," *The National Journal of Criminal Defense* 2 (Fall 1976): 287-316. Nathan Hakman's "Old and New Left Activity in the Legal Order: An Interpretation," *Journal of Social Issues* 27 (1971): 105-21 and "Political Trials in the Legal Order: A Political Scientist's Perspective," *Journal of Public Law* 21 (1972): 73-126, are also helpful in gaining an understanding of radical litigation strategy, but their author tends to make sweeping generalizations on the basis of very limited historical evidence, and the reader is likely to learn more from works that examine the part which Communists played in particular criminal cases, especially from Dan T. Carter's superb *Scottsboro: A Tragedy of the American South* (Baton Rouge: Louisiana State University Press, 1969), Richard H. Frost's extremely detailed *The Mooney Case* (Stanford, Calif.: Stanford University Press, 1968), Charles H. Martin's perceptive *The Angelo Herndon Case and Southern Justice* (Baton Rouge: Louisiana State University Press, 1976), and Francis Russell's entertaining *Tragedy in Dedham: The Story of the Sacco-Vanzetti Case* (New York: McGraw-Hill Book Co., 1962). The classic theoretical work on political justice is Otto Kirchheimer's brilliant *Political Justice: The Use of Legal Procedure for Political Ends* (Princeton, N.J.: Princeton University Press, 1961), but the introduction and articles in Theodore Becker, ed., *Political Trials* (Indianapolis and New York: Bobbs-Merrill Co., 1971), also provide an analytical framework within which to examine the Communist cases.

The literature on the passage of the Smith Act is far less impressive than that on political justice. Indeed, the only real legislative history of that law is a chapter in Chafee's *Free Speech in the United States.* This account is based on published sources only, and Chafee overlooks some of the more important of those. Edward S. Stocker, "Federal Legislation: Alien Registration," *Georgetown Law Journal* 29 (1940): 187-93, is a vigorous attack on the Smith Act written just after its passage. A far less useful contemporary article is "Recent Anti-Alien Legislative Proposals,"

Columbia Law Review 39 (1939): 1207-23. "Federal Sedition Bills: Speech Restriction in Theory and Practice," *Columbia Law Review* 35 (1935): 917-27, on the other hand, is excellent on both proposed national legislation and state statutes already on the books when it was written. John McCormack, "Personal Liberty," *The Annals of the American Academy of Political and Social Science* 185 (1936): 154-61, August Raymond Ogden, *The Dies Committee: A Study of the Special House Committee for the Investigation of Un-American Activities, 1938-1944* (Washington, D.C.: The Catholic University of America Press, 1945), and James T. Patterson, *Congressional Conservatism and the New Deal: The Growth of the Conservative Coalition in Congress* (Lexington: University of Kentucky Press, 1967), all contribute modestly to an understanding of attitudes in the Congress which passed the Smith Act.

On the first prosecution under the new law see Thomas L. Pahl, "G-String Conspiracy, Political Reprisal, or Armed Revolt? The Minneapolis Trotskyite Trial," *Labor History* 8 (1967): 30-51. Maximilian St. George and Lawrence Dennis, *A Trial on Trial: The Great Sedition Trial of 1944* (Washington [?]): National Civil Rights Committee, 1944) examines the second big Smith Act case from the defendants' point of view, while O. John Rogge, *The First and Fifth with Some Excursions into Others* (New York: Thomas Nelson and Sons, 1960), shows the perspective of the man who prosecuted it.

The development that turned the Smith Act against the CPUSA, the onset of the Cold War, has inspired in recent years an outpouring of historical literature far too vast to survey here. The best short synthesis of this work is Walter LaFeber, *America, Russia and the Cold War 1945-1975*, 3rd ed. (New York: John Wiley and Sons, 1976), while the work which most effectively relates the deterioration of U.S.-Russian relations to American attitudes on communism is John L. Gaddis, *The United States and the Origins of the Cold War* (New York: Columbia University Press, 1972). Both Richard Freeland—in *The Truman Doctrine and the Origins of McCarthyism* (New York: Alfred A. Knopf, 1972)—and Athan Theoharis—in *Seeds of Repression: Harry S. Truman and the Origins of McCarthyism* (Chicago: Quadrangle Books, 1971) and in "The Escalation of the Loyalty Program" and "The Rhetoric of Politics: Foreign Policy, Internal Security, and Domestic Politics in the Truman Era, 1945-1950," both of which appear in Barton J. Bernstein, ed., *Politics and Policies of the Truman Administration* (Chicago: Quadrangle Books, 1970), at pages 242-68 and 196-241 respectively—argue that the development of McCarthyism was due to America's adoption of an anti-Soviet foreign policy and to the means utilized by the Truman administration to mobilize support for this program. These men may go too far toward charging the President and his backers with *deliberately* stirring up hostility toward *domestic* communism. Alan O. Harper, *The Politics of Loyalty: The White House and the Communist Issue 1946-1952* (Westport, Conn.: Greenwood Publishing Co., 1969), on the other hand, fails to mention some of the administration's less laudable actions. Alonzo Hamby, in his *Beyond the New Deal: Harry S. Truman and American Liberalism* (New York and London: Columbia University Press, 1973), also rejects the Freeland-Theoharis thesis. Earl Latham, *The Communist Controversy in Washington: From the New Deal to McCarthy* (Cambridge, Mass.: Harvard University Press, 1966), attributes the development of McCarthyism to the frustrations of conservative politicians, while Walter Goodman, *The Committee: The Extraordinary Career of the House Committee on Un-American Activities* (Baltimore: Penguin Books, 1969), subjects to critical analysis the body that led the Republican attack on the Truman administration.

Other books that help to set the political scene for the first Smith Act prosecution are Cabell Phillips, *The Truman Presidency: The History of a Triumphant Succession* (New York and London: Macmillan Co. and Collier-Macmillan, 1966), Burt Cochran, *Harry S. Truman and the Crisis Presidency* (New York: Funk & Wagnalls, 1973), and the old, but still useful, Eric Goldman, *The Crucial Decade and After* (New York: Alfred A. Knopf, 1960). Irwin Ross, *The Loneliest Campaign: The Truman Victory of 1948* (New York: New American Library, 1968), is an entertaining overview of its subject, while Curtis MacDougall's *Gideon's Army*, 3 vols. (New York: Marzani & Munsell, 1965), is the most detailed treatment of the Wallace candidacy. Allen Yarnell's considerably overrated *Democrats and Progressives: The 1948 Presidential Election as a Test of Postwar Liberalism* (Berkeley: University of California Press, 1975) assesses the extent to which the Wallace movement influenced the President and his party.

Unlike the 1948 campaign, the Foley Square Smith Act trial has received little attention from scholars. The only book on the subject is George Marion's polemic *The Communist Trial: An American Crossroads* (New York: Fairplay Publishers, 1950), which has a strong pro-Communist bias. Equally lacking in objectivity, but slanted in the opposite direction, is Hawthorne Daniel's *Judge Medina: A Biography* (New York: Wilfred Funk, 1952). Medina's own *The Anatomy of Freedom*, ed. C. Waller Barrett (New York: Henry Holt & Co., 1959), includes one speech by the judge which discusses the Communist trial at length, and his *Judge Medina Speaks: A Group of Addresses by Harold R. Medina, Judge, United States Court of Appeals*, ed. Maxine Boord Virtue (Albany and New York:

Mathew Bender & Co., 1954), contains a useful analysis by the editor of the letters which Medina received from the public after the trial. Of higher quality than any of these books is Nathaniel L. Nathanson's article "The Communist Trial and the Clear-and-Present Danger Test," *Harvard Law Review* 63 (1950): 1167-75. Richard Arens, "Conspiracy Revisited," *Buffalo Law Review* 3 (1954): 242-68, and the anonymous student note "The Conspiracy Dilemma: Prosecution of Group Crime or Protection of Individual Defendants," *Harvard Law Review* 62 (1948): 276-86, are good on conspiracy law at the time the Eleven were tried. Roger M. Williams, "A Rough Sunday at Peekskill," *American Heritage* 27 (April 1976): 74-80, is a lively but not entirely accurate account of the riot that threatened to disrupt the Foley Square proceedings.

Unlike the trial, the *Dennis* appeal has inspired a flood of scholarly writing. The best treatments of the Court of Appeals decision in the case are the sharply critical "Learned Legerdemain: A Grave But Implausible Hand," *Western Political Quarterly* 6 (1953): 343-58, by Francis Wormuth, and the more sympathetic analysis in *Learned Hand's Court* (Baltimore and London: The Johns Hopkins Press, 1971), by Marvin Shick. Less valuable are Kathryn Griffith, *Judge Learned Hand and the Role of the Federal Judiciary* (Norman: University of Oklahoma Press, 1973), and Robert Samuel Lancaster, "The Jurisprudence and Political Thought of Learned Hand," Ph.D. dissertation, University of Michigan, 1954, both inadequately researched and a bit naive in their analysis of Hand's decision making. For favorable reaction to the judge's opinion see "Clear and Present Danger Re-Examined," *Columbia Law Review* 51 (1951): 98-108. Two of Hand's own books, *The Bill of Rights* (New York: Antheneum, 1964) and *The Spirit of Liberty: Papers and Addresses of Learned Hand*, ed. Irving Dillard (New York: Alfred A. Knopf, 1952), are helpful in gaining some understanding of the mind that remodeled the clear-and-present-danger test, as is Gerald Gunther's "Learned Hand and the Origins of Modern First Amendment Doctrine: Some Fragments of History," *Stanford Law Review* 27 (1975): 719-73. For an assessment of the law Hand upheld that differs considerably from his see Osmond K. Fraenkel, "Is the Smith Act Constitutional?" *Lawyers Guild Review* 10 (1950): 181-84.

The most telling critique of the Supreme Court's *Dennis* decision is Louis B. Boudin, " 'Seditious Doctrines' and the 'Clear and Present Danger' Rule," *Virginia Law Review* 38 (1952): 143-86 and 315-56, but Eugene V. Rostow, "The Democratic Character of Judicial Review," *Harvard Law Review* 66 (1952): 193-224, is effective also. The Court's

most intelligent and articulate defender is Wallace Mendelson, author
of "Clandestine Speech and the First Amendment—A Reappraisal of
the Dennis Case," *Michigan Law Review* 51 (1953): 553-59, and "Clear
and Present Danger—From Schenck to Dennis," *Columbia Law Review*
52 (1952): 313-33. Other significant articles which analyze or comment
on the *Dennis* decision are Chester James Antieau, "Dennis v. United
States, Precedent, Principle or Perversion?" *Vanderbilt Law Review* 5
(1952): 141-49; Edward S. Corwin, "Bowing Out 'Clear and Present
Danger,' " *Notre Dame Lawyer* 27 (1952): 325-59; David Fallman, "Constitutional Law in 1950-1951," *American Political Science Review* 46
(1952): 158-99; John A. Gorfinkel and Julian W. Mack II, "Dennis v.
United States and the Clear and Present Danger Rule," *California Law
Review* 39 (1951): 475-501; Robert McCloskey, "Free Speech, Sedition
and the Constitution," *American Political Science Review* 45 (1951):
662-73; Alexander Meiklejohn, "What Does the First Amendment
Mean?" *University of Chicago Law Review* 20 (1953): 461-79; Elliot
L. Richardson, "Freedom of Expression and the Function of the Courts,"
Harvard Law Review 65 (1951): 1-54; and Raymond L. Wise, "Is Dennis
Really a Menace?" *University of Florida Law Review* 15 (1962): 369-83.
In *Prophets with Honor: Great Dissents and Great Dissenters in the Supreme Court* (New York: Alfred A. Knopf, 1974), Alan Barth devotes a
chapter to lauding Douglas's attack on the majority position in *Dennis.*
As Sidney Hook's *Heresy Yes—Conspiracy No!* (New York: John Double-
day Co., 1953) demonstrates, however, many intelligent contemporaries viewed the Smith Act far differently from the way Barth sees it now.

There are a number of general works on the Supreme Court and civil
liberties that can assist the reader to understand why the 1940 sedition
law was adjudged constitutional. Much the most important of these is
C. Herman Pritchett, *Civil Liberties and the Vinson Court* (Chicago: Uni-
versity of Chicago Press, 1954), but Milton R. Konvitz, *Fundamental
Liberties of a Free People: Religion, Speech, Press, Assembly* (Ithaca,
N.Y.: Cornell University Press, 1957), and Martin Shapiro, *Freedom of
Speech: The Supreme Court and Judicial Review* (Englewood Cliffs, N.J.:
Prentice-Hall, 1966). are good too. Of lesser value are Samuel Krislov,
The Supreme Court and Political Freedom (New York: The Free Press,
1968), Walter Gelhorn, *American Rights: The Constitution in Action*
(New York: Macmillan Co., 1960), Osmond K. Fraenkel, *The Supreme
Court and Civil Liberties* (New York: Oceana Publications, 1960), Henry
J. Abraham, *Freedom and the Court: Civil Rights and Liberties in the
United States*, 3rd ed. (New York: Oxford University Press, 1977), and
Walter Berns, *Freedom, Virtue and the First Amendment* (Baton Rouge:

Louisiana State University Press, 1957). Paul L. Murphy, *The Constitution in Crisis Times 1918-1969* (New York: Harper & Row, 1972), is an excellent survey of twentieth-century constitutional history which emphasizes civil liberties problems.

Besides such books there are also a number of works by and about members of the Court which contribute to an understanding of the *Dennis* decision. The most important of these is Leon Friedman and Fred L. Israel, eds., *The Justices of the United States Supreme Court: Their Lives and Major Opinions* (New York and London: Chelsea House & R. R. Bowker Co., 1969), which includes biographical sketches that range from excellent to awful. Liva Baker, *Felix Frankfurter* (New York: Coward-McCann, 1969), is a competent biography and of far greater value to one interested in *Dennis* than is Helen Shirley Thomas's *Felix Frankfurter: Scholar on the Bench* (Baltimore: The Johns Hopkins Press, 1960). Unfortunately, two of the major works on Hugo Black's Supreme Court career were written before the Communist case was decided, and another, Stephen P. Strickland, ed., *Hugo Black and the Supreme Court: A Symposium* (Indianapolis, Ind.: Bobbs-Merrill Co., 1967), tells the reader little he could not learn by reading the *United States Reports* for himself. Likewise, most of the numerous published collections of opinions and/or extra judicial writings and speeches of Supreme Court justices who participated in the case are of little value in understanding *Dennis*. But William O. Douglas, *Being an American* (New York: John Day Co., 1948), is revealing with respect to its author's views on communism, and Edmond Cahn, ed., *The Great Rights* (New York and London: Macmillan & Collier-Macmillan, 1963), does contain a lecture by Black that sets forth in concise fashion his philosophy concerning the Bill of Rights. Hugo L. Black, *A Constitutional Faith* (New York: Alfred A. Knopf, 1969), is of marginal value.

Henry M. Christman, ed., *The Public Papers of Chief Justice Earl Warren* (New York: Simon and Schuster, 1959), and David L. Shapiro, ed., *The Evolution of a Judicial Philosophy: Selected Opinions and Papers of Justice John M. Harlan* (Cambridge, Mass.: Harvard University Press, 1969), on the other hand, are absolutely essential to an understanding of why the first two men Eisenhower named to the Supreme Court voted in 1957 to restrict the Smith Act. There are several biographical works on Chief Justice Warren, none of which comes close to being definitive. They range from Leo Katcher's fact-filled *Earl Warren: A Political Biography* (New York: McGraw-Hill Book Co., 1967), through John D. Weaver's readable but not very deep *Warren: The Man, the Court, the Era* (Boston and Toronto: Little, Brown & Co., 1967), to Luther A. Huston's simply awful *Pathway to Judgment: A Study of Earl Warren* (Philadelphia and New York: Chilton Books, 1966). More informative than any of these biographies with respect to differences between the Vinson Court and the one that decided *Yates* are John P. Frank, *The Warren Court* (New York: Macmillan Co., 1964), and C. Herman Pritchett, *The Political Offender and the Warren Court* (Boston: Boston University Press, 1958).

The best article on the many cases intiated between *Dennis* and *Yates* is Robert Mollan's exhaustive "Smith Act Prosecutions: The Effect of the Dennis and Yates Decisions," *University of Pittsburgh Law Review* 26 (1965): 705-48, but the unsigned note "Post-Dennis Prosecutions Under the Smith Act," *Indiana Law Journal* 31 (1955): 104-19, is also perceptive and informative. On the other hand, Thomas Michael Holmes's chapter on the Honolulu case in "The Spectre of Communism in Hawaii, 1947-53," Ph.D. dissertation, University of Hawaii, 1975, is neither well researched nor well thought out. Dalton Trumbo, *The Time of the Toad: A Study of Inquisition in America* (New York: Harper & Row, 1972), contains a chapter on the Smith Act which focuses on the Los Angeles case and was originally published as a pamphlet by the California Emergency Defense Committee in 1956. Although his research on the prosecutions is rather superficial, Charles Goodell's *Political Prisoners in America* (New York: Random House, 1973) provides the reader with some intelligent analysis. John Somerville, *The Communist Trials and the American Tradition: Expert Testimony on Force and Violence* (New York: Cameron Associates, 1956), and "Law, Logic and Revolution: The Smith Act Decisions," *Western Political Quarterly* 14 (1961): 839-49, set forth the views of a philosopher who testified at several post-*Dennis* trials, whereas Ann Fagan Ginger, ed., *The Relevant Lawyers: Conversations Out of Court on Their Clients, Their Practices, Their Life Style* (New York: Simon & Schuster, 1972), includes an interview with Mary Kaufman, who appeared as defense counsel in a number of these proceedings. Herbert Packer, *Ex-Communist Witness: Four Studies in Fact Finding* (Stanford, Calif.: Stanford University Press, 1962), contains a good discussion of John Lautner, while Albert Kahn, "National Scandal: A Warning from the McCarthy Era" (a forthcoming work presently in proof) is excellent on the Harvey Matusow affair. Also of interest is Harold W. Chase, *Security and Liberty: The Problem of Native Communists 1947-1955* (Garden City, N.Y.: Doubleday & Co., 1955). The book that is most informative on the political context within which the later Smith Act prosecutions took place is Herbert S. Parmet, *Eisenhower and the American Crusades* (New York and London: Macmillan Co. & Collier-

Macmillan, 1972), but Charles C. Alexander, *Holding the Line: The Eisenhower Era* (Bloomington & London: University of Indiana Press, 1975), is useful too.

The best discussion of the reluctance of attorneys to undertake the defense of Communists during the McCarthy era is that in Jerold S. Auerbach, *Unequal Justice: Lawyers and Social Change in Modern America* (New York: Oxford University Press, 1976), but the reader should compare his extremely negative assessment of the bar with the more favorable one in my own "The Fight for the Right to Counsel," *Ohio History* 85 (1976): 28-48. Also valuable are Milnor Alexander, "The Right to Counsel for the Politically Unpopular," *Law in Transition* 22 (1962): 19-45, and the same author's identically titled 1962 Bryn Mawr Ph.D. dissertation. The best contemporary explanation of the difficulty which radical defendants experienced in obtaining attorneys is the anonymous article "The Independence of the Bar," *Lawyers Guild Review* 13 (1953): 158-73. David L. Weissman, "Sacher and Isserman in the Courts," *Lawyers Guild Review* 12 (1952): 39-47, the same author's "Sacher, Isserman and the Courts: Note II," *Lawyers Guild Review* 14 (1954): 65-77, and Fowler Harper and David Haber, "Lawyer Troubles in Political Trials," *Yale Law Journal* 60 (1951): 1-55, are all good on the legal and professional difficulties of the Foley Square defense attorneys. Also useful are Joseph Edward Downs and Alvin C. Goldman, "The Obligation of Lawyers to Represent Unpopular Defendants," *Howard Law Journal* 9 (1963): 49-67; Fowler Harper, "Loyalty and Lawyers," *Lawyers Guild Review* 11 (1951): 205-13; and William O. Douglas, *An Almanac of Liberty* (Garden City, N.Y.: Doubleday & Co., 1954). For criticism of the ACLU's performance during these years see Mary Sperling McAuliffe, "The Red Scare and the Crisis in American Liberalism," Ph.D. dissertation, University of Maryland, 1972, and "The American Civil Liberties Union During the McCarthy Years," in Robert Griffith and Athan Theoharis, eds., *The Specter* (New York: New Viewpoints, 1974). More favorable to that organization, but a far less competent work than either of McAuliffe's, is Charles Lam Markmann, *The Noblest Cry: A History of the American Civil Liberties Union* (New York: St. Martins Press, 1965).

For invaluable insights into the public opinion which long intimidated both lawyers and the ACLU, see George H. Gallup, *The Gallup Poll: Public Opinion 1935-1971* (3 vols.: New York: Random House, 1972), and the articles entitled "The Quarters Polls" that appeared in each issue of *Public Opinion Quarterly*. Also informative on this subject are Herbert W. Hyman and Paul B. Sheatsley, "Trends in Public Opinion on

Civil Liberties," *Journal of Social Issues* 9 (1953): 6-16, and Samuel
Stouffer, *Communism, Conformity, and Civil Liberties* (Garden City,
N.Y.: Doubleday & Co., 1955).

When, reflecting changes in public opinion, the Supreme Court handed
down its *Yates* decision in 1957, that ruling excited far less scholarly
comment than had the *Dennis* one six years earlier. Although the West
Virginia, U.C.L.A., Minnesota, and Washington University law reviews
all ran student case notes on *Yates*, and the *Harvard Law Review* included a discussion of it in a summary of the Supreme Court's 1956 term, the
decision did not inspire a single major law review article. Before the high
tribunal ruled, however, Osmond K. Fraenkel did analyze the issues involved in *Yates* and several other cases in "The Smith Act Reconsidered,"
Lawyers Guild Review 16 (1956): 149-54. There are also a few relevant
comments in Jack W. Peltason, "Constitutional Liberty and the Communist Problem," in Alfred H. Kelly, ed., *Foundations of Freedom in the
American Constitution* (New York: Harper & Brothers, 1958). Frank
Ober, "Communism and the Court: An Examination of Recent Developments," *American Bar Association Journal* 44 (1958): 35-38, 84-89,
reflects the hostility which *Yates* and similar decisions aroused in some
circles. On the attitude of the ABA see Ross L. Malone, "The Communist Resolutions: What the House of Delegates Really Did," *American
Bar Association Journal* 45 (1959): 343-47. The best study of Congressional efforts to overturn *Yates* and other controversial rulings of the
Warren Court is Walter F. Murphy, *Congress and the Court: A Case Study
in the American Political Process* (Chicago: University of Chicago Press,
1962), but C. Herman Pritchett, *Congress Versus the Supreme Court
1957-1960* (Minneapolis: University of Minnesota Press, 1961), and
Donald G. Morgan, *Congress and the Constitution: A Study of Responsibility* (Cambridge, Mass.: Belknap Press, 1966), are also useful on
this subject.

Strangely, though it was less significant than *Yates*, the Court's 1961
Scales decision provoked far more comment. The best articles on that
case are "Communism and the First Amendment: The Membership Clause
of the Smith Act," *Northwestern University Law Review* 52 (1957): 527-
50, and James R. Phelps, "Judicial Technique and the Communist Party:
The Internal Security and Smith Acts Construed," *University of Cincinnati Law Review* 31 (1962): 152-72. Also helpful are Thomas I. Emerson,
"Freedom of Association and Freedom of Expression," *Yale Law Journal* 74 (1964): 1-35, and a student case note by Paul J. Driscoll, which
appeared in the *Notre Dame Lawyer* 37 (1962): 239-45. Other good
analyses of *Scales* are provided by Lucius J. Barker and Twiley W. Barker,
Jr., *Freedoms, Courts, Politics: Studies in Civil Liberties* (Englewood

Cliffs, N.J.: Prentice-Hall, 1965), and Herbert Aptheker, *Dare We Be Free: The Meaning of the Attempt to Outlaw the Communist Party* (New York: New Century Publishers, 1961). Both the *Ohio State Law Journal* and the *Maryland Law Review* carried unsigned student case notes on the post-*Scales Hellman* decision. For an excellent summary of all court cases and legislation involving the CPUSA from 1940 on see Kathleen L. Barber, "The Legal Status of the American Communist Party: 1965," *Journal of Public Law* 15 (1966): 94-121.

No survey of literature relating to the Smith Act attack on the Communist Party would be complete without some mention of the many books on that long-time foe of American radicalism, the FBI. The best of an uninspiring lot is Don Whitehead's *The FBI Story: A Report to the People* (New York: Random House, 1956), a competently researched but poorly documented house history which sings the praises of the Bureau. On the anti-FBI side are Max Lowenthal, *The Federal Bureau of Investigation* (New York: Willard Sloan Associates, 1950); Fred J. Cook, *The FBI Nobody Knows* (New York: Macmillan Co., 1964); and Ovid Demaris, *The Director: An Oral Biography of J. Edgar Hoover* (New York: Harpers, 1975). Harry Overstreet and Bonaro Overstreet, *The FBI in Our Open Society* (New York: W. W. Norton & Co., 1969), and Norman Ollestad, *Inside the FBI* (New York: Lyle Stuart, 1967), also deal with the Bureau during the period of the prosecutions, but neither is of any real help on them. The full story of the FBI's operations against the CPUSA, like so many facets of the attack on domestic radicalism during the 1950s, of which the Smith Act prosecutions were only a part, remains to be told.

Index

ABOUT THE AUTHOR

Michal R. Belknap, assistant professor of history at the
University of Texas, Austin, specializes in twentieth-century
American legal and political history. He has written articles
for numerous journals, including the *California Historical
Society Quarterly, Ohio History, The National Journal of
Criminal Defense,* and *Crime and Social Justice.* He is present-
ly researching material for a book-length study of the impact
of war on the United States Constitution.